Decolonization and the Remaking of Christianity

DECOLONIZATION AND THE REMAKING OF CHRISTIANITY

EDITED BY
Elizabeth A. Foster
and Udi Greenberg

PENN

UNIVERSITY OF PENNSYLVANIA PRESS

PHILADELPHIA

Published by
University of Pennsylvania Press
Philadelphia, Pennsylvania 19104-4112
www.upenn.edu/pennpress

Printed in the United States of America on acid-free paper
10 9 8 7 6 5 4 3 2 1

Hardcover ISBN: 978-1-5128-2496-4
eBook ISBN: 978-1-5128-2497-1

A catalogue record for this book is available from the Library of Congress.

CONTENTS

INTRODUCTION

Elizabeth A. Foster and Udi Greenberg

Albert Tévoédjrè was a man of decolonization. Born in the French West African colony of Dahomey (today's Benin) in 1929, he spent the 1950s in Paris in pursuit of higher education. He became an ardent anti-colonialist, using his position as editor of *L'Étudiant noir*, the mouthpiece of the Federation of Black African Students in France, to call for African independence. In 1958, Présence Africaine, the publishing house at the intellectual center of the negritude movement, released his book *L'Afrique révoltée*, a title that suggested that Africa was both revolting against and revolted by European domination. Its frontal attack on Europe's "civilizing mission," which Tévoédjrè decried as a cover for economic exploitation and deprivation, made him a major figure in African political thought at midcentury.[1] Tévoédjrè also complemented his words with activism: the same year that his book came out, he co-founded the African National Liberation Movement, which denounced France's efforts to preserve its links to its colonies and campaigned in favor of full political independence.[2] When Dahomey ultimately declared its independence in 1960, Tévoédjrè became a prominent writer and politician. He was the secretary of the national teachers' union, helped found a museum of indigenous art, and served as the minister of information for three years.

Rather than a seamless story of political triumph, however, Tévoédjrè's life also illustrated some of decolonization's ambiguities and tragic consequences. He participated in the government's repression of the opposition (he banned the publication of its main newspapers), and in 1963 became himself a victim of a military coup, which disbanded Benin's democratic institutions and led to Tévoédjrè's brief exile.[3] In the decades that followed, he continued to navigate the aftershocks of independence in his country and in Africa as a whole. Doubly disappointed by persistent economic disparities between Europe and its former colonies in Africa and by Benin's trajectory of instability, he published works on global inequality and remained involved in national politics, including a 1991 presidential campaign.[4]

While it has not always been recognized, Albert Tévoédjrè was also a man of Christianity. Indeed, his intellectual and political trajectories were inseparable from his life as a devout Catholic. Tévoédjrè's early education took place in the St. Gall seminary at Ouidah, run by the French Society of African Missions, and, decades later, he would join that society as a brother. He developed his critiques of European colonialism as he questioned the Catholic Church's Eurocentric views, which he considered a betrayal of Jesus's promise of universal salvation. He dedicated an entire chapter in *L'Afrique révoltée* to the topic of "The Church and the colonial problem in black Africa." In it, Tévoédjrè decried the yawning gap between the ideals of a church, which, he claimed, "in *principle* cannot be a vessel of a system of domination," and the day-to-day reality of Christianity in French Africa. The latter, he mourned, featured European rituals, songs, and saints, as well as frequent cooperation between French authorities and a clergy still dominated by European missionaries. According to Tévoédjrè, a failure to support African independence was not only a betrayal of the church's teachings, but a threat to its very existence. If Christians did not align themselves with anti-colonialism, there would be no future for Catholics in Africa: "Either our religion is tied to the fate of French colonialism, and thus we will be liquidated along with French hegemony," he wrote, "or the church will be African in Africa and Christians must work towards African independence."[5]

Such anxieties motivated Tévoédjrè and many other African Christians to embark on a bold effort to reform Christianity. During the 1950s, 1960s, and 1970s, he and others labored to "indigenize" Christian liturgy by incorporating local traditions, reorient Christian social teachings, and expand African representation in international Christian organizations. It was at least in part thanks to these initiatives that Tévoédjrè's warnings of liquidation did not materialize. In fact, the opposite occurred: while Catholics comprised 9 percent of Benin's population on the eve of decolonization, by the twenty-first century they had become the country's largest single religious group, claiming the adherence of 25 percent of its people. Protestant communities followed a similar trajectory of steep growth, and today almost half of Beninese identify themselves as Christians. This demographic trend, to be sure, had multiple sources, including patterns of migration and education. In the eyes of believers, however, stripping Christianity of its colonial baggage was one of its most important preconditions.[6]

In blending these two projects—transforming both international politics and global Christianity—Tévoédjrè was hardly alone. For countless Christians across the world, the unfolding of decolonization and the remaking of their faith were deeply linked: they were parallel assaults against Europeans' exercise of power and claims to embody universal values in the domains of politics, religion, knowledge, and beyond. The decades after World War II witnessed a revolution in Christian life, one of comparable significance to its initial spread in the ancient Roman Empire or to the Protestant Reformation in the early modern period. Inspired by the global revolt against European supremacy, Christians in Africa, Asia, and Latin America launched campaigns to reconcile Christianity with local cultures and ways of life, challenging Westerners on issues like racial discrimination and economic distribution in the process. These efforts contributed to a dramatic shift in Christianity's center of gravity. While adherence to Catholicism and various strains of Protestantism sharply declined in the 1950s and 1960s in their historical centers in Europe, it exploded in Asia, in Latin America, and especially in Africa. Indeed, even though Christian missions had labored to convert non-Europeans since the fifteenth century, the postwar period witnessed a breathtakingly rapid expansion of the number of believers in the Global South. These dynamics continue to shape global Christianity, which is now in the midst of a stunning reversal of colonial-era migration. In response to the calls of desperate church leaders, African, Asian, and Latin American Christians are increasingly filling pulpits and taking over the leadership of seminaries, missionary orders, and charities in the heart of Europe, a dynamic most notably illustrated in Pope Francis's election as the first non-European pontiff in 2013. As historian Philip Jenkins put it, "the era of Western Christianity has passed within our lifetimes."[7]

This collection explores the many intersections between political and Christian transformations in the era of decolonization, which prepared the ground for these dramatic developments. It shows how the collapse of formal colonialism, the political rise of the Global South, and the remaking of global Christianity all influenced each other. The contributions focus on the pivotal years from the 1940s through to the 1970s, covering the era that began with independence in Asia and came to a close with the end of Portuguese rule in Africa. Overall, the book argues that both the dismantling of formal European empires and the wider cultural challenges to Western hegemony it helped inspire transformed Christianity and helped set it on its current trajectory. Because Christianity was so often associated with colonization—Frantz Fanon famously lambasted Europeans for trying to mold the African subject into "a good Christian and a good slave"—many Christians felt compelled to rethink many of its tenets at midcentury.[8] It would only survive in a new era of indigeneity, many claimed, if its rituals, institutions, and social teachings could be divorced from their colonial roots and their Western bias. The essays assembled in this book chart how new organizations, theologies, and political engagements emerged from this process. They also reveal how Christianity became a powerful tool that believers could deploy in support of decolonization: many used its claims to universality and the messages of the Gospel to call both religious and political leaders to account. Thus Christianity, long a prop of Western power, itself became "decolonized" through the efforts of diverse adherents around the globe. New voices and new ideas did not go uncontested, however, nor were they always triumphant. This collection also reveals how European and North American Christians sought to respond to these developments, whether through accommodation or stubborn resistance, and shows that even amid sweeping changes, important threads of continuity persisted from the colonial past.

This is the first book to examine Christianity and decolonization on a truly global scale, ranging across a variety of contexts to reveal the tremendous scope of the transformations it describes. The subject is well suited to a collaborative approach, since no one place, region, or denomination could capture Christianity's transformation in this era. To do justice to the diversity of Christians' experience while highlighting commonalities across geographical and denominational boundaries, the scholarship here considers both Catholicism and Protestantism across five continents. It is premised on the contention that change unfolded not only in regions of Asia and Africa that were formally colonized, but also in China and Latin America, where there were not processes of political decolonization per se. Even Christians outside of areas that were formally decolonized in the postwar period were impacted and influenced by the extraordinary global realignment of decolonization, which created dozens of new sovereign states. The collection therefore offers explorations of Christianity in colonial spaces, such as Vietnam and Mozambique, but also traces how Latin American Christians linked their efforts to resist North American hegemony to Afro-Asian liberation, and how Christians in China navigated the triumph of Communism. Moreover, it investigates debates in Europe and the United States, where Christian leaders and missionaries had to redefine their organizations' historical association with racism and the "civilizing mission."

All these transformations were linked to each other, as Christian leaders and communities responded to the same worldwide ferment.

In addition to its expansive geographical scope, this collection brings together an array of methodological approaches. The essays here interrogate Christianity and decolonization through a variety of archives and from a range of vantage points. Nonetheless, in order to facilitate comparison and make the collection a coherent whole, they all focus on forms of institutional Christianity. Some contributions examine the Christian communities in the Global South and their political fortunes amid decolonization. Others highlight the importance of international organizations—both religious (the World Council of Churches) and secular (the United Nations)—in political and religious transformations. Others still focus closely on the sphere of ideas by tracing important developments in both Protestant and Catholic theology in the period. Some essays use the tools of biography to place significant individual lives in context, while others bring a fine-grained attention to economic and social history to the volume. Taken together, these diverse approaches aim to capture the multidimensional nature of the era's drama, but they by no means exhaust it. If anything, this collection reveals that vast fields of inquiry beckon additional scholarship on Christianity and decolonization, whether by incorporating new geographical examples or by the exploration of additional methodologies, such as close examinations of popular culture.

The cast of characters in these pages is broad and varied, and includes figures both well-known and obscure from the ranks of the clergy and the laity across denominations. It includes Christians who, like Tévoédjrè, were among the central actors of state decolonization, but it also features a panoply of individuals and communities who witnessed it from some distance. Readers will encounter Barthélemy Boganda, the first Catholic priest ordained in Oubangui-Chari (Central African Republic), who began his career by clashing with French missionaries over the legitimacy of forced labor, and then moved on to become his country's first president. Other Catholic clergy include Luxian Jin, a Chinese bishop who trained in Europe at midcentury and then spent over two decades in prison in China, before finding accommodation with its Communist regime. The book simultaneously explores the dilemmas of Western missionaries, both male and female, charting how they intensely debated their responses to the violent anti-colonial struggles in Mozambique and Algeria. The book also offers multiple studies of the laity. Among others, it explores Protestant Naga activists who deployed Christian language at the UN to try to evade the sovereignty of India, and Christian Progressives in Swaziland (now

Eswatini) who lost out to a much more conservative absolute monarchy that deftly mobilized the vocabulary of Christianity. Finally, theologians in these pages include Richard Shaull, the leftist American evangelical with ties to Latin America; the Catholic Sri Lankan critic of the West, Tissa Balasuriya; and a group of influential ecumenical protestants in the West who embraced the idea of secularization in the wake of decolonization.

Our hope is that this book provides a new departure point for the rich literature on Christianity and global politics. Of course, scholars of Christianity have long recognized that Christian thought, practice, and policy were frequently the product of international interactions. Few Christian communities, whether in Europe, the United States, Africa, Asia, or Latin America, were untouched by the missionary project, whether through donations, publications, or personal encounters. Yet, over the last two decades, historians of Christianity have followed the broader scholarly interest in empire and focused mostly on the era of colonial expansion in the nineteenth and early twentieth centuries. The main thrust of their efforts has been to chart the complex and shifting relations between Western missionaries, indigenous communities, and colonial authorities. As this scholarship has shown, even though Christian missionaries frequently had different priorities than secular officials, their views on labor, race, and sexuality were nonetheless often saturated with colonial ideas of hierarchy. The majority of European Christians envisioned the projects of evangelizing and "civilizing" as mutually constitutive, a stance that alienated many Christian colonial subjects as they sought to navigate missionaries' vast apparatus of schools, hospitals, and research centers.[9]

While this focus on colonial relations has been enormously generative, it has diverted attention from the radical changes that followed decolonization. Only very recently have scholars begun to explore how imperialism's formal *collapse* impacted Christian faith, practice, and institutions, and their work thus far has largely been regionally and nationally confined. They have noted that many Christian organizations went through important shifts between the 1940s and the 1970s (most famously the Catholic reforms of the Second Vatican Council), and they have explored the rise of anti-capitalist and anti-imperialist Christian theory as part of the broader project of "liberation theology" that emerged in Latin America in the 1960s and 1970s. Yet they have rarely reflected on how those changes were shaped by the sweeping global phenomenon of imperial collapse and by new and interregional postcolonial encounters.[10] The contributions here are among the first to shed light on these dynamics. They explain how the remaking of global politics during decolonization changed Christian communities, ideas, and organizations in the postcolonial states, former metropoles, and elsewhere. As they show, it is difficult to grasp some Catholics' efforts to reconcile with Islam (epitomized by the Vatican's proclamations about interreligious tolerance in 1964) without accounting for Catholic experiences during the traumatic end of French imperialism in North Africa. Similarly, it is hard to explain why so many leading Western Protestant intellectuals embraced secularization in the 1960s without understanding their thinking about Christianity's fate in post-colonial contexts. Focusing on decolonization, in short, opens new vistas for our understanding of Christianity and international history.

Decolonization, of course, was not the only global drama that helped shape Christianity in the postwar decades. It often intersected with the global Cold War, with far-reaching consequences. In the twentieth century, the European churches and the missionary organizations they helped sustain were bastions of anti-Marxism, routinely condemning the Communist secular and "materialist" worldview as an existential danger. Throughout the postwar era, Christian organizations drew on this tradition to join the struggle against Communism, launching a flurry of publications, exhibitions, and public campaigns to oppose what Pope Pius XII lambasted in 1949 as the Communists' "anti-Christian teachings."[11] As several contributors here show, these sentiments frequently informed Christians' suspicion of anti-colonial movements. Because revolutionaries often adopted Marxism, and, in places like China and Guinea, leaders also attacked Western missionaries as stooges of colonialism, many Christians around the world worried that anti-colonialists' triumphs would bring about Christianity's demise. Such fears were sometimes reinforced by the paternalist belief that only Western tutelage could secure anti-Communist resistance. This, for example, was a major factor behind church authorities' opposition to anti-colonialism in Mozambique. In other locations, however, the pressure to free Christianity of its colonial links were in tension with and even transcended Cold War calculations. In China, for example, Christian thinkers labored to reconcile their teachings with Marxist ideas, and, in Vietnam, anti-Communism helped accelerate the Vatican's willingness to support "indigenization." The collection therefore shows how decolonization helped refract the Cold War's impact on Christians.

This book has implications well beyond the history of Christianity, however. It can also enrich our understanding of decolonization and its many legacies. Due to the shifting balance of power away from the Global North and to other parts of the world, the emergence of independent Asian and

African states from the ruins of European empires have become the center of scholarly attention over the last few years. Historians have begun to explore how anti-colonial activists established new political organizations, how they utilized international organizations (especially the UN) to articulate new visions of global order, and why they chose the nation state (and not broader federative structures) as their preferred endgame. They have also highlighted forgotten efforts to expand political liberation to the sphere of economics. They resurrected the calls of African, Asian, and Latin American diplomats and economists to end colonialism's lasting effects and radically remake global trade and property rules with a set of 1970s proposals known as the New International Economic Order (NIEO). Scholarship has also begun to recognize the far-reaching impact that hostility to decolonization had among policymakers in the Global North. We now know that European and North American elites' efforts to deflect the NIEO helped fuel their shift to decrease investment in development programs and reduce regulation of global finance and trade, which in the long run created new forms of domination. Alongside the Cold War, decolonization emerged as one of the postwar era's greatest dramas. Some, like author Pankaj Mishra, have come to describe it as "arguably the most important event of the twentieth century."[12]

As this collection aims to underscore, however, decolonization transcended state institutions, global politics, and economic designs as it unfolded unevenly around the globe. It also entailed efforts to resurrect and invent cultural traditions, new solidarities and hierarchies, and even new subjectivities. As the essays here demonstrate, the Christian churches were central forums for these efforts. In congresses of Christian thinkers, meetings of missionary organs, and over the pages of Christian magazines, countless people debated the nature, scope, and consequences of ending European rule and overturning Western hegemony writ large. In fact, several key players in decolonization's political struggles first developed their social visions in the world of Christian institutions. Léopold Sédar Senghor, Senegal's first president, was a product of missionary schools and a member of Catholic organizations, while Kenneth Kaunda, who led Zambia to independence, was the son of a Church of Scotland minister. Some contributors therefore explore the role of Christian vocabularies and institutions in decolonization. They show how senior political leaders (sometimes heads of state), thinkers, and clergy sometimes first developed their ideas about property, political rights, and economic relations in missionary settings, before transferring them to the non-Christian sphere. In similar fashion, some essays trace how Christian organizations and individuals provided ideological justification for radical anti-colonialism. They reveal for example how some American Protestants used the language of Christian salvation to explain their financial support for armed guerrilla movements like Robert Mugabe's Patriotic Front in Zimbabwe.

Equally important, by bringing together case studies from around the globe, this collection aims to capture decolonization's conflicting impacts. It seeks to demonstrate how the process of ending European dominance—both political and cultural—was not just one of liberation and progressive possibilities, but also one of repression and disappointment. On the one hand, decolonization was the key catalyst for making Christianity a less Eurocentric project. As Phi-Vân Nguyen shows, the specter of anti-colonial revolution (and the traumatic expulsion of Western missionaries from Communist China in 1951) helped "indigenize" the Catholic Church in Vietnam. It led Catholic authorities to incorporate local rituals, images, and clergy into institutions that were once run exclusively by the French (a process that repeated itself elsewhere around the world). Decolonization could also empower those who challenged the churches' ties to paternalist visions. Darcie Fontaine demonstrates how the disintegration of French rule in Algeria, Morocco, and Tunisia led many lay men and women to develop a new conception of their churches' mission. Figures like Catholic thinker André Mandouze initiated dialogue with Muslims and strove to involve the church in the project of post-colonial nation-building. Meanwhile, Charlotte Walker-Said demonstrates how Christianity provided the conceptual tools for opposition to the ongoing colonial use of forced labor for economic exploitation in Oubangui-Chari (Central African Republic) in the 1950s. David C. Kirkpatrick extends a similar framework to Latin America, where Evangelical theologians such as Peruvian Samuel Escobar launched a campaign to end what they conceived as their churches' colonial submission to North Americans in the 1960s. They especially sought to counter Billy Graham and his supporters' anti-Communist fixation with an alternative social theory, one more amenable to economic redistribution.

On the other hand, the experiences of Christians can also help cast a harsher light on decolonization's legacies. Against triumphalist narratives of emancipation, some of the essays gathered in this collection chart how Christian networks and ideas helped empower autocratic or neo-colonial power dynamics. The most brutal case was Eswatini, where liberal and feminist Protestants sought to replace British rule with a constitutional regime. As Joel Cabrita shows in her contribution, decolonization led to their decisive defeat by a conservative and patriarchal vision, one that was led by messianic Christian preachers and which coalesced around the country's hereditary paramount chief, Sobhuza II, making him a de facto autocrat. Meanwhile, Lydia Walker reveals how Christian networks and languages were used to preserve paternalist visions of Western hegemony. Her essay uncovers how the leaders of the Naga people, who sought to achieve independence from India, used calls for Christian solidarity to mobilize British and American Protestants against India's government. Telling decolonization's story from a Christian perspective, then, helps expose some of its limitations and less progressive dimensions.

What is more, this collection's focus on Christianity helps highlight the complex roles of imperial networks and metropolitan centers during and after decolonization. As several historians have recently noted, the mobility that was offered to some under colonial rule was, ironically, central to the development of anti-colonialism. Figures from Ho Chi Minh to Kwame Nkrumah studied in Europe and the United States, where they met other anti-colonial activists, published texts against white dominance, and together developed ideas for resistance.[13] As some of the contributors here show, this dynamic was not restricted to the sphere of political organization. Forums and institutions that were designed by colonialism's supporters often became a training ground for its opponents from the global south. Albert Wu's essay demonstrates how the Chinese Jesuit Luxian Jin spent many of his formative years in the Catholic centers in Paris and Rome. Rather than training him to accept European hegemony, however, those centers led him to encounter reformatory ideas supporting the empowerment of Chinese lay people in the church. Gene Zubovich and Justin Reynolds similarly highlight how the World Council of Churches, whose founders often held deeply paternalist views of non-Europeans and non-white people, became a central site for anti-colonial mobilization. Figures like Indian theologian M. M. Thomas used it to advocate for far-reaching reforms and economic reparations. Also here, however, the vibrancy of Christian networks at times had a contradictory effect, by helping to preserve, rather than diminish, colonial frameworks. As Walker reveals, when Naga leaders appealed to Anglo-American Christians in their quest for independence from India, they helped resurrect paternalist and colonial ideas about the need to "uplift" non-Europeans.

Finally, the collection helps us see decolonization's long and sometimes less-explored legacies. Unlike some histories, the collection does not conclude in the early 1960s, when most African countries gained their formal independence. Eric Morier-Genoud's essay explores the prolonged struggle over Portugal's rule in Mozambique, which lasted well into the 1970s. As he shows, the churches' stance on this conflict was hardly a marginal story. The violence in Mozambique drew attention from multiple international Christian organizations, which fiercely debated their approach to it. Similarly, Sarah Shortall uncovers how decolonization's formal conclusion in the political sphere did not end the intellectual efforts to separate Christianity from its European heritage. With a focus on the Ecumenical Association of Third World Theologians, a group of prominent theologians from across the Global South that began to operate in the 1970s, she traces how Asian, African, and Latin American thinkers continued to debate which rituals, ideas, and institutional frameworks still needed to change. For some members, who were disappointed by political decolonization's inability to transform global hierarchies, an even more radical rethinking of Christianity's teachings was still necessary. Sri Lankan Catholic theologian Tissa Balasuriya went so far as to question Mary's virginity (which he considered a European invention designed to subjugate women) and the notion of original sin (which he decried as a European scheme to oppress the weak).

Together, then, the stories assembled in this collection explore the broad forces that molded Albert Tévoédjrè's life trajectory. They chart how decolonization helped transform Christianity but was also inflected by Christian ideas, networks, and communities. From China to Switzerland, Algeria to Peru, many contemporaries understood imperialism's formal end as a Christian event, one that opened new possibilities and solidarities while foreclosing others. In many ways, the legacies of those pivotal decades are still powerful. From clerics to laypeople, writers to politicians, Christians are still debating whether their churches have adjusted to the post-imperial era, or whether, as Latino theologian Miguel A. De La Torre put it in 2021, the task of "decolonizing Christianity" is just beginning.[14]

CHAPTER 1

Apostles of Secularization: The Ecumenical Movement and the Making of a Postcolonial Protestantism in the 1950s and 1960s

Justin Reynolds

> The Christendom idea was dependent on the power of the West to rule. But today independent countries have emerged and their governments are undertaking major responsibility for social and economic change based upon their own criteria of national interest. A Western Christendom approach may not have been entirely unrealistic in the India of Lord Irwin or the Africa of Lord Lugard, but it is irrelevant as a Christian strategy in the Asia of Nehru and Mao Tse-tung and in the Africa of Nkrumah and Sekou Touré.
>
> —Paul Abrecht, *The Churches and Rapid Social Change*

> The coming of Christ is a secular event. . . . [Consequently,] what was invited by this secular event, the thing we usually call Christianity, cannot be anything else but a secular movement, a movement in the world and for the world. It will always be a dangerous perversion of the truth to make Christianity into some sort of religion.
>
> —Hans Hoekendijk, "Christ and the World in the Modern Age"

In the 1960s, Protestant intellectuals underwent a transformation that continues to puzzle commentators. After decades decrying the declining influence of Christianity in modern life, many of them began to see "secularization" as a positive development, even a normative project whose implementation was necessary to advance the cause of Christ in the world. By secularization, they did not mean protecting religious freedom or the separation of church and state—principles that had long been used to achieve and extend Protestant dominance in public life. Rather, they welcomed the decline of religion itself, its retreat to the margins of society, and the formation of a new, "pluralistic" public sphere in which human beings would act, deliberate, and create their social arrangements free from the control of religious faiths, including Christianity. The advocates of this view were not fringe figures, but rather leading voices in the Protestant-led ecumenical movement, a campaign to promote global unity of churches that had galvanized the leadership of established and "mainline" churches in Europe, North America, Asia, Africa, and Latin America since the early twentieth century. Remarkably, and in manner that seemed almost unbelievable to their critics, these ecumenists now argued that Christianity ought to embrace its marginal status, or—more radically—was itself a "secular movement," as the Dutch missionary intellectual Hans Hoekendijk declared at a gathering of Christian student groups in 1960.

The reasons for this transformation have never been adequately explained. One recent account, put forward by the historian David Hollinger and others, finds them in a long history of Protestant "accommodation" to the Enlightenment. In this story, the defining feature of ecumenical Protestantism, in contrast to evangelical and fundamentalist counterparts, was a willingness to reformulate religious beliefs to incorporate scientific knowledge and a cosmopolitan respect for others' customs and religions, gained through cross-cultural encounters in diversifying Western societies and missionary settings abroad. From this point of view, Protestants' postwar embrace of secularization came as something like a moment of self-consciousness, when habits of "self-interrogation" finally got the better of evangelical commitments.[1] Neat as it is, the narrative has difficulty explaining why the turn to secularization occurred at the precise moment it did. Granting that "self-interrogation" has had a hand in reshaping Protestant belief and practice over time, how did embracing secularization become a feasible—even attractive—option for Protestant church elites who had never considered it up until that point? After all, by the 1960s, Christianity had a long record of encounters with other cultures, yet none of these earlier moments had led Protestant church leaders to suggest that a "secular society" in which religion would be relegated to the margins of public life was a desirable, or Christian, arrangement.

This chapter suggests an alternative interpretation. It traces how what I term a "theology of secularization" emerged from efforts to redefine the singular and exclusive truth of Christianity in a world after European colonial empires. My argument is that Protestants embraced secularization in response to decolonization and in an effort to co-opt the politics of self-determination to their advantage, at a moment when they could no longer depend on the support of colonial governments. The birth of "secular Christianity," it turns out, has little to do with Protestants' alleged "accommodation" to non-Christian ways of life and religion; rather, it was a product of debates *within* the ecumenical movement. Its genesis illustrates how attempts to manage political difference and subordinate it to shared religious purpose within the space of international Christian organizations generated new accounts of Christianity and its place in the world. While these accounts could authorize robust forms of anti-colonial activity, they also laid the groundwork for inventive new attempts to reestablish the West's world-historical leadership. That was exactly the purpose behind the theology of secularization, as elaborated by thinkers such as Hoekendijk, Willem A. Visser 't Hooft (the first General Secretary of the World Council of Churches), and theologians such as Harvey Cox and John A. T. Robinson, along with other prominent advocates.

The story that follows tracks how these two dynamics, anti- and neocolonial, interacted with each other. The key conceptual innovations grounding the theology of secularization were first forged by politically radical ecumenical thinkers, primarily from the Global South, whose participation in anti-colonial struggles led them to reject a traditional view of Christianity as the basis of social "order." Instead, they argued, God acted through revolutionary change, extending His grace through humanity's participation in movements to emancipate itself from existing religious and political authorities. In the 1950s, these ideas were co-opted by more conservative, predominantly Western ecumenists who were apprehensive about Third World nationalism and socialism, and sought to retain, in various ways, Western tutelage of non-Western peoples. For them, affiliating Christianity with revolution made sense as a strategy for minimizing the churches' ties with colonialism, even if they lamented the loss of control over the destinies of the post-colonial world. With the theology of secularization, Western ecumenists sought to creatively reclaim that control. Effacing the Afro-Asian origins of their ideas, they presented global movements for postcolonial emancipation as the heritage of Western secularization driven by Christianity.

This chapter has four parts. To set the stage for this investigation, it will be necessary, first, to highlight central features of interwar ecumenical Protestantism, in particular its polemic against secular "emancipation" and how this shaped ecumenical attitudes toward empire. In part II, I will explore how the effort to incorporate decolonization within a Christian theological framework led to a new, positive assessment of emancipation and its globalization in the ecumenical milieu in the 1950s. In part III, I show how this revaluation of emancipation enabled Protestants, predominantly in Europe and the United States, to embrace secularization as a Christian project, highlighting two variations on this theme: a moderate version that sought to prepare Christian churches for a new status as creative "minorities" within pluralistic societies, and a more radical version, calling on Christians to break out of the institutional carapace of the church altogether. Part IV investigates the neocolonial impulses that shaped the Western elaborations of "secular Christianity," showing how their celebration of one figure in particular—the German theologian Dietrich Bonhoeffer—concealed the intellectual movement's actual debts to non-Western ecumenical thinkers while inscribing decolonization as an achievement of the West's Christianizing global history.

I

Recent scholars have begun to recognize the Protestant-led ecumenical movement as a main vector of Christian thought and activism in the twentieth century.[2] Protestantism's dominant international expression from the late nineteenth century to the 1960s, the movement claimed an array of influential clerics, statesmen, activists, and thinkers among its leading figures, such as the Swedish Lutheran archbishop Nathan Söderblom; the archbishop of York (later Canterbury) William Temple; the Swiss jurist Max Huber, president of the Permanent Court of International Justice at the Hague; the British politician and later ambassador to the United States Philip Kerr; and the American statesman (and later Republican Secretary of State) John Foster Dulles, as well as leading intellectuals and theologians such as T. S. Eliot, Paul Tillich, and Reinhold Niebuhr. Despite growing recognition of the movement's significance, however, much less is known about the content of the global ideas that the movement's leaders developed, and how these ideas shaped the movement's relationship to Europe's colonial empires in particular. It is worth outlining how movement leaders understood the role of Christianity in global affairs in the high imperial and interwar period, in order to appreciate shifts that occurred in the era of decolonization.

One thing that makes postwar ecumenists' embrace of secularization so puzzling is that it seems to go against everything their movement stood for up until the 1940s. From its beginnings in the late nineteenth century up through the aftermath of World War II, ecumenists had viewed the decline of religion as the source of catastrophic social and spiritual "disorder," while defining organized Christianity as disorder's sole remedy. The movement's founders, such as the American missionary organizer John Mott and the German Professor of Missions Gustav Warneck, demanded that Protestant missionaries of all nations and denominations coordinate their efforts to ensure that the evangelization of Asian and African masses would keep pace with the ballooning of Europe's colonial empires in the late nineteenth and early twentieth centuries. According to this view, articulated in the reports of the movement's breakout gathering (the World Missionary Conference, held in Edinburgh in 1910), the penetration of modern Western civilization would destroy indigenous religions and create a "spiritual vacuum" that, if not filled with Christianity, would push Africans and Asians to embrace the most destructive forms of Western life: "habits of self-indulgence," economic competition and rapacity, and "infidel and rationalistic ideas and materialistic views."[3] As one participant of the Edinburgh conference, the Scottish missionary and theologian J. N. Farquhar, put it, "There is only one [religion] which satisfies all the religious instincts and yet can be held by modern thinking man. Every religion except Christianity is incredible. . . . Clearly Christianity will be the one religion of man, or else there will be no religion."[4]

Following World War I, the movement's fears of civilizational collapse shifted from the colonized world to the Western metropole. Ecumenists attributed the fratricidal conflict between so-called "Christian nations" to the de-Christianization of Western life and declared that a new post-Christian worldview of "secularism" had displaced non-Christian religions as the faith's chief global rival. Interwar ecumenical intellectuals characterized secularism as modern man's "emancipation" from religion and subsequent attempt to organize spiritual and social life according to his own reason and will. Abandoning God, wrote the Swiss Reformed theologian and leading ecumenical light Emil Brunner in 1930, modern civilization had installed humanity in its place, making it the center of morality and achievement.[5] In the decade that followed, this idea was amended to incorporate a polemic against totalitarianism: though Nazism and Communism rejected the autonomy of the individual subject, they only radicalized modernity's quest for independence from God by forming "secular religions" that deified the race, the nation, or the proletariat. The result of the multi-front secularist revolt was an unprecedented collapse of civilization in Christianity's historic heartland. As one report of the defining event of the 1930s movement, the World Conference on Church, Community, and State held in Oxford in 1937, put it: "Traditional pieties and loyalties and standards of conduct have lost their unquestioned authority; no new ones have taken their place. As a result, the community life of mankind has been thrown into confusion and disintegration."[6] Restoring God's "order" was the ultimate objective of what ecumenical leaders called the "world church," a solidarity of Protestant and Eastern Orthodox churches from "all nations, races, and classes" that would serve as the instrument of Christian influence throughout the globe. Resting on the equation of religious decline and disorder, this secularization script continued to organize ecumenical consciousness through World War II and the beginnings of the Cold War. When ecumenical leaders were planning the inaugural conference of a new flagship organization, the World Council of Churches (WCC), in the late 1940s, they adopted the theme "Man's Disorder and God's Design."[7]

One outgrowth of ecumenical anti-secularism, as the historian Udi Greenberg has suggested, was a novel defense of anti-colonial activism. Though ecumenical Protestants had been staunch supporters of empire before 1914, many began to argue that Western imperialism was an obstacle to the global spread of Christianity. With the belief that modern civilization was secular and materialistic came a critique of Europe's civilizing mission: abandoning God, European powers had "lost [the] right to dominate other continents."[8] These discourses cleared the ground for a Protestant embrace of decolonization after the War. But for Protestants living through the collapse of colonial empires in the 1950s and 1960s, they left crucial questions unanswered. How could now apparently triumphant movements for Afro-Asian self-determination be incorporated into a Christian theological framework that most such movements denied? Similarly, it was not immediately evident how the upshot of decolonization—the creation of post-colonial nation-states in Asia and later Africa—served Christianity. In these new societies, Christians were often a small minority, and the religion itself was stained by its association with empire. In some areas, it seemed that Christian missions might be whipped out altogether without colonial support—a fear realized, for instance, when foreign missionaries were expelled from Communist China in 1951.

II

The conceptual apparatus ecumenists developed to address these questions profoundly shaped the postwar direction of ecumenical Protestant social thought. Beginning in the late 1940s, ecumenists incorporated anti-colonial struggle within a theological framework by positing social "revolution" as a providential event. This idea was pioneered among Asian Christians involved in anti-colonial movements, and it marked a profound revision of existing ecumenical concepts. Ecumenists had traditionally used the term "revolution" to refer to *Communist* revolution, yet in the late 1940s it acquired a wider meaning, denoting not an ideological choice but a process: the rapid and comprehensive transformation of social, political, and economic life.[9] In 1948, C. W. Li (Li Chuwen), a secretary of the Chinese YMCA who sided with the Communists against the Kuomintang, wrote in an ecumenical student journal that "[a]lthough it would be a disastrous mistake to think that the revolution is God's will and plan, yet I for one cannot but believe that the wide awakening and rise of one billion people in Asia is another benevolent act of our Father, evoking new hope and new life among His vast human family."[10] The concept's most important architect was the leftist Indian theologian M. M. Thomas, a leader of student Christian movements in Travancore who, during the war, sought to reconcile Communist politics with theology. Though he abandoned his Communist loyalties after Indian independence, Thomas remained a proponent of aggressive land reform and state-led economic planning, while insisting on the priority of class and anti-colonial struggle as a practice of Christian obedience. In a 1949 report of the World Student Christian Federation (WSCF) co-written with the Anglican intellectual Davis McCaughey, Thomas claimed to perceive the "righteous hand of God" behind the struggle of oppressed "classes, nations, [and] races, demanding not simply the amelioration of their lot, but participation in the total life of society" through "the exercise of power."[11] This immensely influential report, later published by the WSCF in 1952, established the central claims of a generation of left-leaning ecumenical figures. It resonated powerfully among Asian, African, and Latin American Christians who challenged the dominance of Western ideas and complacency within the movement. In the hands of anti-colonial church leaders like Rena and John Karefa-Smart (the latter a future foreign minister of Sierra Leone) the theology of revolution became a framework for promoting African Christian support for anti-colonial action and post-colonial nation-building, while theologians such as Richard Shaull, Mauricio Lopez, and Emilio Castro developed similar lines of thinking in Latin America in the 1950s and early 1960s.[12]

Significantly, however, it was not just the movement's left wing that embraced the theology of revolution. Even those who tended to fret the rise of Afro-Asian nationalism and foregrounded the global threat of Communism came to embrace it, for a simple reason: it offered a language in which churches could bury their prior association with colonial rule and present Christianity as an ally of peoples struggling for independence from alien rule. The report of one missionary conference in 1947, for instance, spotlighted the threats of ethno-nationalism and Communist advances in China in its review of the missionary field. Nonetheless, it saw potential advantages in the "revolution" sweeping Africa and Asia as a force that "freed [Christianity] from ties that were embarrassing to it."[13] The influential British missionary writer and Anglican bishop of Tirunelveli, Stephen Neill, similarly christened anti-colonial agitation in Asia the "greatest revolution that has ever happened in the history of mankind" and celebrated the liberation of Christianity from its captivity to Western secular culture—even as he derided the "neurosis" of Asian nationalism.[14] Most significantly, the theology of revolution was taken up at the highest levels of the WCC. At the World Council's "East Asia Christian Conference," organized in Bangkok in December of 1949, Thomas played the key role in authoring a report endorsed by forty-five delegates drawn from the Council's staff, Asian churches, as well as Western missionary associations. The report welcomed the "social revolution" sweeping Asia, and declared that the church must play its part in "the struggle for and the attainment of political freedom" that had "awakened the hitherto submerged peoples of East Asia to a new sense of dignity and historical mission."[15] The idea of revolutionary providence performed a crucial service, enabling Protestant intellectuals to distinguish the principle of self-determination from the particular, political aims that Asian and African self-determination movements articulated. The wide uptake of "revolution" as a term distilling the theological significance of decolonization derived from its capacity to occlude political differences, foreground a common desire to distance Christianity from its colonial past, and announce the productive role that churches would play in post-colonial development.

In the 1950s and 1960s, the idea of revolutionary providence guided a proliferation of church activities and study groups in the Global South. By 1954, it was obvious to the Swedish director of the WCC's Study Department, Nils Ehrenström, that "the social problems of underdeveloped countries" constituted the 'most important social problem confronting the churches today, whether in the East or West, and should be given attention to the exclusion of all other questions."[16] Two years after the Bangkok conference, a second gathering held in Lucknow, India, outlined an agenda to study Christian responsibility in relation to four areas: land reform, industrialization and urbanization, support for the self-determination struggle, and dilemmas of international involvement.[17] The 1950s brought a succession of conferences in India, Indonesia, and the Philippines. In 1952, the first pan-African ecumenical conference convened in Kampala, Uganda, and was followed by similar gatherings in Ghana immediately after its transition to independence in 1957. In 1955, the WCC centralized much of this activity under the umbrella of an initiative called the "Program on Common Christian Responsibility Toward Areas of Rapid Social Change," funded by member church contributions and grants totaling over $200,000 from the Rockefeller Foundation.

During the seven years of its existence, the Rapid Social Change program (RSC) became the main arena where radicals, moderates, and conservatives debated Christian approaches to political, economic, social, and religious issues of the decolonizing world.[18] Ensuring that the influence of radical voices would be contained, the WCC's Executive Committee, headed by General Secretary Willem A. Visser 't Hooft, appointed two representatives from Western churches, the American Baptist minister and economist Paul Abrecht and the Dutch agronomist Egbert de Vries, to lead the program. Abrecht, who studied under Reinhold Niebuhr while at Union Theological Seminary in New York, had virtually no background in Asian, African, or Latin American affairs when he started the job. De Vries, for his part, had risen to prominence as a colonial official in the Dutch East Indies, where he had developed agricultural training programs to integrate modern practices of credit, cooperatives, and money wages into traditional village economies. After fleeing the colony on the eve of independence, he became head of the Economic Resources Section and advisor to the World Bank.[19] While Thomas and Shaull spoke of "revolution" to conjure subaltern agencies, de Vries focused on defining its effects in terms of problems—such as agricultural modernization and overpopulation—amenable to scientific study and technical interventions.[20] Along with fellow RSC participant and Anglican economist Denys Munby, De Vries represented an approach to the decolonizing world steeped in Western debates over economic development.[21] Like their Catholic contemporary, the Dominican Father Louis-Joseph Lebret, they hoped to carve out a Christian "third way" to the rival "materialistic" theories of development proffered by Soviet officials and American intellectuals such as W. W. Rostow, offering a vision that prioritized the role of churches in fostering spiritual community and responsibility to address the dislocations of social upheaval.[22] RSC study groups also accommodated (primarily Western European) participants who highlighted the perils of Third World nationalism, on the grounds that it incubated the idolatrous tendencies that had led to fascism in Europe.[23] Notwithstanding differences among these positions, together they reflected a belief in the West's responsibility, deriving either from superior scientific and technical knowledge or political "maturity," to guide non-Western peoples in the wake of formal independence.

Yet it would be impossible to say that Western representatives dominated the program, or that Abrecht and de Vries made a concerted effort to suppress more radical perspectives. A group of non-Western "consultants," including Thomas along with John Karefa-Smart and the Japanese theologian Daisuke Kitagawa, played a comparable role in crafting RSC agenda and reports, which also often reflected the views of anti-liberal Westerners such as Shaull and the German theologian H.-D. Wendland. One outgrowth of the RSC program, the "World Conference on Church and Society" held in Geneva in 1966, drew roughly half its four hundred twenty delegates from Asia, Africa, and Latin America; for the first time at a large ecumenical gathering, participants from Western countries were not in the majority. Organized by Abrecht and chaired by Thomas, the conference was a raucous affair. Calls for wealth transfer from the North to the South, state-led economic redistribution, and Christian participation in violent anti-colonial resistance garnered the most attention, and Third World luminaries such as Bola Ige, the Nigerian lawyer and politician, and Kwame Nkrumah, Ghana's first prime minister, delivered keynote speeches.[24] While Abrecht sought to find a middle ground between Third World radicals and the representatives from more cautious Western churches, some critics of the Geneva Conference, such as the American theologian Paul Ramsey, forthrightly condemned the Council's "domination" by progressive currents. Ramsey rued that in marginalizing more centrist voices, the WCC had supplanted the "office of political prudence," depriving policy makers of the rights of conscience and responsibilities in the application of Christian principles.[25]

Rather than resolving intra-movement disputes, the centering of decolonization in the ecumenical consciousness consolidated a new post-colonial ecumenical theology. From the mid-1950s through the mid-1960s, the RSC network became the site of a remarkable reinterpretation of the problem of emancipation, understood broadly as liberation from authority and human responsibility for individual and collective action. Where interwar ecumenists had equated emancipation with rebellion against God, RSC intellectuals—regardless of where they stood politically—presented it as a preparation for the Gospel: a means through which God was working humanity into a position to receive Christianity. The new line was already present in the founding statement of the RSC program, written primarily by Abrecht. The end of empire, it declared, was not merely the abolition of alien rule; it was a "movement for emancipation from oppressive political and economic systems as well as social and religious structures."[26] Within this movement, "Christian conception of man" and society could be made "directly relevant to the search for new foundations of society" by offering "a new pattern of community life" for peoples struggling to liberate themselves "from traditional social customs and moral codes."[27] In this way, the theological framework within which ecumenists interpreted the struggle against colonialism brought about a curious reversal in the ecumenical worldview that had authorized anti-colonial action in the first place.

III

It was on this ground—the positive valuation of emancipation as a condition enabling newly independent peoples to encounter the Gospel—that a new approach to the "secular" emerged in the late 1950s and early 1960s. Looking to advance Christianity in a post-colonial world, some ecumenists began to argue that religion's influence in social and political life ought to be circumscribed in order to clear a space for revolutionary activity to remake men and societies. This idea was first articulated in India. Its later elaboration by Protestants in Europe and the United States underscores both how powerfully the agenda of crafting a Christianity for the post-colony shaped the trends of global ecumenical thought, as well as the ways in which Afro-Asian movement leaders diverged from Western counterparts in their political and intellectual priorities.

Though the Rapid Social Change program established a far-flung network of study groups and local initiatives in Asian, African, and Latin American countries, India was where its ambitions were most fully realized. Headed by Thomas and the theologian Paul Devanandan of the Church of South India, and run out of the Christian Institute for the Study of Religion and Society (CISRS) that they directed in Bangalore, the Indian branch organized a series of consultations among Christian thinkers as well as "dialogues" between Christians and non-Christian Hindus and "atheists" on topics ranging from the welfare state, land and family law reform, election reports, and the foundations of Indian democratic life and institutions.[28] The report of one of these consultations, held in 1957 in Nagpur on the theme "Revolution and Reconstruction," argued that Christians had a responsibility to join with Hindus and atheists in the search for a new "social philosophy" for India.[29] Further, the report advanced a theological defense of secularization as the separation of religion, not merely from the state, but from society as a whole. "There is a deep Christian truth in the secular protest" against religious domination of society, wrote Thomas in a summary of the document, "namely that the different spheres of human life have a real autonomy and must not be regimented into a narrow unity easily achieved through the religious integration of society." Thomas justified this position by distinguishing between the power of the church and the "Lordship" of Christ, who worked not merely through the proxy of a particular religious community but in wider field of social relations. It was a "grave mistake to allow all spheres of life to pass under the authority of the community of religion. The Church has no business to dominate or control the State, the university, the family, and the arts, and when it has done so, it has perverted itself and stifled the fulfillment and growth of the natural purposes of secular society." Hence "true religion," Thomas concluded, "gives society an abiding faith in that ultimate unity of all things which eludes its own grasp."[30]

Despite receiving its founding articulation in the Indian context, Thomas's vision of a pro-Christian secularization was not taken up widely among Asian, African, or Latin American ecumenists. To be sure, many Third Worldists in the movement echoed the emphasis on the need for Christians to cooperate with non-Christians, as well as the urgency of ensuring that post-colonial states were "neutral," free of any formal religious establishments (which were likely to be non-Christian). But it was rare for figures outside the West to conceptualize the decline of religion as advantageous to Christian purposes. Instead, the arguments Thomas pioneered were taken up in the United States and Europe. There, the theology of secularization developed into two conceptually distinct varieties, one focused around adapting Christian churches to their new "minoritarian" role, the other suggesting that it was perhaps necessary to break out of church structures altogether in order to practice Christianity in the age of universal emancipation.

An example of the first, more moderate strain came in an article published by the American Protestant theologian Martin Marty in *The Christian Century*, the main organ of mainline American Protestantism, in 1961. With the election of President John F. Kennedy, Marty wrote, the era of Protestant hegemony in the United States was officially over—and this was good news. In a "pluralist society," Protestants would be able to present their Gospel in sharper outline against the prevailing culture. While earlier Protestant gestures toward solidarity with American Catholics and Jews had appealed to a shared antipathy toward secularism and Communism, Marty's article broke new ground by defending the virtues of belonging to a "minority faith."[31] Shedding the baggage of informal establishment, Protestantism would no longer be a default option for Americans; it would become "something to join and be committed to." Christian communities "must learn the arts, sciences and nuances of speaking to the newly exposed pluralist-secularist orders, of cooperating with other minorities, of becoming more firmly and clearly confessional and articulate than in the past."[32] By the mid-1960s, Visser 't Hooft, now nearing his second decade as General Secretary of the World Council of Churches, was heralding the virtues of "pluralism" on similar grounds. In an article published in 1966, he rejected the idea of an "integrated Christian society in which all would be expected to regulate their lives by the teachings" of Christianity as a pipe dream. Assailing its defenders—including conservative Catholics and erstwhile ecumenical supporters such as T. S. Eliot—Visser 't Hooft argued that the "fact" of pluralism was not just to be tolerated but welcomed on the grounds that, "rightly understood," it "creates for the church a situation in which it is in less danger of falsifying its own nature and in which it is better able to manifest its calling."[33] Testifying to the new ecumenical dispensation, in 1968 the WCC initiated a program to promote "Dialogue with Men of Living Faiths and Ideologies," focusing on the "possibilities and problems" confronting churches in "a pluralistic world." "The meeting with men of other faiths or of no faith must lead to dialogue," announced the program's founding document, adding that this posture in no way denied the "uniqueness of Christ," but constituted the condition in which that uniqueness could be apprehended.[34]

Such "moderate" defenses of secularization praised pluralism as a new, vitalizing environment for churches: as one group among many in a diverse society, Christians could find "space to breath," as Marty put it, and present a more demanding, authentic expression of the Gospel. Other Western thinkers called, more radically, for a thoroughgoing secularization of Christianity itself, at times going so far as to question the validity of the church, or Christianity, as distinct communities. Hans Hoekendijk's 1960 speech declaring Christianity a "secular movement"—quoted at the beginning of this chapter—was delivered at a gathering of student groups alongside speakers from Europe, North America, Asia, Africa, and Latin America attesting to the "crisis" of supernatural belief, and calling on listeners to fulfill their Christian duty through participation in political struggles for social justice.[35] Three years later, in Britain, the Anglican economist and RSC intellectual Denys Munby declared that it was the "peculiar glory of Western Christianity" to have created the social and spiritual conditions necessary for an escape from religion. He heralded the secular society as one "which explicitly refuses to commit itself as a whole to any particular view of the nature of the universe and the place of man in it."[36] In a similar vein, the Dutch Protestant intellectual and former missionary Arend van Leeuwen forthrightly declared that Christianity would triumph not as the universalization of a religious community but the universal separation of civilization from religion—a development begun with the Hebrew Prophets and destined to be finally achieved in a completely secularized modernity.[37] While van Leeuwen's now little-read, nearly five-hundred-page tome became a set text for Christian secularizers of the day, the basic message was popularized in shorter works by the Anglican bishop John A. T. Robinson and the American Baptist theologian Harvey Cox. Cox's blockbuster of 1965, *The Secular City*, celebrated secularization as the liberation of man from "religious and metaphysical control" and the discovery of human responsibility for history. For Cox, the traditional name of "God" was so misleading that he proposed a moratorium on its use.[38] "We must learn," he wrote, "to speak of God in a secular fashion and find a nonreligious interpretation of biblical concepts,"[39] and suggested that, in the meantime, "perhaps, like Moses, we must simply take up the work of liberating the captives."[40]

IV

The Western apostles of secularization are often classed as both theological and political radicals, whose works ushered a generation of Christian leaders toward left leaning causes, while also fatally polarizing organized Protestantism, whose "rank and file" were indifferent to the heady talk of liberation and scandalized by the call to abandon religion.[41] The impact of figures such as Robinson and Cox was undeniable: their books sold hundreds of thousands of copies, and they played central roles in refashioning Protestant intellectual life in the final decade of Christianity's social and cultural ascendency in Europe (and, more ambiguously, in the United States as well). Engaging their works, American Protestant theologians William Hamilton and Thomas Altizer went so far as to outline a new form of Christian atheism in the highly publicized volume of essays they published in 1966, *Radical Theology and the Death of God*.[42] "Radical theology," however, implied no necessary commitment to Third World or anti-racist struggles, though it did in some cases. In fact, the secular Christian movement incubated neo-colonial impulses of its own, above all in its proponents' efforts to advance a new vision of Western Christianity's world-historical significance.

By the mid-1960s, it was clear that the emerging intellectual movement of secular theology and church-based support for socialist and revolutionary nationalist Third World struggle were two distinct, if at times overlapping, configurations. The leading figures in the Death of God movement, including Hamilton and Altizer, were only glancingly associated with the international ecumenical movement, and the pressing political issues of the day were not especially central to their work, in contrast to the increasingly radical engagements of the World Student Christian Federation and the World Council of Churches. Especially in comparison with the explicitly political commitments urged by leftist Christian movements at the time—whether in the WCC's 1966 conference on "Church and Society," Catholic liberation theology, or Black theology—their work remained conspicuously unpolitical. Robinson's politics focused on domestic cultural issues. Though he elsewhere endorsed liberal sexual ethics—notoriously defending the Christian bona fides of *Lady Chatterley's Lover* when the British government charged its publishers with violating anti-obscenity laws— Robinson's 1963 *Honest to God* made no attempt to link its themes to social or political struggles against class, racial, or colonial domination.[43] To be sure, this pattern was not universal: Cox remained significantly engaged with ecumenical activities, playing an important role in the 1966 "Church and Society" conference in Geneva, and was an advocate of politically "revolutionary" action that sought to generate solidarities among anti-colonial struggles in the Global South and North. Hoekendijk similarly marked struggles in Africa and Asia against Western imperialism as sites of revelation, and student groups in Britain, the United States, and Europe also found the theology of secular action a guide in struggles against racism and South African Apartheid.[44] Nonetheless, it is remarkable that secular Christianity succeeded most in precincts far removed from the theological innovations that first made it possible. It was primarily a European and American discourse, and had few important advocates among African and Asian theologians.

Why was this the case? In fact, the Western theologies of secularization were not indifferent to decolonization but evinced a particular way of responding to it and the Western anxieties it provoked. A remarkable feature of many of these texts is the way in which the concept of secularization was deployed to occlude the agency of Africans and Asians whose politics and theological innovations laid its very groundwork. Flowering in the decade that brought independence to thirty-two African states and Afro-Asian ascendency in the UN General Assembly, the secular Christianity movement was also a bid to domesticate Third Worldism as a robust and—to many—threatening new force in global affairs. While de Vries's and others' visions of Christian development from the prior decade advocated concrete technical or political measures to shape Afro-Asian societies, European and American theologians of secularization sought to establish the Christian West's proprietary claim to emancipatory struggle in the very act of acknowledging post-colonial peoples' autonomy to chart their own future. The upshot was a comforting vantage point from which to make sense of the collapse of Western global prestige, by presenting Afro-Asian struggles for independence as the efflux of Christian energies emanating from the West. Refashioning the once-abominated secularization of the West as an instantiation of divine will, Western theologians presented their own society as the avant-garde, the privileged location of God's grace, and the model for other nations to follow.

One of the most striking examples of this kind of argument came in van Leeuwen's *Christianity in World History*. In a stunning reversal of the earlier ecumenical perception of Asia and Africa as the key sites of providential revolution, van Leeuwen now claimed it was the West that had guarded the flame of "revolution" all along. In fact, from the ancient beginnings of the Western church up through the present day, Occidental history had been dynamic and creative while other religions and cultures (especially Islam) had remained mired in "ontocracy," van Leeuwen's term for a spiritual absolutism that denied individuality and history by construing them as emanations of an unchanging cosmic essence. The critical attitude of "modern science," the technical achievements of the industrial revolution, the collapse of integrated religious society of Christendom, and finally the arrival of non-Western peoples at a capacity for autonomous self-development all revealed the presence of a God whose historical incarnation in Jesus Christ was the driving force of historical transformation and creativity. "The impact of the West goes from strength to strength," van Leeuwen wrote; "it is the dynamic factor behind the 'awakening' of the non-Western world; it supplies the backbone of world history in the present age."[45] Echoing the sentiment, Munby argued that the efforts to forge "secular states" in post-colonial societies of Asia and Africa played catch-up with the West's more advanced form of secularized Christianity; the globalization of "secular society," in his estimation, "may be seen as largely the product of the Christian West."[46] Not surprisingly, given the Indian context in which he had first advanced an explicitly Christian defense of secularization, Thomas bristled at the Western triumphalism of such accounts. In a review of van Leeuwen's book, he assailed the author's condescending portrayal of unchanging Eastern religions. While acknowledging that social change in Indian culture today was taking place "through the impact of the West," Thomas insisted that current upheavals were "not altogether discontinuous with the genuine struggles within the traditional Hindu religion and culture."[47] Non-western cultures themselves had been sites of struggle and change, while the West was hardly immune to its own forms of spiritual absolutism. Other redoubts of Third World theology in the ecumenical movement, such as the WCC's "Dialogue with Living Faiths" or "Program to Combat Racism," whose activities included funding Marxist guerrilla insurgents in Zaire, had little use at all for the writings of the Western secular Christians.[48]

The neo-colonial tendencies of secular Christian thought were not always as explicit as they were in van Leeuwen's study. More often, they manifested in the erasure of ecumenism's formative 1950s engagement with anti-colonialism, in preference for a home-grown genealogy of secular Christianity's key insights. This move was most evident in the extraordinary preoccupation of most theologians of secularization with the writings of Dietrich Bonhoeffer, the German Lutheran theologian executed by the Nazis in 1945. In a series of writings and letters completed while in prison for his role in opposing the regime during World War II, Bonhoeffer had written enigmatically on the possibility of "religionless Christianity." Mankind, he averred, was "coming of age," and after nineteen hundred years of religious history had entered a new spiritual dispensation, in which God's activity would manifest in a hidden way within human activity. In 1951, his friend and correspondent Eberhard Bethge posthumously published Bonhoeffer's prison letters and notebooks in Germany, where they were received with interest among theologians, but hardly constituted a popular literary event.[49] An English translation followed in 1953, but it was not until the early 1960s that Bonhoeffer became a celebrity Christian thinker—attaining a place that he still holds today, as one of the most widely recognized Western theologians of the twentieth century.[50] While Martin Marty helped to jumpstart the craze with an edited volume devoted to the Lutheran theologian's life and work in 1962, Bonhoeffer's pioneering popularizer in the English-speaking world was Robinson, who declared in 1965 that, though Christ's death had always been a central event in the Gospel, it was "to Bonhoeffer we owe two other phrases not till now heard on Christian lips: the death of God and the death of the Church."[51] Cox echoed the sentiment, citing Bonhoeffer as one of the key inspirations of his work.[52] Elisabeth Adler, Associate General Secretary of the WSCF, declared in 1963 that young Christian activists in Europe today "are all good disciplines of Bonhoeffer and therefore enthusiastic about a 'religionless' interpretation of the Bible."[53] Few would have disputed the 1965 verdict of Visser 't Hooft, that "hardly any man of his generation has more influence than [Bonhoeffer] on the Christian Church today."[54]

While 1960s theologians enabled Bonhoeffer's lasting fame, the ideas they attributed to him were in important ways distinct from those the German "martyr" espoused himself. As more recent scholars have emphasized, Bonhoeffer's key themes were not the ones that made him famous a decade and a half after his death. His passing comments on "religionless Christianity" and man's "coming of age," contained mostly in a short sequence of letters from the late spring and early summer of 1944, were not attempts to configure a Christian understanding of "revolutionary" social transformation, much less were they an argument for reducing or eliminating the social role of churches. The Bonhoeffer scholar Christian Gremmels has argued that "religionless Christianity" and man's "coming of age" were not the theologian's main themes, but rather "auxiliary concepts facilitating the task of witnessing the presence of Jesus Christ in the present."[55]

Whatever the powerful uses to which a later, post-colonial era put them, Bonhoeffer's suggestive reflections were products of their own time. The theological critique of "religion"—defined as a human construct obstructing obedience to God's word—had been a mainstay of the so-called "crisis theology" movement originating in the writings of Karl Barth and Emil Brunner in the 1920s and 1930s, the milieu in which Bonhoeffer placed himself and to which he addressed his writings. Along with virtually all figures in the international ecumenical movement at the time, Barth, Brunner, and Bonhoeffer saw the decline of Christianity and secular emancipation as a package deal bringing chaos and disorder. What set the post-colonial cohorts apart was their embrace of emancipation and the moral and social responsibility that came with a secular society. When they cast Bonhoeffer, or indeed other "crisis" theologians,[56] as the progenitor of this view, they concealed the role of the ecumenical movement's engagement with Afro-Asian "revolution," and especially the Asian theologians who first invested anti-colonial "revolution" with theological significance, in shaping subsequent currents of Christian thinking. In this way, they made decolonization an achievement of the Christian Occident, reclaiming Western authorship of world history at the moment it was challenged by the defeat of European colonialism.

V

The etiology of the theology of secularization sketched here suggests three concluding points. First, it underscores how profoundly Protestant ideas, institutions, and practices were shaped by challenges to European colonialism. Within the leadership of the ecumenical movement, there was universal urgency to establish the relevance of Christianity to anti-colonial activism and define its place in post-colonial societies. Significantly, it was Third World ecumenists, aligned with anti-colonial movements, and often collaborating with socialist and Communist parties, that developed the crucial concept of revolution as a providential event, displacing "order" and installing social transformation as the site of God's activity in history. This theological framework proved useful in the 1950s even to more conservative Western ecumenists who rejected political radicalism in favor of melioristic or Western-led developmentalist approaches to social change in the global South. It enabled the movement as a whole to claim that Christianity was not tainted by its prior associations with colonial regimes.

Second, on a methodological level, this story suggests the importance of attending to a specific global milieu, rooted materially in international ecumenical organizations, when tracing how dominant Protestant voices understood the meaning and significance of decolonization. This milieu did not, of course, shape all forms of elite Protestant religiosity, nor all forms of it equally. It did, however, have a pervasive influence rooted in its elite membership and claim to represent the global diversity of a universal faith. Recovering the international formation of ecumenical ideas shows how little they comport with narratives of the self-transcendence of Protestant chauvinism: even when Protestants *embraced* secularization they did so to vindicate, rather than challenge, the exclusive truth of historical Christianity—and the legitimacy of its Western incarnation. Recognizing the abiding salience of Christianity's hierarchical commitments precisely in their reformations illuminates the limitations of sourcing it as an inspiration of secular politics or values, even while it highlights the genuinely "revolutionary" politics Christian faith could, at times, authorize.

Finally, the story also sheds light on the sources of ecumenical Protestantism's decline in Europe (especially) and the United States (to a lesser extent) since the 1960s. The theology of secularization was one important ingredient in Protestantism's Western collapse, since it could authorize, for some, an exit from the organized churches altogether, while at the same time contributing to processes of political polarization already underway. Its provenance in Western post-colonial anxieties and neo-colonial aspirations only underscores how deeply tied was the demise of ecumenical Protestantism in the West to the collapse of Europe's colonial empires. That the counterpart of this story—Protestant Christianity's phenomenal growth in the Global South since the 1960s—was enabled in part by that same collapse underscores the multivalent importance of decolonization in shaping patterns of global Christianity down to the present.

CHAPTER 2

From Order to Revolution: American Ecumenical Protestants and the Colonial World, 1900–1970

Gene Zubovich

Beginning in 1970, the World Council of Churches, the largest Protestant and Orthodox body in the world, began sending aid to militant, Marxist organizations fighting colonialism and white minority regimes in Southern Africa and across the world. Organizations like the African National Congress of South Africa, the Patriotic Front of Zimbabwe, and the Black Panthers of the United States received small payments for humanitarian projects from the World Council. While the payments were small, a powerful Christian body signaling its support for these Marxist movements against colonialism and taking sides in complicated political disputes dramatized the newfound exuberance for decolonization among a branch of Protestantism.

The American participants in the World Council of Churches played an important role in engineering this influential human rights mobilization. Why they did so, and how they became staunch critics of colonialism, demands an explanation. After all, Christianity had long been associated with the imperial project and American Protestants had been cheerleaders for US colonialism overseas. This chapter traces the changing attitudes among American ecumenical Protestants from the early 1900s, when they cheered the colonization of the Philippines, through the late 1960s, when they committed to sending political and financial aid to militant independence movements.[1] It argues that for much of the mid-twentieth century American ecumenical Protestants pursued an orderly decolonization, which would be administered by the United Nations and premised on Christian notions of human rights. Orderly decolonization downplayed self-determination in favor of stability, procedure, and international agreement. This limited commitment to decolonization was evident in the movement for "world order" in the 1940s, which framed imperialism as inimical to the creation of a post–World War II peace centered on the United Nations. These attitudes toward colonialism transformed in the late 1950s and 1960s, when American ecumenical Protestants began to embrace revolutionary movements. The transition between those two historical moments signaled changing attitudes about the importance of international organizations, nonviolence, order, and universalism. By the 1960s the justification for opposing colonialism, and the tactics to fight it, had shifted. Protestant advocates of decolonization now stressed that anti-colonial revolutions, even if they were disorderly and violent, were providential.

Among the most important reasons ecumenical Protestants dropped a colonial mindset and donned a postcolonial one was the role of race. Ecumenical Protestants' engagement with anti-racist movements in the United States influenced how they viewed colonialism. The experiences of Japanese internment, the Civil Rights movement, and the Black Power movement shaped how predominantly white Protestant organizations responded to demands for self-determination in the Global South. So too did encounters between Americans and Christians in Africa, Asia, and Latin America, who were often more critical of imperialism and more willing to accuse Christianity of being its handmaiden. Moreover, international religious networks, like the World Council of Churches, mediated and reshaped discussions of race and colonialism. The postcolonial mindset of American ecumenical Protestants emerged through the intersection of anti-racist movements and transnational ecumenical networks.

This chapter builds on a broad body of scholarship that emphasizes the links between race in the United States and American foreign affairs.[2] Scholars working in this area have largely focused on how decolonization and Cold War competition in the "Third World" shaped the US Civil Rights movement. By contrast, this chapter emphasizes how anti-racist mobilizations from the 1940s through the 1960s in the United States aided the movements for decolonization. It highlights the role international religious networks played as a conduit for American anti-colonial activism overseas, as well as for the reception of criticism and reevaluation of the ideas undergirding such activism.[3] This chapter also adds to the growing body of scholarship that shows the centrality of anti-racist movements to the popularization of human rights in the late twentieth century.[4]

The emphasis American ecumenical Protestants placed on race distinguished them from European Protestants and Catholics, whose discussion of decolonization did not feature race as prominently. In Europe in the 1940s and 1950s, Protestant leaders reluctantly accepted the inevitability of decolonization and refocused their energy on European unity as the basis of a new identity.[5] European Catholics were split on decolonization into the 1950s, unable to choose between the civilizing mission of Catholicism and the desire to maintain links with faithful Catholics in places like Africa.[6] American evangelicals largely opposed the anti-racist and anti-colonial figures with whom ecumenical Protestants were in dialogue. Evangelicals defined their international movement in opposition to the politics of the ecumenical movement.[7] American ecumenical Protestants took a distinctive path in coming to terms with decolonization, which wound through transnational networks and was reshaped by encounters with anti-racist movements.

This chapter begins with the first popular articulation of anti-colonial thought by US ecumenical Protestants in the 1940s. American leaders focused on building a post–World War II order around the universal values of human rights and an international government that would guarantee autonomy to subject peoples. It was also marked by ambivalence about decolonization. The chapter then proceeds to the 1950s and early 1960s, when the Cold War reshaped the debates about colonialism and cast suspicion on postcolonial leaders as potential allies of the Soviet Union and the People's Republic of China. During the Cold War, the discourse on imperialism continued to focus on its racial dimensions but it also drew upon initiatives to combat McCarthyism in the United States. Theologian Daisuke Kitagawa, who had participated in American anti-racist programs before taking a post with the World Council of Churches, was a revealing figure, whose ambivalence about race, imperialism, and nationalism laid bare divisions within the broader ecumenical movement about how to respond to decolonization in the late 1950s and early 1960s. Pushed by pastors in the Global South to more forcefully condemn imperialism, Kitagawa's writings revealed the important role of encounters with colonized peoples as a key dynamic in the reevaluation of imperialism in the 1960s. The chapter concludes by showing that by 1968 new theological formulations about "just revolution" formalized the decades-long reevaluation of imperialism by the global ecumenical movement and its American participants.

The Growth of US Protestant Anti-Colonialism

Protestant Christianity had long played an important role in settler colonialism in British North America and the United States. Church leaders justified American settlement of Indigenous lands by appealing to providence, the spread of Christian civilization, and the conversion of "heathens" to Christianity.[8] The religion continued to play that role as the United States became an overseas empire at the end of the nineteenth century. After the United States defeated Spain in the War of 1898, a debate broke out about the status of Spanish colonies. Some had argued that the United States ought to refrain from acquiring colonies in order to maintain its republic. The Protestant evangelist and perennial Democratic Party presidential candidate William Jennings Bryan was among the leading voices opposing the colonization of the Philippines, which he did partly on racial grounds.[9] But the predominant sentiment among Protestant leaders was expressed by Congregationalist reverend Adolphus J. F. Behrends, who called the question of Filipino sovereignty "settled" in favor of American colonialism. "For better or for worse," he announced to an overflowing crowd in Carnegie Hall in 1900, "the white man's burden is on us."[10]

Behrends was speaking at the Ecumenical Conference on Foreign Missions in New York City, which had brought together American missionaries to cooperate across denominational lines. "Your denominational banners—riddled with shot, torn into tatters—put them in your glass cases—stow them away in the shelves of some theological museum—and then let us all go out together, and preach only Christ and him crucified," said Behrends to thunderous applause.[11] This feeling that denominations should cooperate and move toward a united and truer Christianity emerged partly in this colonial context. Ecumenism found expression in the creation of the Federal Council of Churches of Christ in America in 1908. Two years later, in Edinburgh, Scotland, Protestant leaders from across the world met to pursue cooperation across national boundaries.[12]

In the United States, ecumenical Protestantism revolved around the Federal (after 1950, National) Council of Churches. Dozens of American denominations joined this ecumenical organization, including the Northern Methodists, Northern Presbyterians, Northern Baptists, Episcopalians, and Congregationalists. These were predominantly white denominations, whose membership was concentrated in the Northeast, the Midwest, and on the West Coast. African American denominations did join the ecumenical movement but their members were rarely placed in positions of authority. Ecumenical

Protestants viewed overcoming denominational boundaries as a Biblical commandment to uncover a true, universal form of Christianity underneath the contingencies of European and American history.[13] It was also appealing because ecumenism encouraged cooperation among missionaries and made overseas proselytizing more efficient. As these denominations joined the ecumenical movement, their Christian universalism was also rooted in the tradition of the social gospel and liberal theology, which emphasized social reform as a central Christian practice.[14] Therefore, the impulse to cooperate and the impulse to enact social reform was inseparable for American ecumenists.

Only during the interwar era did debates about imperialism come to the fore among white ecumenical Protestants. Following World War I, a large and left-leaning pacifist movement emerged, the leaders of which sometimes drew on both theological and Marxist critiques of imperialism.[15] The evangelist Sherwood Eddy, who was a pacifist and socialist, lamented in 1928 that, only a few years before, "we felt a divine call to go from our own favored 'Christian' nation to the backward 'heathen' nations lost in darkness." But now he recognized this cultural arrogance was "complacent, paternalistic, imperialistic."[16]

While Eddy took the pacifist and socialist route to anti-imperialism, others came to decolonization through engagement with the missionary movement. Harvard philosopher William Ernest Hocking did not share Eddy's politics, but he nonetheless concluded that imperialism was coming to an end. Hocking was an important figure in the early twentieth century movement to reform American missions in light of increasing nationalism throughout East and South Asia. He urged missionaries to focus on what we today would call development work—building universities, sharing agricultural knowledge, constructing hospitals—instead of proselytization. His views were rooted in the theology of ecumenism and the philosophy of personalism, both of which emphasized the commonality of the world's peoples and the universality of science, religion, and industry. Hocking equated American modernity with a "universal" culture and conditioned his acceptance of decolonization on the promises postcolonial leaders made to modernize their nations. But he also stretched the notion of ecumenism by finding cultural and theological value in Asian religions, which sometimes resulted in public confrontations with European neoorthodox theologians.[17]

For all the acknowledgement among missionaries and pacifists that imperialism was dying, and that American Christianity must accommodate this new reality, American ecumenical Protestants in the 1930s did not take a consistent approach to imperialism. Organizations like the Protestant-backed

Institute of Pacific Relations, the international YMCA, YWCA, and the Student Volunteer Movement were institutional homes to anti-colonial activists and educated the US public about anti-colonial movements. But the emerging coalitions of pacifists, socialists, African American activists, and missionaries in the early 1930s had by the end of that decade splintered apart over the wars in Asia and Europe.[18]

During World War II, anti-colonialism reemerged as a pressing issue for ecumenical Protestants but in a new context. The discourse on anti-colonialism became part of a wartime movement to reform what American ecumenical Protestants called "world order." In this globalist context, colonialism became a problem because it undermined the prospects for peace and order once hostilities ceased. Although church leaders had split about American entry into World War II, they came to agree that creating a peaceful postwar order required a world government. "This League-of-Nations-with-teeth," as *Time* magazine called the Protestant proposal, would be "a duly constituted world government of delegated powers: an international legislative body, an international court with adequate jurisdiction, international administrative bodies with necessary powers, and adequate international police forces and provision for enforcing its worldwide economic authority."[19] The World Order movement was led by Presbyterian layman and future US secretary of state John Foster Dulles, who rallied millions of Protestants across the country.

The movement was guided by the principles of the "Six Pillars of Peace," which included "assurance, through international organization, of ultimate autonomy for subject peoples." The phrase was a carefully chosen alternative to self-determination, because "autonomy" could be achieved within the imperial system or under the supervision of an international body. "Ultimate" autonomy could signal that American Protestants were in no hurry to free the peoples of Asia and Africa from colonialism. Debates about the scope, scale, and speed of autonomy raged between leftists like A.J. Muste, who emphasized US complicity in imperialism and called for immediate self-determination, and Dulles, who told State Department officials in 1945 that ecumenical Protestants "were satisfied in all their statements with self-government or autonomy as objectives of the trusteeship system and had never insisted on independence."[20]

Imperialism also received considerably more attention by ecumenical Protestant leaders because, in their view, it was linked to the anti-racist mobilizations under way in the United States during the 1940s. Ecumenical Protestant organizations, like the Federal Council of Churches, were among the very few groups to oppose the internment of Japanese Americans and to work for its hasty end.[21] The president of the Federal Council wrote to Roosevelt in 1942 to condemn internment as "totalitarianism and discrimination."[22] Prejudice against African Americans during World War II was an even greater concern for American ecumenical Protestants. In 1942 the African American press launched the Double-V campaign—victory against fascism abroad and racism at home—and the Federal Council of Churches soon came to their aid. Prominent ecumenical Protestants staffed high-ranking positions in the Fair Employment Practices Committee. They were key players in the creation of the President's Committee on Civil Rights and its pathbreaking report, *To Secure These Rights*.[23] Therefore, it was no surprise that in 1946 the Federal Council of Churches became the first large, predominantly white organization in the United States to call for the immediate abolition of segregation. The organization's pledge to "work for a non-segregated Church and a non-segregated society" came years ahead of other white liberal groups.[24]

Diminishing racism and colonialism remained a contentious issue among ecumenical Protestants, even as the World Order movement popularized the values of anti-racism and anti-colonialism and empowered activists. Dulles, for example, helped engineer the domestic jurisdiction clause of the United Nations, which frustrated African Americans' appeals to the global body in the late 1940s. Dulles' lobbying was aided by the realist theology of Reinhold Niebuhr and his allies, who sought to reign in the earlier enthusiasm for world government.[25] Rather than seeing this as the decline of Protestant commitments to anti-colonialism and anti-racism, we should instead see this as a moment of adoption of orderly decolonization.[26] Ecumenical Protestants, caged in by a commitment to order, actually expanded their initiatives to combat racism and colonialism in the 1940s.[27] As the UN turned a deaf ear to claims by African Americans and the World Council of Churches became dominated by realists, and later neoorthodox theologians, American ecumenical Protestants continued to carry the banner of anti-racist human rights. In 1948, the Federal Council of Churches issued a statement on human rights, which was modeled on the UN's Universal Declaration. But the American organization emphasized the racial dimensions of the political, social, and economic rights and its implications for the United States. Human rights "cannot be obtained under a system of racial segregation," it announced.[28]

Ecumenical Protestants continued to push for the creation of a mandates system for colonial territories under the United Nations with more explicit protections for colonial peoples and for guarantees of independence within definite time frames. But the emphasis ecumenical intellectuals placed on order and international governance limited their commitment to anti-colonialism. Ecumenical Protestants wanted to work with the UN, to bolster its standing, and to reform the organization so that it more closely resembled the world government they had advocated during the war. Their desire for order, peace, and international machinery meant that they were committed to working through the UN, despite the lack of interest in decolonization among the majority of permanent Security Council members.[29]

American ecumenical Protestants were also hampered by their reliance on US foreign policy elites, who sometimes emerged as spokespersons for the World Order movement. For example, when the Federal Council of Churches announced the Six Pillars of Peace in 1943, they issued press releases on each of the six propositions, which ran in hundreds of newspapers across the country. These pieces were written by public figures like *New York Times* publisher Arthur Sulzberger, Undersecretary of State Sumner Wells, and Princeton University president Harold Dodds. The statement on the pillar calling for autonomy for subject peoples was written by Francis B. Sayre, the former US colonial administrator of the Philippines. Sayre warned that there was "no easy and quick solution" to colonialism. Thinking back to his own time in the Philippines, he recalled the "slow and arduous and baffling task of preparing the Filipino people for ultimate autonomy"—a goal he was not confident the United States had achieved over the past forty years. Sayre endorsed progressively handing over greater responsibility to locals and called for some measure of international control in colonial territories. But he ignored racism as the basis for colonialism, the relationship between imperialism and segregation in the US, and the generally self-critical outlook ecumenical Protestants had been developing. In this way, much of the American public beyond church circles encountered ecumenical Protestants' ideas as an endorsement of the US government's position in international affairs. The desire of ecumenical Protestants to be politically relevant, their alliances with prominent governmental officials, and their focus on the UN competed with the more critical discourses on race and colonialism circulating in their community.

From World Order to Revolution

In the 1950s and 1960s, discussions of decolonization changed in important ways among the leadership of American ecumenical Protestantism. Their aversion to disorder gave way to a tolerance, and sometimes an outright embrace, of militant revolutionary movements. Their commitment to universalism made more room for national contexts. And the locus of their activism shifted from the United Nations to working directly with anti-colonial leaders. These new attitudes were partly shaped by a response to the collapse of the anti-Communist consensus, the Civil Rights movement, the Black Power movement, and the rapid decolonization of Africa.[30]

But before ecumenical Protestants would embrace decolonization, they had to break free from the Cold War framework that had enveloped nearly all aspects of American life by the start of the Korean War in 1950. Politicians and civil society figures proclaimed that the competition between the United States and the Soviet Union was a war between religion and atheism.[31] The United States began being called a "Judeo-Christian" nation, one that now welcomed Catholics and Jews as stewards of a nation that had long been assumed to be Protestant.[32] In the 1950s, religious language spread to US currency, the pledge of allegiance, and the new national motto, "In God We Trust." The Catholic Church and Catholic organizations, like the Knights of Columbus, were especially enthusiastic about the religious nationalism sweeping the country but a broad array of Protestant organizations promoted the religious fervor as well. Amid the enthusiasm for the Cold War, new laws, loyalty oaths, and public hearings created a chilling effect on leftist members of unions, universities, civil rights organizations, and media. This "McCarthyism," as it became known, did not target Protestant organizations initially. Only in 1953 was the liberal Methodist bishop G. Bromley Oxnam forced to appear before the House Un-American Activities Committee. That same year, Senator Joseph McCarthy's aide J. B. Matthews proclaimed that "the largest single group supporting the Communist apparatus in the United States today is composed of Protestant Clergymen."[33] The Protestant churches were able to weather such accusations better than other groups in the United States. Nonetheless, facing McCarthyism encouraged some ecumenical Protestants to turn away from Cold War orthodoxy and become more sympathetic to liberation movements in the Global South, despite the prominence of Marxism in those movements.

American Protestant theologians also had to contend with the realist theology of Reinhold Niebuhr, who was among the most ardent supporters of the US-led Cold War in the 1950s. Niebuhr had once been a committed pacifist, but he broke with this community in the lead-up to World War II and became a public critic of political and religious liberalism. He lambasted liberals as the "children of light," whose naïve confidence in rationality and progress blinded them to the persistent problem of sin in the world. Liberals needed to learn from the hardball tactics of the "children of darkness," those totalitarian states like the Soviet Union, without losing sight of the ultimate ends of liberalism. This balancing act between good intensions and muscular politics animated Niebuhr's view of America's role in the world. Niebuhr shared in the ecumenical consensus on international order and structure but took it in a more hawkish direction than many of his fellow theologians. For example, Niebuhr forcefully endorsed NATO while the broader US ecumenical leadership was split on the issue.[34]

Alongside McCarthyism, the international ecumenical movement also pushed some American Protestants to undercut the logic of the Cold War. The ecumenical World Council of Churches was created in the 1930s, but the organization's founding was delayed by World War II until 1948, when Protestant and Orthodox denominations gathered together in Amsterdam. At its inception, the global religious body focused its attention on Cold War tensions, postwar reconstruction, displaced persons, religious freedom, and theological questions. It said little about decolonization or about racism. Nonetheless, from the outset, the World Council of Churches attempted to circumvent some Cold War divisions because it wanted to maintain communion with churches in Eastern Europe and in China, both of which had come largely under Communist control. The universalism of ecumenism—"that they will all be one," as John 17:21 instructed—created an incentive to maintain dialogue and cooperation with churches in Communist countries and to maintain good relations with places like Czechoslovakia, Hungary, and (after 1949) the People's Republic of China. At the 1948 Amsterdam meeting, the World Council proclaimed a new theology of the "Responsible Society," an economic view that steered a middle course between capitalism and communism in a concerted attempt to counteract Cold War divisions.[35] For European theologians, the new outlook fit with the burgeoning Christian Democracy movement in postwar Europe. In the United States, however, the Responsible Society was received in the context of anti-Communism and forced US theologians into debates about the Cold War.

While the World Council of Churches addressed the Cold War from its inception, the organization did not intervene in the debates over racism in a substantial way until 1954. It criticized segregation at that time largely because it was meeting in the United States a few months after the pivotal *Brown v. Board of Education* Supreme Court decision, which declared segregation in schooling unconstitutional. African Americans took on the role of critic of racism and imperialism partly because in the 1950s the World Council of Churches remained dominated by Europeans and Americans, with few delegates from the Third World holding leadership positions. In 1954, Benjamin Mays, an African American educator and mentor to Martin Luther King Jr., took the lead in pushing the World Council to condemn segregation.[36] Mays had served as a vice president of the Federal Council of Churches in the 1940s and was instrumental in that organization's stance against segregation, first announced in 1946. At the World Council meeting, Mays drew on the universalist discourse promoted by the ecumenical movement as he argued that race was an artificial barrier to the unity of Christianity. He cited church historians, who demonstrated that, until the modern era, Christians paid little attention to racial differences and worshipped across color lines. Armed with this usable past, Mays called on Christians to return to an allegedly primordial theological insight that the fatherhood of God demanded the brotherhood of mankind.[37] Mays' demand for a "new Pentecost" swayed the World Council of Churches.[38] The organization drew on the language developed by American ecumenists in the 1940s as it called on Christians across the world to "renounce all forms of segregation or discrimination and . . . work for their abolition within their own life and within society."[39]

Because African American activists were bringing the issue of race to the global body, and because they drew upon the universalism of the ecumenical movement, the implications of the World Council's pronouncement would have an effect well beyond America's shores. South African theologian Ben J. Marais, an Afrikaner and member of the Dutch Reformed Church, understood the implications of Mays' criticism for his home country. Marais defended apartheid publicly at the 1954 World Council meeting. "Different churches based on language or race may be useful and even preferable in some extreme cases," Marais cautioned. Drawing on the rhetoric of order and disorder, he argued that forcing integration on South Africa "would only lead to a rich harvest of chaos and disaster."[40] Marais' warnings did not stop the World Council of Churches from condemning racism or from taking further steps to combat it.

The efforts by Black delegates from the United States to highlight the problem of racism drew attention to South African apartheid, an issue the World Council's executive secretary Willem Adolph Visser 't Hooft had hoped to keep quiet. Visser 't Hooft was no apologist for apartheid, but he consistently prioritized maintaining good ecumenical relations with the South African Dutch Reformed Church, which was a vocal supporter of white supremacy. The theologian believed that anti-racism was implicit in ecumenical relations. Drawing in white South African churches into a universal Christian movement would dispel racial myths, create community, and lessen racial antipathy more effectively than any proclamation or program that promoted antagonism toward white minority rule, Visser 't Hooft believed. Preferring quiet diplomacy over attention-grabbing proclamations, he traveled to South Africa in 1952 after a multiracial delegation from the World Council of Churches was banned from the country. His report was dull in tone and an attempt at what he considered even-handedness. While detailing the plight of Bantu laborers, he framed his report in ways that would not be off-putting to white churches that supported apartheid. The system of racial segregation did not necessarily imply "discrimination," he wrote. "It can mean separate development of the races so that each may have the fullest opportunity for growth."[41] In this way, Visser 't Hooft promoted the logic of separate-but-equal that had been rejected in the *Brown v. Board* decision. He remained opposed to taking special initiatives to combat white supremacy beyond the promotion of a universal church.

American evangelicals resisted condemning apartheid more tenaciously than did Visser 't Hooft. The modern US evangelical movement was organized in 1942 with the founding of the National Association of Evangelicals. Evangelicals remained steadfast opponents of the World Council of Churches. With roots in the fundamentalist movement of the early twentieth century, and affinities with the anti-modernist movement of the late nineteenth century, American evangelical identity was largely forged in opposition to the theological and political liberalism of the US participants in the ecumenical movement. Evangelist Billy Graham served as the movement's public face and the magazine *Christianity Today* (founded in 1956) served as its most important mouthpiece.

US evangelicals remained sympathetic to the apartheid state, and especially to its religious supporters. "It has become a popular pastime with long-distance mud-slingers to besmirch the name of the Dutch Reformed Church in South Africa," lamented Anglican theologian Philip Edgcumbe Hughes in the pages of *Christianity Today*. Hughes had grown up in South Africa before moving to the United Kingdom and finally settling in the United States. His role in the US Episcopal Church demonstrated that many adherents of the "mainline" churches remained sympathetic to apartheid even as the ecumenical movement was becoming more critical. But what is particularly striking is that *Christianity Today* invited Marais to act as an analyst of South African affairs after he was repudiated by the World Council of Churches. For example, Hughes paraphrased Marais approvingly in 1958. "The oneness of all believers in Christ cuts across and transcends (although it does not necessarily abolish) racial and social distinctions."[42] Marais was invited back for an interview later that year.[43] He was also published regularly in the journal, including a two-part series on South Africa, and he sometimes worked as a correspondent for the paper. Marais was among the most influential figures shaping US evangelical opinion on apartheid.[44]

While the evangelical *Christianity Today* cultivated sympathy for apartheid and its religious supporters, the World Council of Churches took incremental steps toward organizing against racism through the establishment of the Department of Racial and Ethnic Relations soon after the Evanston meeting. In retrospect, this initiative marked a transition from the universalist, ecumenism-as-anti-racism attitudes expressed by Visser 't Hooft to an action-oriented, anti-colonial approach that became dominant by the late 1960s.

The Department of Racial and Ethnic Relations was headed by Daisuke Kitagawa from 1960 to 1962. Kitagawa was born in Taihoku, in Japanese-occupied Taiwan, in 1910 and immigrated to the United States in 1933 to attend an Episcopalian seminary. He began his career as a minister in Seattle, Washington, in 1938. Like so many other Japanese Americans, Kitagawa was interned during World War II, at Tule Lake, where he headed the pastoral program for the Episcopal Church. After leaving the camp, he settled in Minneapolis, Minnesota, where he ministered to Japanese Americans and joined local civil rights groups. His experiences in an internment camp gave his words gravitas in ecumenical Protestant circles.

Kitagawa was a transitional figure between the UN-centered views of the 1940s and the postcolonial outlook of the late 1960s. His Department of Racial and Ethnic Relations acted as an information center and coordinating body that focused attention on racial tensions.[45] For example, when a political crisis occurred in Rhodesia and Nyasaland in 1960, Kitagawa brought together local politicians, business leaders, and teachers to discuss the situation.[46] The Department's approach was bureaucratic, proceduralist, and oriented toward promoting dialogue and mutual understanding. Nevertheless, it offered a venue for critics of imperialism to voice their concerns, including for individuals who otherwise had few political resources. The Department's work would help transform the ecumenical movement.

Kitagawa's position required him to travel across the world and partake in listening sessions with local ministers. In his writings about his travels, he frequently lambasted the shameful racism of white South Africans, Americans, and Europeans. But he was also suspicious of ethnic nationalism among non-white peoples. He recalled a conversation with an Indonesian student, who explained to Kitagawa in fluent Japanese that he was grateful for the Japanese occupation of the islands during World War II because the "Japanese have demonstrated to us that we Asians can be just as good as Europeans." To Kitagawa, this was a troubling sign of "counter-racism" ascendant among Asians and Africans. And he believed that these attitudes were also becoming reflected in international politics. The 1955 Bandung conference, a meeting in Indonesia of twenty-nine Asian and African nations, was one sign that "militant racism" was uniting the "colored races" against whites in "retaliation to the white man's past discrimination against them," according to Kitagawa.[47]

The growth of nationalism in the colonial and postcolonial world worried Kitagawa because of its threat to the ecumenical movement and to the UN-centered vision of international politics. He had experienced a virulent form of nationalism during World War II, when the US interned him for several years. Armed with skepticism, Kitagawa counseled Christians to see nationalism "as a threat to the ultimate unity of mankind and world peace, and even more, as a threat to the integrity of the Christian church."[48] The central purpose of Kitagawa's warnings was to chastise white Christians for their racism and to encourage them to combat prejudice before racial tensions became so extreme that dialogue was no longer possible. "The existence of these rabid racists among the people of colored races is an indication that the masses of colored people have cast the vote of nonconfidence in the Christian leadership among white people," he explained.[49] Nonetheless, Kitagawa's writings in the early 1960s showed that he viewed nationalism with suspicion and postcolonial societies as potential threats to world peace and order.

Kitagawa's writings in the early 1960s also documented new ways of thinking about revolutionary movements in the Third World among Africans, Asians, and increasingly among members of the global ecumenical movement. In 1960 he met with African pastors in the British colony of Southern Rhodesia (now Zimbabwe), to discuss nationalist movements fighting British rule. They spoke about nationalist leaders whom today we might call post-Christians—those who grew up in Christian institutions but have disaffiliated themselves in adulthood. This was common among African independence leaders in the 1960s, who were often educated in missionary schools but came to see Soviet or Chinese models of development as attractive alternatives to Western modernization theory. When anti-colonial leaders disaffiliated with Christian institutions, it was because "the church has alienated them rather than the reverse," the African pastors explained. According to Kitagawa, the pastors declared their solidarity with the nationalists, who are "risking their lives to put into practice what we have been preaching all these years." Nationalist leaders "are still within the church," the pastors stated emphatically, "and we not only have pastoral responsibility over them but we are prepared to follow them even into jail."[50] In other words, these pastors gave full endorsement to anti-colonial movements for liberation and urged greater pastoral care for revolutionaries. They criticized simplistic distinctions some of their fellow believers made between "Christian" and "secular" groups and called for the ecumenical movement to see the ways Christian values could be lived by disaffiliated (and sometimes explicitly anti-religious) movements.

These unnamed African pastors articulated in 1960 ideas that would be more fully embraced by the ecumenical movement at the end of the decade. As in other instances, the contributions of figures in the Global South to ecumenical thought remained muted in accounts like those of Kitagawa's. But they were there, nonetheless. The encounters between ecumenical leaders and Asian, African, and Latin American ministers and laypersons profoundly shaped the attitudes of Americans involved in the ecumenical movement and added to the work African American ministers had been doing in the United States. Kitagawa did not agree with the unnamed African pastors' analysis, but he was clearly moved by his encounter with such bold theological claims. He encouraged readers of his travelogue to be more understanding of what he called the chauvinistic tones of African nationalist movements. He called white Christians to forgiveness—to ask for forgiveness for "past racism" and to forgive Africans' "counter-racism." Forgiveness was not a passive act, he argued, but part of a broader action of accepting nationalism, acknowledging their "new national identities," and integrating their new nations into the "emerging one world community."[51]

Kitagawa's reluctant acceptance of nationalism, his endorsement of self-determination, his willingness to engage with independence movements that were not Christian (or were openly hostile to Christianity), and his greater appreciation for national pluralism reflected shifts among American ecumenical leaders and the broader global ecumenical movement. During the 1950s, a growing number of American ecumenical Protestants had come to similar conclusions. They shared three interlocking goals: to find an alternative to the Cold War framework, to combat American racism, and to promote self-determination for victims of Western imperialism. This could be seen most clearly in discussions by the officials of the US-based National Council of Churches of the Communist takeover of mainland China. This discourse framed the creation of the People's Republic of China as primarily an expression of nationalism, not communism. Figures like historian Kenneth Scott Latourette and theologian John Mackay, both of whom played key roles in formulating the ecumenical movement's policy toward East Asia, emphasized that events in China needed to be understood in the context of a long history of Western imperialism in East Asia and they called for the United States to diplomatically recognize the country and to stop blocking its entry into the United Nations. They emphasized that engagement with the Communist leadership of China was necessary for the creation of an orderly international system.[52]

Like the National Council of Churches, missionary networks and international student organizations also moved in the direction of accepting revolutionary movements and taking more seriously the notion of self-determination. This transition came in the guise of a new theology of revolution, which became more widespread in the 1950s. One of the key figures in this theological innovation was the missionary and educator Richard Shaull, who split his time between Brazil and Princeton Theological Seminary. Like Kitagawa, Shaull was moved by views he encountered abroad. Many of his Brazilian students were drawn to Marxism because it offered a better explanation and clearer solutions to the poverty the students saw all around them. Moved by their appeals, Shaull called on Americans in the mid-1950s to recognize the providential revolutions taking place across the world and for Christians to organize political alternatives to Communist movements that would nonetheless deliver many of the same things to the poor and marginalized: land reform, economic sovereignty, and control over their lives. His many writings and public appearances in the United States promoted socialist ideas to the American public as religious imperatives. Shaull also stressed the economic component of self-determination, an issue that was central to postcolonial nations, and he focused attention on the lowest rungs of colonial and postcolonial societies. Shaull became a fixture at American student gatherings in the late 1950s, alongside anti-colonial activists from the Third World, such as Nigerian lawyer Bola Ige.

In this internationalist context, students in the American ecumenical movement heralded a theological shift that would become more evident among the ecumenical leadership by the end of the 1960s. The National Student Christian Federation, whose members were joining the sit-in movement in 1960, explained that God was acting "in the far-reaching movement of liberation of Asian and African peoples from imperialist and colonial status to independence with dignity" and in the movement for "racial freedom and dignity" in the United States.[53] Many of these ideas would later fall under the broad banner of "liberation theology."[54]

The theology of revolution had been worked out in the 1950s and early 1960s by people who were wrestling with international events and taking part in transnational Christian networks, and who were often motivated by the US civil rights movement. By the mid-1960s the Black Power movement, the decolonization of Africa, liberation theology, and the Marxist-inspired activism of the "global sixties" created a context in which revolution became more widely accepted among ecumenical Protestants. These developments came to a head at the 1968 World Council of Churches meeting in Uppsala, Sweden. The theme of the meeting was "Behold, I make all things new," which was a fitting title for a conference that represented a dramatic shift in thinking about colonialism. African American writer James Baldwin (who replaced the recently assassinated Martin Luther King Jr.) lambasted the hubris of racists and imperialists in an address at Uppsala. Echoing the Black nationalist movement in the United States and the American liberation theologian James Cone's idea of Christ as a Black man, Baldwin endorsed "black power" and chastised clergy for creating a Christ with "blue eyes and blond hair."[55]

Baldwin's speech was well-received by a meeting rocked by student protests and increasingly vocal Third World delegates. As a marker of this transformation, ecumenical leaders admitted the Church of Christ on Earth, the first African-initiated—that is, not founded by Western missionaries—denomination, into the World Council.[56] Some of the white delegates from the United States had been rethinking decolonization and were receptive to the criticism at Uppsala. The conservative writer Ernest Lefever was ungenerous in his depiction of the Uppsala meeting as an "orgy of Western confessions of guilt, especially within the U.S. delegation."[57] But it did capture the self-critical attitude of many white American participants and the important role of figures like Presbyterian minister Eugene Carson Blake in leading the charge against colonialism and white minority regimes.

The new postcolonial mindset among ecumenical Protestants was most clearly articulated in the theology of "just revolution." In prior decades theologian Reinhold Niebuhr had developed a "just war" theology for Protestants, who had largely lacked such a tradition prior to World War II. But as critics took issue with Niebuhr for allegedly sanctifying an unequal distribution of power on the world stage, they began to call for a theological justification for revolutionary movements. Under what conditions is a revolutionary movement justified in deploying violence against the colonial state? What is the role of Protestants in revolutionary situations? The discussions around these questions were transnational, with figures like Shaull and Indian theologian M. M. Thomas offering the most nuanced theological defenses of revolution.[58]

Thomas understood the nature of the church through the function of the church in the world, which was to promote human dignity and unity in an effort to build the Kingdom of God. "The Work of Christ and His Kingdom is discernible in the secular social and political revolutions of our time," he explained in an address at the 1968 Uppsala meeting. And the "Church's function is to discern it and witness to it."[59] A revolution was "just" if democratic participation or nonviolent protest had been foreclosed by colonial authorities, thereby making violent struggle the only option. Thomas did acknowledge the longstanding ecumenical concern for orderly decolonization. He urged fellow Christians to take note of whether the revolutionary movement has the potential to control the chaos that revolutions often unleash. But he emphasized justice in his analysis. The World Council should consider whether a revolutionary movement has the will and means to empower a greater number of colonial subjects (or, as was the case in some Communist movements, it is likely to replace one group of elites with another). By recognizing just revolutions and supporting them, Christians had the potential to minimize hatred by reminding revolutionaries of the humanity of their adversaries, encouraging dialogue as soon as possible, and emphasizing the humanistic goals that the revolutionary movements proclaim. In this way, the Church can "call for revolution where the status quo is inhuman or unjust and even participate in the ideologies and strategies of the revolution, without absolutizing them or losing the resources of prophetic criticism in relation to them."[60]

The theology of just revolution gave the World Council of Churches a justification and blueprint for aiding some of the last anti-colonial movements in Southern Africa against Portuguese colonialism in places like Angola and

Mozambique, and against white minority regimes in Rhodesia and South Africa. The details of the ensuing human rights mobilization, which lasted until the fall of apartheid in 1994, are beyond the purview of this chapter.[61] But it is important to note that the theological justifications of revolution facilitated concrete, material commitments to aiding anti-colonial movements. That the World Council of Churches called its initiative "the Programme to Combat Racism" was a product of the intertwined discourses of anti-racism and anti-colonialism, a link that was especially pronounced in the United States.

CHAPTER 3

Vietnamese Catholics' Search for Independence, 1941–1963

Phi-Vân Nguyen

In 1963, *Informations catholiques internationales* enthusiastically covered how the world embraced the ideas of the Second Vatican Council, except perhaps for Vietnam.[1] Catholics, there, had accomplished great achievements. The nomination of a Vietnamese Catholic, Ngô Đình Diệm, as the prime minister of the State of Vietnam in 1954 capped a ten-year struggle to liberate the country from French domination, "clearing" the name of Catholics often accused of working for the colonialists. But this success turned into triumphalism. Priests acted like the kings of small fiefdoms. Bishop Ngô Đình Thục, the prime minister's brother, confused religion with politics. Catholics formed little enclaves, similar to the French, Spanish, or Canadian churches overseas, and failed to live in harmony with the rest of the society, the article concluded. Why did the decolonization of the Vietnamese Church expand its outreach so far outside the realm of the spiritual? Had it gone too far?

We often reduce decolonization to a single event, such as the signature of a treaty. But the transition toward independence involves different processes when we look at the political, social, cultural, or economic autonomy of a colony. What happened in Vietnam is no different. The decolonization of Catholicism involved the transformation of a Western religion into a genuinely Vietnamese faith, a greater representation of Vietnamese priests and bishops, and the creation of a hierarchy directly connected to Rome, standing on par with other national churches. These achievements did not happen overnight, nor did they coincide with Vietnam's political independence.

While these developments unfolded at a different time and pace, they influenced the role of Catholics in the struggle for independence and their relationship with the postcolonial state.

Studies of the Vietnam Wars suggest that Catholics either acted like pawns in a struggle against Communists or obeyed their Catholic prime minister like little soldiers. The Vatican's aversion to atheism remains the core reason for the Vietnamese Catholics' opposition to Communism and involvement in political, economic, and cultural projects.[2] Missing from that interpretation is their struggle to decolonize their faith. This chapter argues that Catholics disagreed and competed against each other over how to best transform this Western religion into a Vietnamese one. To the Japanese military and later Chinese Communists, the decolonization of the church involved a total break with the West. Vietnamese Catholics, fearing the expansion of Communism would generate a schism, launched political and social initiatives to decolonize their faith differently. Finding the right ideas, institutions, and reforms to express the evolution of a Vietnamese church entirely independent from colonial or Western domination would not only guarantee the survival of the church, it could also become a rampart against Communism and serve as a model for other Catholics across the globe.

From a Peaceful to a Violent Decolonization

The first Catholic communities emerging in the Đại Việt empire in the sixteenth century had grown to roughly 1.6 million people by 1945.[3] Rome's calls for the creation of national churches echoed aspirations from local priests to take over the responsibilities traditionally held by Western missionaries. In the wake of this transformation, Catholics created publications and organized local celebrations, such as festivals or pilgrimages.[4] Missionaries from Québec, Spain, or the United States slowly took over positions held by the Foreign Paris Missions. By the 1930s, a decolonization of the church had already started. But this quiet transition changed when Vietnam headed toward a violent decolonization. Catholics debated whether they should support the overthrow of colonial rule and a more radical adaptation of Catholicism. This division did not emerge with the Communist revolution, but under the Japanese occupation of Indochina in 1940.

The rise of the Japanese empire in the 1930s challenged the status and practice of Catholicism in Asia. Tokyo pressured its subjects to express their absolute loyalty to the empire, which compelled Catholics to reconsider how their faith was practiced in Asia. Debates on the compatibility of ancestor worship had ended in the eighteenth century, when Rome chose the propagation of a Europeanized faith, rather than adaptation to the local culture and customs.[5] Now that Japan was taking over the territories of Western empires, its demands on its subjects brought the risk that the Catholic faith would be outlawed.

In the 1930s, missionaries initially complained about a policy of requiring churches to display a shrine to the goddess Ameratsu, the imperial family's ancestress.[6] But Tokyo's pressure forced the Vatican to revise this policy.[7] Rome nominated indigenous bishops in Japan. It also lifted the interdiction to hold rites for ancestors in Manchukuo in 1936, in Japan the following year, and in China with the 1939 decree *Plane compertum est*.[8] The Vatican could not afford to lose these Catholics. As the Japanese empire extended its reach over a growing number of the faithful, Rome moved toward creating national churches and opening the Catholic faith to local variations.

The French reacted similarly when Japanese troops occupied Indochina in 1940. Cut off from the rest of the empire, colonial authorities agreed to deliver resources and let Japanese troops station in Indochina. This kept French rule intact. But Japan's call to give "Asia to Asians" emboldened anticolonial sentiments among the Vietnamese. Worse yet, Japanese troops exacerbated "xenophobic" feelings, and urged Vietnamese people to develop self-reliance.[9] They even encouraged Catholics to separate from the rest of the hierarchy. A Japanese cultural center, created in 1943 in Hanoi, advertised that the Japanese church had eliminated financial ties with Europe and the United States.[10] The more Japanese propaganda spread, the more the French feared that all Vietnamese, including Catholics, could turn against them.

In response, colonial authorities insisted Indochina was a joint venture, benefiting the Vietnamese and the French.[11] Similar to Vichy France's *Révolution nationale*, several youth programs, sport events, and cultural initiatives tried to reinvigorate Vietnamese bodies and restore morality.[12] Cultural campaigns drew parallels between historical figures, such as Joan of Arc in France and the Trung sisters, who resisted foreign invasions.[13] The Japanese creation of a Pan Asian Buddhist association also prompted the state to sponsor religious groups, Confucian studies, and exhibitions on the Đại Việt empire. Japan's call for Asians to rise against the West pushed the French to support more initiatives exploring Vietnam's past and future history.

Catholics also took advantage of this attention. Alexis Cras, a French Dominican, believed this was the opportunity to bring a more Vietnamese interpretation to the Catholic faith. He ordered the painting of the Nativity scene, displaying Vietnamese characters, animals, and a landscape reminiscent of the Northern highlands, to give the impression that the birth of Christ had occurred in Vietnam.[14] He also created the Cercle Renaissance, in 1941, to organize lectures on Vietnamese history and introduce French philosophy, such as Jacques Maritain's existentialism and Emmanuel Mounier's personalism, to students of the University of Hanoi. He pioneered the introduction of Western philosophical ideas using examples drawn from the Vietnamese classics or literature, believing it was the only way Western ideas and the Catholic faith could become "an incarnation that would become genuinely Chinese, Annamite [the word then used to refer to the inhabitants of the Đại Việt empire], or Japanese."[15] This cultural adaptation could prevent a brutal rupture with the West.

The greatest impact of the Japanese occupation, however, came unexpectedly. The Japanese overthrew the French on March 9, 1945, rounding up all nationals and civilians from Allied countries, including missionaries. This brought the church to an unprecedented situation, as Vietnamese priests assumed all the responsibilities previously held by missionaries for the first time. Some Catholics worried about the arrest of their priests. But the general reaction to the coup suggested that Vietnamese Catholics' attitude toward colonial rule had changed.[16] The French lamented: "While indigenous Catholicism had been a source of order, social stability, and an element loyal to the protecting power, the events which followed March 9 have shown that the clergy and Tonkinese Catholics had become very nationalist and rejected French sovereignty over their country."[17] Some Catholics participated in the government created by the Japanese or prayed "for the soul of Japanese officers and soldiers, and Annamite volunteers fallen in the struggle for the liberation of Vietnam."[18] Regardless of their position regarding the colonial state, priests had to assume new responsibilities as local administrators because a famine reaped the lives of a million persons, roughly 8.3 percent of the population of Tonkin and 7.9 percent in the Northern Central provinces.[19] They oversaw everyday matters, handled food distribution, and organized self-defense militias because the new government, at the local level, was nowhere to be seen. This situation had a profound impact on Catholics' role in Vietnam's independence, when the Việt Minh, an anti-fascist front created by the Indochinese Communist Party in 1941, came out of the maquis to seize power.

Defining Independence

Five months later, the Việt Minh overthrew the government backed by the Japanese and proclaimed the creation of a new state, the Democratic Republic of Vietnam (DRV), on September 2, 1945. Over the previous weeks, they had occupied governmental offices, police headquarters, and telegraph and rail stations in most cities, but not everywhere. Catholics controlled large patches of territory and seized townlets in the diocese of Phát Diệm on August 20, 1945, hours before the Việt Minh's arrival.[20] The DRV's survival would depend on their support. Hồ Chí Minh had been praising them for years. To him, Vietnamese bishops were meant to head the church entirely: "On a total sixteen bishops in the country of Annam, only three are Annamites in the present; when Vietnam will be independent, all sixteen bishops will be Vietnamese." Once the Việt Minh seized power, he exhorted Catholics again: "For nearly a century, many Annamite heroes have poured their blood for independence! They followed, without knowing, the example of Jesus Christ who died for the salvation of humanity."[21] The creation of the DRV could bring a new dawn for the decolonization of the church.

Catholics initially welcomed Việt Minh rule. Virtually all the seminarists of Saint-Sulpice in Hanoi attended the proclamation of the DRV, whereas Catholics elsewhere, gathered in numbers—almost 30,000 in the city of Vinh alone—to celebrate the new state.[22] Vietnamese bishops sent a letter to Rome asking the Pope for his benediction: "Our government made the auspicious decision to mark the celebration of our Annamite martyrs, authorized by the Holy See, as a national day for Vietnam."[23] Everything suggested the Catholic Church and the DRV stood united for Vietnam's independence.

The presence of DRV officials, including notorious Communists, at the Lê Hữu Từ's ordination as the bishop of Phát Diệm in October 1945, confirmed that Catholics and the DRV had become close partners.[24] This alliance translated into formal arrangements. Hồ Chí Minh invited Msgr. Lê Hữu Từ to become a supreme advisor to the DRV. Two dioceses, Phát Diệm and Bùi Chu, continued to run their own administrative organs and militias.[25] The Christmas cover of a Catholic publication, *Đa Minh* [Dominicans] even showed the five-pointed star to remind both of the announcement of the birth of Christ and the flag of the DRV.[26] Catholics had become a pillar in Vietnam's struggle for independence and could even remain autonomous within the DRV.

Over time, the relationship proved more complicated. The Việt Minh represented an anti-fascist front, but everyone knew the Indochinese Communist Party was behind its creation. Communists held the Ministry of Interior, National Defense, Foreign Affairs, and Finance. Despite Hồ Chí Minh's attempts to dissipate concerns by ordering the party's dissolution in November 1945, the DRV's liquidation of Nationalist leaders who criticized the Communist leadership cast doubts on the Viet Minh's true nature.

From the outset, the Việt Minh accused any Catholic criticizing Communists of national treason. The bishop of Phát Diệm knew that challenging Communist influence could turn against Catholics. Therefore, he ordered the creation of the Federation of Nationalist Catholics (*Liên đoàn công giáo quốc gia*), to become an alternative to the Catholics for National Salvation (*Công giáo cứu quốc*), for fear the latter organization would place Catholics under Việt Minh control.[27] Bishops also forbid lay Catholics from speaking or acting on behalf of the church without authorization.[28] But these tensions became an open confrontation with the outbreak of the Cold War.

The turning point came with the transformations of the Catholic Church in China after 1949. After winning the civil war, Chinese Communists gathered first Protestants and then Catholics into a patriotic association, which passed a resolution denouncing imperialism and declaring their determination to achieve the Three-Self Movement in 1951.[29] This included financial independence by refusing funding from abroad; administrative independence by removing foreigners from the hierarchy; and apostolic independence, by taking charge of evangelization without the assistance of foreign missionaries.[30] The following year, the government expelled all foreign missionaries and Chinese Catholics resisting the association. For the first time, the independence of the church meant the violent departure of all missionaries, the nationalization of the church, and a separation from the world church hierarchy. Rome insisted that faith in God did not contradict patriotism. Pope Pius XII's letter, *Cupimus Imprimis*, on January 18, 1952, declared: "[The church] does not reject, refuse the particular genius of diverse people, their mentality, their art, or culture; in fact, it welcomes them with enthusiasm, and adoring all this diversity, becomes joyfully embellished."[31] It was unnecessary to seek more independence because the Vatican was already supporting—not hindering—decolonization. Despite this reassurance, the Chinese patriotic association maintained its decision, which led Rome and the rest of the Catholic Church to denounce it as schismatic.

Vietnamese Catholics feared they would endure the same fate. While the expulsion of missionaries from China was an earthquake for the Christian world, it was particularly concerning to Vietnam for several reasons. Many Vietnamese Communists, including Hồ Chí Minh, lived in Southern China in the 1920s. Some underwent training at the Whampoa academy, marched alongside Mao to Yunan, and even became officers in both the Chinese People's Liberation Army and the Vietnamese People's Army.[32] Victory in China meant new support for Vietnamese Communists, who intensified their war effort by taking over the Việt Minh and launching land reforms in specific areas. Abandoning the broad front policy, Communists purged the army, the state, and the front from bourgeois elements, and clashed with allies, including Catholics.[33]

Chinese support for Vietnamese Communists prompted an avalanche of diplomatic recognitions. Beijing's and Moscow's backing of the DRV met Washington's, London's, and Rome's support of the Associated State of Vietnam (ASV), which the French created in 1949 to give a new purpose to their war effort. This turn, however, meant something different to Catholics. The separation of the Catholic Church in China raised the question of how to best achieve the decolonization of Catholicism. Could a church become fully independent while remaining attached to the rest of the hierarchy? Could it affirm its independence without separating from Rome?

While many Catholics had no categorical answer to these questions, two trends emerged. One part declared a total loyalty to the Việt Minh and claimed that anything else was a betrayal. While a few priests embraced Marxism, others insisted that nationalism remained the main reason Catholics should support the DRV. Father Phạm Bá Trực, a priest from the Red River Delta trained in Rome, served as chair of the DRV's National Assembly. From the early days of the DRV, the Việt Minh's main line of attack against Catholics was to claim they remained subservient to the West and hindered Vietnam's independence. "If we unite, we will survive, and if we divide, we will die! This is the motto to oppose those who divide, sabotage, and sell the country for their honours."[34] Father Phạm Bá Trực, too, insisted on unity. For Christmas 1948, he recalled that Christ himself had declared: "Then they will be one with each other, just as you and I are one," urging all Catholics to "rise together with our compatriots and resist, to reclaim independence, unity, and real freedom for the Fatherland (as this [was] God's natural law)."[35] The French calls for Catholics, especially from the autonomous dioceses of Bùi Chu and Phát Diệm, to join the ASV, was another attempt to divide the country. Father Phạm Bá Trực warned that France had already used religion to "steal" the country, by using the excuse of retaliating for the execution of Spanish missionaries to conquer the Đại Việt empire in 1858.[36] To him, religion and the state had to remain separated by reminding that Jesus had said to "Render unto Caesar the things that belong to Caesar, and unto God the things that belong to God." This saying went beyond the separation of divine and worldly matters, he believed, and applied to national independence: "Nowadays traitors claim colonialists protect their religion and give them the mandate to question the Lord, then the Lord answers: 'Render to Vietnam what belongs to the Vietnamese!'"[37] Returning from a visit to China and Korea, he insisted religion remained free, but the main danger hiding behind the French was, in fact, American imperialism.[38] Any Catholic rejoining the French behaved like "Judas betraying the Lord."[39] According to Phạm Bá Trực, God himself urged Catholics to defend their nation.

Other Catholics, however, considered that Communism was the greatest threat to their faith and that Rome itself stood by them. China's victory transformed the war in Indochina because it revealed the true face of Communists hiding behind the Viet Minh. The Legion of Mary, a lay association originating in Ireland and developing in China as an underground organization resisting Communist repression, also found fertile ground in Vietnam.[40] From its creation in Hanoi in 1948, other "squads" appeared elsewhere in the Red River delta by 1952.[41] Their periodical, *Đạo Bình Đức Mẹ*, reported on the repression of the clergy in China and Korea, and published essays from Chinese Catholics in exile, criticizing the state's intrusion in the church's affairs.[42] Moreover, Catholic refugees from China came to Vietnam to seek shelter in 1951. Their testimonies confirmed these fears. The church had been hijacked from within, dismantled, and humiliated. Eventually, Vietnamese Catholics would experience the same fate. But their war was not over yet. Unlike Chinese Catholics, they could prevent this from happening.

The church hierarchy reacted to this new turn of the war. In 1951, bishops of Indochina issued a letter urging Catholics not to engage in any activity that could facilitate Communism.[43] Bùi Chu and Phát Diệm joined the ASV. While the army absorbed Catholic militias, the two dioceses remained distinct provinces and Msgr. Lê Hữu Từ appointed priests and laypeople to run the civil administration.[44] Vietnamese bishops also insisted there was no incompatibility between nationalism and the Catholic faith. A pastoral letter, in 1952, declared that "becoming a member of the Church, does not mean that one abandons the tradition and civilization of its homeland," while a message, the following year, claimed that "the Church is a common Church for the entire world."[45] Vietnamese did not need to separate to become fully independent.

The Vatican also increased representativity in the hierarchy.[46] In 1945, only three apostolic vicariates, Phát Diệm, Bùi Chu, and Vĩnh Long, were placed under the authority of Vietnamese priests. Four more were nominated in 1950 and 1951 alone.[47] These elevations resonated well beyond Vietnam: Trường Cao Đại's ordination as the bishop of Haiphong did not happen in that city but in Hong Kong, where many Chinese Catholics had sought refuge. The presence of religious and political figures suggested the ceremony's significance.[48] "For us Catholics, the concept of Church and the concept of Homeland are so closely related that one cannot exist without the other. Because it is impossible to serve our Church without serving our Homeland. And it is impossible to serve our Homeland without serving our Church," declared a Vietnamese representative.[49] These Catholics were determined to show that their faith reinforced their commitment to protect national independence.

Confirmation that Communists considered Catholics as traitors came at the end of the First Indochina War. The Geneva ceasefire signed on July 20, 1954, divided Vietnam at the seventeenth parallel and gave the North to the DRV. Catholics in the DRV zone faced the choice of either leaving for the South or staying under Communist rule. Although the Vatican did everything to maintain relationships with the new government, many Catholics feared retribution. The Vatican informed Msgr. Trịnh Như Khuê, the bishop of Hanoi, that priests had to remain and only those who had received an authorization from their superior could go to the South.[50] However, priests departed in larger proportions than lay Catholics. Between 11 percent and 72 percent of them left, depending on the province, leaving certain parishes without clergy.[51] The local DRV authorities' refusal to deliver travel authorizations for Catholics led to confrontations. In Thanh Hóa, parishioners locked themselves inside the church demanding to be transported to the South until three military sections of the People's Army came to scatter them.[52] Other Catholics left in secrecy. The French Navy rescued an entire group on the verge of drowning from a sandbar.[53] Of all 850,000 civilians who left for the South, 60 percent were Catholics, a massive departure.[54] This gave the impression that the church left the North.

The situation of those remaining was bleak. The DRV insisted it respected of freedom of religion and instructed local cadres to organize mass where the priests had left, or repair damaged or stolen religious artefacts.[55] Despite that, Catholics saw their worst nightmare become a reality. In March 1955, priests loyal to the DRV created the Catholic National Liaison Committee, whose purpose was to "free Vietnamese Catholics from the influence of imperialism and restore dignity to the Fatherland and the nation."[56] The following day, the apostolic delegate in Hanoi declared this committee was "foreign to the Church" and threatening its unity.[57] But there was nothing he could do to prevent the Committee's rising influence. Soon after the DRV launched a land reform, foreign missionaries remained under house arrest, leaving their confinement to say mass or give sacraments. The Committee gathered signatures of patriotic Catholics demanding their expulsion. In 1958, the remaining twenty-one missionaries left the DRV, and so did the apostolic delegate the following year. Unlike their Chinese counterparts, Vietnamese Communists did not launch a Three-Self movement. But the party had taken over the church and isolated it from the rest of the hierarchy.

This convinced the Catholics who had left for the South that their fight for independence was not finished. It transformed into a struggle against Communism. "It is not sufficient to escape French domination; we must strive to escape from Communist rule," which "sells the country to Chinese Communists and the Soviet Union," declared a priest.[58] The best way to prevent Communists from taking over the church was to counter the claim that it was a vestige of colonial rule. They had to find an innovative path to decolonize the church and demonstrate its independence, without creating a schism.

Becoming a Model for Others

If Vietnamese Catholics wanted to remain within the church, they had to determine how they could transform this Western religion into a Vietnamese one. South Vietnam was the best place to explore the scope and reach of this spiritual decolonization, because it became a hub for Catholics facing Communist expansion in East Asia.

The situation in China worsened. By 1958, priests excommunicated by Rome headed twenty-six dioceses. And, of all 102 apostolic vicariates, only three were held by legitimate bishops. Twenty-five bishops had been imprisoned since 1951, and fifteen of them were still in jail in 1958.[59] Vietnamese Catholics, in contrast, nearly doubled in the South after 1954, forming a critical mass. These 1.6 million Catholics seemed insignificant compared to the three million Catholics and seven hundred thousand Protestants in China in 1950.[60] But they accounted for ten percent in Vietnam, while Catholics made up only 0.5 percent of China's population. Apart from the Philippines, Vietnam had the largest proportion of Catholics in East Asia.

Moreover, foreign Catholic money and activists converged toward Saigon. Christians from across the globe donated to "refugees of Communism" who left the North in 1954. Central to this was an existing network of Chinese Catholic refugees and missionaries, expelled from the mainland, who had established contacts with American Catholics. Francis Spellman, the archbishop of New York, provided diplomatic support to the ASV and channeled American Catholic generosity toward Asia.[61] Catholic exiles who fled Chinese Communists also gathered in South Vietnam. Belgian missionary Raymond de Jaegher, who famously recounted his escape from a Japanese prison in China before being expelled by the Communists, came to Saigon.[62] He ran the Free Pacific Association connecting Chinese Catholics on both sides of the ocean, and contributed to the columns of *Free Front*, the English-language publication of the Asian People's Anti-Communist League. Father Patrick O'Connor, who covered the Korean War for the Catholic News Service, also settled down in Saigon. The convergence of key activists made South Vietnam a center in the spiritual search for a solution against Communism.

Catholics also enjoyed unique governmental support. During the war, many Catholic intellectuals became interested in personalism, Emmanuel Mounier's philosophy calling for a social revolution that would respect the spirituality of human beings.[63] This facilitated the rise of one of Vietnam's oldest Catholic families to the highest ranks of the church and the state: Ngô Đình Thục, the third Vietnamese priest to be nominated as bishop, held an influential position in the hierarchy; Ngô Đình Nhu, the architect of Vietnam's Personalist Revolution oversaw the creation of a Labor party; and Ngô Đình Diệm eventually became the president of the new Republic of Vietnam, which replaced the ASV and remained entirely detached from French ties.[64] Spirituality was enshrined in the constitution, because it marked South Vietnam's opposition to Communism. The Republic remained secular but encouraged the growth of spirituality, which allowed the development of Catholicism, Buddhism, and the introduction of new faiths, such as the Baha'i in South Vietnam.[65] This propitious environment propelled Catholic experiments to determine how far the inculturation of their faith should go, and what role Catholicism could play to protect Vietnam from Communist rule.

Catholic priests continued the work of Vietnamizing Western ideas, which had started in the 1940s. This included exploring commonalities between religions.[66] The possibility that Catholicism could complete Confucianism was appealing to them. Alexis Cras, who was familiar with finding commonalities between Vietnamese classics and Christian values, wondered if the latter could complete the former. Confucianism brought important teachings and imbued the Vietnamese society, but it was "incapable of responding to the configuration of modern life and to the aspirations of men today. This is where Christianism could intervene, as this would be the only way to correct, develop, and complete Confucianism."[67] Fernand Parrel, a French missionary and Personalist advocate, went further:

> It is necessary to remind the teachings of the Christ himself: I did not come to abolish the Law, but to complete it. The Confucian basis was valuable, and we could have constructed something solid on it. Why had nothing been tried in this respect to this day? Without a doubt, this is unfortunate. However, nothing is lost, and a synthesis remains possible. Isn't Saint Thomas Aquinas said to have baptized Aristotle? Why wouldn't we witness the same baptism of Confucius?[68]

An Asianization of Catholicism and a modernization of Confucianism might bring the two together. The race against a Communist decolonization and Saigon's Personalist Revolution placed the Catholic faith in an unprecedented situation. It was time to push the frontiers of what was possible.

The Catholic faith could also contribute to the social and cultural development of the country. Father Parrel translated economic and social essays produced in French Catholic circles and wrote columns on social inequalities in Africa, Latin America, and in Vietnam.[69] He advised Ngô Đình Nhu to use the services of Economie et humanisme, a movement headed by Dominican Father Louis Lebret, whose vision of development relied on French philosopher Jacques Maritain's concept of integral humanism.[70] After Lebret visited Vietnam in 1955, his team conducted a four-year-long survey of its social and economic situation. In their report, religious membership and spiritual depth were not mere sociological identifiers, but criteria to measure the development of South Vietnam, alongside economic data.[71] More than ever before, perhaps, Christian ideas could play a role in the future of the postcolonial state.

The church prepared the ground to train new intellectuals. Plans for a Catholic University dated to the war. While de Lattre de Tassigny imagined a university in Hanoi staffed with clergy expelled from China, the bishops of

Indochina sent a Belgian missionary to establish a partnership with the University of Louvain in 1953.[72] Yet these plans materialized only four years later when the Catholic university in Dalat received Cardinal Spellman, who came to say mass at the inauguration of its library.[73] The university trained new soldiers, the minister of information claimed, leading a spiritual and intellectual fight against Communist expansion.[74] Education thus reinforced Saigon's struggle against Hanoi.

This intellectual energy and indirect pressure from the government may have increased conversion to Catholicism. Leaving aside children, the number of adult conversions grew from 16,323 in 1956–1957 to 27,385 in 1958–1959 and reached 37,429 (with 111,324 additional catechumens) in 1960–1961.[75] Catholicism had not just survived the Communist infiltration—it was thriving.

The Vatican was careful not to embolden Vietnamese Catholics. Many Vietnamese priests had ignored Rome's orders to remain in the North in 1954. So, Rome nominated two moderate priests rather than fierce anti-Communists as the apostolic delegate in Saigon and bishop of Cần Thơ.[76] In contrast with Chinese Catholic refugees, for whom Rome nominated an apostolic visitor to the overseas Chinese in 1953, the Vatican urged priests from Northern Vietnam to integrate into local dioceses.[77] But the outstanding growth of the church and the changing military situation in South Vietnam led Rome to overcome its reservations. In December 1959, Vietnamese Communists resumed the armed fight. Bishops in South Vietnam reminded their faithful about what happened to China and quoted a document Saigon intelligence intercepted, showing Communists were ready to "divide and rule." Infiltrating the church by using "patriotic associations" was one step "to separate the faithful from the unity of the church."[78] The resumption of the war also prompted another step in the decolonization of the church. On November 24, 1960, the Pope eliminated the apostolic delegation for Indochina and created a hierarchy. Vietnam had twenty dioceses, gathered around three provinces: Hanoi, Saigon, and Huế. The Vietnamese Church was finally standing as an equal among others. It was a church freed from Western rule, determined to oppose Communism, and convinced it could become a model for others.

This consecration confirmed Catholics could also lead the country's fight against communism. The elevation of the church of Lavang, a place where farmers claimed to have seen the Virgin Mary, into a minor basilica in 1961 was an opportunity to honor past successes of the church and project its future ambitions. Over two hundred thousand pilgrims came to Lavang, as did representatives of the government and Catholic allies across Asia.[79] The celebrations were significant for religious and political reasons, since the Virgin Mary "could grant Vietnam the possibility to unite its territory with justice, freedom, and benevolence."[80] Ngô Đình Thục's opening speech declared that this was a shrine to the Vietnamese nation and not just one to the Virgin Mary. Hence, "all Vietnamese brothers and sisters, regardless of their religion or political party, should take part in this pilgrimage to honour Our Lady at the temple of the Person, a shrine which was constructed with the joint contribution of Catholics and non-Catholics of the North, the Center and the South."[81] The Catholic faith should become a model for all Vietnamese.

This success also had influence overseas, where Communism threatened the church. In 1962, an article revealed Chinese Communists were making recommendations to Cubans about a three-stage process to eliminate the Catholic Church.[82] First, went the plan, political authorities impose a total subordination of Catholics. Second, the party creates a schismatic church, including a separate episcopate and a distinct liturgy. Third, the transition of religion from being a collective responsibility to an individual practice achieves the ultimate aim: the progressive eradication of all religion, as generations go by. Communism aimed to eliminate national churches, one by one. Yet South Vietnam's success could serve as a stepping-stone for a counter-offensive. Catholic publications claimed Lavang was now famous in "a worldwide fight against Communism, and one in particular in Southeast Asia, threatening Tibet, India, Ceylon, Burma, Thailand, all the way to Cambodia. Communism has found, in Buddhism, the path of 'compassion,' a convenient way to surround Asia and dominate the world from the East, the North, and the South."[83] Christianity seemed to be the only strong faith to resist Communism, and South Vietnam was a beacon of light in Asia.

Vietnamese Catholics believed they could help others decolonize their faith and prevent Communist expansion. Could Vietnam transition from being a mission country to one sending missionaries overseas? Msgr. Ngô Đình Thục dreamt of creating the Vietnamese equivalent of the Paris Foreign Missions, to train missionaries with unique sensibilities toward other decolonized people.[84] Vietnamese priests also wondered whether they could play a role in the decolonization of Africa, where the propagation of the faith was the fastest.[85] Father Nguyễn Tiến Huynh, a Vietnamese priest ordained and living in France, articulated this idea in November 1962. Africa, much like Asia, had experienced "white man rule and white man economic exploitation," and the propagation of the faith continued with the work of "white missionaries," he claimed. Yet many of these states now turned to the "yellow skinned man" to receive technical support, often believing Mao Zedong's promises. Hence, thousands of cadres from Communist China came to "help" African countries. For these reasons, Asian priests had to strive:

> It is time—it is already very late—that yellow Catholics of Southeast Asia roll up their sleeves and strive for the evangelization of Africa. Now more than even before, we need to use the trust of African people toward yellow people to serve the Church in Africa. Besides, since Africans have lost their confidence in the white men because of history, only yellow Catholics can participate in the race against time, in the competition with communists in Africa. Only they can save the situation and bring the hope of the ultimate victory.[86]

Asian Catholics had to replace Western missionaries to propagate the faith. Of all Asians, only the Vietnamese had both experienced Communist rule and achieved a full decolonization from the French empire. Vietnamese priests would know "how to be an African among Africans." The opportunity was there. Not only had the Vietnamese Church overcome its own challenge, it could become a model for the rest of the decolonizing world.

Conclusion

In the views of many, the experimentations to decolonize the church in South Vietnam had gone too far. In May 1963, protests in most cities opposed the government and the church's disproportionate influence. Western observers, including missionaries familiar with Asia, also criticized the anti-Communist stance of many members of the Vietnamese clergy who had mistaken religion for politics. While many Southern Vietnamese Catholics remained silent on that matter, a group of priests publicizing the principles arising from the Second Ecumenical Council indirectly criticized the politicization of the Catholic faith in Vietnam. Its intransigent stance against Communism contradicted the calls for establishing a dialogue with other religions and living in peace with others in the society.[87]

This overview of Catholic debates over the decolonization of the church shows that the Vietnam wars were not just a hot spot of the Cold War or a civil war opposing different political groups to lead the country. There was also a religious war opposing different interpretations of the role of Catholics in the struggle for independence and the status of Catholicism in the new nation-state. This conflict not only pertained to the creation of or opposition to a schismatic church. It materialized in a competition about defining what a successful decolonization of the Catholic faith truly meant. These questions not only involved Vietnamese Catholics, Rome, and the colonial state. Regional developments such as Japanese calls to break up from the West and the victory of Chinese Communists also influenced the possibilities, the reach, and objectives of this decolonization.

CHAPTER 4

Jin Luxian, Chinese Catholicism, and the Horizontal Networks of Decolonization

Albert Wu

In 1947, Aloysius Luxian Jin (金魯賢) boarded a ship headed for Marseille—incidentally, the same vessel that twenty years earlier had carried a young Deng Xiaoping to France. Unlike Deng, who worked in an iron and steel plant in the suburbs of Paris, Jin was headed to Europe to complete his training as a Jesuit. His four-year stay would take him to the centers of Jesuit learning in Europe—Paris, Rome, Innsbruck, among others.

Jin had almost been denied the opportunity. Months before he left, he had served as a guide for Marcel Bith, the Jesuit provincial superior of Paris, who toured China as part of a regular inspection of Jesuit holdings in China. Taken by Jin's talent, Bith announced that he wanted Jin to finish his studies in Europe. Jin's supervisors in Shanghai vehemently rejected the proposal. At an open meeting, one Jesuit missionary "struck the table with his fist and told Bith that Chinese who went to Europe did not follow orders and on return no longer respected the French missionaries. He also said that Chinese were not qualified to teach theology."[1] Bith—an independent-minded anti-racist who had been a member of the French Resistance—overruled the opposition.[2]

Curious and peripatetic, Jin made the most out of his European adventure and paid a visit to almost every major center of Jesuit thought. Through his Jesuit affiliations, Jin came in contact with a dense network of progressive Catholic thinkers and activists. His memoir constitutes a "who's who" of leading figures who would later influence the agenda of Vatican II. In Innsbruck, he took walks with Karl Rahner. In Paris, he visited Pierre Teilhard de Chardin. In Lyon, he stayed in a room next to Henri de Lubac. He heard worker-priests give sermons.

In a counter-factual history, one can imagine Jin becoming a figure like the Senegalese Alioune Diop, who, as Elizabeth Foster has shown, profoundly shaped discussions at the Second Vatican Council.[3] Yet the victory of the Chinese Communist Party in 1949 transformed China's relationship to the global Catholic community. Arrested in 1955, Jin spent the next twenty-seven years in jail. He did not even learn of the momentous changes that the ecumenical council brought to the church until 1982, the year he was freed from prison.

This rupture between Chinese Catholics and the global Catholic Church has been reflected in the historiography of Chinese Catholicism.[4] Preoccupied by the Cold War question of why Christianity had "failed" in China—and, conversely, why Chinese Communism had succeeded—Chinese Catholicism has been written as an exceptional story, disconnected with other histories of decolonization. Jin's "controversial" career has largely been situated within that literature, and he has been seen as either a collaborator or silent resister to the Chinese Communist attack on religion.[5] His memoir, in turn, has been read largely as an attempt to defend his decisions and actions. In this chapter, I draw on Jin's memoir, but I sidestep the questions of resistance or collaboration. Rather, I argue that Jin's writings can help us to sketch out the place of Chinese Catholics and, by extension, Chinese Catholicism within progressive Catholic networks of decolonization. In doing so, I hope to put the history of Chinese Catholicism more firmly in dialogue with global histories of decolonization.

More broadly, as the historian A. G. Hopkins has noted, China has gone missing from narratives of decolonization. While "China features prominently in studies of the Cold War," Hopkins notes, "it rarely features, except as 'background,' in the literature on post-war decolonization."[6] This neglect, Hopkins argues, is largely due to the peculiar history of European imperialism in China, where most of the country experienced informal, rather than formal, colonization.[7]

But the Catholic Church's history in China brings the analytical categories of colonization and decolonization into sharper focus. A series of unequal treaties in the nineteenth century placed all Catholics in China under the jurisdiction of the French Religious Protectorate, an entity the historian Ernest Young has called an "ecclesiastical colony."[8] The French Jesuit missions, moreover, enjoyed an elevated position within this world. As Steven Pieragastini has shown, the new Jesuit mission, established in 1842 in the wake of the First Opium War, became an "empire between empires" (*imperium inter imperia*), and in particular an "extra-governmental power holder" in Shanghai. Benefiting from the unequal treaties and the fragmented administration of the treaty ports, the Jesuits accrued a vast amount of real estate in Shanghai. They established a parallel set of state-like institutions: schools, hospitals, orphanages, and other charitable institutions. They were important players in Shanghai civil society, running their own printing press, newspapers, and, later, radio stations.[9] In other words, the Catholic Church did "colonize" the areas where it operated in China.

And when the Chinese Communist Party came to power after 1949, it subjected these Catholic institutions to a violent process of confiscation and removal. Chinese Catholics thus had a similar experience to Algerian and Vietnamese Catholics, encountering something akin to the decolonizing encounters in places with a more overt history of colonization. Jin's memoirs are a vivid account of this process of decolonization, and how individual actors responded to this dramatic global story.

Moreover, Jin's memoir also points us to the centrality of China as an important *node* in the immediate postwar moment of decolonization, both in the region and globally. Before the Second World War, China was a central place for missionary training, as Christian missionaries from throughout the world traveled to China to work, study, and teach there. The Jesuits facilitated horizontal movement between empires, as Jesuits circulated between Europe, the Americas, Africa, and Asia. Both in China and in Europe, Jin encountered a worldwide network of dissidents who criticized Catholic Eurocentrism and its connection to European imperial power.

After the Communist victory in 1949, these horizontal networks ensured Catholicism's survival in East Asia, as Chinese priests traveled to places like Taipei and Manila, hoping for an eventual return to China. Decolonization, while configured by the metropole-periphery relationship, was also profoundly constructed through a wide range of horizontal nodal connections. In this story, nodes like Lyon, Innsbruck, or Bruges become just as important—or perhaps even more important—centers of Catholic ferment than traditional centers, such as Rome or Paris. Jin's story points us to a series of horizontal nodes that shape the intellectual geography of global Catholicism as much as the traditional metropole-periphery relationship that has populated our historiographies.

Thus, I seek to place Jin within a global cohort of Catholic intellectuals who worked to challenge the church's Eurocentrism. Like so many of his contemporaries, Jin's early thought was shaped by the central currents of anti-imperialism, his career molded by the Catholic Church's attempt to indigenize the episcopacy in China. During his time in Europe, his thinking of Catholicism's place in the world was transformed by his encounter with other Catholic thinkers who were examining and thinking about decolonization globally. When he returned to China, his life's trajectory was altered by the shocks of decolonization in China: the expulsion of European and American missionaries from China in the wake of the Communist victory and the nationalization of the Catholic Church's assets in China. Situating Jin's story, and the Chinese Catholic Church's story, within a global history of decolonization moves beyond narratives of Chinese exceptionalism. It further helps to illuminate where the Chinese case diverges and converges with other places.

The Contradictions of Chinese Catholicism

Jin's early life reflects the multiple tensions and conflicts that Chinese Catholics faced in the early twentieth century. On the one hand, Catholicism represented the triumph of foreign imperialism, as the unequal treaties that Western powers had imposed on China in the nineteenth century granted Christian missionaries access to inland China. Even in his youth, Jin understood how his Catholicism was connected to the wider humiliation of China on a global stage. Jin Luxian begins his memoir: "I was born at a time when the people of our country were suffering from the chaos of civil disorder and foreign occupation. So during my youth there was . . . only national disgrace."[10]

On the other hand, by the early twentieth century, Catholicism had developed into an intensely local, enclosed identity, shaped by its minority status as well as successive waves of anti-foreign violence that spread through China out of anger about the treaties. Jin, for instance, was born in 1916 into a village where all the inhabitants shared the same last name and same Catholic faith. He had no family tree, which indicated that he came from a poor family with little social status. Jin writes in his memoir that he suspected that his "ancestors were peasants for generations back."[11] Catholicism gave Jin's family access to a world previously inaccessible to Chinese peasants. Jin's paternal grandfather was a devout Catholic who had been forced by the Taiping rebel army to work in their logistics corps.[12] His father, born in 1885, attended St. Ignatius College, where he learned English and French. Because he spoke foreign languages very well, he found a lucrative job as a Chinese comprador for the British import-export company Hutchison. But he lost his wealth from a ruinous moment of trying to speculate on foreign currencies. Jin remembers his father as "very Westernized"; he wore Western trousers and smoked Havana cigars. His mother, a devout Catholic, took him and his brothers to attend mass daily, and from a young age told him that she wanted to raise him for the priesthood.[13]

At the age of ten, Jin entered the same Jesuit-run elementary school his father attended, launching a lifelong relationship with the order. The Chinese Catholic institution that he entered was itself undergoing a revolution. In the wake of World War I, in 1919, Pope Benedict XV issued the papal encyclical *Maximum illud*. Fearing that Europe would soon no longer have the will nor financial resources to continue to support overseas missions, Benedict XV exhorted missionaries in China to transfer more power and responsibility to indigenous clergy to prepare for the day when the Chinese church no longer had to rely on funding from Europe. Progressive European missionaries in China and Chinese Catholics, dissatisfied with the fact that the episcopacy in China was dominated by Europeans, had been influential voices in shaping the policies in *Maximum illud*. The pope argued that the church in China needed to accelerate its pace in ordaining Chinese clergy and dissociate itself from European imperial power. The Vatican was partly motivated by a sincere desire to develop indigenous clergy, but it also wanted to undercut the power of the French Religious Protectorate by developing a direct relationship with the Chinese regime. Chinese bishops, they believed, would facilitate that diplomatic exchange.[14] In 1926, the same year Jin entered St. Ignatius, Pope Pius XI ordained the first six Chinese bishops.[15]

Within the Jesuit order, reaction to *Maximum illud* was mixed. As the historian Ernest Young has shown, the Jesuits "publicly ignored" *Maximum illud* in China, refusing to publish the text.[16] The French Jesuits who opposed *Maximum illud* supported the Pope's exhortations in principle but argued that Chinese clergy were not ready for higher positions in the episcopacy. But the encyclical found enthusiastic supporters among Chinese Catholics. Ever since its reestablishment, the Jesuit order in Shanghai had produced some of the most influential Chinese Catholic theologians and public intellectuals, who dominated Chinese Catholic public discourse.[17] Many of these Chinese Catholics were ensconced in Jesuit educational institutions, tasked with educating Chinese Catholic youth.

In high school at St. Ignatius College, Jin came under the tutelage of the influential Xu Zongze, who edited the *Revue catholique* [*Shengjiao Zazhi*], the most important Chinese Catholic journal of the first half of the twentieth century. In his journal, Xu advanced a two-pronged attack.[18] On the one hand, Xu wrote to rebut his European Jesuit superiors, arguing that Chinese Catholics were ready for church leadership. He analyzed the work of Celso Costantini, the first apostolic delegate to China, who was tasked to implement the indigenizing agenda set out in *Maximum illud*. He reported on the readiness of Chinese Catholics for church leadership, while extolling the compatibility of traditional Confucian thinking with Catholicism. Xu's argument about the affinities between Confucianism and Catholicism was also a move to respond to secular Chinese critics of Catholicism. In the 1920s and 1930s, Chinese nationalists increasingly criticized Catholics as handmaidens of Western empire. Throughout his writing, he wanted to show how Catholicism and Chinese-ness were, in Chloë Starr's words, "integrated identities, not alternatives."[19] He sought to demonstrate the centrality of Roman Catholicism in Chinese history, highlighting the work of early Chinese converts—all converted by Jesuits—such as Xu Guangqi. Endorsing Chiang Kai-shek's nationalist "New Life Movement," Xu adopted a critical stance toward Communism and socialism in his writing.

That is not to say that all Jesuits whom Jin encountered were pro-Guomindang nationalists. As the war with Japan intensified, some of Jin's teachers at seminary voiced their criticisms of Chiang Kai-shek for betraying the United Front and prioritizing his campaign against the Chinese Communists over the war against Japan. Furthermore, as Jin advanced through his studies, he encountered Chinese Jesuits who were embedded within the progressive and left-leaning reform movements that were sweeping through the church during the interwar years. Jin's rector at the Jesuit novitiate was Wang Changzhi, perhaps the most important Chinese Catholic intellectual in the first half of the twentieth century. Born in 1899, Wang joined the Jesuits at twenty-three, and was sent to France to study from 1927 until 1937. He entered the recently reestablished theologate in Lyon. There, he became lifelong friends with Gaston Fessard and Henri de Lubac. In Lyon, Wang produced path-breaking works that showed the compatibility of classic Chinese thought and Christianity, as well as a theological treatise arguing for the possible salvation of non-Christians.[20] Long before Vatican II, he began to develop a theory of Chinese Catholic indigenization. Later, when Jin met Henri de Lubac in Lyon in 1947, de Lubac asked after his old classmate Wang. De Lubac called Wang a "real genius" whose "achievements in theology have been remarkable." When told that Wang was teaching Chinese literature to juvenate students and was editing a children's magazine, de Lubac responded, "How can this be? This is to hide the light under a bushel."[21]

Jin credits the primary force holding back Wang's career in the Jesuit hierarchy to European racism. In his memoir, Jin singles out Yves Henry, the father superior of the Jesuits in Shanghai, for blame. When Henry took over leadership of the Shanghai Jesuits, he halted publication of Chinese nationalist magazines and transferred Chinese priests to less important positions.[22] Wang Changzhi, for instance, had applied to teach theology many times, and, each time, Henry rejected his application. "Wang Changzhi was truly a talent without any outlet," Jin laments in his memoir.[23]

Wang was not the only one whose career suffered under Henry's watch. Under Henry, Jin writes, "the Shanghai diocese took a big step backwards" in turning over more power to indigenous clergy.[24] The seminary in Shanghai remained a bastion of conservatism, untouched by progressive trends. "In those days," Jin writes, "the course of study at Xuhui School of Theology was very traditional. All the theology was as per the Council of Trent and the First Vatican Council."[25] One professor forbade students from learning about evolution. Jin recounts meeting with Pierre Teilhard de Chardin, who sought common ground between Catholic theology and evolution, in 1947. "After talking with me for an hour," Jin writes, Teilhard de Chardin sent him away "with a pat on the shoulder, saying: 'My brother, you are at least 40 years out of date.'"[26]

Jin contrasts Shanghai with the Jesuit seminary in the north, in Xian County, not far from Beijing, where Jin studied philosophy from 1941 to 1942. Under the direct control of Jesuits from Champagne Province, the seminary at Xian County became a center of Jesuit progressivism in China. Pierre Teilhard de Chardin, for instance, was based there before the Vatican banned him from teaching. The Jesuits in Xian County were also forerunners in the move to indigenize the episcopacy. By the 1930s, they had ordained a Chinese bishop, and in the 1940s, a Chinese priest became father superior.[27] In contrast, the Parisian Jesuits in Shanghai, Jin writes, "were unwilling to transfer power" to Chinese priests even on the eve of the Chinese Communist victory in 1949, which further gave the Chinese Communists cause to expel them from China.[28]

Jin's experiences remind us of one important fact: the embeddedness of China within the global Jesuit network. In Xian County, he studied philosophy with Jesuits from Spain, Canada, Hungary, and France. He was introduced to the work of Bergson and of Blondel, and encountered the philosophies of Kant and Hegel, "as well as a shallow critique of Marxism."[29] In Shanghai, Jin studied for four years with a hundred other students and faculty from all over the world, including "Canada, the United States, Mexico, Colombia,

Uruguay, Chile, France, Ireland, Italy, Spain, Hungary, Switzerland, Holland, Austria, Germany, Portugal, Belgium, and Indonesia."[30] Shanghai's particular status in World War II—the French were able to carve out a zone of neutrality in China from Japanese aggression—made it an important node within the Jesuit global network. Jesuits in other war-torn countries were able to travel to Shanghai to continue their formation.[31]

Jin's Travels in Europe

And China was, of course, just one node in the Jesuit global network, as the Jesuits facilitated Jin's travels in Europe. Jin's account of his time in Europe fits into a longer historical tradition of Chinese travelogues of the West, dating back to the nineteenth century. Hoping to push for reform and change in China, Chinese travelers detailed the technology, the culture, and the political institutions that they encountered in the West. An important trope within the tradition of Chinese travelogues is that of the provincial ingenue who is astounded by the wider world. Jin's travelogue certainly fits into this mode, as we see him document his delight as he walks along the Seine, hikes in the Alps, and tours the ruins of Pompeii. But the Catholic pilgrimage also adds another layer to this trope: we see Jin visit the Notre Dame in Paris, the Cologne Cathedral, the Grotto of Lourdes. His memoir also helps us to map out centers of learning that mark Jesuit formation: Rome, Paris, Innsbruck, and Lyon.

Unlike nineteenth-century Chinese travelogues documenting Western modernity, in Jin's memoir the European landscape is in convulsion, still reeling from the devastations of World War II. Upon arriving in Paris, Marcel Bith, the provincial superior who had encouraged Jin to travel to Europe, told Jin to apply for bread rations from the state. The food, Jin notes, "was worse than in Shanghai." Arriving in Germany in 1949, Jin remarks, "I could sense the misery of people's lives. Many wore old, threadbare clothes and some children went to school barefoot. There was insufficient grain to go around. It was hard to maintain even the lowest standard of living. . . . People told me that a whole set of encyclopedias could be exchanged for only a few loaves of bread."[32]

But Jin's travelogue also reminds us of the incredible amount of movement and vibrancy in the aftermath of the Second World War. "There was a constant flow of Jesuits coming to Paris—on business, for tourism, as immigrants," Jin writes in his memoirs. The rector of the Parisian Jesuits told Jin that over two thousand Jesuits had come through Paris in 1946. "According to the daily number of visitors, he needed to arrange for them all to say mass once a day. He collected no extra fees, but according to the Jesuit rule of *Ubi Missa, ibi Mensa*, each visitor expected an altar at which to say mass and a table at which to dine."[33]

While Jin encountered immiseration in the daily scenes around him, Jin also arrived in France at a moment of extraordinary dynamism and fervor for Catholic thought. As the influential Dominican theologian Yves Congar remarked, "Anyone who did not live through the years 1946 and 1947 in the history of French Catholicism has missed one of the finest moments in the life of the Church."[34] In France, the Dominican Saulchoir school of theology, centered around the figures of Marie-Dominique Chenu and Yves Congar, as well as the Jesuit seminary in Fourvière, Lyon, served as the poles of intellectual ferment. Catholic thinkers involved in the *Ressourcement* movement—referred to by its opponents as *nouvelle théologie*—launched new journals and attempts to reform the liturgy.[35]

The Jesuit Inter-Provincial Peace Conference in 1947, which Jin attended, offered a vivid instance of new progressive ideas in Jesuit thinking. Bith, who had himself been a member of the French resistance, opened the conference. The list of the main speakers at the conference illustrated the increasing importance of progressive voices among the Jesuits: Gaston Fessard (1897–1978), who had developed a theory of resistance to Nazism and totalitarianism more broadly; René d'Ouince, the publisher of *Études*; the theologian Henri-Marie de Lubac (1896–1991); and Teilhard de Chardin.[36]

Jin's time in Europe from 1947 to 1951 was marked by meetings with progressive figures who would later shape Vatican II and, in turn, the global Catholic Church. As a student in Rome, he spent time at the German College, where he met Hans Küng, who taught Jin German. Küng and the other German seminarians impressed him: "They were the sharpest minds in each diocese, both clever and lively."[37] In Innsbruck, he stayed at the Canisianum, where he became quick friends with Karl Rahner. They went for a "walk together every afternoon, discussing theological problems, the challenges of the Church and many other topics."[38]

Jin's discussion of befriending future theological heavyweights is impressionistic: he does not dwell long on their ideas. One encounter, however, left an imprint: his meeting with the worker-priest movement. Begun in the early 1940s by two Catholic chaplains who feared the increasing dechristianization of Europe, the founders of the worker-priest movement believed that Europe needed to be seen as a land where Christian missionaries needed to operate and work. As Sarah Shortall has shown, supporters of the worker-priest movement believed that it marked a dramatic shift in approach to missions: it "represented a clear departure from the interwar lay apostolate, abandoning its logic of conquest and conversion in favor of a commitment to dialogue and *témoignange* (bearing witness)." Shortall writes that missionaries needed to approach bastions of secularism as "site[s] of an '*indigenous Christianity*' that had to be nurtured with [their] own internal resources, much as foreign missionaries sought to foster indigenous Churches in Africa and Asia."[39]

The worker-priest movement made a deep impression on Catholics in Jin's generation. As Piotr Kosicki has shown, the young Karol Woyjtla, later Pope John Paul II, then a PhD student studying in Rome, also came across the worker-priests in 1947 and found them a "revelation."[40] Jin, similarly, writes in his memoirs that one Jesuit worker-priest "really inspired me and has remained with me." A priest of about forty years old "wore workman's clothes" and gave a quasi-socialist reading of the church's relationship to political economy. France, the priest explained, was once an "agricultural country and the Church rooted itself among the farmers." The church found a center within the lives of an agrarian society. But the industrial revolution destroyed the lives of many farmers and, as a result, the "rural population moved to the towns, losing their lands and gaining no property, instead living in cheap workmen's cottages built for them by the capitalists." The church, afraid of the rise of socialism, sided instead with the aristocracy and the capitalists. As a result, the urban poor "became estranged from the Church and the parish priest."[41]

The worker-priest argued that the "Church needed to proselytize the proletariat, not preach the Gospel to everyone but the workers. Also, we should join the workers, use our bodies as witness, spread the Gospel anew. The priests should not ape the manners of the bourgeoisie, but should become workers, work alongside workers, share the lives of workers so as to be accepted by them, gain their attention, their trust, and bring them back into the Christian fold." Jin remembered one detail from the priest's talk: a worker found a dead rabbit in a waste bin, cooked it, and invited the priest to share in a meal with them. "The priest was obliged," Jin recounts, "to share in the worker's pleasure at this special meal." "In my heart," Jin writes in his memoir almost sixty years after that encounter, I retain great respect for those worker-priests."[42]

As Darcie Fontaine has shown, during the period that Jin was in Europe, "the worker-priest project was at the center of the 'progressivist crisis' in the French Catholic Church."[43] At its heart, debates revolved around the question of whether the Catholic Church could accommodate Marxist-oriented political circles. As Shortall writes, more broadly, the debate around the worker-priest movement reflected "an emerging tension between progressive Catholics who were open to some form of engagement with the left and those who refused any such collaboration. Far more than just a conflict between right and left, this dispute revived the old prewar debate about whether Catholics could work with nonbelievers to achieve shared political goals."[44]

In 1947, the Dominican friar Réginald Garrigou-Langrange launched his first attack on the group of Jesuits engaged in what he called *nouvelle théologie*, seeing them as compromising the core principles of Catholicism. In 1950, Pius XII delivered the papal encyclical *Humani generis*, attacking the progressive outlook of *nouvelle théologie*. Institutional assaults on the new theologians followed. Henri de Lubac, for instance, was removed from his teaching post in Lyon and forbidden from publishing. Pierre Teilhard de Chardin was disciplined by the Jesuit superior general and sent to New York. By 1954, the Vatican issued an ultimatum, banning the worker-priests from continuing their work.[45] Jin, in his memoirs, recounts these dramatic episodes, indicating his awareness of the vitality of theological debate in European Catholicism after World War II.

China in Europe

Jin's memoirs point to another fact of mid-twentieth-century Catholic life in Europe: the ubiquity of China within European Catholicism. Everywhere he traveled in Europe, Jin came across either a Chinese person living in Europe, or a European who had deep ties to China. Among the Chinese he encountered, a substantial group were Chinese students who lived and worked in France. In the wake of World War I, the French government used portions of the Boxer Indemnity funds to set up the Lyon Sino-French Institute. The institute was the first Chinese degree-granting entity outside of China. The Jesuits set up an organization to aid Chinese students and, every Sunday, Jin visited with Chinese students, both secular and religious, there.[46] Of course, Jin also met Chinese students studying at seminary. And he encountered yet another group of people who connected Catholic Europe to China: Chinese nuns. In Switzerland, Jin visited an eldercare home, where he met a Chinese nun from Shanghai who managed the kitchen. "In Europe many of these places used to have Shanghainese nuns," Jin comments in his memoirs.[47]

Throughout his time in Europe, Jin encountered Europeans who had once spent time in China. In Paris, the head of the missionary department of the Paris province had once served as a missionary in Shanghai. In Belgium, he met a priest who had formerly served in the hospital in Xian County.[48] In London, he ran into a former teacher, who was wearing a Chinese gown on the street. His teacher had been sent to China due to outspoken opposition to the Nazis; the Jesuit leadership had ordered him to go there to escape possible persecution in Germany. "He spoke enthusiastically about China, saying how much he had liked my country and that he wore a Chinese gown to prove his point."[49] In Rome, he met Pasquale d'Elia, chair of missiology at the Gregorian University. Previously a missionary in Shanghai, d'Elia had produced several historical studies of the Jesuits in China. In Ireland, his English tutor had served as a missionary in Hong Kong. And at the Vatican, he paid a visit to Celso Costantini, the main architect behind the push to indigenize the clergy in China and who had since been appointed to become secretary of the Congregation for the Propagation of the Faith.

Yet, within this density of the networks in Europe, the ideological orientation of the important "China hands" in Europe were all overwhelmingly anti-Communist. The influential missionaries that Jin mentioned all had close ties to Chiang Kai-Shek's Guomindang (GMD). D'Elia, whose work focused on Matteo Ricci and the history of the Jesuit missions, had translated Sun Yat-sen's Three Principles into English and defended the compatibility between Chinese nationalism and Confucianism. Costantini was close to the GMD during his years in China, praising the Chinese nationalists for unifying China. And Father Lu Zhengxiang, who lived as a Benedictine monk in a monastery in Belgium and was the most pre-eminent Chinese Catholic in Europe, previously had been a premier of the Republic of China. He had led the negotiations at Versailles and retained ties to the Chinese nationalists.

This proximity to the GMD, Jin suggests in his memoirs, led the Vatican and other church leaders to underestimate the durability of the new Communist regime. Jin suggests that the Vatican made a tactical mistake in 1949, with the Chinese Communist Party (CCP) on the cusp of victory. The Congregation of Rites delivered an anti-Communist decree, stressing that Catholics were forbidden to read Communist newspapers, publications, or listen to radio transmissions. They were prohibited from participating in any activity that promoted Communism. In his memoirs, Jin writes that he thought even then that "such a blanket instruction would be hard to enforce." Moreover, it placed Catholics in a difficult position in relation to the new regime: "At that time I thought that from then on it wouldn't be easy to be a Catholic in China."[50] He observed pointedly: "I realized that the Vatican only paid attention to the reports of missionaries who had been expelled from China and had no understanding of the religious policies of New China or the challenges of the Chinese Church."[51]

Jin's Return to China

The wishful thinking of anti-Communist Catholics became evident to Jin when he returned to China in 1951. Ignatius Kung Pin-Mei, who had been appointed bishop of Shanghai in 1950, told Jin that he believed the Communist regime would collapse within five years. Jin was not as confident. He told Kung: "As the days pass, the Communist government is getting stronger and the hope that the US and Chiang Kai-shek will return gets smaller."[52] Unlike many of his other fellow Catholics, he predicted that "the Chinese Communists would also succeed and rule China for a long time."[53] Meanwhile, Jin thought that Kung—surrounded by "thoroughly anti-Communist, stubborn, and hard-nosed" counselors—had delusions that he was "bound to become cardinal archbishop" if he maintained his resistance to the CCP. Kung, like other hardliners in China, were "controlled by the Frenchmen and didn't trust the CCP," Jin charges. "As for me, I had returned from Europe, where the East was already Red, and the Western European workers and intellectuals all tended towards communism; thus, I had no illusions about any return of the US and Chiang Kai-shek."[54]

While critical of the Chinese Communist Party for its assault on organized religion, Jin blames the Chinese Catholic leadership for ratcheting up tensions with the CCP. Jin later believed that the Catholics could have compromised with the CCP on its plan to develop a "Patriotic Church." The CCP's stated goal was to indigenize Christian churches "into the Chinese people's own self-governing, self-propagating, and self-financing religious enterprise."[55] These terms—self-governing, self-propagating, and self-financing—constituted the core principles behind the "Three Self Movement." Originating in elite Protestant circles during the interwar years, the CCP co-opted the "Three Self Movement" as a national religious policy; the proposed formation of a "Patriotic Church" amounted to a form of accelerated decolonization. In the name of anti-imperialism, the CCP pushed Protestant and Catholic churches to wean themselves off foreign personnel and money. Protestants, led by the national director of the YMCA, Wu Yaozong, embraced the policy and adopted the Three Self Manifesto at the 1950 National Christian Council held in Shanghai. "The Shanghai diocese," Jin writes in his memoirs, "could not produce a personage such as the Protestant Wu Yaozong, who could stand up and publicly embrace the government."[56]

The Catholic leadership made it clear that any accommodation with the CCP's Three-Self Patriotic Church was impossible. Antonio Riberi, the apostolic nuncio, stated in an address to all Chinese Catholics that "any so-called 'national Catholic church,' in an exclusive sense, is simply a schismatic church, and not the true and one Catholic Church."[57] Fernand Lacretelle, the Jesuit mission superior, also took a hardline stance: any Catholics who joined the Communist Party would be excommunicated, children who joined the Communist Youth League were to be denied Communion. Catholics were even discouraged from reading Communist newspapers or marching in Communist parades.[58] When China entered the Korean War in October 1950, Bishop Kung instructed the faithful not to contribute to the war effort, including donations for military funding. Bishop Kung continued his outspoken critique of the regime until his arrest in 1955.

Jin comments in his memoir that the decision to resist the CCP placed an almost impossible burden on the lay Catholic faithful, most of whom were poor and living in rural areas. Jin writes:

> It really was tough to be a Catholic. Meanwhile, we the priests were living in comfortable rooms, drinking milk and eating steak while both instructing and propagating these callous and unfeeling instructions, not sparing the faithful from a hopeless outcome, causing them to miss school, become unemployed, or even risk losing their liberty. While I was in jail, I thought these things over, and felt that we had let down the faithful. We ought to have given more thought to the great numbers of the faithful and the common people, allowing them to survive under communist rule, to study hard and to work alongside the rest of the people.[59]

In 1955, the Chinese Communist Party launched an aggressive attack on the "Kung counter revolutionary" clique. Several thousand Catholics were rounded up and thrown into jail. Jin was one of those arrested and spent the next twenty-seven years in various prisons. In 1957, the Chinese Catholic Patriotic Association was established, becoming the officially sanctioned church organization. Church leaders and the faithful who refused to denounce their ties to the Vatican were driven underground.

Horizontal Networks in Action

While the Catholic communities in China came under increasing assault from the Chinese Communist Party, the horizontal networks of global Catholicism kicked into gear. Months before the official victory and establishment of the People's Republic of China in October 1949, the Jesuits began evacuating their personnel, who numbered close to a thousand people throughout China. The majority went to Hong Kong and Taiwan, where the Guomindang had evacuated most of its military forces and established the seat of its government.

But the Jesuits also fanned out across East Asia. The largest number of priests went to the Philippines, which had achieved independence in 1946. Catholicism had long established a stable presence in the Philippines, and its Jesuit mission had, by 1949, been occupied largely by Americans. President Elpidio Quirino, elected in 1948, was an outspoken anti-Communist, and he had granted a special request from the American cardinal Francis Spellman to accept Jesuits who wanted to leave China. The Jesuits decided to move their Chinese novitiate and juvenate to Manila, and in the months preceding the Communist victory in 1949, more than a hundred Jesuits arrived in the Philippines.[60] A smaller, but nonetheless substantial, number of Jesuits travelled to Indonesia, Portuguese Timor, South Vietnam, and Thailand.[61] By 1957, the Jesuits established a new Far East Province, comprised mostly of people formerly involved in the China missions.

Many of Jin's friends, teachers, and colleagues left China, finding refuge throughout East Asia. Wang Changzhi, Jin Luxian's old teacher and Henri de Lubac's classmate, went to the Philippines, where he taught philosophy and published a series of popular books introducing Chinese readers to Catholic dogma. A classmate of Jin's at Xianxian, Pierre Tritz, also went to Manila, where he became a famous philanthropist working with the urban poor. Another classmate, Luis Ruis Suárez, went to Macau and set up an organization that offered direct aid to refugees from China.

Besides diverting their resources to East and Southeast Asia, the Jesuits also used their power to influence popular perception of the plight of Catholics under Chinese Communism. In 1957, for instance, Jean Lefeuvre, who was ordained by Bishop Kung in 1952 and arrived in Taiwan in 1955, published *Les Enfants dans la ville: chronique de la vie chrétienne à Shanghaï (1949–1955)*. The book detailed the Communist assault on Catholic life in Shanghai and, more broadly, the "virtual extermination of religious life" in China.[62] When the book was published in France, it became an immediate bestseller and garnered multiple reprintings. As Anthony E. Clark has shown, the book enraged Premier Zhou Enlai, and he asked his friend Simone de Beauvoir to write a rebuttal to the book, which she did in her book *The Long March: An Account of Modern China*. Both books went on to become bestsellers.[63]

Other Jesuits in Jin's networks came to shape the way Europeans and Americans thought about China. Perhaps the most prominent was László Ladány, a Hungarian-born Jesuit who fled to Hong Kong in 1949. There, he edited the *China News Analysis*, and his weekly dispatches became essential resources for "China watchers." As Simon Leys wrote in 1990, "China News Analysis was compulsory reading for all those who wished to be informed of Chinese political developments—scholars, journalists, diplomats . . . the factual information which he supplied was invaluable and irreplaceable."[64] Ladány, a vociferous anti-Communist, set the tone for much of the Church in Europe's approach toward Chinese Communism, as Church leaders in Europe argued that any accommodation with Chinese Communism meant a betrayal of the global Catholic Church. Ladány lobbed especially harsh criticism at Jin Luxian after Jin was released from prison and was ordained as an auxiliary bishop in the Chinese Patriotic Church. In 1987, Ladány described Jin as "a brilliant theological student, a charming character liked by everybody, but not a man of strong will."[65] Ladány accused Jin of betraying the Catholic Church in return for preferential treatment in prison.

Conclusion

Ladány's account of Jin's life—and this is certainly the dominant mode of thinking about him—focused on labels of "resistance" and "collaboration." But placed within the broader framework of decolonization, Jin's story points us to a different set of narratives. Jin belonged to a generation of Catholic leaders who came of age in the 1940s and became leaders of the church in the 1980s. For an earlier generation of Chinese Catholics—Jin's teachers—the central intellectual problem they faced was the conflict between nationalism and Catholicism. Accused of being traitors to China, Chinese Catholics wanted to demonstrate that Chinese nationalism and Catholicism were compatible. Jin's generation, on the other hand, was bound together by the ravages of far-right militarism. In Jin's case, Japanese militarism wreaked havoc on his country, and in the case of European Catholics, the Nazis devastated the continent. The central conundrum for Jin's generation was how to keep the church relevant in a landscape where an alliance with far-right nationalism had been largely discredited. As recent work on the Catholic Church has shown, these conflicts were ones that all Catholics faced during the interwar years, not just those in China.

The process of decolonization in China, then, mirrored much of the other decolonizing movements and moments globally. As Jan Jansen and Jürgen Osterhammel argue, decolonization was more than a technical process through which Europeans hoped they could manage the withdrawal of European power.[66] Decolonization was also a cultural process of dismantling racial hierarchies. Jin's story mimics these broader political and cultural trajectories—a provincial figure becoming radicalized by progressive movements in the metropole.

But Jin's story also does not fit neatly into a metropole-periphery story. The Jesuit missions point to the existence of a dense horizontal transnational network, where surprising nodes, like Bruges, Manila, or Xian County, emerge as centers. Of course, the world was not flat; persistent racial hierarchies permeated even the narratives that sought to dismantle them. Jin, for instance, hardly pays attention to developments in the Latin American or African churches; his reference points were all rooted in Europe and China. While he did mention the existence of fellow Africans or Latin Americans, the idea of a global, universal church remained limited for Jin. Nationalism, and Europe, still bounded his imagination. Moreover, these horizontal networks helped Chinese Catholicism survive after the Chinese Communist victory. The Chinese Jesuits throughout East Asia became the first people to help reestablish the church in the 1980s, after China's reform and reopening. For instance, a former Jesuit colleague who ended up in the Philippines sent Jin money annually after 1982 to reestablish the seminary in Shanghai.[67]

Finally, Jin's story also reminds us of the importance of China as a node before the Second World War. Jin's travels through Europe illustrate the density of Chinese networks, of not only Chinese living in the diaspora, but also of Europeans whose lives had been shaped by their time in China. It reminds us of the importance of China as a training ground for missionaries throughout the nineteenth century. Missionaries had developed a comprehensive network of state-like institutions, as well as a complex web of connections with the broader global church. Decolonization delivered a significant blow to this network, severing connections between Chinese Catholics and members of the global church. Moreover, the expulsion of Christian missionaries from China also signaled the dramatic transfer of people and resources out of China.

The experience with failure and defeat in China had a decisive effect on the way that missionaries began to consider the place of Catholicism in the world. Jesuits who had received their training in China began to reflect on why they had failed. Some, like Laszlo Ladány, argued that the main culprit was the Communist enemy. Others began to turn their critical lens inward, seeking to reform their practices. Take, for instance, the work of the Austrian Jesuit Johannes Hofinger, who studied theology at Innsbruck and traveled to China after completing his doctoral dissertation.[68] In China, he taught at the seminary in Xianxian, publishing works in Latin and Chinese. In 1949, along with other Jesuits, he fled the impending Communist victory by catching a plane for Manila.

In Manila, the Jesuits at first devoted their resources to maintaining the Chinese mission, thinking they were eventually going to return to China. They established Chinese schools and opened a center for Chinese learning. By 1953, it had become clear that the Chinese Communist Party's power was going to last. The Jesuits were forced to change track. Hofinger, along with other Jesuits from the Chinese mission, created the Institute for Mission Apologetics. In his founding statement for the institute, Hofinger wrote that because of the "enforced exile" from China, missionaries had been pushed to "reexamine the whole problem of religious instruction in pagan lands." By holding onto the hope of an eventual return to China, the Jesuits had become disconnected from its actual congregants in the Philippines. Moreover, Hofinger argued that missionaries needed to *"re-think* the *Christian message itself*, in order that, by the grace of God, we may give to our fellow-beings, children and adult, a living faith."[69]

Through the Institute, Hofinger pushed for a radically different approach to religious education and mission. Hofinger drew upon ideas emerging from cultural anthropology, applied psychology, and liturgical movements. At the heart of his message was that the essential Christian message (*kerygma*) needed to be indigenized or inculturated, made relevant to the immediate context where it was being preached. The institute, which later became the East Asian Pastoral Institute, emerged as one of the central places for discussions of "liturgical inculturation" and the training ground for priests throughout East Asia. Hofinger also became an important figure behind the Second Vatican Council. He served on the committee meeting in Rome in 1961 to prepare for the council, and his activism directly influenced three documents at the council—the Constitution on the Sacred Liturgy, the Decree on Missionary Activity of the Church, and the Declaration on the Relationship of the Church to Non-Christian Religions.[70] Horizontal networks proved central to the Second Vatican Council's formation.

When Jin went to prison in 1955, the progressives he had met in Europe were banned by the Vatican. "Who would have guessed," Jin writes in his memoir, "when John XXIII opened the Second Vatican Council, Chenu, de Lubac and Rahner and their young fellow-thinker Ratzinger, among others, would be invited to the council as expert advisors?"[71] The tragedy of Jin's story—and that of Chinese Catholicism—is that while the Communist victory in China had helped to catapult the insurgent progressives into the mainstream, individual Catholics in China like Jin were absent from the world stage. They were not there to bask in their friends' victory.

CHAPTER 5

Decolonizing Global Evangelicalism: The Latin American Evangelical Left in the Shadow of the Cold War

David C. Kirkpatrick

"Socially and economically, Latin America is passing through a revolution, which is shaking it to its very foundations. . . . If Latin America should go Communist, I seriously doubt if the United States could maintain its present freedom and present status as a democracy and a republic. We could not bear . . . a Latin America gone into the Communist camp."[1] In 1962, American evangelist Billy Graham watched, worried, and wondered if waves of change in Latin America would soon lap onto the shores of the United States. After returning from a pathbreaking South American tour that year, Graham preached on his radio program *Hour of Decision*, connecting Latin American political trends with the future of the United States. For Graham himself, political danger arose, however, from particular *religious* practices in Latin America, as well: "Wise Latins are becoming aware that there is some relationship between their neglect of true religion and their problems. And herein lies a hope for improvement and progress."[2] Latin American political problems, and corresponding dangers to the United States, had spiritual origins *and* spiritual solutions. Communism, in Graham's public words, could only be combatted on the battlefield of hearts and minds; personal conversion to Jesus Christ was the only solution to the temptation of errant politics, fitted in the form of US evangelical religion. Only these converted individuals could save the world from impending doom, embodied by radical protests, political assassinations, and social unrest across the world during the tumultuous decade. Of course, privately, Graham hedged his bets, pressing successive US governments to intervene militarily in Latin America.[3]

For both mainline and evangelical Protestants, the pressure for change arrived, in large part, due to the shifting demographics of global Christianity and emerging leadership in the Global South. Former "mission fields" spoke back to sending countries with demands for change. But precisely because political problems required *spiritual* solutions, evangelicals decried the leftward drift of their mainline Protestant counterparts, who doubted evangelical solutions to these social problems. In the minds of many American evangelicals, Christian confusion over mission, theology, and institutional leadership, then, posed an existential threat not only to churches but to the United States itself. Here, in the tensions and promise of the 1960s, American evangelicals sharpened their voice and contribution to US foreign relations. Historian Andrew Preston has clarified how American evangelicals reimagined foreign policy in what he called "evangelical internationalism"—a "fundamental shift in American internationalist thought," which rejected a consensus model for a more robust US engagement shaped by American goals and values.[4] In this chapter, the stories and experiences exported from Latin America to the United States helped construct not only evangelicals' imagination of the world but also their understanding of how to engage with it.

In the 1960s, global Christianity splintered over demands from coreligionists in Africa, Asia, and Latin America. Many US mainline and evangelical Protestant leaders listened with heightened attention, vexed by how to respond. Many global evangelical organizations and institutions lagged in their release of power to coreligionists in the Global South, setting the stage of conflict and negotiation regarding the terms of decolonizing their institutions even after formal decolonization ended. In the case of mainline and evangelical Protestant communities, the answers many Global South Christians provided were religiously and politically inconvenient for leaders in power. In a culmination of sorts, the World Council of Churches (WCC), an ecumenical, inter-church organization comprised of 235 mostly mainline Protestant denominations, met in Uppsala, Sweden, in 1968.[5] Rather than seeking to extinguish the fire of revolution, mainline Protestant organizations were breathing oxygen into the flames. Uppsala 1968 provided evangelicals with plenty of reasons for concern; their consternation went far beyond unfounded alarmism. Mainline Protestant leaders debated the acceptability of violence to provoke social change and direct funding for political liberation movements, including those engaged in guerrilla warfare in the Global

South. The WCC did not simply dip their toes in the water of revolution; they dove in, head-first.

As seen in the earlier chapters of this volume, reaction was particularly swift toward the WCC "Programme to Combat Racism" (PCR). *Christianity Today*, the flagship American evangelical magazine, founded by Billy Graham, fixated on the events preceding and proceeding from Uppsala with titles such as "Will the WCC Endorse Violence?" "Will Uppsala Trigger a Radical Shift for Protestantism?" "Back to Violence as Usual?" and "Uppsala: Awkward Ecumenical Timing."[6] At Uppsala, the World Council of Churches embraced radical proposals, reshaping their mission and purpose in the face of pressure from Global South and US minority Christians. Fearful of appearing apathetic toward Global South pressure, the WCC began to provide direct funding to political liberation movements in South Africa and Black Power organizations in the United States. According to Udi Greenberg, "The WCC went so far to support the violent over-throw of anti-socialist regimes, and even provided funds for guerrilla organisations in Africa."[7] Ultimately, the WCC gave over $4 million "directly and without strings"—over $100 million in today's money.[8] For many American evangelicals, the WCC traded Christian mission for leftist political praise.

Throughout the 1960s and early 1970s, US leaders like Billy Graham faced pressure both outside the gates of American evangelicalism and within its constructed borders. In the face of the mainline churches' radical departure from what evangelicals saw as traditional Christian emphases, Graham and leaders orbiting him began to search for evangelical voices in the Global South to combat this perceived drift. But within their own communities, a restless generation of African, Asian, and Latin American evangelicals also pushed for change *within* evangelical circles, providing dissenting voices to long-held political and theological assumptions in the United States. In particular, a Latin American evangelical *left* provided a stark contrast to widespread white evangelical politics and their full-throated support for American interventionism in the region. An entire generation of evangelicals was shaped by the global Cold War on both sides of the Rio Grande and across the political spectrum. These two pressures, both dipped in themes of violence and decolonization, cross-pollinating and overlapping, would change the direction of American Christianity and the political coalitions that would emerge later in the 1970s. As the 1960s progressed, even prior to Uppsala 1968, evangelicals watched as many of their worst theological fears were confirmed by ideas emanating from Latin America. The resulting tensions, structures, and coalitions set new trajectories for these global religious communities. These shifts occurred especially at the grassroots level, beyond the gaze of political observers. Yet the implications would rise to the level of US foreign relations as evangelicals took their place at the table of political influence.

Decolonizing Latin American Christianity

The Cold War impacted global Christianity in a series of stark contrasts. The Roman Catholic Church reeled from the loss of influence and land in Cuba and the spread of Marxist-inflected ideologies across many Catholic-majority countries. In response, the Catholic hierarchy rearranged their theological furniture in the largest remodel in nearly a century. Pope John XXIII began the Second Vatican Council (1962–1965) with prescient words: "open the windows and let in the fresh air." But which type of air they allowed to flow, which they filtered, and which they would block entirely became the subject of fierce debate over the coming decades within Catholic circles. Many cheered the council for its "turn toward the poor," the linguistic shift in the mass from Latin to local languages, and a vow to combat a top-down mentality—a "pilgrim church," the council called for. At the first session of Vatican II, 601 of the 2,778 delegates (21.6 percent) arrived from Latin America.[9] Given this representation, it is not difficult to see why the council impacted Latin America so profoundly. In terms of Latin American Christianity, many observers mark the Latin American Episcopal Conference (CELAM) meeting in Medellín, Colombia in August 1968 and the publication of Gustavo Gutiérrez' monumental 1971 work *Teología de la liberación* as the beginning of this new era of local Latin American theologies reflecting an emphasis on liberating the poor and creating new social Christian structures. But theologies of revolution and liberation percolated long before they were codified in print and gained attention from the Global North. They built momentum throughout the 1950s and 1960s south of the Rio Grande. In Latin America, an international group of young theologians took the lead in a conversation that was anything but a Latin American or Catholic monologue. This story resists a South to North binary, with many US and British Christians involved in the development of Global South theologies and independent religious construction.

Richard Shaull, a US Presbyterian missionary to Colombia and Brazil and subsequently a professor at Princeton Theological Seminary, was one of the most important organizing forces in Latin American social Christianity. He would also later become a focal point of Latin American evangelical attacks. His own "theology of revolution" and organizing prowess helped prime the pump, especially within the World Council of Churches. In 1955, the WCC inaugurated a ten-year conference series in Latin America titled "Christian Responsibility Toward Areas of Rapid Social Change." Perhaps most importantly, it produced a strategic discussion forum titled "Iglesia y Sociedad en América Latina" (ISAL).[10] ISAL became a magnet for increasingly radical ideas on Marxism and Christian participation in revolution—including the use of guerrilla warfare to produce social and structural change. For the newly launched conferences, Shaull invited individuals with whom he had worked in the WCC's Student Christian Movement (SCM) in Latin America—students José Míguez Bonino, Rubem Alves, and Julio de Santa Ana, among others. These young leaders would later become leading liberation theologians, publishing critical material together over the coming years.[11]

Reports from the ISAL gatherings became increasingly radical in nature. In 1962, Shaull wrote back to the Committee on Cooperation in Latin America, pushing for the WCC to embrace revolution, both spiritual and political, and indicting the "sins" of the United States: "The need at this moment is for people who are free to live in a situation of almost total insecurity, in which everything is in a state of flux; people who are able to understand why they are disliked as North Americans and live by the forgiveness of their sins in such an atmosphere." This also applied individually to those watching revolutions from abroad in the US: "The present moment demands men and women who are able to understand the revolution sympathetically, and to deal imaginatively, in terms of Christian faith, with the issues and dilemmas which people face in it. . . . Through the work of the Holy Spirit they may discover how their participation may be of service at this time; they will almost certainly learn much more than they contribute."[12] The implications of Shaull's suggestions were clear: Western leaders should not clutch the status quo of dusty, old ideas, politics, and theologies, but rather provide freedom for a new generation of leftist ideas to win the day. Faithful Christian practice may actually require participation in revolution alongside.

Shaull's political theology within ISAL only radicalized as the decade continued. By 1964, ISAL began to argue that "social change in Latin America *demanded* participation in revolution" and by late the same year, "revolution had become almost a monochord in ISAL publications" (italics mine).[13] Shaull's 1966 plenary speech in El Tabo, Chile, entitled "Social Justice and the Latin Churches" also called for the liberation of Latin American theology.[14]

But more importantly for English-speaking audiences, he gave a barn-burning speech at a 1966 WCC conference in Geneva, where he embraced guerrilla warfare as a means for social change. At a time when Martin Luther King Jr.'s ideas were particularly salient within these WCC circles, Shaull rejected the idea of "exclusive reliance on non-violent action" and rebuked those who "insist that Christians should have no participation in the use of violence."[15] Instead, Shaull made his point clear: "There may, in fact, be some situations, in which the threat or use of violence can set the process of change in motion." For Shaull, small-scale, guerrilla violence with a goal of "constant struggle for limited change in society" was promising. "The formation of such 'guerrilla' units, with a clear sense of self-identity, a vision of a new social order, and a commitment to constant struggle for change, inside or outside certain social structures, may offer one interesting prospect for building a new society at this time."[16] Historian Lilian Barger described Shaull's view well: "he did not rule out the judicious use of violence at strategic points in the system." Shaull's speech was later published in the *Princeton Seminary Bulletin*, assuring a wider reading among ecumenical Protestants.[17]

Shaull's influence was wide and the pressure emanating from ISAL significant. As historian Alan Neely concluded, "It is doubtful if any theologian has more consistently and directly contributed to the shaping of the thought of the contemporary Protestant theologies of liberation than Richard Shaull."[18] But perhaps most importantly, Shaull helped remove the taboo against violence in mainline Protestant circles and opened a wider conversation on its use in particular political situations. This influence also highlights a broader reality: the influence of the Latin American context on shifting political and religious loyalties in the postwar period. It should also be noted that the embrace of theologies of revolution and liberation was far from uniform. Many leaders within mainline circles disagreed with this presentation of Christian participation in violent revolutions, of course, alongside the voices of many evangelical Protestants. This set the stage for a raucous and tumultuous global assembly of the World Council of Churches and an equally fierce backlash.

Platitudinous Drivel

The World Council of Churches assembly met with a sense of urgency, pressure, and solemnity in Uppsala, Sweden, in 1968. One commentator in the flagship ecumenical publication *Christian Century* wrote in advance, "We can be sure that Uppsala will be no holiday . . . and post-Uppsala will be a picnic only for anti-ecumenical forces. All things considered, the faint-hearted had better stay away and bargain-hunters looking for 'cheap grace' had better look somewhere else."[19] The assembly gathered an all-star cast of influential religious and political leaders, including writer James Baldwin and Zambian president Kenneth Kaunda, and subsequent consultations included US senator George McGovern; Oliver Tambo, acting president of the African National Congress (ANC) in South Africa; and Milwaukee civil rights activist and priest James Groppi, among many others. Dr. Martin Luther King Jr. was scheduled to give a keynote address but instead was assassinated in April of that year. At the assembly, organizers played a previously recorded address from King, impacting the tone and temper of the gathering.[20] In other words, violence and the pressing need for structural change was evident from the outset. But King's absence also appeared to be symbolic of the WCC's approach to issues of decolonization and violent struggle. *Time* magazine reported, "The mood of the delegate, white and black alike, was as militant as the resolutions," even if one African American minister railed against "the same old platitudinous drivel."[21]

Uppsala was also a watershed moment for Global South participation and leadership. This was true numerically and thematically.[22] According to Risto Lehtonen, "The Assembly went all out to rid the WCC, its programs, and its image, of any signs of Western domination or of vestiges of colonial attitude." This played itself out in the form of a discouragement of "critical discussion" as the forum "imposed a kind of self-censorship on representatives from the North in all matters of concern for the South."[23] White delegates were often widely silenced or they self-censored. The reality of new voices from the Global South meant differing views on politics, economics, and theology. In other words, the decolonization of global Christianity arose front and center. Overall, the WCC "forcefully linked the anti-colonial and anti-capitalist struggles, claiming that both were demanded by the Gospel."[24]

Instead of King's message of nonviolence, however, the ideas of leaders like Shaull appeared to win the day, especially within the later Programme to Combat Racism (PCR). The wide embrace of funding political violence became a dividing line for evangelical Protestants. Historian Brian Stanley put it directly: "Many conservative Christians in the northern hemisphere regarded the PCR as evidence that the WCC had departed from Christian orthodoxy and fatally succumbed to the political pressures of the secular and anticolonial age."[25] Evangelical and mainline Protestant leaders faced overlapping but divergent pressures. Mainline Protestantism experienced a significant decline in missionaries in the Global South that their evangelical counterparts did not. Thus, trends from the WCC were not simply the result of mainline Protestant desire to amplify diverse voices in the global church. They had fewer and fewer voices from Europe and the United States on traditional mission fields. If they wanted voices from these regions, it necessitated local leaders and correspondingly divergent opinions. With this ceding of authority came dissenting economic views, as well.[26] As US Christians gave more intellectual and organizational control to their coreligionists in the Global South, boundary lines began to shift. Uppsala ultimately rejected traditional Christian mission, replacing conversion with humanization. In fact, its official pronouncements called seeking conversions "the very opposite of mission."[27] These shifts away from traditional Christian mission emphases, and the endorsement of revolutionary liberation movements, set the evangelical world alight.

Many US evangelicals watched with mouths agape. With a provocative title, "Back to Violence as Usual," the news section of *Christianity Today* indicted mainline Protestants in a widening battlefront: "1968 may go down as the year in which the world tried to cope with a rising tide of violence while ecumenical assemblies sought to encourage it."[28] For many American evangelical leaders, how mainline Protestants handled the issue of violence and Christian mission revealed their true spiritual nature. They had lost the plot of the Bible and the Gospel message alongside it. Violence split Protestant Christendom down the middle.

American evangelical leaders like Graham began to realize that in the global battle over hearts and minds, US Christians needed like-minded thinkers in strategic positions abroad. American evangelicals, in their own way, turned to their coreligionists in the Global South to confirm their fears and fight their battles. Yet some of the most vociferous disagreement came not from across the border but from within Latin America itself—among those most affected by the realities of revolution at home. Fierce debates broke out within emerging progressive Latin American circles, shaping internal and external trajectories in the region.

A Dissenting Voice

White Americans were not the only evangelicals watching and worried about radical trends within the World Council of Churches and Roman Catholic Church. During this decade, an eclectic but increasingly vocal coalition of progressive Latin American evangelicals began to emerge in various parts of the Protestant world. They often shared in common a suspicion of American imperialism and conservative political loyalties in the US, but also skepticism toward the leftist theological and political convictions of organizations like ISAL and the WCC in the region. Progressive Latin American evangelicals defined themselves primarily against two perceived ideological excesses: Marxist inflected theologies of liberation and the conservative political loyalties of the Religious Right. Thus, the emerging coalition of the Latin American evangelical left was theologically conservative and evangelical but pushed boundaries on socially progressive ideas, especially in politics. This linguistic designation should not be used to mask its diversity, however. The emerging progressive evangelical coalition in Latin America was as diverse as the denominations and organizations that they represented, similar to a wide spectrum within the so called religious right. The glue that held together this emerging coalition of progressive evangelicals was their brand of social Christianity—their local answer to a changing and tumultuous context.[29]

The Peruvian Samuel Escobar, Ecuadorian René Padilla, and Puerto Rican Orlando Costas were principal theologians here, each with their own emphases and concerns. Escobar and Padilla were longtime staff members with the International Fellowship of Evangelical Students (IFES) in Latin America, founded in 1947 at Phillips Brooks House at Harvard University in Cambridge, Massachusetts. IFES is the worldwide representative body that arose out of the Inter-Varsity Fellowship (IVF), later known as the Universities and Colleges Christian Fellowship (UCCF) in Britain, and InterVarsity Christian Fellowship–USA (IVCF). Costas was a missionary and professor at Seminario Bíblico Latinoamericano in Costa Rica, later becoming the first Hispanic American endowed chair at an evangelical institution as the Thornley B. Wood Professor of Missiology and director of Hispanic Studies and Ministries at Eastern Baptist Theological Seminary (later named Palmer) in 1980. In the mid-1960s, the Latin American evangelical left arose as a formidable force against the managerial status quo of global evangelicalism. Latin American evangelicals had already taken leadership of global organizations in the region, as well. This reality—that many Latin Americans were just emerging into their own intellectual independence, and a growing restlessness and wariness over leftist trends—set the region on a crash course in terms of global Christianity.

Rather than responding to the rise of theologies of liberation, progressive evangelicals began to respond to a shared cluster of political and social forces that were reshaping postwar Latin America: rural-urban migration, the resulting complications of urbanization, and the rapid expansion of the universities, where Marxist ideas of revolutionary change were of growing appeal to students.[30] Since Padilla, Escobar, and Costas were all based on university campuses in the region, their proximity to unrest provided ample materials for theological construction. Already in 1966, Padilla had decried "the almost complete absence of a social concern and of a realistic approach to social evils, the frequent identification of the Gospel with foreign ways of life and thinking."[31] He rejected the market conditions that brought imported Christianities to the region, and the content of those goods, which were almost entirely spiritual but not social. He also began to ascertain the need for social action within evangelical Christian mission: "We are concerned for an evangelism in which man does not abstract himself from Secular City [sic] in order to become a self-righteous bigot, but remains as man among fellow men—taking his share in the sufferings of the world, actively engaged in the fight against social evils—yet ever endeavoring to take 'every thought captive to obey Christ.'"[32] But Padilla's own solution was similar to Graham's at this time: changed hearts and minds.

While rejecting what he saw in white US evangelicalism, Padilla found little help within the writings or trends of the Roman Catholic Church or mainline Protestantism. Padilla described Catholic trends as an attempt by the hierarchy to "dispel the common notion that for Roman Catholicism God always sides with the rich over against the poor and to show in practical ways that the church not only favors change but is ready to promote it." Padilla's attitude toward these new developments was one of skepticism. Though he acknowledged that "these are undeniable signs of the church's awareness of the demands placed upon her by the new situation" he wondered if it were simply "a change of tactics on the part of a losing party, a renewed effort to maintain whatever power the church still has and sees rapidly slipping from her hands." Thus, he concluded morbidly, "It is difficult to avoid the feeling that . . . the Roman Catholic Church is already a corpse."[33] A flatlined Catholicism, then, left young people "hanging in the air, the object of all sorts of modern ideologies, from Communism intent to change things by means of violence to a 'beatnik' existentialism lost in Nausea."[34] Padilla rejected violence for social change but also the ideologies that supported those conclusions. In doing so, Padilla reflected the broader beliefs of an emerging Latin American evangelical left at this time: a recognition of a toothless evangelicalism but the rejection of solutions found within other Christian communities.

Padilla would later sharpen his critique and aim directly at ISAL. Evangelicals across the world needed "immediately to recognize that 'ISAL theology' is a Latin American version of the 'secular theology' (read 'anthropology') manufactured in Europe and the United States in these last years" (parenthetical in original).[35] Padilla undoubtedly had Shaull in mind, as well as the influence of European Political Theology. Padilla then aimed directly at the heart of ISAL ideologies: "The equation of ideology (Marxism) and faith (Christianity), the erasing of the boundary between the church and the world, the sanctification of the revolution, the rejection of biblical authority—these are the strands with which the theology of ISAL is woven. It does a favor to no one, and even less to the cause of Jesus Christ, to overlook the profound differences between this theology and any other that attempts to find its source in the biblical message."[36] Even for progressive Latin American evangelicals like Padilla, the political theology of the WCC went too far in its "sanctification of the revolution."

Orlando Costas, for his part, was optimistic about Christian participation in revolution. He would later write, "The church cannot remain neutral any longer. It must become involved in the struggle of the Latin American masses if it is ever to live up to its nature and fulfill its mission."[37] Costas concluded with words that echoed many of his mainline and Catholic counterparts: "The reality of revolution in Latin America indicates that the church cannot hide any longer behind the excuse that it has only a spiritual mission. No longer can it be affirmed that all we need to do is change the heart of men and everything else will take care of itself." In his conclusion, Costas also shared a warning: "The fact is that the Latin American masses will not wait for the church to come and change their hearts before they act. They want now to change the systems that have kept them in oppression for so long! They want justice and freedom now!"[38] Samuel Escobar, for his part, thought Costas was naïve and blamed Costas' distance as a US citizen and time spent in Costa Rica, a country that largely avoided the political tumult of its neighboring countries. Escobar, more conservative politically than both Padilla and Costas, still viewed dialogue with Marxists as essential, writing his own book, *Cristo y Marx*, in 1967.

The emerging Latin American evangelical left spent the decade of the 1960s sharpening their critiques and contributions to a decolonizing evangelicalism. This meant increasingly raising their voices against US evangelical ideologies in the region and supposed solutions to Latin American problems. Padilla made this clear in the first article dedicated to liberation theology to appear in *Christianity Today*.[39] While he rejected liberation theology in the first half of the article, Padilla also accused "evangelical circles" of allowing theology "to be a cover-up for an ideology marked by political conservatism and conformity to the status quo." He concluded, "The need for a liberation of theology is then as real in our case as in the case of the theology of liberation."[40] The article's final words revealed that neither theologies of liberation nor current conservative evangelical theology answered Padilla's question: "Where is the evangelical theology that will propose a solution with the same eloquence but also with a firmer basis in the Word of God?"[41] For American evangelicals like Graham and Carl F. H. Henry, Latin Americans simply needed to embrace the faith that Americans brought to the region. For their coreligionists like Padilla, Escobar, and Costas, the answer was not so simple and would ultimately arrive after decolonizing its core theologies and institutions.

In the 1960s, Billy Graham required no convincing regarding the need for evangelical alternatives to ecumenical Protestantism. Uppsala was simply the nail in the coffin. After the WCC's radical turn at the assembly, where did Billy Graham turn to cauterize the perceived spreading wound? Not surprisingly, the BGEA first turned south of the border to Latin America, where pressure appeared most acute, communism seemed to be gaining ground, and liberation movements multiplied with each passing day. Latin America became the location where the WCC sought to grow cultures from the petri dish of revolution *and* where evangelicals sought to destroy them. But while the Latin American evangelical left was sharpening its own critique and local ideas to counter ISAL, Henry, Graham, and the white evangelical establishment grew impatient. Off the back of a global gathering in Berlin in 1966, US evangelicals planned an intervention in Latin America. Rather than successes, their failures set the tone for the direction of global evangelicalism in the decades following.

American Intervention, Global War

Billy Graham's alarm rang across the southern border of the United States in the late 1960s. The Billy Graham Evangelistic Association (BGEA) invited nine hundred twenty hand-selected delegates to Bogotá, Colombia, from November 21–30, 1969, for what they called the First Latin American Congress for Evangelization (Congreso Latinoamericano de Evangelización, or CLADE I)—organized and funded by the BGEA.[42] The title of the congress publication was "Acción en Cristo para un continente en crisis" (Action in Christ for a Continent in Crisis). The BGEA carefully curated their message by hand-selecting conference speakers at CLADE, seeking only those who would echo their theological and political concerns. From the perspective of an emerging Latin American evangelical left, this accentuated the conference's foreignness and stubborn American insistence on managing the world. In a broader sense, CLADE laid a foundation for the evangelical left to reject how Americans sought to control processes of global religious decolonization.

While the explicit goal was the "evangelization of the whole of Latin America," Graham was also motivated by evangelistic zeal, anti-Communist anxiety, and perceived liberalizing shifts in mainline Protestant organizations such as the WCC.[43] CLADE was also a BGEA attempt to combat what they viewed as theological liberal advancement within Latin America through Tercera Conferencia Evangélica Latinoamericana (CELA III), which was held earlier in the year through the WCC.[44] As they prepared for their own conference, evangelical CLADE organizers worked behind the scenes to determine who was theologically *safe* and who was *dangerous*. In doing so, they not only sought those who were theologically and politically conservative, but also to block Latin American pastors from affiliating with the World Council of Churches.[45] For CLADE organizers and backers, joining the WCC was a matter of spiritual life and death.

At CLADE, the BGEA also distributed literature to carve boundaries around individual Latin American leaders. Each participant of CLADE I received a copy of American missionary Peter Wagner's book, *Teología Latinoamericana: Izquierdista o evangélica? La lucha por la fe en una iglesia creciente* (*Latin American Theology: Radical or Evangelical? The Struggle for the Faith in a Young Church*).[46] Wagner's book was distributed free of charge to every attendee at CLADE I, denoting BGEA's confidence in its contents.[47] Wagner rejected calls for addressing social needs and structures alongside the Gospel and his analysis drew heavily on stereotypes, lumping more evangelically minded thinkers such as José Míguez Bonino, Emilio Castro, and Justo Gonzalez together with more radical ecumenical theologians like Rubem Alves and Richard Shaull. Orlando Costas later wrote, "We were offended by the purpose, content and methodology of the book."[48] In a 2013 interview in Valencia, Spain, Samuel Escobar called it "an embarrassment."[49] Padilla objected not only to Wagner's book but also to the "pre-made package," a thirty-year plan for evangelizing Latin America, presented by CLADE co-president Carlos Lastra.[50] Lastra called it an "integral plan" to "evangelize Latin America"[51] Referring to American paternalism,

Padilla called this "typical of the way in which work was done sometimes in the conservative sector."[52] In a private letter, Billy Graham later wrote to US president Richard Nixon asking for Lastra to be appointed "US Ambassador to Latin America."[53] This is perhaps the clearest example of Graham's approval of CLADE and Lastra's work as co-president with Clyde Taylor, Executive Secretary of the Evangelical Foreign Missions Association (EFMA). For Padilla and the emerging Latin American evangelical left, the reality of the conference and plan being "made in the USA" was an affront to their decolonization efforts. Padilla published a scathing article in response and began to organize like-minded leaders for a response.[54]

While the BGEA went to significant lengths to present a united front against leftward shifts in religion and politics, one speaker slipped through the cracks. Samuel Escobar's paper was titled "The Social Responsibility of the Church" and spoke directly to the sociopolitical tumult in the region. It also provoked a prolonged standing ovation from the crowd. Even Peter Wagner admitted, "By general consenus [sic] the most enthusiastically received address was the one . . . by Dr. Samuel Escobar. . . . [H]is paper should be widely circulated throughout the world. When he concluded, the assembly could not contain their urge to signify their approval by a thunderous standing ovation."[55]

In his plenary speech, Escobar addressed the tumultuous Cold War context, as well as the soul-saving mission of his evangelical forebears. In doing so, he echoed a uniform refrain of the Latin American evangelical left: rejecting *both* theologies of liberation and US conservative evangelical theologies. "Christ did not come to preach an armed revolution to break unjust structures. But he expected from his disciples a revolutionary behavior characterized by the spirit of service and sacrifice. Such a thing is possible only if man allows God to change him, if he converts. Let's not convert the gospel into a method of 'being happy and living without worry.'" Escobar also spoke of an awakening of political conscience among the evangelical community in Latin America, spurred on by the work of British missionaries, who had helped them discover the "social dimension of the gospel."[56] Escobar, however, also affirmed the centrality of evangelization: "The comprehension of evangelization as the central task should not lead us to close our eyes to other urgent tasks."[57] He said, "We should affirm that evangelization is *one* of the tasks of the church, it is not the only task of the church and it does not end in proclamation" (italics in original).[58] Social structures affected the church and the reception of the gospel—not to recognize this "disfigures" the gospel and "impoverishes the Christian life."[59] For Escobar, the Latin American context demanded a fresh breeze through the church's windows. Escobar's talk and its discordance with official conference literature foreshadowed clashes to come.

CLADE was an abject failure from the perspective of the BGEA conference organizers and provoked fierce backlash due to two primary factors: the perception Americans continued to dictate the terms and content of Christian mission and local politics, and a perceived distance from the sociopolitical tumult of the era. Specifically, when BGEA gathered speakers and leaders, many were perceived as aloof from this "continent in crisis." The speakers at CLADE largely came from stable democracies: Puerto Rico, Costa Rica, and Hispanic communities in the United States. In other words, for Padilla, Escobar, and others, the BGEA lacked surface area for reactions to sociopolitical unrest. In our wider story, CLADE provoked the Latin American evangelical left to intervene in their own way, rejecting how Americans curated experiences of global violence and poverty.

Perhaps more important than the conference itself were the relationships that were formed as a result of BGEA funding the travel of Latin American leaders across the region. Many Latin American pastors and theologians met each other for the first time and found common ground in a struggle for relevant and timely theological and pastoral production. In the face of perceived paternalism, Samuel Escobar recalled in a 2013 interview, "We said, now is the time that we as Latin Americans decide who is *evangélico* in Latin America and what it means to be *evangélico*. And as always, these ideas delayed, were discussed, debated, talked till midnight. . . . From there came the idea of the Fraternity."[60]

The Latin American Theological Fraternity (Fraternidad Teológica Latinoamericana, or FTL) was the brainchild of Peruvian-born British missionary Peter Savage, Samuel Escobar, René Padilla, and a few others who met at CLADE I to discuss the formation of a Latin American evangelical theological organization. This ad hoc group reunited the next year from December 12–18, 1970, in the town of Carachipampa, located just outside Cochabamba, Bolivia—though in later press releases, the nearby city of Cochabamba was named for clarity.[61] There, they formed the FTL, which became the most influential evangelical thinktank in the region. The FTL was a precursor to the evangelical left gathering in downtown Chicago on Thanksgiving weekend, 1973, and an emerging pipeline of social Christian materials. In Chicago, the FTL was also well represented. The now-disgraced Anabaptist ethicist John Howard Yoder, a leading voice in the evangelical left and early member of the FTL, had just returned from Buenos Aires when he joined the Chicago gathering. In Latin America, he spoke at strategic gatherings and produced collaborative literature. Escobar also attended the Chicago gathering, as did Costas' later colleague Ron Sider. Two years prior, the FTL was a construction site, building an early intellectual framework for the evangelical left.

South of the Rio Grande, American evangelicals such as the BGEA found confirmation of a global war on their religion; Christianity was under attack and the radical shifts within Latin America confirmed the consequences of inaction. But here, a surprising challenge to American evangelical political and theological loyalties also arose from the shadow of the Cold War—from the same generation and location as Pope Francis and theologies of liberation. The FTL was most influential because Latin American leaders across the region brought their nascent brand of social Christianity with them. At these early gatherings, justice was *essential* rather than *optional*, as religious thinkers sought to mold their message to fit their contextual reality. Yet progressive Latin American evangelicals were not content with keeping these ideas hermetically sealed within the borders of Latin America; they dragged them to the global stage. As they sought to bring these ideas into the global evangelical spotlight, they faced further headwinds prior to the epochal evangelical gathering called the Lausanne Congress of 1974.

Latin American Evangelicals on the Global Stage

In July 1973, Carl F. H. Henry, leading US evangelical theologian and movement architect, planned a forty-five-day trip to eight Latin American countries.[62] Beneath the umbrella of the newly founded Fraternidad Teologica Latinoamericano, Henry planned a hurried lecture schedule of more than sixty speaking engagements.[63] On paper, one could imagine an emerging generation of Latin American evangelicals embracing this high-profile engagement. As one historian recently opined, "While Billy Graham was the front man for the evangelical movement, Henry was the brains behind the operation."[64] A visit from Henry could undoubtedly help fundraising, publishing, and even church growth. Yet, behind the scenes, leaders of the FTL expressed hesitancy at an American interloper threatening their fragile intellectual independence. The Cold War had begun to shift the power dynamics of global evangelicalism.

Prior to the trip, Padilla wrote a personal letter to Henry, highlighting the embarrassing lack of contextual theology in the region: "Young people [ask] questions regarding the Christian attitude towards a Marxist regime, while the pastors [discuss] the length of the skirts that girls are wearing in church. A social ethic—we have none."[65] It is no surprise, given Henry's expertise, to see a separate letter from Henry to Peter Savage, expressing a desire to teach and promote the study of "ethical teaching and the believer" in Christian mission—the very gap that Padilla highlighted and the specific expertise of Carl Henry.[66] Padilla wrote further to Henry, "We fear however, that the glowing reports from Latin America often fail to point out . . . main problems which threaten to turn the church into a mere sect, unable to make a Christian impact on society."[67] These words hearken back to Henry's own worry in his influential *Uneasy Conscience of Modern Fundamentalism* (1947), which many credit as sparking the neo-evangelical movement and its separation from fundamentalism.[68] Yet, when Padilla wrote to Henry requesting Henry cover certain topics, the request arrived with a rebuke and a warning.[69]

Instead of seeking Henry's advice and expertise, Padilla sharply warned Henry: "We would hesitate to ask you to try to place too much emphasis on specific answers in the field of social ethics, (which may not betoo [sic] well received, coming from a North American)."[70] The message was clear: the Cold War changed the calculus and Latin Americans were taking control of their own religious destiny. Much of the history around these events highlights the shocking words and rebukes of Latin Americans at the epochal Lausanne Congress of 1974. But careful attention to the archives and personal papers of these main characters also reveals that this private spat at the edge of Lausanne was simply one of many fierce battles between white evangelicals such as Henry and progressive Latin Americans. Given this backstory in Latin America, no one should have been surprised by the fireworks in Lausanne in 1974.

In 1974, Billy Graham summoned evangelical leaders to accelerate the evangelization of the world. In response, he nearly reaped an evangelical civil war. That year, evangelical leaders huddled in Lausanne, Switzerland, in a meeting that rivaled Vatican II in terms of influence; nearly twenty-five hundred Protestant evangelical leaders from over one hundred fifty countries and one hundred thirty-five denominations gathered. *Time* magazine called it "a formidable forum, possibly the widest-ranging meeting of Christians ever held."[71] Rather than the evangelization of the world, an emerging evangelical left seized the moment and thrust global evangelicalism into conflict. As American leaders mapped strategies for "mission fields," leaders from these countries demanded a seat at the table, bringing contexts of poverty, inequality, and widespread injustice.

At Lausanne, Padilla's plenary speech fueled a fiery protest, providing inspiration and an intellectual framework for the future of a global evangelical left. Padilla rebuked American missionaries for exporting a deadly cocktail of capitalist rhetoric and evangelical salvation. He also rejected their brand of the "American Way of Life," embracing instead a gospel for the poor, what he called "*misión integral*" or "integral mission." On the global stage, the Latin American evangelical left sought to strip evangelicalism of its white, middleclass American packaging. In response, many conservatives heard the language of the "godless Communists" they feared creeping into their community. Lausanne shined a spotlight, exposing fractures and fissures across this eclectic religious coalition.

In the story of postwar global evangelicalism, Latin Americans took a leading role, converting Cold War pressure into activist energy. While the Catholic side of this story is widely known, the overlapping and shared context is widely overlooked in the drama of Protestant evangelicalism. An entire generation of Latin American evangelicals insisted that the Christian church should center on the poor—in Pope Francis' words, to build "a Church which is poor and for the poor." In doing so, they challenged widespread American evangelical loyalties to conservative politics.

In the United States, this renaissance of evangelical social Christianity ushered in a brief moment of progressive political activism and a lasting era of global evangelical relief organizations that command billion-dollar budgets. While the political edge rounded with white evangelical adoption, it also sharpened among a significant moral minority. A Cold War generation of African, Asian, and Latin American leaders, inspired by Lausanne, rejected American global religious hegemony, and rose to intellectual and organizational independence on previous "mission fields." Many evangelicals of color in the US also embraced this story, drawing inspiration to challenge broad sympathies for the Republican Party. Through a global lens, an alternative image of the evangelical left comes into focus, revealing victories and defeat, negotiation and resistance.

Conclusion

In the 1960s, global violence and decolonization confirmed the fears and assumptions of many white evangelical Protestants. In response, many turned inward, battening down the hatches and preparing for a worldwide battle over the boundaries and contours of global Christianity. But US evangelicals also gazed into the world and saw a global family in need of their intervention—not only theologically but also politically. Prominent leaders such as Billy Graham could publicly claim apolitical work but privately press politicians to intervene in Latin America. In historian Axel Schäfer's words, evangelicals "learned to stop worrying and love the state."[72]

Behind this story lies hidden fractures and fissures surrounding the role of US leaders in Latin America and the world. Together, these events tell the story of a battle for decolonizing evangelicalism—its theology, its structures, and its specific mission around the world. The entire preceding decade placed a particular question mark over foreign intervention and boundary-policing in politics and religion. An emerging generation of progressive evangelicals in Latin America wielded their hybridized biographies, marked by anti-Protestant violence, missionary paternalism, repressive US-backed military regimes, and a growing restlessness over foreign incursion. Latin American Protestant *and* Catholic theologians rejected paternalistic structures and incorporated ideas emanating from a shared social location within the Cold War. In the case of the Latin American evangelical left, the Cuban Revolution (1959) played an outsized role within evangelical battles over mission, theology, identity, and politics. The failed Bay of Pigs invasion in the early 1960s only served to confirm what Castro's forces had already signaled—American imperialism was anything but invincible or inevitable. The Cuban Revolution, and events surrounding it, heightened radar in multiple directions.

For many US evangelicals, "godless communism" was not just a political threat but a rival religion that sought to exterminate Christianity. Many forms of social Christianity, especially those emanating from the World Council of Churches (WCC), seemed like attempts to weaken the walls of Christianity for communism's steady advance. In turn, many Latin American evangelicals, especially those within the Latin American evangelical left, viewed US attempts to police *their* theological boundaries as neocolonialism, paternalism, and a breach of trust in what should have been a global partnership. Gone were the days of a US monologue, as Christianity increasingly shifted southward. Evangelicalism's power balance, however, teetered between a financial and educational anchor in the Global North and an increasingly ascendant Global South.

CHAPTER 6

At the Crossroads of East and West: Christianity and the Legacy of Colonialism in Postcolonial North Africa

Darcie Fontaine

Ruins of historic Christian sites of the Roman Empire, including Hippo and Carthage, dot the landscape of North Africa, a constant reminder of the centuries-long Christian presence in the Maghreb. The French colonization of North Africa in the nineteenth and twentieth centuries further embedded Christianity in the region. Between 1830 and 1962, Algeria held a unique position in the religious landscape of the French empire as France's largest settler colony; there were approximately one million European settlers there at the outbreak of the Algerian War of Independence in 1954, and 800,000 of them would have described themselves as Catholics.[1] Morocco and Tunisia, later additions to the French empire, also had significant populations of European Catholic settlers: on the eve of independence, an estimated 250,000 Catholics resided in Tunisia, and 325,000 in Morocco.[2] Yet neither this historic legacy nor the powerful presence of the Catholic settler population could counter the force of decolonization in the 1950s and 1960s. Consequently, the decolonization of the Maghreb led to the stunning exodus of more than 75 percent of the European settler community from all three countries, leaving the presence and power of the Catholic Church visibly diminished in North Africa after independence. While Christians were not expelled by force, as many had feared, the reality was that Catholicism in the Maghreb was nearly decimated as a result of decolonization, and those Catholic institutions that remained were dramatically transformed after independence.

The shadow of French colonialism weighed heavily over the post-decolonization Catholic Church. But in Morocco, Algeria, and Tunisia, Catholic leaders and laypeople sought to engage in both symbolic and practical actions that would demonstrate their willingness to reject the old system and to reinvent a more just and modern form of Catholicism. At the forefront of this project in all three countries were leftist Christians, who had, since the late 1940s and early 1950s, engaged in theological, social, and political movements that sought to demonstrate solidarity with the poor and colonized populations of the Maghreb and, to a lesser extent, North African nationalist movements in their fight for justice and independence. I argue that the main reason Christianity was not expelled by force from the Maghreb in the aftermath of decolonization was largely due to a complex series of negotiations by Christian institutions and individuals with postcolonial governments relating to questions of nationality, education, and religious freedom as well as the dramatic renunciation of Catholic wealth and power through the transfer of nearly the entirety of Catholic Church property to the state. This situation was highly unusual in the decolonizing world and occurred simultaneously with a full renegotiation of the role of Catholic institutions and individuals in the political and social structures being built in the new Maghrebi nation-states. Drawing support from the theological innovations of Vatican II, Catholics in the Maghreb in the 1960s and 1970s envisioned their church as one that should "incarnate" the values of Jesus through presence and service to the North African Muslim population, solidarity with the oppressed, and dialogue with ideas and faiths outside of Catholicism. While in some ways it seems counterintuitive, this tangible realignment of practices and values, in tandem with the church's acceptance of its visibly diminished profile and power in the new postcolonial states, enabled the survival of Christianity in the Maghreb after decolonization.

Christianity and the French Colonial Regime in the Maghreb

Catholicism played an essential role in the expansion of the French empire in North Africa. The European settler population of Algeria grew steadily over the nineteenth century and French Catholics sought to expand their own influence within the territory. In 1838, the diocese of Algiers was established under the authority of the French hierarchy, which undertook a massive expansion of Catholic institutions, including schools, hospitals, and churches, built primarily for the use of the Catholic settler population.[3] The French missionary presence in Algeria was modest compared to other European colonies, as missions to convert the Muslim populations of Algeria to Christianity had largely failed.[4]

The expansion of the French empire into Tunisia and Morocco also led Catholics to invest more heavily in Africa. In the 1880s, Cardinal Charles Lavigerie, the archbishop of Algiers since 1867, shifted his attention to the new French protectorate in Tunisia.[5] In line with his vision to restore the Catholic Church in North Africa to its former Roman glory, Lavigerie lobbied Pope Leo XII to reinstate the ancient see of Carthage. In 1884, the pope created the Archdiocese of Carthage, making Lavigerie the archbishop and primate of Africa. In contrast to Algeria, the French were a minority among the European settlers in Tunisia, and Catholics there were never fully integrated into the French hierarchy, remaining much more autonomous in their relations to power (both church and state).[6] In Morocco, Maréchal Lyautey, the veteran colonial officer and first resident general of the French Protectorate, formally outlawed proselytism by missionaries and wrote a clause into the 1912 Treaty of Fes stating that France committed to protect the Muslim religion and its institutions; like the early colonizers of Algeria, his motivation was not theological respect for Islam or the Muslim population of North Africa but rather to maintain order in the colony.[7] Consequently, Catholic institutions in Morocco were also primarily organized around the European settler population, which remained a significant minority through the entire colonial period.

By the interwar period, Catholics in all three colonies sought to capitalize on their power and promote their ties to the colonial regime. In Algeria, the centenary celebrations of the French conquest in 1930 sought to showcase a triumphant settler regime, and Catholics enthusiastically participated. That same year, in Tunisia, Catholic officials were overjoyed that Pope Pius XI chose Carthage as the site of the thirtieth International Eucharistic Congress.[8] Wary French authorities noted, however, that the ostentatious performance of Catholic power (and the government support it received) upset the Muslims of North Africa: Tunisian anti-colonial activist (and future president) Habib Bourguiba wrote in the nationalist Destour party's newspaper that the parades of Catholic children dressed as crusaders were an "affront to Tunisia's Muslim personality."[9] In response to yet another eucharistic congress, held in Algeria in 1939, Algerian nationalist Messali Hadj's newspaper

El-Ouma denounced the congress as a "provocation," a "colonialo-Catholic manifestation."[10]

Yet, by the late 1940s there were significant ideological and political divisions within the Catholic communities across the Maghreb over issues like the church's support for the colonial regime and its role in the oppression of the Muslim population. Conservatives (including a growing far-right movement) were by far the largest and most powerful population of Catholics in North Africa. Nevertheless, inspired by growing anti-colonial activism across the Maghreb and discussions taking place among Catholics globally about decolonization, a minority of leftist Catholics openly discussed the injustices of colonialism and the historic role of the Catholic Church in supporting the French colonial regime. Leftist Catholic periodicals such as *Esprit*, which were widely distributed in both France and Algeria, published extensively about colonial racism in the Maghreb, the war in Indochina, and the uprisings in Madagascar in 1947.[11]

The most significant influence on the burgeoning leftist Catholic minority of the Maghreb in the 1940s, however, was the arrival in North Africa of more progressive French Catholic theologies that challenged traditional hierarchies and offered new visions for how Christians could relate to the Muslim population of North Africa.[12] In France, the most radical versions of these movements and theologies (known broadly as *progressiste*, or progressivist) came under increasingly harsh criticism in the early 1950s from both conservative French Catholics and the Vatican for their "materialist" (i.e., communist) political engagements. One target of conservative Catholic critique was the Mission de France (MDF), a French "internal missionary" movement that began in 1941 as a seminary to train priests as missionaries to the working classes.[13] The MDF built on the Catholic project to combat the "dechristianization" of the working classes through efforts to convert the Catholic Church to the modern world. Early on, the MDF participated in the controversial "worker-priest" experiment, in which Catholic priests went undercover in factories to "incarnate" the values of Christianity through solidarity and direct social and political engagement with the working classes. When the Vatican condemned and shut down the "worker-priest" project in the 1950s, MDF priests found other methods to pursue their personal engagement with the working classes, and several of them moved to North Africa.

A settler priest named Jean Scotto, from the working-class parish of Hussein-Dey in Algiers, brought the MDF to Algeria in 1949 with the intention of working directly with impoverished Muslim populations. Alongside mostly women parish workers, the MDF priests organized a social center to provide basic medical care and education in a shantytown in Hussein-Dey that became the model for a much larger government-run organization known as the *Centres sociaux*. MDF teams spread into eastern Algeria (Souk-Ahras) and Tunisia in the early 1950s, where they sought to make connections and provide support for the impoverished Muslims they lived among.[14] These actions earned strong animosity from local authorities and Catholic settlers; Scotto and the MDF priests quickly gained a reputation for being dangerous "progressistes" and sympathizers with anti-colonial nationalist movements across the Maghreb.

Another group that gained notoriety among conservative Catholics in Algeria was the *Association de la jeunesse algérienne pour l'action sociale* (Association of Algerian Youth for Social Action, or AJAAS), which brought Christian, Muslim, and Jewish youth movements together to discuss and find solutions to the social and political problems of colonial Algeria.[15] The political awakening that took place across religious and class boundaries among AJAAS members led numerous Christian and Jewish members to take up action in support of Algerian independence, with some even joining the Algerian nationalist Front de libération nationale (National Liberation Front, or FLN).[16] In November 1956, for example, AJAAS member and Catholic university student Evelyne Lavalette was arrested in Oran after transporting FLN tracts from Algiers and was sentenced to three years in prison; the tracts had been printed on a roneo machine in the Algiers apartment of a Jesuit priest named Père Jules Declercq, who had also helped print some of the first issues of the FLN's periodical *El Moudjahid*.[17]

Certainly not all Catholics in the Maghreb who questioned the injustices of the colonial system openly supported independence or anti-colonial nationalist movements. Most of them would fall into the category of what were called the *libéraux* (liberals) of North Africa, who sought reforms of the colonial system; as with the vast majority of French citizens on both sides of the Mediterranean, they never imagined that the French colonies of the Maghreb could be anything but French. Yet, the outbreak of the Algerian War of Independence in November 1954 hardened the ideological and political divisions within the Catholic communities of the Maghreb, setting off a near civil war within the Catholic community of Algeria. As the conflict became progressively more violent, both astute Catholic leaders inside North Africa and outside observers from institutions like the Vatican became increasingly alarmed that a victory for the Algerian nationalist FLN could mean the expulsion of the entire Christian population from the Maghreb. If that was the case, other decolonizing territories might follow suit, which would be an unthinkable disaster for global Christianity. That this did not occur in Algeria (or Tunisia and Morocco) was largely due to a handful of Christians in North Africa and their efforts to both disentangle Christianity from its colonial ties and transform its theology and institutions to reform social, political, and economic injustices, rather than to create and preserve them.

Catholicism and the Collapse of French North Africa

Between 1954 and early 1957, both French Catholic leaders and the Vatican notoriously said very little about the escalating violence in Algeria. Public statements from Algerian Catholic leaders and from the Assembly of Cardinals and Archbishops (ACA), the organization that represented the French Catholic hierarchy, tended to be quite vague, with general calls for peace and justice. Catholic leaders explicitly refrained from suggesting political or "technical" solutions to the Algerian problem, as this was "outside their competence."[18] Although there were a handful of notable supporters of Algerian independence among French and Algerian clergy, French Catholic leaders generally believed that, even with its flaws, French Algeria was far preferable to an Algeria run by Muslims or communists.[19]

The positions of Pope Pius XII on Algeria were similar. By the mid-1950s, decolonization had become one of the Vatican's main preoccupations and, in many colonies, the solution was support for the establishment of indigenous clergy and hesitant support for the transition away from European-led churches (even if that was not exactly the situation on the ground).[20] There was little trust that African and Asian churches could manage on their own, however. In his message of June 13, 1957, Pius XII stated "it seems necessary that Europe maintains in Africa the opportunity to exercise its educative and formative influence."[21] Given the context of the Vatican's positions on Africa and decolonization, it is easy to see why the Maghreb, with its settler colonial Catholicism, failed missions, lack of indigenous Catholics and clergy, and growing violence, presented a problem for the Vatican.

Caught in the midst of all of these tensions was Msgr. Léon-Étienne Duval, the archbishop of Algiers. Duval was installed as archbishop in March 1954 after serving as bishop of Constantine and Hippo since 1947. Initially, Duval followed the lead of the Catholic hierarchy in France and argued that it was not the role of the church to get mixed up in "political questions."[22] The clergy in Algeria remained bitterly divided throughout the war, with the vast majority remaining staunch supporters of French Algeria, yet Duval ordered his clergy to stay united behind him and prohibited them from adding anything to his directives. Although Duval was working behind the scenes from 1955 onward to protest the French military's actions in Algeria, including direct correspondence and meetings with both political and military leaders on topics such as the use of torture and summary executions of prisoners, he appeared to many to be staying carefully neutral, frustrating Catholics across the political spectrum.[23]

Everything changed in 1957 with the highly publicized trial of the "progressivist Christians" in Algiers. In the midst of the battle of Algiers, during which the French military used torture, "disappearances," and summary executions to destroy what they described as the urban "terrorist" networks of the FLN, a group of twelve French Christians was arrested and charged in the military tribunal of Algiers with "undermining the security of the French state" for their alleged participation in Algerian nationalist activities.[24] Among them were a number of prominent Catholic figures connected to Père Scotto, including Mission de France priest Jean-Claude Barthez and a former AJAAS leader named Pierre Chaulet, who, as a medical student, had treated wounded members of the maquis and then joined the FLN in 1955. They also included four Catholic social workers who worked in the Centres sociaux. All four of these women had been arrested in early 1957 and held at the notorious Villa Sesini in Algiers where they were tortured by the French military for the alleged crime of sheltering a French communist named Raymonde Peschard, whom the French military wrongly accused of being the "blonde woman" responsible for the infamous Milk-Bar bombing in Algiers.

Major newspapers in both France and Algeria printed daily summaries and editorials about the trial, with growing debate about whether it was Christians' moral duty to protest the French military's use of torture or to support the project of French Algeria, no matter the cost.[25] The trial shifted the opinions of right-wing Catholics firmly against Msgr. Duval, as he carefully refused to condemn the Catholics on trial, which conservatives understood as support for the "progressivist" position. He received hundreds of furious letters from Catholics across Algeria and was nicknamed "Mohamed Duval," for his perceived privileging of the Algerian Muslim population over his own Catholic flock.[26]

In the aftermath of the trial, Duval seemed to realize that it was no longer possible to remain neutral about the moral and even the political issues related to the war. He more openly condemned torture and military violence in his public statements. In the face of a growing number of attacks directed at him from the partisans of French Algeria, he made public gestures to demonstrate his solidarity with "progressivist" Christians like Jean Scotto, who stood at his right side during the mass for the death of Pope Pius XII in 1958.[27] Additionally, he gained a powerful ally in the newly elected Pope John XXIII. Unlike his predecessor, John XXIII had direct experience with Algeria, having toured the country in 1950 as papal nuncio to France; during that trip he had spent a significant amount of time with Msgr. Duval, then bishop of Constantine, who had taken him on a tour of the region that included meetings with Jewish and Muslim religious leaders. Although John XXIII never publicly expressed support for Algerian independence before 1962, he did privately send a telegram to Msgr. Duval in April 1961 expressing his support for Duval's strong stance against the Generals' Putsch and for "the Algerian population . . . to whom we wish with all our heart the realization of their legitimate aspirations in justice and liberty."[28]

In 1961, as the French and Algerians prepared to negotiate the terms of Algerian independence, the settler militia known as the OAS (Organisation de l'armée secrète) used violence and terror to intimidate and prevent European settlers from leaving Algeria, but that plan backfired in a number of ways.[29] By late summer of 1962, more than 800,000 settlers had fled Algeria for France (a country many of them had never even visited), often with little more than what they could carry in their suitcases.

The process of decolonization was far less violent and drawn out in both Morocco and Tunisia. France sought to quell nationalist uprisings in both protectorates by granting "internal autonomy," in the case of Tunisia, and full independence to Morocco, where the Sultan Mohammed V was recognized as king in March 1956.[30] Christianity also played far less of an ideological role in the decolonization of Morocco and Tunisia than it did in Algeria; the significantly smaller size of the European settler populations there, and consequently of Christian institutions, meant that they had far less power to wield with the French government than was the case in Algeria. Yet the political and ideological divisions that bitterly divided the Catholics in Algeria during the 1950s also emerged in Morocco and Tunisia, if on a less dramatic scale.

In Morocco, European "liberals" and even Moroccan nationalists praised the 1952 apostolic letter of Msgr. Louis-Amedée Lefevre, archbishop of Rabat, which suggested the Christian presence in Morocco could only be justified by three reasons: the human law of hospitality; the economic development of the country; and the desire to engage the population in the spiritual life of the country ("without aggressive proselytism, by the example of authentic Christian behavior"). He further specified that it was the responsibility of Christians to "adapt" to the Moroccan culture, not the other way around.[31] Lefevre's open support for leftist Catholic publications and workshops that directly addressed the political, social, and economic problems of colonialism earned him the nickname "the Red Bishop," and the vocal criticism of the far-right settler population in Morocco.[32]

Despite their individual paths through decolonization, the fates of all three French Maghrebi colonies remained linked, both during and after decolonization. Morocco and Tunisia also saw an exodus of the majority of the European population in the aftermath of independence; in contrast to Algeria, however, it was less abrupt and occurred over the subsequent decade.[33] Algerian refugees and violence seeped across the borders of both Morocco and Tunisia, contributing to widespread feelings of insecurity in both countries. To formerly colonized Muslims across North Africa, comparatively wealthy European landholders and symbolic institutions like the Catholic Church were viewed as representatives of French imperialism, which was on its way out. Consequently, civilian uprisings in support of the Algerian nationalists and attacks against European landowners increased after independence in Morocco and Tunisia, where a significant number of European settlers owned agricultural lands.[34]

In late 1961 and early 1962, when it was clear that Algeria was moving quickly toward independence and that the vast majority of the European settler population was not willing to stick around to adapt to life in the postindependence Maghreb, Catholic leaders in all three countries tried to envision the future of their churches, and of Christianity more generally, in their new political situation. It was clear to everyone within the institution, from the Vatican to laypeople on the ground, that without the structural support of the French colonial regime and the European settler population, the survival of the Catholic Church in North Africa would depend on a "decolonization" of the church as an institution, into one that would be of service to the Maghrebi population, not just the European settlers.

Reinventing Catholicism in the Postcolonial Maghreb

Just as it had been under colonialism, the situation of Catholicism in the Maghreb after independence was unusual, with no indigenous clergy or European settlers to anchor the church in majority-Muslim countries that actively discouraged missionary activity and proselytism. Greatly diminished in size, wealth, and institutional power, the church transformed over the next several decades to focus primarily on providing education and social services to the Maghrebi population and creating spaces and opportunities for Christian-Muslim dialogue. Few of the Catholics who remained in North Africa after decolonization were theologians and instead claimed their engagements and vision for the postcolonial church were a response to events on the ground. Yet church leaders also took inspiration from the theological innovations of Vatican II, particularly the directives supporting Christian-Muslim dialogue, development, and the enactment of the "progressivist" missionary theologies that directed Catholics to "incarnate" the values of Jesus in their daily interactions in the world. By the turn of the twenty-first century, the "decolonized" Catholic Church in the Maghreb looked almost nothing like it had a century earlier.

In Morocco, the installation of a socially conservative king (Mohammed V) as head of state after independence meant that, for Catholics, the transition from the colonial regime was less abrupt than in Algeria or Tunisia. Morocco faced many of the same economic and political problems that the other two countries did at independence, including massive illiteracy and low education rates, extreme poverty, and competition for power among nationalists.[35] Rather than instituting radical democratic changes or nationalizing and redistributing the property of European colonizers, Mohammed V spent several years battling left-wing nationalists to consolidate his power; by 1959, the monarchy emerged as the pillar of stability and opposition movements were fairly decimated.

Mohammed V maintained good relations with Msgr. Lefevre and the leadership of the Catholic Church. Although he never instituted any specific legal accords on the status of Christianity or the Catholic Church in postindependence Morocco, he saluted the solidarity of the Catholic and Protestant Churches with the Moroccan people during their fight for independence and served as patron for interconfessional events at the Toumliline monastery in the Atlas mountains (a Benedictine monastery created in 1952, dedicated to prayer and a "meeting place" of Christianity and Islam).[36] After Mohammed V's unexpected death in 1961, his French-educated son Hassan II became king, and set about developing a constitution modeled on that of France. Islam was enshrined as the official religion and Arabic the official language, but the Jewish community was recognized as an integral part of the nation; Christianity and other religions were henceforth viewed as "foreign" religions, although freedom of thought, expression, assembly, and the right for everyone to conduct religious affairs was enshrined in the constitution as well. From 1962 onward, the law prohibited anything from infringing on its laws about Islam, and both forbade attacks on Islam and created penalties for proselytism (or attempts to convert a Muslim to another faith).

In the years before independence, Msgr. Lefevre and others had begun to imagine the role of the Catholic Church in Morocco as one of presence and service to the Muslim population, rather than as an institution focused solely on the European settlers. Like many leftist Catholics in the Maghreb, Msgr. Lefevre was an adherent of the ideas of the Catholic mystic and desert explorer Charles de Foucauld, whose approach insisted on respect for the Muslim religion, Christian-Muslim dialogue, and living closely with Muslim populations.[37] As Msgr. Lefevre noted in documents to his parishioners and to the Vatican, with the departure of Catholic settlers after independence, the church transformed into a place of refuge for the often itinerant Christians who passed through Morocco.[38] But its secondary role was to "encourage meetings and contacts between Christians and Muslims on a human scale"—to form connections between the two religions, between East and West.[39]

Msgr. Lefevre and his successor, Msgr. Jean Chabbert, who became archbishop of Rabat in 1968, also enthusiastically adopted the vision of the Second Vatican Council. In practice, this meant that the majority of the resources of the church and religious congregations went toward education, social services, and institutions to promote interreligious and ecumenical dialogue. Reorganized as "associations" after 1962, religious congregations continued to provide medical services in hospitals, clinics, and other institutions, many of which carried over from the protectorate. Catholic schools were integrated into the Moroccan educational system, teaching primarily Muslim children and employing mostly Moroccan faculty and staff; their distinction from state-run schools, however, was the language of instruction, as Catholic-run schools typically used French as the language of instruction after primary school. The country faced significant political and economic instability during Hassan II's reign, and even more Europeans left the country. Numerous churches closed and were handed over to the state or local authorities, and most of the time became spaces for social or cultural activities. Although the Toumliline monastery closed in 1968, the church opened new institutions to promote Christian-Muslim dialogue, including an inter-faith research and study center in Rabat in 1980–81 and supported the formation of the Groupe de Recherche Islamo-Chrétien in 1977, which still exists today.[40]

In 1969, Hassan II opened a correspondence with Pope Paul VI regarding the growing violence in Israel after the arson at the Al-Aqsa mosque in Jerusalem. But it was the conflict with Western Sahara that pushed the king to a further rapprochement with the Vatican, as he sought to counter the influence of the Polisario Front (the Sahrawi nationalist movement that had proclaimed the independence of Western Sahara from Morocco and Mauritania in 1976) and Algeria. In 1980, Hassan II made a diplomatic visit to the Vatican, the first head of state from a Muslim country to do so. He met with Pope John Paul II, who returned the visit in 1985, where the pope held a large interfaith gathering for some 80,000 young Muslims in the stadium of Casablanca. One significant consequence of this rapprochement was that Hassan II issued a royal proclamation (Dahir) in 1984 creating a statute for the Catholic Church in Morocco, assuring it the freedom to "publicly and freely exercise its spiritual mission and its own activities, such as worship, the magisterium, internal jurisdiction, good works, religious education, and aid to prisoners; assuring everyone religious liberty and the ability to live in faith in a society concerned with coexistence and cooperation."[41] In 1997, Morocco opened an embassy in Vatican City and, despite growing tensions in recent decades over a government crackdown on proselytism by evangelical Christians in Morocco, Pope Francis visited Morocco in March 2019, where he met with Muslim leaders and sub-Saharan African migrants, who are currently the largest population of Christians in Morocco.

In contrast to Morocco, Tunisia's transition to independence was far more disruptive to the status quo of French colonial rule, both for European settlers and for Tunisians. Nationalist leader Habib Bourguiba became the first president of Tunisia in July 1957. By June 1959, Bourguiba had consolidated nearly all state power under his own authority, creating what has been described as a "presidential monarchy."[42] While his main opponent had sought the support of Muslim religious leaders for the Neo-Destour movement, Bourguiba sought to minimize their power in the new regime, claiming that he was "modernizing" Tunisia.[43] He claimed that he was not so much sweeping aside Islamic law as reinterpreting it, although Muslim religious leaders were profoundly disturbed by his early "secularizing" reforms.

The establishment of the Tunisian republic in 1957 left the Catholic Church in a legal limbo, and Catholic leaders were unsure how to proceed. Msgr. Maurice Perrin, archbishop of Carthage, followed advice from the Vatican and engaged in some conciliatory gestures to the new government. He removed the statue of Lavigerie from the entrance of the Tunis medina and halted construction on new chapels.[44] He sought to signal to the government that the Catholic Church was a willing and enthusiastic participant in the new independent Tunisia and hoped to encourage this spirit among the entirety of the Catholic population.[45] Yet this attitude was not shared widely and the majority of European Catholics left the country. Out of approximately 260,000 Catholics in Tunisia just before independence, only 102,000 remained at the end of 1956. Bourguiba's nationalizations of property (particularly rural agricultural land) and the Bizerte crisis of 1961, during which the Tunisians blockaded the French naval base in Bizerte in an attempt to force the French out of the country, were the catalysts for even more departures; by 1965, only 20,000 Catholics remained in the country.[46] The departure of the settler population both destabilized the church itself but also seemed to give a further impression to outsiders of the continued ties between the church and the colonial regime, as the European settlers seemed incapable or uninterested in pursuing life in Tunisia without the protection of the colonial regime.[47]

Although the 1959 Tunisian constitution guaranteed the "respect of human rights and equality of all citizens" as well as the "inviolability of the human person, and the protection of the free exercise of religion, as long as it does not trouble public order," a series of events over 1959–60 unsettled the Catholics who remained.[48] First, the government banned the annual August 15 Assumption procession in Tunis as well as Catholic prayer meetings that were taking place at a private venue in a suburb of Tunis. Even more dramatic was the state's seizure of the church and presbytery of Kairouan, a city in the northern desert that was an important center of Islamic scholarship. Just a few months later, the school run by the White Sisters was closed and the congregation expelled from Kairouan.[49]

In reflecting on these events, the Tunisian Mission de France teams suggested a handful of possible reasons for the government's actions. The first was a reaction against the colonial ties of the church, made more visible by the departure of the settler population. More plausible, however, seemed to be the secularizing policies of the government more generally, since Muslim institutions were also being targeted. Their report to the MDF leadership in France noted that the government did not seem to be targeting individual Catholics, but rather institutions, an important distinction. By contrast, they noted, large numbers of Catholics who remained in Tunisia were actually working for the government in the education and medical sectors (including members of religious congregations).[50]

This crisis inaugurated a period of intense reflection on the role of the church among the Catholics who remained in Tunisia. Catholic bishops created diocesan committees and MDF priests worked closely with parishioners in Tunisia as well as "progressivist" Catholics in Algeria to consider how the new missionary theologies they espoused could respond to the various political, social, and theological issues at stake for Catholics in Tunisia.[51] In a 1960 document, for example, a reflection group connected to the MDF in Tunisia wrote: "The Church must become part of the aspirations, worries, and preoccupations on every level (religious, national, familial, social) to the efforts, the struggles, the mentality, the life of this country. . . . This means sharing in the lives of the poor (like the Fraternities of Charles de Foucauld), whether through various forms of cooperation in the construction of the country (culture, technical), or every possible form of sharing (with neighbors, etc.)."[52] On a more official level, diplomatic meetings between Bourguiba and the Vatican beginning in June 1959 signaled a willingness on the part of the Tunisian government to officially recognize the legal status of the Catholic Church in Tunisia.[53]

The convention known as the *Modus Vivendi* was executed in 1964 and laid out the conditions for the continued existence of the Catholic Church in Tunisia. The Tunisian government guaranteed the free exercise of the Catholic religion in Tunisia, provided that the church refrained from engaging in any political activities. The convention also allowed for the teaching of Catholic doctrine in prescribed locations such as churches and Catholic schools (but only to Catholic students and with parental permission) and forbade proselytism. The church was allowed to manage its own internal affairs, including publications, provided Catholics followed the laws of the state. The Catholic hierarchy would henceforth be dependent on the Vatican, which had the authority to name new prelates. The Tunisian government took control of a significant portion of Catholic property, but gave assurances that all religious buildings would only be used for "public interest purposes that are compatible with their previous use."[54]

Only a handful of churches, hospitals, and schools remained in the hands of the Catholic Church after 1964, while symbolic concessions, such as the suppression of the title of "archbishop of Carthage, primate of Africa," and the transfer of the cathedral in Carthage to the Tunisian government, provided a demonstration of the church's willingness to shed its colonial trappings.[55] There is an inherent recognition in the *Modus Vivendi* that the balance of power lay in the hands of the Tunisian government, rather than in the hands of Europeans; it was Bourguiba who demanded the suppression of the archdiocese of Carthage, as he had long viewed its resurrection in 1884 as a violently colonialist act.[56] Not all Catholics in Tunisia found this situation acceptable, particularly the loss of the archdiocese of Carthage and its cathedral, and some lamented the destruction of the Catholic Church in North Africa. Not unrelated, the period just after the publication of the *Modus Vivendi* accord in 1964 saw the final significant mass emigration of Catholic settlers out of Tunisia during the postindependence decades.[57]

Msgr. Perrin announced his retirement as archbishop of Tunis in 1965 and was succeeded by Msgr. Michel Callens, a White Father and trained sociologist who was fluent in Arabic and familiar with Tunisia; he remained in the post until 1990. Callens presided over the July 1968 diocesan assembly, which had followed an extensive survey of Catholics across the country to collectively redefine the mission of the postcolonial church in the wake of decolonization and Vatican II. The result was a reorientation of the church to the "modern world" (i.e., secular society) and one in which Catholics sought to "incarnate" the true face of Jesus, while living in service among the Muslim population, rather than just focusing the church's actions on the existing Catholic population.[58] For the most part, Catholics have kept a fairly low profile in Tunisia since the 1960s as "missionaries without converts," focusing their efforts on maintaining a Christian presence among the Muslims and, as in Algeria and Morocco, serving a Catholic population that is largely made up of sub-Saharan African migrants. This transformation of the church into what sociologist Alexis Artaud de la Ferrière describes as a "transliminal institution" ("neither fully integrated within its national context, nor fully exposed to the mainstream Catholic world") in many ways echoes its evolution in Morocco and Algeria, although with some significant distinctions.[59]

Between May and July 1961, French government officials negotiated the terms of Algerian independence in a series of meetings in Switzerland with representatives of the Algerian provisional government (GPRA), resulting in a treaty known as the Évian Accords that was signed in March 1962. Under the terms of the treaty, the European settler population was guaranteed religious freedom and the right to choose their country of citizenship (France or Algeria) after a period of three years. Despite growing numbers of European settler departures in the face of OAS violence, the French government assumed that the majority of European settlers would remain in Algeria after independence and was completely unprepared for the mass exodus that occurred in the spring and summer of 1962.[60] For the Catholic Church, the departure of the majority of its congregants (and a significant number of clergy) had numerous material consequences, but unlike in Morocco and Tunisia, the Catholics who remained did not face significant hostility from the Algerian population, nor from the provisional government.

In the summer of 1961, Msgr. Duval informed the French government that the Catholic Church would hold its own negotiations with the Algerians on the future of Catholicism in Algeria because the church did not want its interests to be conflated with those of the French government.[61] In July 1961, Duval sent Jean Scotto on a secret mission to Genoa where he met with Pierre Chaulet, who had been working in Tunisia for the FLN after the 1957 trial of the "progressivist Christians." The discussions centered on a report that Chaulet had written in collaboration with two priests who had also joined the FLN in Tunisia (Abbé Alfred Berenguer and MDF priest Pierre Mamet), which proposed three key points of transformation for the Catholic Church in postindependence Algeria. First, it requested that the church return to the Algerian state all of the Islamic religious buildings that French Christians had taken over since the conquest, notably the Ketchaoua Mosque (Saint-Philippe Cathedral) in Algiers. Second, it encouraged the church not to maintain Catholic schools as an essential institution of its existence or to oppose any measures that fell under national sovereignty (such as family planning). Finally, it suggested an eventual attachment to the Congregation for the Oriental Churches, which would permit Arabic to become the liturgical language. Although the Catholic leadership rejected the third point, they were open to the first two suggestions, which had already been under discussion among groups like the Mission de France across the Maghreb.[62]

In contrast to the very tenuous status of the Catholic Church at independence in both Morocco and Tunisia, the Catholic Church in Algeria was on a much stronger footing with the FLN and the new Algerian leaders. In late 1961, the GPRA sent an official letter to the bishops of Algeria in which it declared, "Never will we forget the understanding, the sympathy, and the support that we found, during the years of struggle, from the most conscious and authentic Christians, outside of Algeria, but also in Algeria. Nothing on earth would make us desire that these Christians do not feel at home with us. Finally, we are convinced that Christian values that are seriously lived in real-life can only increase the spiritual patrimony of our country."[63] In this letter, the GPRA assured the bishops that even though the Catholic Church was losing its privileged position in society, Christians would have a place in

Algeria where they "would feel free and respected." But this was also the same moment when the OAS was stepping up its murderous rampage against both Algerian civilians and Europeans who were seen to be sympathetic to Algerian independence. Thus, as numerous commentators noted, it was essential that the Catholic Church demonstrate in both symbolic and meaningful actions its commitment to rejecting its colonial past.

Just after independence, Msgr. Duval gave an interview to *Le Monde* in which he stated, "The Church in Algeria has chosen not to be foreign, but to be Algerian." In a later interview, he explained that the Catholic Church in Algeria was not going to be just a church for the embassies, or Catholics in transit, but that it would be "open to the population and to the realities of the country."[64] In the spring and summer of 1962, Msgr. Duval and his adjutants restructured the dioceses and negotiated with French and Vatican officials to detach Algeria from the French episcopate. On the day after Algerian independence, Msgr. Duval proposed to the Algerian authorities that the Catholic Church return to the new state all of the Catholic churches that had been mosques before French colonization. In doing so, his adjutant noted, the church would "demonstrate [its] warm feelings toward the Algerian nation and its desire to alleviate what could become a source of conflict."[65] As with the Carthage cathedral in Tunisia, the most symbolic property transfer for the Algerians was the Cathédrale Saint-Philippe, which had been converted from a mosque to a church in 1832 and was the seat of the archbishop of Algiers.[66]

On the eve of independence, a small group of Christians (both Catholics and Protestants) who had decided to stay in Algeria formed a study group called the Association d'études with the goal to consider how best, as Christians, they could integrate themselves into postcolonial Algeria. The first meetings of the Association d'études were held in Algiers in June of 1962 and, for the next few years, the group met nearly every month to discuss issues like the sociopolitical environment of postindependence Algeria and their position in it and the economic and social role of Christians (and the church) in a socialist, Third-Worldist nation. At first, the Christians who remained in Algeria after independence were concerned about how to distinguish themselves (in the minds of Algerians) from the "mass of Europeans" who had fled back to France and who remained emotionally tied to the legacy of French colonialism. Their first steps would need to be to separate themselves from institutions and behaviors associated with the colonizers, and to recognize their own complicity in the colonial system. Only from there could they reenter Algerian society on a more humble and equal footing.[67]

In the early months of independence, Catholics who remained in Algeria debated practical measures they could take to integrate themselves into the Algerian nation. Many were concerned about whether they would need to learn Arabic to be able to work and what it would mean to apply for Algerian nationality (the Évian Accords did not allow for the possibility of double nationality for Europeans born in Algeria). There was also concern about whether they would need to give up personal property to demonstrate their full cooperation with the socialist projects of the government. Some pointed out that Christians were going to be constantly watched and judged, especially in the early years after independence. It was necessary, they argued, for Christians not to shut themselves off in a European "ghetto," as they had done during the colonial period, but to live among the Algerians, even if that meant giving up some of the material benefits and privileges they had enjoyed under the French regime.[68]

The mass departure of the European settler community opened up numerous economic and job opportunities for both settler Christians who stayed in Algeria and for the tens of thousands of *coopérants* who were recruited from abroad to help rebuild the country after independence, a significant number of whom were Christians who saw an opportunity to engage in a radical project of Third-Worldist development.[69] As in Tunisia, the necessity for white-collar labor and the vast expansion of the education sector meant that Europeans typically filled these jobs until Algerians themselves were fully trained to undertake them. Numerous Catholics went to work for the Algerian government, including priests and members of religious orders, often training workers in industry and education. The Boumediène years between 1965–75 saw the culmination of the leftist spirit of cooperation, but also its eventual demise in the face of Arabization and nationalization policies that put many Europeans out of work.

While much of the leftist Catholic energy of the immediate postindependence years had started to wane by the late 1960s, the events and ideas circulating at the Second Vatican Council (1962–65) illustrated that the work of Algerian Catholics was not occurring in a vacuum. Msgr. Duval was an active participant in Vatican II, and noted in his interviews with journalist Marie-Christine Ray that the event that most helped him "become African" occurred on the second day of the council, when bishops were divided by region in their study commissions; the Algerian bishops realized that they should join the bishops of the African region, rather than those of France.[70] In 1965, Pope Paul VI then named Msgr. Duval a cardinal, an honor that was particularly well received by the Algerian people, and he remains a symbol of Algerian Christianity long after his death. Trusted collaborators like Jean Scotto and Henri Teissier, who had long worked for dialogue and reconciliation between Christian and Muslim populations in Algeria, also rose in the Catholic hierarchy. Scotto became the bishop of Constantine in 1970, and Teissier the bishop of Oran in 1973 and, later, the archbishop of Algiers upon Msgr. Duval's retirement in 1988.

As the European Catholic population continued to diminish through the 1970s, the Algerian Catholic Church turned its attention to social and educational service projects for the Algerian population and its largely sub-Saharan African parishioners. Catholics became visible targets in the 1990s for Islamist terrorists seeking to challenge the authority of the Algerian government. Although the "Dark Decade" of the Algerian Civil War (1991-2002) forced most of the remaining European Catholics into exile outside of Algeria, Catholic leaders and numerous clergy determined that they would stay in Algeria, alongside the Algerian Muslim population. This remained their position even after the brutal assassinations of some nineteen priests and nuns, including Pierre Claverie, the bishop of Oran, and seven Trappist monks from the Tibhirine monastery in 1996. As during the Algerian War of Independence, the solidarity of this small group of Catholics with the plight of the Algerian people during a time of great suffering has helped the Algerian Catholic Church maintain its overall positive reputation and presence in Algeria.

Conclusion

For Catholics in the Maghreb, decolonization forced a dramatic re-evaluation of the role of the church and of individual Catholics in majority Muslim societies in which Christianity was no longer supported by a powerful colonial regime. The church itself was decolonized both through the mass exodus of European settler Catholics from all three countries in the wake of independence and the complete restructuring of power relations, wherein the Catholic Church voluntarily renounced nearly everything that had previously sustained its power. For Catholics who remained in the Maghreb after independence, the break from colonialism offered an opportunity to demonstrate the "true face of Christianity," as Père Jean Scotto of Algeria suggested. Building on leftist Catholic theologies that sought to revitalize the Christian missionary effort and push Catholicism itself to adapt to both their mission field and the "modern world," Catholics in postcolonial Morocco, Algeria, and Tunisia saw their continued presence in the Muslim world, and in the Maghreb specifically, as a means to transform the Christian-Muslim relationship from one of violence to one of dialogue and friendship without either overt or covert proselytism.

It was no coincidence that these efforts were taking place at the same moment as Vatican II, which offered theological support to Catholics in the Maghreb who sought to transform the role of the church in the wake of colonialism. The bishops of North Africa participated in the council as representatives of the African churches, a symbolic break from their previous ties to the French episcopate. Msgr. Callens, the bishop of Tunis, wrote in 1974 that the 1964 dogmatic constitution, *Lumen gentium*, which addressed the doctrine of the church and role of Catholics in the modern world, was the "guiding spirit of the Catholic Church in Tunisia."[71] In Algeria, Msgr. Duval and the Catholic community actively responded to surveys on Schema 13, which became *Gaudium et spes*, the 1965 pastoral Constitution on the Church in the Modern World and reoriented the mission of the church to those outside the Catholic faith, rather than just focusing on Catholics themselves.[72] Msgr. Henri Teissier, successor to Msgr. Duval, noted that *Nostra aetate*, the 1965 declaration on relations between Christians and non-Christians, provided concrete justification for the numerous efforts at Christian-Muslim dialogue that Catholics instigated in the Maghreb in the decades after independence.[73] For Catholics in North Africa who sought to rebuild the church in the aftermath of decolonization, the modernizing and global focus of the Vatican in the 1960s and 1970s provided the theological support to maintain their path through many challenging circumstances.

CHAPTER 7

Church and State in the Struggle for Human Rights and Economic Dignity in Central Africa at the End of Empire

Charlotte Walker-Said

The final straw that created an irreparable rift between Barthélemy Boganda, Oubangui-Chari's first African ordained priest, and the vicar apostolic, Msgr. Joseph Cucherousset, followed a dispute over a relatively small amount of money.[1] Although Father Boganda had for years sharply criticized the head of the Vicariate of Bangui, as well as European missionaries and his colleagues in the French colony's Catholic schools over their militant racism and demeaning treatment of African students, seminarians, and catechumens, it was Boganda's claim to be entitled to keep and spend his congregation's donations within the Grimari Mission in Ouaka that ultimately provoked his suspension from the clergy in 1949.[2]

Father Boganda was raised by missionaries of the Congrégation du Saint-Esprit in M'Baïki after the age of ten, after his parents were murdered by concessionary company militias in the late 1910s for not meeting the rubber quota.[3] Boganda's region of origin, Lobaye, was ravaged by the extreme brutality of colonial rule in Moyen-Congo and Oubangui-Chari,[4] which included merciless labor conscription, displacement by village removals, tsetse-borne diseases and smallpox, famine, and local warfare provoked by colonial and concessionary competition. However, Boganda grew into adolescence and adulthood in relative isolation in the mission school at Saint Paul des Rapides in Bangui, the *petit séminaire* of the Jesuits in Lemfu (Belgian Congo), and the Benedictine *grand séminaire* in Mvoylé (Cameroon).[5] Boganda's personal journals, which are housed in the archives of the Congrégation du Saint-Esprit in France, reveal a Eurocentric educational formation but also a pious sensibility that veers from standard missionary inculcations, in that his writings evoke a consciousness of the dignity of the human person and its vulnerability: that one's humanity could be destroyed by subordination and deprivation.[6] While deeply devout, Boganda sharply clashed with Catholic Church leaders in Oubangui-Chari both before and after his defrocking over what he perceived as the church's blindness to the inhumane conditions of life for Africans under French colonialism and its adherence to hierarchical systems rather than to principles of human rights.[7]

Boganda's entry into the priesthood in 1938 was followed by his election as a Parliamentary *député* for the French colony of Oubangui-Chari in 1946. He later gained a seat in the Oubanguian Territorial Assembly in 1952, became mayor of Bangui in in 1956, was president of French Equatorial Africa's Grand Conseil in 1957, and, finally, rose to the position of prime minister of the Central African Republic in 1958, when Oubangui-Chari became an autonomous territory under French suzerainty.[8] Despite this meteoric rise, Boganda realized by the late 1940s that acquiring political prominence was not attendant with either the power to enact changes that improved the lives of his fellow Africans or the authority to manage any aspect of Oubangui-Chari's wealth. His criticisms of what he described as the "violence" of French colonialism—lived as starvation, taxation, and forced labor—and his attempts to create economic opportunities for Central Africans eventually led to his expulsion from the priesthood, condemnation in French parliament, arrest in Oubangui-Chari in 1951, ridicule by the ecclesiastical elite, and, finally, death in a suspicious airplane crash in 1959.[9] However, Boganda's discourses on ethics, and particularly on the relationship between economic rights and human dignity, which he presented in parliaments and state assemblies, were startling in their originality and their unrestrained condemnation of poverty as the defeat of moral self-determination. Boganda's demand for a "true" decolonization that included economic restitution and the recognition of Africans as equally entitled to a life of material dignity was as much ethical as it was political, although both the colonial government and the Catholic leadership in French Equatorial Africa perceived it as dangerously ideological.

This chapter details Barthélemy Boganda's formulation of an economic rights doctrine, which was borne out of his formation in the Catholic priesthood, his work as a mission leader and teacher, and the influence of the French political party that supported his entry into politics: the Mouvement

Républicain Populaire (MRP), which, he argued, "understands that civilization is not only defined by better material and intellectual conditions, but also satisfying spiritual aspirations."[10] His vision was also rooted in equatorial African cosmology, particularly the belief in the metaphysical power of the Earth and its productive capacities.[11] Weaving together these various intellectual currents, Boganda formulated a theory of economic justice that aimed to restore full humanity—in essence, the *imago Dei* and dignity of the human soul or person—to Africans, through control over *séssé* ("earth" in the Sango language), truly free economic competition, the abolition of forced labor, and cooperative financial enterprises.[12]

As this chapter will demonstrate, Boganda did not merely engage in dialogue. He also launched successive efforts to support a more productive African-centered economy by (1) forming agricultural cooperatives on mission land and surrounding villages; (2) establishing the Société cooperative de l'Oubangui-Lobaye-Lessé (SOUCOULOLE), a coffee cooperative that also sold local goods in regional markets; and (3) meticulously documenting the use of forced labor and persistently writing to government leaders, the Vatican, and the international press about this abject form of oppression in Oubangui-Chari.[13] European Catholic leaders' strong opposition to Boganda's economic and human rights initiatives reveal a politically shrewd and morally compromised church at the end of the French empire, in which ecclesiastical leaders misconstrued African discourse and action on economic justice as Marxist, anti-colonial, and anti-Christian, perhaps willfully, and used it as evidence for the necessity of continued imperial and ecclesiastical control, even if granting territorial sovereignty was unavoidable.[14]

In many ways, the 1949 financial dispute between Fathers Boganda and Cucherousset is emblematic of broader struggles at the end of empire in Central Africa over the true meaning of African self-determination and whether incorporation of colonized peoples into higher levels of political and religious governance would mean the acceptance of racial equality as a human value. If African pastors could not decide their churches' expenditures nor have authority over the use of mission land, Boganda argued, how could they "help preserve the conditions of their congregants' existence and guard against their suffering?" And if Christian communitarianism did not "raise Africans' spiritual, moral, *and* material aspirations, how then, would they . . . measure their own dignity?"[15] These sentiments were echoed in halls of government as Boganda fulminated against French authorities over the punishing effects of French trading monopolies on African cotton producers, the extensive use of forced labor, and a barbarous law enforcement system that engaged in widespread extrajudicial killing and arbitrary corporal punishment.[16]

This chapter concurs with much of the recent scholarship that advances the argument that decolonization was fundamentally a process dominated by conservative initiatives—in essence, it was an era where Europe advanced, rather than withdrew, its claims to command "hard power."[17] Historians have also accurately noted that, within the Catholic Church globally in this era, there was a diversity of imperialist, anti-colonialist, xenophobic, and non-racialist voices.[18] However, the Catholic ecclesiastical leaders in Oubangui-Chari moved in particularly close lockstep with the French administration, demonstrating an unusually stolid posture on French superiority and attributing the accursed state of affairs in the colony (such as the very poor state of schools and few trained graduates) to African deficiencies.[19] What angered Father Boganda most was the church's refusal to acknowledge the problem of forced labor in Oubangui-Chari—which continued into the 1950s—and its complicity in the territorial administration's rationalization of the practice as merely an occasional undertaking in limited geographical zones.[20] Both church and administrative leaders responded ambivalently, even when Boganda brought overwhelming evidence of specific incidents of the use of forced and unpaid labor, as well as capital punishment and arbitrary killings of Africans without due process, throughout the territory in the late 1940s and 1950s.[21] The French religious and political establishment remained largely convinced that the region's depopulation, demographic collapse, and displacement resulted from "tribalism" and local warfare, polygamy, and disease, rather than colonial labor policies or profoundly disruptive and coercive economic programs such as the building of the Congo-Océan Railway and forced cotton cultivation.[22]

In an even broader sense, Boganda's arguments for religious and political recognition of African economic freedom, dignity, and equality are ideologically analogous to the debates of social reform Catholicism of the nineteenth century and human rights Catholicism of the mid-twentieth century. As scholars like Paul Misner and Samuel Moyn have shown, Catholic Church leaders in these eras did not always embrace religious thinkers who considered the social implications of the industrial economy, nor did they believe that human rights should lay the groundwork for social justice.[23] Boganda's own brand of liberalism—predominantly framed as economic rights for African people—met with this familiar resistance within the Catholic Church hierarchy. Attention to both Boganda's discourse and his career and life trajectory reveals that despite the prehistory of the development of social teaching, compassion for labor, and even support for human rights and democracy within the church, Catholic leaders in Central Africa at the end of empire supported "independence" for African states not as freedom from colonial rule, but rather as a transition to a new governance structure with French-designated African political leaders facilitating the continuation of European domination in the region.

Colonial Trauma and African Poverty

It would be difficult to overstate, or perhaps even correctly estimate, the true toll of the violence of colonial rule in the first half of the twentieth century in Oubangui-Chari. Scholars like Catherine Coquery-Vidrovitch and J. P. Daughton have explored the considerable brutality that was attendant with the virtual enslavement of rural populations in Equatorial Africa for infrastructure development and rubber harvesting after World War I.[24] Daughton has even revealed the heretofore obscured processes by which tens of thousands of Africans were forcibly removed from their homes, separated from their families, and coerced into performing physical labor along railway lines and concessionary worksites—often until they expired from exhaustion, disease, or starvation.[25] A 1946 report on labor in French Equatorial Africa (AEF) confirmed that forced labor was "necessary" to create transit systems and expand agricultural development in Oubangui-Chari and neighboring Moyen Congo, and that payment was often lacking for laborers, even though conscripts were, by law, to be remunerated at a set fee in each colony.[26] One French missionary observed while discussing insurrectionist resistance to forced labor in Kouango, "The occupation brigade applied extreme force in 1903, but the soldiers have been called back to again overpower those who will not submit. . . . Hundreds have fled to avoid being restrained and killed or forced to work."[27]

The exhaustion of wild rubber in the late 1920s did not open new opportunities for free enterprise in Oubangui-Chari. Rather, forced labor continued in mostly the same form under emerging cotton production regimes.[28] Laws passed throughout the 1920s and early 1930s in the territory obligated all adult males and females to furnish ten days per annum of *prestation* (obligatory service) for "the accomplishment of works in the public interest."[29] Compulsory unpaid labor was set in law, but legal maximums were ignored by recruiters and cotton plantation managers.[30] While neighboring French colonies also used extensive forced labor, the enforcement practices employed in Oubangui-Chari appear to have been particularly aggressive. For example, armed guards were posted in cotton fields to prevent laborers from escaping or resting and territorial officials enforced pass-card laws, known as the *laissez-passer*, to keep Africans from leaving their assigned districts, restricting freedom of movement far more intensively than in neighboring colonies.[31] Moreover, local officials also either banned or financially strangled village mutual aid societies, depriving the territory's farmers and local producers from building capital, maintaining reserves from which to pay taxes, or expanding production, as other mutual aid societies had in areas like Cameroon.[32] The relative frequency and violence of uprisings against colonial officials and their African militias and enforcement agents in Oubangui-Chari is therefore not astonishing.[33]

Village and regional chiefs as well as other local leaders mobilized mutinies in plantation fields and attacked neighboring villages whose members were part of enforcement brigades or *milices* hired by French officials to marshal laborers.[34] Africans in the *commandement indigène* recruited from Chad and within the Oubangui territory carried out punitive acts dictated by administration officials and concessionary overseers, including beatings, mutilations, incarcerations, and even killings. Ethnic and regional tensions grew over the course of the twentieth century as the administration remained committed to its divisive labor recruitment policies and sadistic disciplinary actions, which often pitted chiefs and local communities against one another.[35] The high number of police forces and non-state militaries entirely comprised of Africans who worked for both public and private entities in Oubangui-Chari meant that African laborers had few means of escape or resistance, as enforcers were both omnipresent and had sufficient familiarity with the territory to hunt down runaways. It also meant that there were considerable hostilities between African regional groups and between Africans designated as enforcers and those designated as laborers.[36]

That the majority of physical violence against laborers, including women and children, was meted out by African soldiers was fundamental to Barthélemy Boganda's conception that colonialism had robbed Africans of the foundation of their morality and of their ability to see the intrinsic worth of human beings.[37] Boganda correctly grasped that private enterprise worked hand-in-glove with the French administration in Oubangui-Chari to maintain an entirely extractive economy with little administrative or humanitarian infrastructure, meaning that the principles of fraternity, development assistance, and modern law were entirely ignored, even after the Brazzaville Conference.[38] Boganda argued that the European presence was experienced through three principal actions: forced labor requisitioning (*prestation* or *corvée*), the head tax, and very low prices of cash crops. And he concluded that this combination left Africans entirely destitute after years of work—making colonialism virtually indistinguishable from slavery.[39] Emancipation, therefore, was not solely about self-rule but also about restoring value—material and metaphysical—to African people. Economic disempowerment more than simply impoverished Africans, it neutralized their ability to exist as a whole human being as the *imago Dei*—capable of following the command to love one's neighbor, build families, sustain ethics, build rational insight, or instruct morals. As he wrote in 1937, "Evangelization has accomplished so little because of the very poor state of the territory. . . . Despair destroys the human essence."[40] For Father Boganda, slavery and deep poverty were the principal causes of inter-ethnic violence, sadistic policing, the low birthrate, and corrupted community traditions. Economic self-determination, by contrast, supported conscientious moral decision-making and was central to both political *and* spiritual liberation.[41]

Economics, Catholicism, and Marxism

For the Catholic Church in Oubangui-Chari, the issue of economic emancipation for Africans at the end of empire was inextricably linked with competing fears over both the spread of communist and free-market capitalist ideologies in African societies.[42] Church projects in the territory in the late 1940s and 1950s aimed at limiting the influences of these and other "anti-Christian" philosophies, and European missionaries fretfully hoped that any advancement in Africans' education or material life would not inspire greater earthly desires or ambitions. The introduction and widespread expansion of the Scouts de France de l'AEF, carefully supervised mission trips and student sponsorships to Europe, and heavy-handed warnings to congregations in the Oubangui-Chari territory all aimed to foster a sense of attachment to the church and also to blunt anti-colonialist discourses and anti-racist agendas for racial equality, labor rights, and student organizing.[43]

Catholic Church leaders aggressively denounced "atheist" Marxism and "materialist" capitalism to their African followers and presented this position as theologically and spiritually rooted.[44] However, the church's hardened stance against economic development discourse as proposed by either Marxist or free-market ideologies troublingly dovetailed with colonialist political agendas that limited African financial and economic empowerment by disenfranchising African agricultural cooperatives, backing French trading monopolies, and maintaining slavery-like conditions of labor.[45] Even when Africans framed economic development in terms of promoting "social evolution," "morality," and "a life of dignity, well-being, and light"[46] (i.e., as Boganda envisioned: a form of material advancement that placed spiritual values at its center), European church leaders in the territory stood equally against it, fearing its "revolutionary" potential and rejection of the colonial status quo.[47]

The deeply conservative social agenda and anti-development position of the Catholic Church in Oubangui-Chari evolved into a French nationalist and neocolonialist posture at the close of French empire and the emergence of an independent Central African Republic. Church leaders in Oubangui-Chari opposed all three of Boganda's economic initiatives for Africans in the territory—mission-sponsored agricultural cooperatives, the SOUCOULOLE, and the abolition of forced labor and the head tax.

These stances prompt a reexamination of Vatican projects to foster and promote "Catholic economic development," which historians have understood as a means of curbing Communism and capitalism while also maintaining France's and the West's relevance in formerly colonized regions.[48] Catholic economic philosophy such as that promoted by Dominican minister Father Louis-Joseph Lebret has previously been discussed as an important component of the church's mediation of nationalism and other revolutionary ideologies at the end of empire as it promoted a social-justice-oriented economic doctrine. Indeed, Lebret's "Catholic Economic Development" theoretically centered social, economic, and moral questions and had the blessing of Pope Pius XI.[49] However, I argue that the "layered" nature of Lebret's philosophy—which arguably was predominantly focused on expanding Catholic influence in colonized regions and only secondarily concerned with the worldly needs of the people in those regions—allowed conservative religious leaders to selectively emphasize the least empowering forms of advancement and legitimize their opposition to social and material improvements for colonized peoples they deemed unprepared for or vulnerable to the moral hazards of prosperity. What resonated most profoundly with church leaders in Central Africa was the dimension of Lebret's development theory that aimed at rebuilding—or maintaining—France's and Catholicism's influence in the wider world. And that priority translated into collective action against Father Boganda's (and later Mayor and President Boganda's) economic agenda.

Giuliana Chamedes has argued persuasively that Catholic thinkers like Father Lebret contributed significantly to postwar economic development discourse and, in the process, refashioned the Vatican's considerations of modernization.[50] Chamedes's work also demonstrates that anti-Communism and anti-capitalism galvanized international Catholic activism in the postwar period when colonialism was increasingly being called into question.[51] What remains to be investigated, however, is how expressly "Catholic" development philosophy influenced missionaries and those working in church initiatives in the colonies in the years leading up to the end of empire. How Europeans received and interpreted Catholic development theories to justify continued Western economic dominance while granting limited political sovereignty reveals much about the process referred to as "decolonization," as well as French politico-religious alliances in negotiations of African self-determination.

Scholarship on the waning years of empire by Jessica Pearson has also recently highlighted the particular anxiety of French national and imperial leaders in the late 1940s, and French efforts to block various other forms of development—including international public health monitoring and service provision—from emerging in Africa.[52] Fears about international organizations' "intrusion" into the privileged sphere of colonial influence were the primary driving force behind the development of exclusive "inter-colonial" modes of cooperation, which purposefully constrained the potentially beneficial capacities of technical organizations and prevented their work in needy territories like French Equatorial Africa.[53] Contrasting insights from this same period by Elizabeth Foster provide insight into the conflicted French Catholic community with ties to Africa, who struggled with and debated the church's historical relationship with its role in the French "civilizing mission" and whether Catholic theology endorsed or condemned colonization, in order to determine whether the church should usher in African self-governance, or instead protect the empire.[54] This chapter's European protagonists held parallel perspectives to many of Pearson's and Foster's conservative French political and religious leaders, who believed a continuing influence of the French state was necessary for keeping Africans devout and guarding against potentially corrupting international or cosmopolitan influences.

Barthélemy Boganda's ecclesiastical and political careers are windows for examining how Africans envisioned spiritual and economic liberation despite the pervasiveness of denigrating racial and cultural narratives and colonial self-interest which guided the administration of Oubangui-Chari in the late 1940s and 1950s. Frederick Cooper has highlighted the differentiated nature of imperial governance, but the way in which Oubangui-Chari was organized and policed sharply contrasts with governance approaches in other regions, even in other equatorial territories, which remained poorer and more deficiently staffed than colonies in French West Africa.[55] In neighboring Cameroon, where the French colonial government was subordinate to the supervisory framework of the Permanent Mandates Commission, a plentiful range of international missionary societies expanded their influence by establishing schools, hospitals, orphanages, and other charitable associations. These institutions supported social and economic improvement and also acted as an oversight committee—reporting on abuses and gross injustice in a systematic way to authorities in the League of Nations.[56] By contrast, the French Congregation of the Holy Ghost operated Oubangui-Chari's sole apostolic vicariate and relatively few missions in close cooperation with the colonial administration, which meant that reports of atrocities in Oubangui-Chari stayed largely within administrative circles until the publication of René Maran's polemic against colonial horrors in Central Africa and André Gide's *Voyage au Congo*, which emerged only in 1926 and 1927.[57] African leaders in Oubangui-Chari's religious and political spheres therefore contended with authority structures that coordinated their methods of African integration and mutually reinforced each other's prejudicial and inaccurate assessments of the colony's hardships and conditions.

Despite Boganda's theologically rooted vision for economic rights for Africans in his territory, church leaders continued to express fears over what they perceived as Africans' "spirit of avarice" and desires for capitalist accumulation. The church's shock at Boganda's economic plan in 1947 to counter settler monopolies with economic competition from African cooperatives later translated into Msgr. Cucherousset's full-scale defrocking of Father Boganda, which coincided with (and was not only a result of) Boganda's rejection of priestly celibacy and entry into marriage with a white French woman.[58] Whether in disputes over catechists' salaries or debates over supporting the economic proposals of indigenous political leaders, the Catholic clergy in Oubangui-Chari were largely suspicious and disapproving of African requests for economic improvement. Relations between Father Boganda, arguably the territory's most popular, devoted, and renowned priest, and the European clergy deteriorated as Boganda amplified his criticisms of African impoverishment at the hands of French traders, plantation owners, and political leaders who dictated economic policy in the colony.[59] By the early 1950s, the white leadership of the Catholic Church hierarchy in French Equatorial Africa, which included French priests and leaders of the Holy Ghost (Spiritaines) Mission, had fully turned against the vicariate's first African ordained priest. Clerical leaders denounced him within the ranks of the church and to the political establishment in AEF and expressed outrage at his economic proposals, decrying his emphases on equality and the improvement of living standards as "decadent," "savage," and "demagoguery leading to bloody revolution."[60]

The history of Barthélemy Boganda's struggle for economic rights and human dignity in Central Africa at the end of the French empire demonstrates that the layered aspect of Catholic development theory envisioned by Louis-Joseph Lebret, which had French nationalist and Catholic institutional ambitions set atop plans for African socioeconomic improvement, allowed for selective and self-serving interpretations of economic development to take root among the European religious and political leaders who were preparing Oubangui-Chari for self-rule in the late 1950s. The French religious and political establishment in Central Africa pursued strategies for mitigating the loss of French imperial power and Catholic institutional authority, which purposefully weakened rising African anti-colonialism by entrenching economic disempowerment and reinforcing unequal and exploitative economic relations between France and Central Africa.

Father Boganda, as well as other progressive African political leaders, envisioned a form of economic development that was anti-communist and spiritually centered, but still failed to gain European adherents at least in part because the church was not genuinely or wholly supportive of decolonization and was led by many high clergy who were motivated by racial prejudice. Moreover, church officials construed Boganda's efforts to form a Pan-Africanist economic and political community (what was originally conceived as *la Républíque Centrafricaine*) as a communist program, contributing further to the motivated reasoning behind implementing a purportedly "Catholic" development agenda that was indeed neither communist nor free-market capitalist, but rather anti-competitive, exclusionary, and neocolonial. Barthélemy Boganda's vision for Oubangui-Chari, based on worker cooperatives, free enterprise, and labor rights, represents a significant contribution to Christian thinking by incorporating a focus on economic rights that supported and justified the interrelationship between dignity and rights. Although rejected by the ecclesiastical elite in the mid-twentieth century, current-day understandings of economic rights not only allow for the harmonization of religious values and economic empowerment theories, they also have a specific focus on racial equity that was glaringly absent in discussions of the church's stance on decolonization.

Cognitive Crisis and Spiritual Restoration: From Depletion to Sufficiency

Jan Vansina was perhaps the first modern scholar to provide a thorough analysis of the Central African forest zone and rightly perceived that changes to the physical environment and cultural patterns considerably disturbed human relationships.[61] Vansina's insights into the "equatorial tradition," or the dynamic nature of precolonial social and legal relations, led him to believe that African kinship, intermarriage, community norms, and authority structures mutated beyond recognition with incorporation into French colonial systems, causing an irreversible crisis of cognitive inadaptability to "unforeseen and hitherto unimaginable events of the colonial conquest."[62] Vansina's work was one of the first among modern histories to candidly depict the trauma of colonialism, which spelled "death" to the equatorial tradition—analogous to Chinua Achebe's renowned depiction of cultural alienation and social decline among the Igbo of Nigeria.[63] In my previous work, I argued that historians should look beyond ontological insecurity and narratives of subordination to locate histories of resistance or accommodation among African societies.[64] However, Boganda's diaries, speeches, and missives openly and vividly bear witness to stark human suffering in Oubangui-Chari on a scale that calls for a reconsideration of whether resistance and adaptation to colonial domination is so plainly universal. Boganda's eyewitness accounts of the merciless debasement of those he considered fellow humans and fellow Christians support Achebe's reflection that "we have fallen apart" and Vansina's discernment of an "inability to cope" among African societies who lived under European rule, presenting evidence that resistance or adaptation are only achievable within certain political and social conditions, and also suggesting that unmitigated persecution is perhaps the more standard pattern in colonized spaces. As an example, the colony of Oubangui-Chari had no nonreligious secondary school for Africans until 1952.[65] The acutely undeveloped state of education is but one of many indications of intentional impoverishment, where European political leaders conceived of and realized a colonial possession that was purely a site of exploitation and extraction.

Boganda's rejoinders, which included cooperative financial projects and local economic endeavors were not—or not only—a means to resist, nor were they examples of accommodation of a subjugating system. Rather, they were a call to recognize that deprivation and misery were not merely material states but also spiritual conditions. Boganda vocally criticized those in the church who stood against economic advancement for Africans on the basis that wealth would threaten African "solemnity and piety," and lead to insobriety and arrogance. In a glaring example of clerical aggression toward African economic improvement, in 1946, Père Aristide Morandeau abolished the Grimari Mission African economic cooperative launched by Boganda in 1942, arguing it "exploited" church property and was under the "questionable guidance of those with anti-colonial attitudes."[66] Boganda responded that church representatives should "open their eyes" to the real exploitation that was occurring throughout the territory and recognize their real responsibility to eliminate destitution and hunger in their congregations.[67]

Father Boganda, like Vansina, perceived French colonialism as a cognitive and intellectual cataclysm for "la société equatoriale" in Oubangui-Chari.[68] But rather than calling for "resistance" or proposing a vision of African futurity based on a simulacra of traditional values and practices that had long since adjusted to new power dynamics, in the vein of Kwame Nkrumah or Leopold Senghor, Boganda argued for Africans' empowerment within the capitalist structure with a simultaneous commitment to Christian social values. Boganda positioned economic rights and wealth accumulation not as threats to Africans' spiritual devotion, but as a means to promote the practices of providence, prudence, dignity, and morality. For the "degradation of man" led to worsening moral conditions "in the intimate relations between humans" and produced improvidence, profligacy, and intemperance. Those familiar with scarcity and violence, Boganda argued, are loath to contribute, nurture, or develop disciplines of piety. It was only in achieving a measure of material dignity that Christian life could be sustained.[69]

For Boganda, the question of economic rights was also an issue of racial equality. If the territory's Europeans could accumulate wealth under a capitalist system and not have their faith questioned, why should Africans be suspected of shallow attachments to Christianity because of their efforts to acquire wealth? Economic rights are often overlooked in histories of decolonization, as well as in accounts of debates surrounding racial equality and self-rule. Examinations of African struggles for political rights have focused on citizenship, nationality, and sovereignty more than on explicit calls for redistribution or wealth transfer, or even the processes of how Africans acceded to positions of economic policymaking. Historians like Elizabeth Schmidt and Jean Allman deftly portrayed the nationalist sentiments expressed by various ethnic and class coalitions who mobilized against the colonial state for political representation and autonomy.[70] Frederick Cooper has recently insisted on a more careful examination of what meanings various agents gave to the concepts of "freedom" and "independence" by showing that African leaders' demands for equality and autonomy did not necessarily convey aspirations for a nation-state. Many among the African political leadership harbored concerns about how their national economies would be sustained if metropolitan centers withdrew their investments, supply chains, or organizational frameworks.[71]

As Cooper has demonstrated for many other political leaders in French West Africa, Barthélemy Boganda was firmly anti-colonialist, but not nationalist in the ordinary, territorially focused sense. His vision of self-determination centered on creating the means for African economic independence *and* economic interdependence between African states or territories, rather than advocating for a theoretical political sovereignty that would mean financial insolvency and economic instability. Boganda's intention for the "*République Centrafricaine*" was a Pan-Africanist vision of an interlinked Gabon, Moyen-Congo, Oubangui-Chari, and Chad (the territories of French Equatorial Africa) that *maintained* economic networks established by France during the colonial period, while granting more autonomy to African business enterprises and, critically, strengthening African property rights and resource governance. It was capitalist and anti-colonialist, but not anti-French or anti-Christian. Indeed, Boganda explicitly and emphatically rejected both Communism and anti-constitutionalism, desiring a continuity within the French Community (*Communauté française*), whose terms reaffirmed the preeminence of France by placing in the *domaine commun* critical functions such as foreign affairs, defense, currency, economic policies, and control of raw materials.[72] Boganda even refused to align with or vote for socialist positions in the Assemblé nationale.[73] Nevertheless, the Catholic hierarchy in Oubangui-Chari and in France largely concurred that Boganda was a radical anti-colonialist who threatened the stability of the church's position in Oubangui-Chari and also inspired materialist and Marxist sentiments among the African faithful.

Boganda's Death and the Birth of Neocolonialism

After proposing several economic policies, both in the Oubangui-Chari territory and in the National Assembly, that expanded agricultural and financial opportunities for Africans and limited French manipulation of trade and exchange terms as part of his vision for a post-colonial transition toward economic self-governance, Barthélemy Boganda was killed in a plane crash under suspicious circumstances, which still today elicits speculation over the intentions of the French government in 1959 to grant its equatorial territories full or genuine independence.

Although the Catholic Church had raised Boganda from childhood and supported his entry into politics and his election to *député* in France's National Assembly, Boganda did not feel so indebted to the institution as to restrain his rebukes against what he perceived as their moral blindness. Boganda insisted that the church recognize the evidence he collected regarding low or unpaid wages for Africans, fixed prices for cash crops, the head tax, the hunting ban, and even the recirculation of Africans' church donations, and his campaigns inspired his formulation of a forceful religious narrative in support of the concept of economic justice as fundamental to protecting human dignity and human rights. Catholic Church leaders in Oubangui-Chari rejected these campaigns, however, and dismissed the assertion they had spiritual and evangelical implications.

Archival evidence demonstrates that Lebret was widely read among Spiritan missionaries and the Catholic clerical elite in Central and West Africa.[74] Notwithstanding this exposure to both papally endorsed, socially conscious Catholic thinking and lived experience within a space of highly visible, undeniable human suffering, Spiritan leaders and the ecclesiastical elite in Oubangui-Chari remained steadfast in their support for the French administration and European presence in the territory. Implementing Catholic human rights therefore has a more complicated and frustrating history—especially in Central Africa—than an examination of church discourse might otherwise suggest.

Father Boganda's published and unpublished writings on the relationship between economic security and human dignity and his greater vision of economic rights for Africans as a means of achieving a spiritually driven liberation are not entirely unrelated to current-day religious movements in Africa that address "epistemological, normative, and ontological insecurity,"[75] whether in the form of the prosperity Gospel or popular churches promising economic as well as spiritual rewards.[76] Moreover, many current-day African Christian churches' emphases on healing and empowerment appear to overlap with Boganda's discourses evoking the "misery," "blindness," "terror," and "starving" (among other states of being) of Africans under oppressive regimes.[77] Ruth Marshall explores how Pentecostalism presents the experience of being born again as a chance for Nigerians to realize the promises of political and religious salvation made during the colonial and postcolonial eras.[78] Marshall demonstrates how African believers at the grassroots mobilize the promises of fuller humanity embedded in revivalist and evangelical Christianity to cope with poverty, corruption, and inequality—which many Nigerians believe were first cemented into the political economy through colonialism—confirming Boganda's contention that there would be no end to colonial domination without an end to poverty and deprivation *and* that only in ending both of these two systems could there be spiritual deliverance as well. African societies' current-day expressions of "a heightened desire for spirituality"[79] are intimately related to ambitions of "progress along a gradient of material achievement" and integration into a wider social world.[80] But one need not point (solely) to structural adjustment or neoliberal reforms for the broader emergence of religious discourses on economic inequality or material consumption.[81] Boganda's conceptualization of national liberation and decolonization was predicated upon Africans finally joining the world community organized by a material hierarchy in which they would direct their own progress (moral, material, and spiritual) through control over the wealth from their own territory. The failure of this to occur has roots in colonial racial and economic domination, which Boganda feared would remain implanted unless a more expansive and non-racist vision of Christian human rights emerged among Europeans. As African nation-states continue to contend with the defeats of decolonization, dreams of twinned prosperity and salvation remain very much alive and continue to plant seeds of progress.

CHAPTER 8

A Fractured Church: Catholicism and Decolonization in Mozambique

Eric Morier-Genoud

Most churches in Africa faced the issue of decolonization around the Second World War. Because of the slow development of the Portuguese colonies, the authoritarian nature of the Portuguese state and its colonialism, and the strictness of its colonial race hierarchies, the issue of decolonization emerged in Portugal's African colonies much later. Discussion within the church in Mozambique began in 1960, the year of Africa's decolonization, and developed substantially only after the launch of a liberation war in 1964. Some individual missionaries became involved in supporting or opposing decolonization rapidly, but collective action only started in 1971—three years before a coup d'état in Lisbon kickstarted the decolonization process. As a result, the debate around Portuguese decolonization and decolonization itself occurred within a very different context, not just because many independence processes had already taken place and the Cold War profoundly reshaped the geopolitics of the region, but also because the Vatican II process was unfolding and changing the dynamics of the Roman Catholic institution worldwide.

The historiography about church and state in the Portuguese empire traditionally presents the church as united and fully allied with the colonial state, with only a few cases of dissidence. Based on the case of Mozambique, the present chapter aims at exploring the diversity of positions that existed within the Roman Catholic Church in relation to decolonization and investigating how positions crystalized and influenced each other within the institution. The aim is to unpack the crude and political version of history that has dominated Mozambican (as well as Angolan and Portuguese) historiography by positing a Catholic pro-colonial "majority" against a few "exceptions"—exceptions that would prove a rule.[1] The text tries also to complicate the teleological view that the church and its members only started to change perspective due to increasing external pressure and the liberation war, by looking at processes of influence inside the institution. Finally, the chapter opens a window into the wider religious world, beyond Catholicism, to see how some Catholic clergy reached out to institutions in the Protestant world and how the latter followed and acted in relation to them.

The chapter deploys a historical and sociological approach. Taking the diocese of Beira as a case study (representative of Portuguese colonies and to some extent Southern Africa where decolonization unfolded much later than in other African territories), it unpacks the trajectory of the church and restores its singular historicity. It does so by looking at all the congregations and other (formal and informal) groups active in the diocese. Research was carried out in Mozambique and Europe, in archives of several congregations and state institutions, and through interviews and life histories collected over a twenty-year period in those places and in the United States. The text starts with a discussion of the diversity of views within the archdiocese of Beira in the 1960s and 1970s—up to 1975 when Mozambique became independent. It then looks at the way collective decisions were taken in relation to decolonization, and how the latter influenced other individuals within a changing, Vatican II–era church. In a final section, the text focuses on the Congregation of the Sacred Hearts of Jesus and Mary, also known as the Picpus Fathers, and their largely unknown and unstudied decision to leave Mozambique in 1974 in protest of the collusion between the church and the colonial state.

From Diversity to Division

Catholicism arrived in Southeast Africa at the end of the fifteenth century with Portuguese explorers on their way to India. Following Vasco de Gama's first voyage, the Portuguese opened a trading post on the island of Mozambique, where a church was built. From there, Dominican and Jesuit missionaries tried to conquer spiritually the kingdom of Monomotapa in what is today Zimbabwe. Having failed, they settled along the Zambezi river, developing major semi-feudal estates whose populations (including slaves) they converted. A full century ensued, with Portuguese missionaries having a firm territorial and spiritual presence in the area. But a bout of extreme regalism in Portugal led to the expulsion of the Jesuits in 1759, after which republicanism, more anti-clericalism, and civil war in the early nineteenth century undermined what was left of the church. By mid-1800s, the Catholic institution in Portuguese East Africa had all but collapsed; in 1855 there were only five missionaries left for the whole of Mozambique.[2] The church rebuilt in the late nineteenth century, with new congregations, new methods, and new means, but growth was interrupted by an anti-clerical republic in 1911. Growth returned in the late 1920s after anti-clericalism came to an end, to expand significantly after 1940 and the signing of a Concordat and Missionary Accord by the Vatican and Portugal.

Thanks to the 1940 Concordat and Missionary Accord, the church in Mozambique, like elsewhere in the empire, began to receive state subsidies and various other advantages. The state paid church salaries and offered retirement plans, land was given for missions, and funds were provided for the building and running of schools and hospitals for Africans. While the Concordat separated church and state in the metropole, the Missionary Accord brought them together in the colonies. The Catholic Church became a quasi-state institution, and the administration did not just support the church, it also repressed and then contained Catholicism's competitors, namely: Protestantism and Islam. As was to be expected, state support led to massive growth of the church, materially, with the building of many mission stations, schools, and health posts, as well as spiritually. Conversion exploded after 1940: in the archdiocese of Beira, baptism increased fivefold over a twenty-year period.[3]

Because Portugal was a small country (pop. of seven million in 1940) and had been faced by several anti-clerical moments since the eighteenth century, the clergy was not numerically sufficient to colonize effectively the whole empire—Angola, Mozambique, Guinea Bissau, Timor, Goa, and a series of islands and port cities. Consequently, most of the territory of Angola was "given" to a French congregation while, in Mozambique, many foreign congregations were called in to occupy and evangelize the land and its people. By the time of independence, there were nineteen different male and thirty-nine female congregations in Mozambique.[4] While the situation varied by diocese, more than 50% of the clergy was non-Portuguese in the archdiocese of Beira. In the early 1950s, Lisbon tried to limit the number of foreign missionaries and it banned Italians, the Dutch, and Germans, all of whom it distrusted because their countries had lost their own colonies. Still, the clergy became very diverse in terms of nationalities and congregations, something that reflected the global church but might have been atypical in comparison to some other countries or colonies.

Within this diverse church, the first anti-colonial views only emerged at the very end of the 1950s. Before then, some Catholic clergy were critical of some aspects of various colonialisms and they might have expressed preference for one type of colonialism over another—for instance, British versus Portuguese colonialism. But their views did not go beyond colonialism. What sparked a change was, of course, the beginning of decolonization in Asia after the Second World War and, more specifically, the 1955 Bandung (Asian-African) conference. This event did not shift perspectives at once, but it planted a seed of doubt among a fringe of the clergy, including the Bishop of Beira, a seed that developed and expanded gradually. It changed the perspectives of the personnel concerned, making them realise that colonialism was time-bound, and this made them think about how the church should prepare and organize for an eventual independence.

A discussion about decolonization took place for the first time in the Mozambican Catholic church in 1960 because of a seminarian articulating, in private, pro-independence ideas at the major seminary. The fact was discovered when the clergy opened the student's correspondence (as was the regular practice at the seminary). The arch-conservative cardinal of Mozambique was outraged and demanded the student be fired. He made a fuss with the archbishop of Beira, whom he held responsible for the affair, since the archbishop of Beira was liberal and the student came from that diocese. The bishop of Beira did not contradict the cardinal but protected the student after his dismissal. The matter aggravated rapidly when the cardinal's auxiliary demanded all seminarians commit to an absolute pro-Portuguese stance. Several young men left the seminary and the colony, some going to study abroad and others joining early nationalist groupings.[5] Missionaries from the Society of the White Fathers became embroiled in the affair as they helped seminarians flee and find scholarship or their way to the liberation movements. This led to the development of a network of White Fathers to help African nationalists flee colonialism and join what by 1964 became a liberation war. A first White Fathers missionary was arrested and expelled from Mozambique for "anti-national" activities in 1965, and several others faced problems in subsequent years. In the process, an increasing number of the White Fathers became favorable to an African independence for Mozambique. Expectedly, White Fathers were influenced by colleagues working in other African countries where decolonization had already unfolded. At the same time, though, this society's priests were all anti-Communists and many eventually took their distance from the dominant Frelimo (Frente de Libertação de Moçambique, or Liberation Front of Mozambique) liberation movement when its leadership shifted to Marxism in 1968.[6]

The White Fathers had a unique position in the archdiocese of Beira. The archbishop saw them as very efficient and he used them to "modernize" his clergy, particularly the "old-fashioned" Goan and Portuguese missionaries. He did this in many ways, not least diocesan synods and other meetings of the clergy where he asked these missionaries to make presentations. The views of the archbishop of Beira, Dom Sebastiao Soares de Resende, about decolonization were not far off from those of the White Fathers. While originally favorable to colonialism and Portugal, his ultramontane beliefs and the social doctrine of the church led him to become critical of Portuguese colonialism and eventually think beyond colonialism. In the 1960s, he toyed with the theory of lusotropicalism (a Portuguese form of multi-racialism promoted by the Portuguese government)[7] but also began to think that independence was inevitable, if not desirable. He never expressed these ideas in public, but wrote them in his private diary.[8] His public positionings were neutral, and he defended all clergy as long as they worked for the good of the church—irrespective of their views. He thus said nothing about exceedingly pro-Portuguese missionaries nor anything about the White Fathers missionaries and others who had pro-independence leanings and activities. In fact, he even went quite far to defend his clergy, traveling on one occasion to Lisbon to meet the prime minister to protect a man he saw as his best missionary, even though he was involved in sending men to the liberation struggle. His view can be seen in the advice he gave to his clergy about politics in 1964:

> I would like to say to all missionaries, and in particular those who are not Portuguese of origin, that they should not get involved in political questions. Priests are not ordained to do politics, but "*ut offerat dona et sacrificia pro peccatis*." Priests are priests for everyone in their parishes, or missions, or dioceses, regardless of which party they are from, or whether they are democrats, socialists, or communists. If they [the priests] ostensibly support one side, they will become incompatible for those who support other parties, a situation that will frustrate their universal mission. God has taught us to "Give God what belongs to God and to Caesar what belongs to Caesar."[9]

The archbishop's inclusive and supportive style of leadership was key to maintaining the church's unity in central Mozambique as differences of views over how to work and relate to the colonial state and its colonialism increased between missionaries in the 1960s. Unfortunately, in January 1967, after twenty years leading the diocese, the archbishop died of cancer. Subsequently, the Vatican chose a new archbishop who was similar in approach, but the Portuguese state vetoed him, as it could thanks to the 1940 Concordat—this was the first time Lisbon vetoed a Bishop (the man was seen as too liberal). This resulted in the Vatican choosing a new archbishop who was not only nationalist and conservative but also not inclusive. Faced with many congregations and a subtle process of change resulting from Vatican II, and an evolving political situation after the start of the liberation war in 1964, the archbishop made several "mistakes" after his arrival, such as selling the cherished diocesan newspaper and not consulting his clergy before taking decisions as his predecessor did. Consequently, his clergy radicalized. Those who wanted a renovation of the church's structures and actions in line with Vatican II felt the bishop was against them and soon demanded his resignation. Those who resisted reform, on the other hand, went to support the archbishop and eventually made an alliance, which led to the nomination in 1970 of an arch-conservative Franciscan as vicar-general (in replacement of a Portuguese liberal diocesan priest whom the archbishop demoted). Thus, within two years, the clergy became very politicized and very divided. "Conservatives" used the political police in their fight against "liberals" who, for their part, called on the Vatican to step in and force the hand of those who refused to apply Vatican II reforms. As things became heated, the new archbishop fled his diocese and the diocese imploded.[10]

Part of this implosion, the White Fathers missionaries decided in 1971 to leave Mozambique as a society, in protest of the collusion between the Catholic hierarchy and the colonial state. The missionaries had seen several of their men expelled or not allowed to return from furlough and they felt the Catholic hierarchy, particularly the new archbishop of Beira, was more in line with the colonial state than with them and their pastoral mission. The decision was taken in April 1971, at the high of the conflict with the archbishop of Beira, by the leadership of the society in Rome after it held a series of consultations with state and religious officials as well as members of the society in Mozambique. Consultations were held also with other congregations in Mozambique and in Rome (see more details in the next section). After the decision was made public, the Portuguese political police decided to preempt the missionaries' voluntary departure and expel them, en masse. This turned the affair into an international global scandal that made the international headlines. Once in Rome, the somewhat spurious distinction between the religious and political motivations for their leaving Mozambique evaporated and their move was interpreted (to support it or denounce it) as a protest against Portuguese colonialism—officially they were only protesting the collusion of the church hierarchy with the colonial state that prevented their evangelical work.[11]

While the White Fathers' departure grabbed worldwide attention, other congregations evolved toward another stance against colonialism. This was the case of the Spanish Burgos missionaries (from the Instituto Español de Misiones Extranjeras), who shifted toward liberation theology in 1969. The shift came because of influences from Latin America where most of the Burgos missionaries worked. In Mozambique, liberation theology led the congregation to rethink their missionary activities at large. First, they moved away from their traditional work in education—which relied on buildings and aimed at conversion—toward an evangelization focused on workers and the creation of "base communities." Second, they shifted to actively support the decolonization of Mozambique. Missionaries went on to contact the liberation movement and eventually work in their favor. By 1971, the missionaries' approach had changed drastically. In a report of a meeting in August, the Mozambican Burgos priests reported that they had now:

- Opted to continue to side with this people;
- Opted in favor of the colonized and exploited people;
- Opted in favor of the urgent education of native clergy;
- Opted in favor of a prophetic testimony in the face of injustice; and
- Opted in favor of a collective pastoral ministry focusing on a united church.[12]

In other words, while in 1971 the White Fathers decided to prophetically leave Mozambique in protest of colonialism, the Burgos Fathers took the opposite but equally prophetic decision to stay in Mozambique to side with the liberation movement fighting for the end of colonialism.

On the Portuguese side, among Jesuits and Franciscans, very few missionaries held liberal views. The majority stood in favor of Portuguese colonialism and/or was quietist. Only a small number of younger missionaries would become more favorable to Vatican II and critical of the colonial situation in the 1970s. Many Franciscans were favorable to the Estado Novo regime because they saw it as having saved the church (and their congregation specifically) from the anti-clerical regime that came to power in 1911. They saw Salazar and his regime as heroic for having put an end to the anti-clerical republic and signed the 1940 Concordat, which brought "religious peace" to Portugal. Additionally, the Franciscans were nostalgic for an earlier period when they controlled most of Mozambique—that is, before dioceses were created, in 1940, when one of their number was the prelate of Mozambique and they owned many properties in their congregation's own name.[13] Consequently, although taking vows of poverty, the Franciscans in Mozambique were very attached to their ownership of land and farms and, pastorally, their approach relied heavily on schools and teacher-catechists. This reactionary view (in the original sense of wishing to return to the past) was not shared by the Portuguese Jesuits who, by the late 1960s, accepted that decolonization was on the horizon. But the Jesuits rejected the models proposed by the White Fathers and the Burgos Fathers of a local church aligned with the Vatican and separate from Lisbon and its patriarch. They saw Mozambique as part of Portugal and wished for a church based in and centered on Portugal (in line with the *Padroado*). Politically, they denounced the decolonization argument as part of an externally fostered (communist) agenda. On the positive side, they wished for a reform of colonialism and empire. In an internal report in 1971, the head of the Jesuits in Mozambique criticized the White Fathers for not seeing any solution other than independence and for refusing to consider the Portuguese solution of a "multiracial integration" of the colonies. Multiracial integration referred here to the lusotropical argument that Portugal ruled benevolently over a racially diverse series of territories—a strand of that thinking would evolve into a political program to reform the existing empire into a Portuguese "federal structure," with autonomy or semi-independence for its territories.[14]

Missionary sisters were in the majority quietist—like many priests in all congregations. Among the eleven female congregations in the archdiocese of Beira (most of them Portuguese), there were sisters who defended colonialism and did not hesitate to denounce priests who were critical of Portugal. This was the case at the Barué mission in 1971, where the sisters denounced a White Father for making a joke about elections, leading to the missionary not being allowed to return to Mozambique after his furlough, and leading the White Fathers to consider leaving Mozambique at once. A more critical position was seen in multinational and foreign female congregations. Three congregations aligned with a program to renovate the church in line with Vatican II and protested officially against the expulsion of the White Fathers in 1971.[15] Among them were the Franciscans of the Divine Mother, the Paulinas sisters (congregation of the Daughters of St. Paul), and the Sisters of the Sacred Heart of Mary. The former worked with the White Fathers in three mission stations and contributed to the Beira catechetic center to reform the church's pastoral ministry and ecclesial approach (see more about the center in the next section). The Sisters of the Sacred Heart of Mary took a stand with the progressive clergy when the latter clashed with the archbishop over pastoral issues. The Paulinas sisters stood against the conservative archbishop too, and one of their missionaries, Sister Maria de Carli, was particularly active in renovating church structures and pastoral approaches, to the point that the Portuguese state prevented her from returning to Mozambique from furlough in 1973 (in effect expelling her from the territory).[16]

Vatican II and the Fracturing Process

The first archbishop of Beira, Dom Sebastião, attended all sessions of Vatican II and was the most active Portuguese bishop at the council (making more interventions than any other Portuguese prelate). Back in his diocese, he published his interventions in the diocesan newspaper, encouraged the renewal of the church, and pushed for the development of structures that brought together the clergy across congregations and genders. In this way, his diocese became a center for the renovation of the church in Mozambique. Many Beira missionaries were involved in the design, development, and direction of "missionary weeks" after 1962, which were held in different dioceses each year to update missionary approaches and methods. After 1968, they additionally initiated "pastoral weeks" to reform the church as a whole, with a conference each year in a different region of Mozambique. Linked to the latter initiative, three catechetic centers were set up across Mozambique in 1969 to train lay men and women (couples) and thus shift Catholic evangelization away from its reliance on schools and teachers-evangelists. In Beira, a catechetic center was opened in Nazaré, in the periphery of the city of Beira. Uniquely staffed by individuals from different congregations, including sisters, the center was particularly dynamic. Portuguese congregations were involved too, the Jesuits having sent one of their young priests as permanent staff.[17] The Franciscans kept their distance, but some younger priests were eventually convinced to participate, if discreetly, by the director of the center, who went to great lengths to ensure that a representative of each key congregation in the diocese was present at the center.

In 1971, the catechetic center of Nazaré opened a Center for Pastoral Investigation (CPI), which became a Mozambique-wide institution to carry research, reflections, and exchanges on renovating the Catholic Church. This initiative articulated with the pastoral weeks just mentioned and added to them. The CPI held conferences, seminars, and soon published a bulletin entitled *Palavra e Sinal* ("Word and Sign"), as well as occasional papers. In this way, the Nazaré center became the cauldron in which missionaries in Mozambique could think collectively about how to renovate the church and implement change. It was a cradle of new thinking as well as a center of influence. A Sister of the Divine Pastor recalled fondly the collective and participatory ambiance of the center: "At night, after dinner: fathers, sisters and catechists met and, together, we had strong moments of praying, reflection, roundtables, celebrations, and other specific activities on the theme proposed for each meeting. It was a real meeting of happiness, union, and brotherly life."[18]

Reflections started on reforming the church but soon ventured onto the issue of decolonization. Most notably the pastoral week meeting of 1972 engaged in a debate about the church's prophetic ministry, freedom, and human rights. The meeting produced recommendations that requested a revision of the Concordat and Missionary Accord, a denouncing of injustice, and a new birth of the church united with the people.[19] Contrary to the usual practice and for the first time since the Weeks began, the Episcopal conference refused to approve the recommendations coming out of the meeting, thus deepening the divisions which existed between the hierarchy and the clergy.

This new collective way of coming to decisions can also be seen in relation to the White Fathers' decision to leave in 1971. Before making a choice on the issue, the superior general of the Society, father Van Asten, travelled to Mozambique to hold consultative meetings with his clergy (whom he asked to vote in favor of or against leaving), with state and religious authorities, with key congregations (Jesuits, Picpus, Burgos, Capuchins and Combonians), and even with catechists.[20] State authorities and the bishops were of course not willing to support the White Fathers' position, because they argued Mozambique was not ready to become independent (according to the bishops) and because Mozambicans were Portuguese and should remain so (according to state officials). Among the congregations consulted, most were supportive of the White Fathers' position, but they themselves were not ready to leave, or they preferred to stay and have an impact from within. As to Mozambican catechists, they explicitly encouraged the superior general to withdraw his society.[21] Thus the decision the superior general eventually took with his directorate in Rome in April 1971 was not just well-informed, it was also consultative. Internally, a majority of the White Fathers voted to leave the territory; externally, only the state and the hierarchy opposed the decision. The whole process, in turn, forced all those engaged to think about their own positions and to articulate them explicitly, if not to formalize them.

A similar process of consultation was initiated by the White Fathers' superior general in Rome in early 1971, within the Union of Superiors General (USG). Created in 1957, the USG is a collective structure joining all Catholic congregations' superiors general; female organizations launched a similar structure in 1965. The White Fathers' superior general, Theo van Asten, organized a first meeting with colleagues before he travelled to Mozambique, and he found much interest among his peers in the option to leave Mozambique. Ironically, one of the superiors general who favored most the White Fathers' idea of withdrawal was the Franciscan superior general who, clearly, did not share his Portuguese province's views.[22] Altogether, there were five meetings between the White Father's superior and other heads of congregations—Burgos, Jesuits, Picpus, Franciscan, Combonians and others who had a presence in other parts of Mozambique. At the first meeting, before the White Fathers left, the priests agreed to write a document to the Bishops in Mozambique and set-up a commission to that end. At the second meeting, with only five heads of congregations present (Jesuit, Franciscan, Capuchin, Comboni and Marist), still before the departure of the White Fathers, they considered leaving Mozambique all together, but a majority reckoned they would have better be expelled, so that those left behind and their priests and brothers in Portugal would not suffer.[23] At the meeting after the White Fathers' council had voted to leave Mozambique,[24] some of the superiors general criticized the White Fathers for having taken their decision unilaterally. Discussions and meetings continued, however, and an attempt was made to offer a common position that was different from the White Fathers' yet still critical of the colonial situation. A message was drafted to be sent to all male congregations in Mozambique; the message said, in one of its last versions—the text was eventually never finalized or sent out—"The superiors general recognise that many of their missionaries suffer from the political situation and of the excessively close connection between church and state in Mozambique. They advise missionaries, however, to stay put, with the people, and act in line with their Christian conscience, and they hope the [Portuguese] government will take measures to recognise liberties and civic rights for all, so as to avoid the revindication of those rights through violence."[25] Just like the consultations in Mozambique, the White Fathers' superior general did not explicitly try to convince other congregation leaders to follow his society's path, but the consultation process influenced other superiors and it did force them to think about their positions and articulate them explicitly.[26]

The Vatican II reforms and the White Fathers' departure (the Burgos decision was kept secret) led the conservative clergy to symmetrically narrow their ties to the church hierarchy and to the Portuguese colonial state. Conservative clergy were mostly Portuguese, but not only. Not all White Fathers wanted to leave Mozambique, for example. A minority of mostly old German missionaries, who had lived through World War II, had been expelled from Tanganyika after the war, and had been well received in the Portuguese colony; they did not support reform or protest. They also voted against leaving Mozambique in 1971. One Swiss White Father voted against leaving and went on to return to Mozambique after leaving the society.[27] Still, the conservative clergy were mostly Portuguese and there was among them a strategy to occupy positions of power to enact their views in favor of a Portuguese-centered church working hand-in-hand with the Portuguese state.

As noted earlier, under pressure from the reformist clergy after his arrival, the second archbishop of Beira passed an alliance in 1970 with the Franciscan missionaries and demoted a popular and inclusive secular Portuguese vicar-general in order to replace him with a reactionary Franciscan superior. According to the Portuguese political police who appreciated him, the Franciscan superior came into the job with the explicit aim of "cleaning" the diocesan structures of their "pernicious" elements. At the level of missionaries, some proceeded to work with the police and the army, in their parish or mission, to fight the "terrorists" of Frelimo and their "allies" within the church.[28] Interestingly, there was diversity of views among conservative clergy, too, as we noted earlier, and there seems to have been little collaboration between the two main congregations, namely the Franciscans and the Jesuits, to combat the "progressive" clergy.

Among African Catholic priests, divisions played out differently. We saw earlier how students from the major seminary clashed with the cardinal of Lourenço Marques and his auxiliary, and several students fled abroad, some joining the liberation war. None of these men continued their religious studies and became priests. Among those who stayed in Mozambique and continued their training to ordination, only two African priests joined the liberation movement. The first, Father Mateus Gwenjere, fled the country in 1967 after the death of his protector, the first archbishop of Beira. He was received as a hero in the liberation movement based in Tanzania, but rapidly clashed with the increasingly Marxist leadership and was soon forced to leave. The second, Father Filipe Couto, joined Frelimo in 1971 while he was studying abroad. He was not as involved as his predecessor and stayed with Frelimo until (and after) independence. Another priest, Father Gonçalo Ferrão, did not join Frelimo, but was jailed in 1968 for his nationalist sympathies and because his bishop refused to send him to Portugal to protect him (as happened with many Angolan priests).[29] Except for these cases, the majority of African priests remained either very discreet or quietist, if not favorable to the status quo or a multiracial option. Some priests were sent abroad by their congregations to study further and "protect" them from politicization. Thus, there were no debates (that we know of) among the African clergy about decolonization before the coup d'état in 1974, which led to independence in 1975. During the transition period, African priests and African sisters came together and organized the Union of Priests and Religious Women of Mozambique (USAREMO) with the explicit aim of Africanizing the clergy and hierarchy, something that came rapidly with independence and the nomination of new bishops. Foreign missionaries, priests of mixed heritage, and Frelimo were unhappy with the move, however, accusing USAREMO of focusing on race rather than the need to reform the ecclesial structures and pastoral approach of a church compromised by colonialism.[30]

Looking at the issue numerically, can we evaluate the importance of the clergy critical of colonialism in Mozambique? Firstly, we can estimate that at least five out of the nineteen male congregations in Mozambique became clearly and in their majority critical of colonialism (the White Fathers, the Burgos missionaries, Comboni missionaries, Capuchins of Bari, Capuchins of Trent), and two, at least, in parts (Sacramentins and Consolata). Diocesan clergy, both Portuguese and African, had many elements who were favorable to decolonization, too, and we saw that there were exceptions in all Portuguese congregations, particularly among younger priests. Among female congregations, there were divisions in at least three congregations out of thirty-nine. As shown before, many sisters were pro-colonialism, but even more were quiescent or disinterested in politics. Secondly, an idea of the percentage of the clergy standing against colonialism can be gained in relation to a crisis in early 1974 around the bishop of Nampula and the Comboni congregation, who declared themselves openly in favor of decolonization and the end of the Concordat and Missionary Accord (see more details below). After their public declarations, and just as the state organized the expulsion of the bishop and the Comboni missionaries, a group of clergy decided to organize a letter of solidarity, which gained 300 signatures, representing 17 percent of the clergy in Mozambique.[31]

Now, 17 percent is quite significant, but it is even more so if we consider, first, that the organiser of the declaration could not reach much of the clergy living in the countryside and, second, that more than twenty members of the clergy had already been expelled or prevented from returning to Mozambique since 1965 (over 5 percent of the clergy). In other words, we can speculate conservatively that at least 30 percent of the clergy stood in favor of decolonization in 1974. Among the hierarchy, the percentage was much lower. Only one bishop (out of eight) pronounced himself in favor of independence (12.5 percent of the bishops)—the one expelled in 1974. The other bishops were pro-colonialist or quiescent, unsurprisingly so if one recalls that they were all Portuguese and vetted by the Portuguese government (as discussed earlier). Most bishops were not reactionary, looking to the past, but, rather, in favor of a multiracial society; in a 1970 pastoral letter, they referred, on the sixth year of the liberation struggle, to a "growing integration of native populations" into the colonial society.[32]

Finally, we may note that the dynamics of the church in the 1970s had ecumenical echoes. The White Fathers' expulsion in 1971 was a world event that called the attention of the Protestant World Council of Churches (WCC). In October 1971, the WCC passed a resolution taking note of the White Fathers' decision to leave Mozambique and it asked the WCC's forty-four member churches to consider the same option should they find themselves in a similar position.[33] The WCC resolution came amid heated discussions in the Protestant world about the stance churches should take in relation to colonialism and racism. In 1970, the WCC had launched a Program to Combat Racism (PCR), which focused specifically on racism in Southern Africa and sided against apartheid and colonialism, going as far as providing non-military help to liberation movements in Southern Africa, including the African National Congress and Frelimo. A vivid debate ensued in the Protestant world about colonialism, violence, decolonization, and racism. In most places, the discussions were theological and political, about violence and Communism, but in francophone Switzerland, the discussion was also practical, as the churches there had a missionary arm, the Swiss Mission, which had a significant presence in both Mozambique and South Africa.[34] In May and June 1971, as the

White Fathers left Mozambique, Swiss Mission leaders were invited at the WCC headquarters in Geneva with a Frelimo delegate to discuss whether the Swiss Mission should also withdraw from Mozambique. The discussion was friendly and consensual, and all present agreed that the Swiss missionaries should stay in Mozambique to evangelize and train professionals for the post-colonial period. Like the Burgos Fathers, then, the Swiss Protestants decided not to leave Mozambique but work instead for independence from within and in secret. The mission leaders explained that their decision had to be kept secret, because the mission took a risk for its missionaries, African pastors, and laity in Mozambique, and they were unsure if regular church members in Switzerland would agree with their choice.[35]

Ripple Effects: The Case of the Picpus Fathers

Picpus Fathers, from the Dutch province of the society, came to Mozambique in 1956. The decision to establish a mission in that territory resulted from the society's desire to establish a seminary for their congregation in Portugal; indeed, the government demanded a presence in the colonies if Catholic missionaries wanted state subsidy in the metropole.[36] This was the first time the priests from the Congregation of the Sacred Hearts of Jesus and Mary went to work in Africa. The first elements went there wholly unprepared and subsequent missionaries had little missiological training, too.[37] They settled in an area north of the provincial capital of Beira, in urban parishes and missions along the Zambezi River. The life of the mission was largely uneventful until the 1970s—for a few years, the missionaries mostly learnt the ropes of their new job. Under the influence of the archbishop of Beira and other congregations, their missionary focus became clearer and they began learning the local language, one of their missionaries becoming a recognized Sena language specialist and translator. The Picpus missionaries were an integral part of the diocese and hence evolved with the rest of the clergy. They held no position of power in the diocese and tended to follow and learn from other congregations. Being foreigners, they tended to align with other foreign missionaries, though they were largely quietist.

Events caught up with the missionaries in 1970. In February of that year, three Picpus priests were expelled from Portugal as reprisal for a petition signed in Holland against Portugal. The petition was signed by 742 priests and pastors demanding Portugal be banned from using NATO armaments in its war against liberations movements in Africa.[38] The Picpus priests were caught off guard by the accusation and expulsion, since none of their priests had signed the petition and some Picpus Fathers had been very close to the authoritarian regime in Portugal—one of their priests was the dictator António Salazar's confidant. Then, in early 1971, came the departure and expulsion of the White Fathers, which demanded the Picpus missionaries take a position on colonialism, something they had not reflected much upon. In February or March 1971, the Picpus missionaries had a meeting with Theo van Asten, the White Fathers' superior general, during his consultation tour in Mozambique. Even though the Picpus missionaries were close to the White Fathers at the time (the congregations' superiors in Mozambique were both Dutch and friends), they decided not to follow the White Fathers' path. For one, the Picpus congregations had missionaries in Portugal, in contrast with the White Fathers, who would have been negatively impacted by the organization leaving Mozambique. For another, they felt the situation was not bad enough to require leaving yet and they felt compelled to stay to support local Christians who suffered from the situation.

A Picpus Father explained the view of the missionaries in the following way—in a letter to his superior in Holland summarising a Picpus missionary meeting held in May 1971:

> We all agree with the White Fathers' departure, because we saw that their motivations are real and just. But, on the other hand, we spoke about a very negative side [to their action]. The fact that the parents leave the house full of children alone. They leave, and nothing else. We decided to stay. We hope for the reaction of the African people and European people, of the ecclesiastic and civil authorities. When, later, our work faces even more obstacles, less freedoms, etc., then we will leave, as well. Is this position coherent? The answer was: yes. Our sole presence is already an attack. After all, those who stay have the same role to accomplish as those who leave. So, to leave or not to leave doesn't make a difference. Only in the perspective of Africans will our staying not be understood. That is why, I was saying at the meeting, it is better to shut up and not explain [our choice] to them, since they will not understand.[39]

Not explicit in this extract is the fact that all Pipcus missionaries did not agree with the position adopted. Later in his letter, Father Verdaasdoonk complained about his colleagues' lack of consideration for, and lack of confidence in Africans.[40]

Political events soon shattered the Picpus's tentative compromise. After 1971, repression increased (in 1973 a Picpus priest was expelled from Portugal for a homily in favor of peace)[41] and the war of liberation reached the area of work of the Picpus. In April 1973, the missionaries referred to infiltration and attacks by the liberation movement near their missions and they expressed fears that "terrorism" would soon reach the cities (which they called a "fourth front").[42] As a result, at the Picpus regional meeting held on August 20–24, 1973, the priests discussed not just the security situation but also the need for Africanization and whether they should leave Mozambique. They feared the villagization policy of the army and the fact that they would soon not be able to travel outside of their mission except in military columns, and they wondered whether they would not soon be perceived as being "complicit in the oppression of the people." They concluded again that they should stay in Mozambique, but they also decided to create "base communities," so as to prepare Africans for their eventual leaving.[43] This shift to base communities was most probably the result of the influence of the Burgos Fathers. After the departure of the White Fathers, the Picpus missionaries became quite close to the Spanish missionaries who were, as we noted before, adepts of liberation theology. In short, then, the Picpus priests decided in August 1973 to stay in Mozambique but also to radicalize their approach and prepare to leave. This was not just a position of principle: the missionaries decided to prepare Africans to live without their presence and give them leadership roles in the church—and to do so immediately.[44]

The situation at the mission of Inhaminga, north of Beira, accelerated the pace of Picpus thinking and actions. The war reached the area at the end of July 1973 and various members of the church were killed in subsequent months as the army tried to repress the Frelimo progress. In February 1974, the secret police began assassinating prisoners, killing a traditional chief and his family, while the army began to use napalm in areas of the mission suspected to be supporting Frelimo.[45] In January 1974, the white settler population began, in turn, to suspect the missionaries of being favorable to African nationalism and tensions rose rapidly, so that by March the missionaries decided to leave the mission alongside the Rhodesian diocesan sisters working with them—they jointly decided to leave on March 22. Drawing from this experience, the regional superior of the Picpus missionaries and his council decided in March 1974 that the congregation should withdraw from Mozambique at once, and he asked the Picpus superior general in Rome for authorization. The latter agreed and sent a letter to Cardinal Villot, the secretary of state, on March 28 stating that "after so much earlier hesitations and uncertainty, the moment to leave has come."[46] To his missionaries, the superior general explained further: "What happened in Inhaminga leaves us no choice."[47] Interestingly, the superior general explained that his congregation received the authorization to leave from the apostolic administrator in Beira, but received no reply from the nuncio. Between the lines, one can read that the superior general did not ask for an authorization from the Vatican and just informed it of its decision.

Always a step behind, the Picpus Fathers' decision to leave Mozambique was interrupted by a coup d'état in Lisbon on April 25, 1974. In what came to be known as the "Carnation Revolution," military officers and soldiers brought down the authoritarian regime in Lisbon. This happened when only half of the Picpus priests had left Mozambique. The first revolutionary transitional government was not clearly in favor of decolonization, even though the main grievance of the soldiers was the "colonial war." Discussions took place about an option to federalize the empire.[48] It took a few months and several other transitional governments before a decision was taken in Portugal to engage in a full decolonization process. Be this as it may, the fact is that the coup d'état in Portugal and the perspective of decolonization created a tricky situation for the Picpus Fathers. Half the missionaries were now back in Holland while half of them were still in Mozambique; the priests remaining in Mozambique therefore became unsure whether they should now leave or not. After much hesitation and discussion, the missionaries still in Mozambique decided to stay, while those in Holland proceeded to try to help the decolonization process from outside.

Building on a meeting on April 29, 1974, in the Netherlands between Picpus theologians and Spanish Burgos liberation theology missionaries who had been expelled from Mozambique, the Picpus Fathers in Holland decided in early 1974 to try to bring together all the Catholic clergy who had been expelled from Mozambique—the White Fathers, the archbishop of Nampula, the Comboni missionaries, some Burgos missionaries, some Sisters of the Calvary, some regular clergy, Sister Maria de Carli, a Franciscan, etc. They sent them all an invitation on May 4, 1974, containing a reflection on the situation, a questionnaire about what should be done "from the diaspora," and a list of contacts.[49] A meeting ensued in Madrid, Spain, on May 12–14 to discuss a strategy for clergy in the diaspora. After two days, the expelled members agreed that: (a) it was not time to return to Mozambique, as the Catholic hierarchy had not changed yet, and (b) they needed to "prepare in Portugal, in Tanzania, and in Zambia African Mozambicans and Portuguese from Portugal and from Mozambique to the conversion from colonialism to the acceptance of the African himself as an independent person who will found an independent African state."[50] They also decided to develop a program of common action, keep exchanging experiences, join relevant publications, set up another meeting, and begin to work with other churches.[51]

Accordingly, the Picpus Fathers reached out to "other churches." On May 22, 1974, they wrote to the aforementioned Swiss Mission, telling them they had learned about the persecution the Swiss Mission had suffered in 1972 (the daughter church's leadership was imprisoned and the president of the synod was killed),[52] that they had themselves left Mozambique, and they hoped for a future "with an ecumenical face."[53] The Protestants answered with a long letter thanking the priests for their contact and hoping for an ecumenical future, too.[54] In the next letter, the Picpus Fathers expressed a desire to meet the Swiss.[55] The latter accepted and offered to meet in Switzerland.[56] A meeting ensued on September 24 in Lausanne, with the leaders of the mission and three leaders of the Presbyterian Church, the daughter church of the Swiss Mission. From the record, the meeting did not unfold well. The Swiss missionaries came with their wives, so there were twelve Protestants to receive two Catholic priests. After presentations, they talked about the Frelimo liberation movement, whom the Presbyterians had just visited in Tanzania, and they discussed ecumenism. The head of Presbyterian church explained that ecumenism would be very difficult in Mozambique, because the Catholic Church was very "compromised." The Picpus Fathers explained that the official church was a problem, indeed, but that their initiative to meet the Swiss, like the earlier meeting in Madrid, was done in their own name and that of their congregations—not the official Catholic institution. At the end, the priest invited the Mozambican pastors and the Swiss to a meeting in Lisbon with progressive missionaries to follow on the Madrid gathering. But the head of the Presbyterian delegation questioned whether these missionaries represented the Mozambican people, while one leader insisted that the Catholic Church was too compromised, citing as an example the extreme case of the archbishop of Lourenço Marques. In conclusion, the Picpus explained that there were two faces to the Catholic Church, the official church and the church of the people. The Protestants concluded that there could only be local collaboration with Catholics, and only about such issues as bible translation.[57]

Conclusion

This chapter looked at the position of the Roman Catholic Church in the face of decolonization in central Mozambique in the 1960s and 1970s. It focused on the diversity of positions among the clergy, explored how different missionary groups influenced each other, and considered the specific case of the Dutch Picpus missionaries. What it uncovered is, first, a great diversity of positions among the clergy, not just in favor or against the church taking a stand about decolonization, but also about how to make that stand (or not). The White Fathers departure from Mozambique in 1971 crystallized the debate and, while many missionaries agreed with the critical stance of the White Fathers, particularly in view of the hierarchy's political conservatism, most did not want to leave Mozambique. Some thought the church should avoid politics, others reckoned they should stay in Mozambique to provide pastoral help to a people affected bywar, and a few decided to stay to proactively help the liberation movement inside of Mozambique. The latter position was that of the Burgos Fathers, who became adepts of liberation theology in the late 1960s and went on to contact and work with Frelimo after 1971.

There were three broad models on how to promote decolonization in central Mozambique—leaving to protest the church's collusion with the colonial situation (White Fathers), staying to try to help shift the situation in favor of decolonization (Burgos missionaries), and staying to help reform colonialism in favor of more racial integration and towards medium-term autonomy or independence. Only the Franciscans were wholly in favor of colonialism and/or opposed to decolonization—and even there divergences began to appear in the 1970s among younger priests. These three options did not exist abstractly only; they were debated within the church in several locations, most of which, we uncovered, had developed as a result of Vatican II—missionary weeks, pastoral weeks, Catechetic centers, and the Nazaré Centre for Pastoral Investigation. These were sites of congregational intermixing and idea exchange intended primarily to update the pastoral approach and ecclesial structure of the church in line with Vatican II; but they led to wider discussions and broader actions, including in relation to politics. It should be said that the archdiocese of Beira was quite unique in Mozambique for its diversity and the vitality of its debate. While it may therefore not be representative of other dioceses, it played the role of the avant-garde for the whole territory and it offers a perfect place to glimpse how change unfolded internally, within a diocese in connection to other dioceses, to the Vatican, and the rest of the world.

In relation to the historiography of Mozambique, the chapter looked at dynamics and debates within the church to understand how change resulted from internal factors. This was intended as an addition and correction to the common view that the Catholic Church in Mozambique (and in the Portuguese colonies) was wholly colonialist and only saw "cracks" (and exceptions) when pressure was applied by the liberation war and the symmetric rise in repression by the Portuguese colonial state, including massacres. Such internal analysis has revealed the role of Vatican II in changing the structures and dynamics of the church in Mozambique and the role of particular congregations in pushing for a debate about decolonization and a stand against it, namely the White Fathers and the Burgos Fathers. Other individuals, including sisters, Portuguese secular priests, and missionaries from other congregations had a role. Outside of the archdiocese of Beira, other congregations and one bishop also played a part, not least the Comboni missionaries and Bishop Manuel Vieira Pinto (who had been involved in the archdiocese of Beira as apostolic administrator), decided to declare publicly in 1974 that they were in favor of independence—they were duly expelled by the Portuguese. In sum, looking at the internal dynamics of the Catholic Church has revealed a more complex picture than known so far and altered the chronology of how the church changed its stance in relation to colonialism, including the fact that change began in the early 1960s, before the liberation war began.

CHAPTER 9

Contesting Christian Nationalisms in Pre-Independence Swaziland

Joel Cabrita

In mid-1960, the future of independent Swaziland (renamed Eswatini in 2018) seemed clear to all. The British were drawing up an interim constitution and making plans for an orderly transition of power to the Swaziland Progressive Party (SPP). This was the country's first Black political party, an organization that had emerged from an association of educated Christian emaSwati in the 1920s. Representing the interests of urban teachers, ministers, lawyers, and doctors, the Progressives stood for universal franchise, the progress of Swaziland along Western democratic lines, and an unwavering belief in education and literacy. British administrators considered these to be sound men (the party was largely, but not solely, composed of male figures). These were individuals recognizable to the colonial administration as modern politicians with whom they could work in Swaziland's transition to independence.

Yet all this was not to be. Within just four years, the educated Christian Progressives were routed by a royalist clique centered around the hereditary paramount chief of the emaSwati, Sobhuza II. Crucial to Sobhuza's success was the religious legitimation he received from a very different source than the Progressives' middle-class Christian respectability. Prophetic indigenous churches known as Zionists lent their support to Sobhuza in claiming his reign was divinely ordained. Zionist prophets lambasted the educated Christianity of the Progressives, claiming that their own spirit-infused Pentecostalism was a more accurate reflection of divine will. The alliance of prophets and king worked. By 1964, in the aftermath of the Swazi protectorate's first elections, the Christian Progressives were ousted, imprisoned, exiled, or co-opted by the monarchy. Their liberal-democratic vision of nationalism had been defeated by a rival version of decolonizing thought, one that vested power in a theocratic monarchy and eschewed the egalitarianism of democratic elections. This proved an enduring state of affairs. To this day (2022), independent Swaziland has never held entirely free elections and it persists in being Africa's last absolute monarchy. Its current ruler, Mswati III (son of Sobhuza II), holds complete power, banning all political parties. Zionist churches continue to offer theological legitimation of the authoritarian monarchy as divinely appointed.

The case of Swaziland invites us to challenge typical narratives of decolonization and, in particular, the role that Christianity played in this process. Scholars have usually cast decolonization in triumphalist terms. Decolonization is commonly framed as a liberatory transition from European to democratic self-rule. Historians have offered a similarly positive reading of Christianity's role in this process. They have showed how, across Africa, political parties very similar to the Progressives—male-dominated associations of Christian mission-educated middle-class elites—gained power as Europeans wound down their flags. Historian E. A. Ayandele argued that this genteel Christianity was a force for good, equipping African converts with political aspirations by teaching them "the intoxicating message of Christian equality and fraternity." More concretely, Ayandele also outlined how the religious associations and publications of mission stations familiarized converts with new modes of political expression, allowing them to gain vital leadership skills through holding religious office and acquiring literate communication skills.[1] Christianity, in other words, was a school that prepared Africans to take leadership of their countries as colonial powers departed.

Ayandele spoke for Nigeria, but others noted similar patterns in the rest of the continent. In neighbouring South Africa, independence would only happen in 1994, but the leadership of the party that assumed power, the African National Congress, was of a near-identical middle-class Christian demographic as that of the Swazi Progressives. Further north, in Zimbabwe, devout Catholic schoolteacher Robert Mugabe would rule over the newly independent country from 1980 under the auspices of ZANU-PF; in Zambia, Kenneth Kaunda, son of a Church of Scotland minister and also a schoolteacher, became the first independent president; in Botswana, Seretse Khama, leader of the Botswana Democratic Party was elected first president of the country in

1966—he was a London Temple–trained barrister and a devout Methodist. It seemed the days of traditional political authorities like chiefs and kings were at an end. The era of modern enlightened progressive rulers, men formed in the classrooms and churches of Christian mission stations, had dawned.

Swaziland does not fit this pattern. The following chapter describes the defeat of modernizing Christian nationalists by a force that many historians assumed had disappeared during the decolonizing era—traditional African monarchy. Swaziland's breaking of the theoretical mould is instructive, inviting us to reconsider the very nature of decolonization. Swaziland's history shows us that decolonization was repressive as well as egalitarian; that decolonization simultaneously liberated African populations and entrenched new elites; and that decolonization both ushered in representative democracy as well as celebrated authority that rested upon inheritance and divine appointment.

Recognizing these contradictions prompts us to reconsider our deeply engrained teleologies of nationalism. Much work has been done to show the limitations of Benedict Anderson's territorially bound version of nationalism, one predicated on the individual's possession of liberal-democratic rights. Recent work by Adom Getachew and Manu Goswami convincingly demonstrates the limits (as well as the non-inevitability) of the nation-state by pointing to expansive transnational imagined communities that existed alongside and often well before the modern nation-state.[2] The role of Christianity in these creative acts of "worldmaking" (to use Getachew's phrase) is well documented. Studies have looked at the role of Christian millenarianism in Marcus Garvey's transatlantic United Negro Improvement League, as well as the religious and political work done by Black Methodist networks in the modern Atlantic world.[3]

Yet still much less understood is a very different variety of "worldmaking" thought. These are forms of political organization that are hierarchical, monarchic, and theocratic, visions of the nation that rely upon the extraordinary powers of divinely anointed individuals rather than the representative nature of an elected individual. Often, they look inward to the importance of ethnic bonds rather than outward to global communities. These religiously inflected forms of statehood eschew the "disenchanted" Christianity of modern Protestantism, and they rebut the liberal politics that often accompany such forms of rational Protestantism. Anderson treated these hierarchical politics as premodern precursors to modern nationalism, and he assumed they would dissolve as modern nation-states came into being. Yet, these theocratic forms of statehood continued to be highly relevant to agents of decolonization in the

1950s and 1960s, including in Swaziland. We cannot dismiss these theocratic states as puzzling anachronisms; rather, the case study of Swaziland invites us to understand them as integral to decolonization and to modern twentieth-century politics.

Eschewing a portrayal of African nationalists as a monolithic whole, what emerges in 1960s Swaziland is the rich variety of indigenous decolonizing discourses, the textured heterogeneity of Swati responses to the end of colonial rule, and the internally contested meaning of independence from the British Empire. Quite simply, not all Africans shared an identical vision for independent Swaziland. In similar fashion, the following chapter also complicates the role that Christianity played in African decolonizing discourses. The case of Swaziland reminds us that Christian practitioners could contribute to repressive—as well as emancipatory—outcomes in an age of decolonization. While many assumed a symbiotic connection between Christianity and modern nationalist movements in Africa, decolonizing Swaziland disabuses us of the notion that Christianity was a predetermined emancipatory force—a spiritual preparation for modern democracy, as historians like Ayandele would have it. Instead, the role that Christianity played in African decolonizing discourses was as multiple and varied as the very nature of Christianity in Africa itself. Christianity possessed no inherent qualities disposing its adherents to liberal democracy on a continent newly free of European rulers. Instead, Swaziland's decolonization process shows us that while many Christians may have opposed British rule, they supported the divinely anointed rule of an illiberal monarch.

The Cream of the Nation

The mid-nineteenth century saw a tiny class of Christian emaSwati emerge in the Southern African territory of Swaziland.[4] Early Christian missionaries (largely Methodists) clashed with traditional authorities decidedly unsure about these new proselytisers.[5] Ousted by the Swati King, Methodist missionaries would only return to Swaziland in 1880. Representatives from other mission churches soon followed. By 1936, there were twenty-three different churches in the territory. Methodists, Anglicans, Seventh Day Adventists, and Catholics had the largest followings, although by the 1936 census nearly 70 percent of emaSwati still defined themselves "heathen."[6] Many Christian converts were drawn from the ranks of commoners. Following a pattern discernible across Southern Africa, traditional aristocrats simply had less reason to convert. Commoners, on the other hand, hoped for greater freedom and equality in the church than in the pronounced hierarchies of Swati society.[7] Many were women who similarly found the promise of greater standing within the church.[8]

These Swati converts exemplified the distinct values of the new Christian African class. These were women and men adapted to Western ways. An individual's possession of property, contrasted against older communal land ownership, was a defining feature (causing tensions with traditional chiefs, who historically controlled access to land).[9] Christian emaSwati were also committed to equality with whites—this despite the fact that Swaziland, a protectorate of Great Britain, had no independent status. Yet, converts felt their possession of Christianity—and the associated skill of literacy—marked them as the equals of any persons in the world. Correspondingly, Christians distanced themselves from non-Christian compatriots, denouncing old traditions as paganism and celebrating their status as "civilized" moderns whom the colonial state exempted from "native law."[10] In the 1930s, the anthropologist Hilda Kuper heard one young Christian man remark of his non-Christian brethren dancing the Incwala (a rainmaking kingly ritual): "Fancy still dressing in skins and feathers. These people are quite uncivilized."[11] Reflecting their sense of superiority over non-Christians, many Swati Christians referred to themselves as "the cream of the nation."[12] This small community of Christians flourished remarkably. Many were teachers and preachers (both professions were employed by mission stations) as well as small independent farmers. Women were almost exclusively teachers and nurses.[13]

In early 1929, Swati Christians formed the Swaziland Progressive Association. The name reflected members' identification with the progressive values of Christianity and literacy, and their belief in eventual attainment of equality with whites. The Progressive Association's precepts affirmed "the essential dignity of every human being irrespective of race, colour, or creed."[14] Membership was "open to any person of adult age and of good character"[15] (despite the rhetoric of egalitarianism, members were exclusively male until the 1960s). Their official language was English, and meetings focused on the commercial interests of the new Christian class, protecting it against racist discrimination from the colonial government.[16] Meetings included topics like "business stands in towns, sale of firearms, Employment of Native Clerks, loans for Natives from Agricultural Loan Funds." The Progressive Association worried about sexual morality as well as the political future of Swaziland, which a land-greedy South Africa had long had its eyes upon; it made submissions to the colonial administration about "hooliganism at private dances and night concerts, seduction of Native girls by Europeans as well as a protest against incorporation of Swaziland into the Union [of South Africa]."[17] It was hardly a radical organization; members stood to observe three minutes' silence after the death of a prominent colonial administrator.[18] It was also a struggling association, largely due to the miniscule size of the Christian intelligentsia relative to the bulk of emaSwati. The Progressive Association's newspaper, *Izwi lama Swazi*, only ran for six months in 1934 before folding. Its largest ever sale was thirty-five issues; average sales were twenty copies per issue.[19]

Despite the limited nature of the Progressive Association, the hereditary leader of Swaziland, Paramount Chief Sobhuza II, worried about its eventual political implications.[20] In particular, Sobhuza expressed anxiety about educated Christian emaSwati cutting themselves off from their compatriots, and that they might "support the government against Swazi institutions."[21] He also claimed, in vocal representation to the British administration on the topic, that the rights of his people were already adequately contained within the traditional Swati constitution. The contours of future conflicts were already emerging: educated Christian emaSwati versus the Swati monarch and the entire edifice of "traditionalism." The British government both stoked disunity between these different factions and, simultaneously, tried to neutralize it, with resident commissioner Ainsworth Dickson maintaining to the Progressive Association that "I regard you, the better educated Natives, as an advance guard of the Swazi Nation but I must emphasize you owe full and direct allegiance to the Paramount Chief."[22]

This Christian elite underwent great growth in the 1940s, with World War II something of a turning point in their fortunes. At the urging of the paramount chief, two thousand emaSwati men were recruited to fight in North Africa.[23] The Christian intelligentsia embraced the decade's jingoistic mood, correctly discerning opportunities for advancement in so doing. Progressives donated to official war funds, organized fund-raising concerts, and offered woollen goods knitted by members' wives.[24] As did elites throughout Africa, the Progressive Association leveraged its support of Britain to argue for rights and eventual independence. Their membership drive of December 1945 linked war participation with the advance of the "intelligentsia": "If you are not members, join today its ever increasing ranks of determined intelligentsia, insistent upon the fact that in this war our comrades shall not have died in vain."[25] J. J. Nquku, the chief inspector of "native" schools, and a leading

Progressive Association member, railed against discriminatory laws by citing Africans' contribution to the war: "It is utter folly at this juncture when the Empire wants our coordinated efforts to win the war yet the relationship between whites and black is further aggravated by undemocratic laws."[26]

Partly in response to demands such as these from across the continent, postwar Britain undertook wholesale economic development of its African colonies. In the case of their Swati protectorate, officials were aware they had spent virtually no money on the territory and that it was woefully "underdeveloped." In a belated effort to invest in the protectorate, an ambitious government-led malaria programme was embarked upon in the 1950s.[27] The postwar years also saw a dramatic rise in capital investment in Swaziland and industry's rapid growth. The British Colonial Development Corporation (created to implement the Second Colonial Development and Welfare Act of 1945) became the primary underwriter for large-scale development projects, including plantation agriculture, irrigation schemes, and mineral extraction.[28] All this meant that the small Christian middle-class, employed in towns and by many of these new industries, grew dramatically. One way to measure this is via the growth in the number of educated emaSwati. In 1929, there were five thousand children attending school; in 1955, there were 21,441.[29] A teacher training college, the first in the country, was opened in Matsapha in 1953.[30]

Paradoxically, the inauguration of the apartheid regime in South Africa also strengthened Swaziland's Black elite. The ascent to power of the Nationalist Party in 1948 hardened Progressives' moral outrage at minority white rule. It also meant that political exiles from the apartheid regime flooded into Swaziland.[31] One was Douglas Lukhele, the first Swati lawyer, who had formerly worked in the law offices of Nelson Mandela and Oliver Tambo.[32] Another was Regina Gelana Twala, the second Black woman to gain a degree from the University of the Witwatersrand. Twala had done ethnographic fieldwork in Swaziland in the 1940s and was well known to Sobhuza. Apartheid police had arrested Twala in 1952 for her activism in the Defiance Campaign. By 1954, as with many others, Twala relocated to Swaziland to avoid further harassment. Many of these new South African exiles would become key figures in the Progressive Association, seeing resistance to British rule in Swaziland as a direct continuation of their fight against apartheid. The African National Congress—to which many had belonged in South Africa—exerted influence across the border. In 1949, the Progressive Association indicted British rule in Swaziland, copying word-for-word from an ANC document created earlier that year.[33]

Throughout the 1940s and 1950s this small elite class continued to grow. These were years of renewed nationalist zeal, full of commitment to the idea of an independent Swaziland. In 1949, the Progressive Association published new resolutions. It not only "expressed its gratitude to Divine Providence" but, for the first time, also directly stated "the ultimate aim in Swaziland should be to prepare the Swazis for self government."[34] In 1949, *Izwi lama Swazi* was relaunched (this time, it would run until 1964) and the Progressive Association launched a new publication, *The Swazilander/Ungwane* (1955).[35] *The Swazilander/Ungwane*'s first issue began with a statement of "religious faith," noting our "only hope lies in the universal following of the teachings of Christ" and declaring itself "standing against all exploitation of the voiceless non-European Swazilander." Progressives stood for "freedom not serfdom" and "democracy not dictatorship."[36] Decolonizing fervor was also evident in the Progressive Association's push for the adoption of a dedicated siSwati orthography and rejection of isiZulu (the widely spoken South African language).[37] Historically scathing of indigenous culture, the Progressive Association now discerned the value of strategic appeals to Swati custom. In 1959, Progressives called for a public holiday on December 16, marking the traditionalist Incwala ceremony.[38]

Progressives signalled their new openness to tradition in other ways. Historically allied with European missions, by the 1940s Progressives were trying to change public perceptions of them as pro-European. Many Christian emaSwati now felt continued European missionary influence was antithetical to the Black elite's interests. Educated emaSwati worried about "denominationalism," the fractured, fragmented, and multiple nature of Christian missions. Thus, leading emaSwati, many of whom were Progressives, decided to establish a new national church led by emaSwati themselves, reflecting the values of their class as well as asserting autonomy from missionaries. In 1944, the United Christian Church of Africa (UCCA) was launched, with its first chairperson John Nquku.[39] The UCCA presented itself as a platform for a unified Swati Christian identity in the service of a nascent nationalism. Christianity and Swati "custom" were affirmed as mutually complementary; the new organization's constitution stated "its foundation is indigenous. . . . It tolerates all national customs so long as they are not inconsistent with Christian principles, and for its aim so far as possible intends to Christianize such customs."[40] Its architects hoped for a distinctly Swati church—sympathetic to "national customs"—while maintaining a focus on educated progressiveness.

Yet the perception nonetheless persisted that the Christian intelligentsia was composed of non-Swatis disloyal to the paramount chief, Sobhuza II. In part, this was a problem created by the British administration. For positions requiring special knowledge, and since the number of educated emaSwati was so small, the colonial government had long recruited individuals from South Africa. There was much controversy that the president of the Progressives, and the first Black inspector of schools in the protectorate, John Nquku, was in fact a Zulu from South Africa. Letters to the *Times of Swaziland* noted, "The next man appointed [native supervisor of schools] must be a Swazi born and grew up in the country, a man who knows the customs of the people and speaks their language. It must not be a detribalized person. It must be a person who acknowledges the Paramount Chief as his Supreme Chief."[41] Suspicion of "detribalized" foreigners in powerful administrative positions was widely shared. Another letter said, "All important positions have to be occupied by Imports only is a serious error."[42] Sobhuza himself worried the Progressives "would be taken over by non-Swazi with different loyalties and ideas."[43]

Throughout the 1950s, tensions simmered between the royalists and the Progressives. Efforts were made to smooth over differences. S. T. M. Sukati, Sobhuza's official representative in the Swaziland administration and a bachelor's degree holder, himself, reassuringly remarked the educated and the uneducated "might be divided like fingers but they were still members of the same hand."[44] Nquku and the Progressives publicly professed loyalty to Sobhuza, referring to the older days when "the conservative mass of our people viewed the Swaziland Progressive Association with suspicion, mistaking it for a rival body to the Swazi National Council [Sobhuza's advisory group]." Yet, in the present, Nquku was emphatic that the situation was quite different: Progressives "stand behind our chief leader, the King of the Swazi, and as intelligentsia, the cream of the Nation, we have pledged ourselves to support him."[45]

At the same time, and despite mouthing support for Sobhuza II, Progressives still named the key hardships of Swaziland as "Tribalism, Witchcraftism, Superstitionism . . . unless these all are done away with, there is little prospect of organizing Swazis. . . . These are the enemies of the Progressive, economically, religiously, socially."[46] John Nquku argued against Sobhuza's mandate to wear "traditional clothes" to royal rituals like Incwala: "To discriminate on the basis of dress would not be good, because it would just divide people."[47] Progressives lashed out against the powerful traditionalist body of the Swazi National Council that advised Sobhuza, with Nquku commenting that "things are working out in other countries like Basutoland and Bechuanaland because the people who represent [the people] are taking instructions from the ordinary people and they do not go to the public with some royal decree."[48] British officials resisted Progressives' efforts to bypass the power of the Swazi National Council, insisting submissions to the government be made solely by Sobhuza. Otherwise, as an ex-resident commissioner put it, Progressives would "usurp the functions of this Swazi authority."[49] Nquku and the Progressive Association reacted angrily, asserting "democracy assures us that no free public expressions would be muzzled. . . . The Association fully believes that in a British Protectorate it is entitled to the privilege of expressing its views undiluted or undistorted."[50]

By 1960, tensions between Sobhuza and the Progressives came to a head. Signalling both their break with the monarchy and their ambitions to lead a future independent Swaziland, in mid-1960, John Nquku and several Progressives inaugurated the Swaziland Progressive Party (SPP), dissolving the Association. They were joined by other educated emaSwati, including the country's first Swati doctor, Ambrose Zwane, as well as educated exiles like Regina Twala (who became women's secretary of the party).[51] The SPP aimed to establish universal suffrage and to adhere to the principle of one man, one vote, eradicating dynastic hierarchy-based politics. In 1960, poised on the brink of independence negotiations with Britain, it indeed seemed the Swaziland's future lay in the hands of the Christian elite.

But "The Cream of the Nation"—as they liked to call themselves—were not the only advocates for independence. They were not even the most numerous representatives of Christianity in Swaziland. As late as 1966, 87 percent of emaSwati were living in rural traditional settings without education, no affiliation to European-style Christianity, and distanced from Progressive-level education.[52] There were thus other rival nationalist visions circulating during these years. Some were also profoundly informed by Christianity, albeit—as we shall now see—of a very different kind.

Tinhlanhla Tami ("My Very Own Crazy Ones")

Progressive Swati Christians punched above their weight. While positioning themselves as significant to the future of independent Swaziland, they did not represent the majority of Christian adherence. By the 1960s, many Christians belonged to a different type of Christian organization, loyal to one or another of the hundreds of Zionist churches in the country. Swaziland's

Zionists (unrelated to Jewish Zionism) were a loose federation of hundreds of evangelical churches, entirely African in leadership and membership, and that had existed in the country since the early 1920s. Zionists stemmed from a controversial faith-healing church in the North American Midwest calling itself the Christian Catholic Apostolic Church in Zion. At the turn of the century, the Illinois-based leader of the church, John Alexander Dowie—the self-proclaimed second incarnation of Elijah the Prophet—had sent testimonial literature and missionaries to South Africa. Dowie's church grew across Southern Africa, many drawn by its promise of bodily health via prayer. By the 1960s, it had spawned thousands of offshoot churches, most with little or no link to the Illinois church. But still in common with the North American church, the Southern African Zionist movement spoke for a populist rejection of educated elites and an insistence on ordinary believers' power to heal bodily affliction.[53] Zionism became especially successful in Swaziland, not least due to the movement of migrant laborers between South Africa and Swaziland. By the 1940s, Zionists accounted for half of all emaSwati Christians.[54]

Despite their popularity, Zionists faced an upward struggle establishing themselves in Swaziland. On the one hand, they faced harassment from European missionaries who correctly perceived them as rivals to their own popularity. Missionaries "had nothing favourable to say about Zionists," dismissing them as hardly Christian.[55] They darkly suspected Zionists' healing powers invoked "pagan" healing techniques. As one missionary put it in 1937, Zionists "are largely taking the place of witchfinders amongst the Natives."[56] On the other hand, Zionists had to also contend with the hostility of the educated Progressive Christians. The League of Churches was an umbrella association of all churches in Swaziland. Heavily dominated by Progressives in the 1940s (not a single Zionist featured among the league's officers),[57] the league frequently portrayed Zionists to the British administration as uneducated, lacking in discipline, and a danger to society. In correspondence with the colonial secretary, powerful John Nquku "doubt[ed] whether it would be correct to encourage the wholesale registration of these churches which are not properly established and under no good governmental control." Damningly, he noted, "I fear by [encouraging Zionists' registration], I may be encouraging mischief."[58] These were tensions largely fuelled by the class-based hostility of educated Progressives toward unschooled Zionists. Zionists' populist values directly contradicted the elitism of the Progressives. One prominent Zionist, J. Mthethwa, complained "the [Progressives] treat the Zionists as if they were children and ignorant. . . . The leaders of these [Progressive] churches must guard against exploiting Zionists because they are illiterate."[59]

Rivalries were further stoked by the fact that Zionists enjoyed a close relationship with the Swati monarchy. In many respects, this alliance between Sobhuza and the Zionists was a surprising one. Despite their mutual mistrust of educated elites, Zionists' evangelical casting aside of traditional medicine and alcohol set them against traditional Swati elders. Zionists' peripatetic lifestyles, continually crossing borders to attend far-flung services, further alienated them from traditional authorities eager to shore up dissolving territorial boundaries. Elderly Swati Zionist minister Soul Sibandze remembered how his father and others would travel on foot for days, hiking over high mountains, to attend Easter services across the border in South Africa.[60] A 1937 survey of Zionists in Swaziland noted they "tend to be resistant to Tribal Authority and go wandering over the country."[61] Moreover, Zionists also incurred the wrath of traditional authorities (and British colonial administrators) on account of their popularity with women, many of whom left homesteads and male relatives to devote themselves to their church. The same 1937 inquiry claimed Zionist men would assert "the Spirit moves me to go into the fields with Mrs So-and-So, and pray. . . . Misconduct then takes place."[62] Swati chiefs were warned by colonial administrators and missionaries that Zionist misconduct in "seducing" young girls should be reported immediately.[63]

Yet, despite the distance between these radical evangelicals and traditional authorities—the former striving for loyalty to God's Kingdom, the latter attempting to secure territorial polities—there were also important convergences between Zionists and ethnic Swati leaders. Sobhuza's sympathy toward Zionists should be situated amid the ethnocultural revivals he pioneered during these years; his warmness toward Zionists was part of his overall effort to preserve Swati autonomy in the face of European governance. A 1923 Swati deputation to London had attempted to reverse the controversial 1907 Land Partition. Its failure led Swati royalists to view ethnocultural revival, rather than territorial integrity, as key to avoiding Swaziland's assimilation within the Union of South Africa and subjection to its racist legislation.[64] Throughout much of the twentieth century, Sobhuza attempted to rebuild the prestige of the Swati monarchy, deliberately reviving old monarchical rituals such as the annual rainmaking Incwala ceremony, as well as the regimental age-grade system, *imibutho*, that required men to serve the paramount chief at a palace. Sobhuza criticized Christian missionaries' provision of Western education for "causing the Swazi scholar to despise Swazi institutions and his indigenous culture."[65] Sobhuza's search was for a Christian identity that would bolster, rather than undermine, nascent cultural nationalism. Indeed, it was largely for all these reasons that Sobhuza viewed the Progressives with such disfavor, seeing their educated ways and disdain for "tradition" as a threat to his effort to reinvigorate Swati custom.

In Sobhuza's eyes, and in contrast to Progressives, Zionists seemed to stand for a uniquely Swati Christian identity, detached from Western-style education and loyal to the monarchy. While mission churches and Progressive Christians stressed book learning as part of the intertwined package of Christianity and civilization, evangelical Zionists insisted the only guidance for the people of God was the Bible and the Holy Spirit. With the exception of Johanna Nxumalo—an important early Zionist leader who was a schoolteacher—leading Zionist figures in Swaziland tended not to be educated. None of the Swati Zionist founding fathers (Daniel Nkonyane, Stephen Mavimbela, Andrew Zwane) were literate, something their Zionist followers to this day emphasize as evidence of their piety.[66] Thus, while Western missionaries criticized Zionists as uneducated "fanatics," for a royal circle increasingly anxious that Christianity estranged emaSwati from their national ways, Zionists' reluctance to enter the educational enterprise was a welcome sign of independence from Western culture. Zionists' reputation as the church for the rural poor and the uneducated grew as the century progressed. A study conducted in the 1970s found most Zionists in Swaziland had education only "between Grade 1 and Standard II" (the earliest years of elementary school) while another counted only one in eight ministers had any theological education.[67] One contemporary Zionist's memory of the church in the 1960s was that "the majority of ministers were not educated, [they] had gone up to maybe primary school level."[68] In contrast to the snobbishness of the educated Progressives, Zionists' lack of learning signalled a humble grassroots piety, in touch with the aspirations of ordinary emaSwati. Simon Mavimbela, grandson of the famous prophet Stephen Mavimbela, commented, "We Zionists [were] willing to go to poor, dirty people."[69]

Furthermore, as the century progressed, Zionists became increasingly willing to sanction aspects of indigenous culture, practices that both European missionaries and Swati Progressives denounced as satanic, including polygamy. Indeed, it was these very practices that formed the bedrock of the Swati monarchy. One prominent Zionist of the 1950s defended his church's adoption of indigenous practices on the grounds of patriotism and national pride: "One was worried whether the customs of the Swazi were found so wanting that it became necessary for customs of other nations to be superimposed on Swazis."[70] As part of the wider traditionalist shift amongst Zionists, the figure of the prophet who invoked ancestral spirits became increasingly powerful in many congregations. In an earlier period, Zionist prophets and ordinary believers were reluctant to admit reliance upon ancestral spirits, although doubtless this did occur. But by the 1950s, prophecy via deceased family members had become more common. This trend was particularly evident in the case of the Jericho Zionists. Founded by a former migrant worker to Johannesburg, the Jericho church grew into Swaziland's largest Zionist church, with around 30,000 members by 1990.[71] Jericho was first and foremost a church of ancestral spirits, with prophets invoking the guidance of their relatives during the whirling of the *siguco* (an energetic circular dance-prayer) and recommending church members pay homage to their ancestors to improve their lot in life. Indicating the respect "Jerichos" accorded to deceased family members, their leader, Elias Vilakati, stated in the late 1970s that "I do not see how you can be a Christian if you do not respect the traditional customs. Even those who are dead should be respected and we should have feasts together with them."[72]

The institution of the prophet signalled a transition to a more hierarchical and secretive religious dynamic, contrasting with the previous egalitarianism of the Zionist church. Afforded regular opportunity for displaying their divinatory gifts during *siguco*, prophets became influential figures, wielding authority over the congregation and even appointed church officials. Prophets were always a small but powerful minority; most Zionist churches only had around 4 percent of the congregation renowned for these abilities.[73] This tiny spiritual elite was largely composed of older men, many with little or no education.[74] Some prophets also occupied leadership positions such as bishop, minister, or evangelist, although this was not necessarily the case, as a prophet's gifts were sufficient to place him in a position of authority regardless of formal appointment.[75] Thus, the institution of prophecy served to prop up enormously powerful and older, largely male, individuals. Suggesting the large reserves of authority available to those who claimed inspiration both from the Holy Spirit and from their ancestors, Vilakati once stated, "I progress through prophecies. . . . Jehovah said I am greater than all people on the earth."[76] My point here is that, throughout the 1950s, Zionism moved closer to the values of the indigenous monarchy: both favored hierarchy, espoused esoteric rather than open knowledge, preferred dynastic male leadership rather than female participation in religious affairs, and advocated for divine appointment rather than democratic election.

Sobhuza, moreover, was viewed by many Swati Zionists as a divinely ordained patron who had rescued them from persecution by the colonial government and hostile white missionaries. In the 1930s, Sobhuza had publicly invited beleaguered Zionist leaders to come under his protection. While Zionists were beset by opposition from European missionaries, Progressive Christians, and the British, Sobhuza positioned himself as the protector of these indigenous Christians. In a famous speech, Sobhuza proclaimed Zionists were "tinhlanha tami" (my very own crazy ones), thus turning on its head the common criticism that Zionists' claims to be inspired by the Holy Spirit meant they were "mad."[77] A common saying amongst Swati Zionists, still in use today, is that "as a hen does to its chicks, so the King protected us under the wing of his arm from the British."[78] For their own part, Zionist ministers were viewed as spiritual protectors of the royal family. In the 1950s, a crisis hit Sobhuza's palace when the hut of one of his wives burned down; this was attributed to witchcraft. Sobhuza called upon Zionists to deploy their spiritual weapons against evildoers. He cast Zionists, armed with divine healing prowess, as a new sacred "regiment," devoted to defending the royal family: "You are an army out to fight a beast, and when it begins to roar, you should say to yourselves: 'I wish I could just get at it with my weapon.' This is a challenge for you and with your weapons of faith and prayer . . . this is your battle as Christians, fight it and win!"[79] While Progressives were Sobhuza's enemy, Zionists were valued allies.

Zionists' ability to connect with a traditionalist constituency helped them grow in power throughout the 1950s and 1960s, outstripping elite Progressives. A 1960 survey found Zionist churches "had grown considerably in numbers" since the 1930s.[80] By the 1950s, in contrast to their prior marginalization by Progressives, Zionists had gained control of the League of Swazi Churches. The election of J. Mthethwa, a Zionist minister, to the league presidency in 1950 both reflected this growing popularity of Zionists as well as gave them new influence within the country's official Christian affairs.[81] In elections for new league officials, in 1954, half the elected individuals were Zionist.[82] In 1959, at the Good Friday Easter meeting of the league, an observer found "other churches were swamped by emaZione [Zionists] and had to withdraw, now calling the League meeting Into ye MaZione [a thing of the Zionists]."[83] John Nquku's United Christian Church of Africa also folded in this decade, largely due to declining membership and internal fractures.[84] In 1950, Progressives admitted their ecumenical aspirations had failed: "The United Christian

Church of Africa is United no longer."[85] The same 1960 survey cited above also revealed that while "the UCCA is sometimes described as the Swazi National Church, it appears to have singularly few adherents." By contrast, the survey found Daniel Nkonyane's Christian Catholic Apostolic Holy Spirit Church in Zion—one of the largest Zionist churches in Swaziland—had a far larger membership than the UCCA.[86]

Not surprisingly, as the Progressives declined in public standing, tensions flared between them and Zionists. Progressives tried to compensate for their dwindling influence by casting aspersions on the Zionists, their key religious competitors. John Nquku used the Progressive newspaper, *Izwi lama Swazi*, to attack Zionists as ignorant, superstitious, and detrimental to national unity. Only the Progressives could be trusted to safely steer Swaziland to independence. Nquku contrasted Zionists' divided state against Progressives' attempts to create a national church: "When churches are divided like this it is a state of affairs so bad that even though believers may pray for the sick, they will not be delivered."[87] Discerning the anti-democratic thrust of many Zionist churches, Nquku attacked Zionist prophets as status-obsessed, lambasting them for pursuing prestige and authority rather than enjoying a true spiritual calling: "Those who seek status will lose the way of Jesus Christ. . . . They cripple the brethren because they speak well, but their deeds are opposed to what they say with their mouths."[88] Lacking the platform of a periodical like *Izwi lama Swazi* or *The Swazilander/Ungwane*, I have no record of Zionist leaders rebuffing these criticisms in print. But they did not need to. They were already on a winning streak.

For Sobhuza, seeking to neutralize the Progressives' vision for a democratic constitutional Swaziland, the Zionists were perfect allies. As we shall now see, the monarchy and the Zionists successfully worked together to undermine and eventually oust Progressives' dreams of a democratic Swaziland once the British had departed. There was little the Progressives could do to withstand this powerful alliance; their elite vision for egalitarian democracy was no match for dynastic theocratic monarchism.

Downfall

British colonial administrators anticipated an independent Swaziland in which the Progressive Party would play a major role. Their vision was for a gradual, orderly transition to a constitutional monarchy in which Sobhuza II would still be active but merely a figurehead. Reflecting the long-standing nurturing the administration had offered the educated elite, the resident commissioner of this period, Brian Marwick, envisioned a one man, one vote constitution in which modern political forces—most of all the nascent nationalist movement led by John Nquku—would play a leading role.[89] He and other officials strongly believed in the necessity of transforming what Marwick described to the anthropologist Hilda Kuper as a "feudal society" and a "top-down monarchy" into a "modern democracy under a constitutional king."[90] The Zionists, it goes without saying, were wholly absent from British officials' thinking. With administrators' limited definition of what constituted "politics," they failed to see these churches as important players in an independent Swaziland.

Sobhuza, unsurprisingly, strongly objected to this roadmap for independence. From the early 1960s, dating to the formation of the SPP, he began to cast the phenomenon of a political party in carefully timed public speeches as "unSwati." One of Sobhuza's most famous utterances was his pithy characterization of political parties as "carbon copying of cultures of other people, like dung beetles who feed on excreta."[91] Sobhuza strategically argued Western-style parties, like Nquku's SPP, were simply not applicable to Swaziland, and that they would breed division. Addressing SPP members, Sobhuza counselled, "The policy of one man, one vote, can only lead us into hardship," calling for the "immediate abolition" of parties.[92] Sobhuza's suspicion of parties as "non-Swati" found widespread support among traditionalists, many in the rural areas, as well as Zionist promoters. There was, for example, the following from an "open letter to all the political leaders" written by A. Z. Khumalo and published in *The Times*: "What race are the political parties going to make us? Black Europeans, devoid of their nationhood, their laws and customs, mere mimics of the Western way of life?"[93] In a speech from July 1960, Sobhuza announced that "the European system of franchise with the principle of one man one vote was totally unfamiliar to the African and there was no good reason why such practices should be forced on the latter."[94]

The British were undeterred. At their instigation, a complex series of negotiations took place throughout the early 1960s in both Swaziland and London. The talks brought together the major players: British officials, Sobhuza and his representatives, the white settler community, and the political parties. Since the formation of the SPP in mid-1960, several rival parties had quickly sprouted up, most constituted by defectors from the SPP. The most significant of these competitors, represented at the talks in London, was the Ngwane National Liberatory Congress, led by Ambrose Zwane and to which Regina Twala had also defected. Negotiations between the British, the royalists, and key parties were fiery and frequently broke down. By 1963, exasperated and impatient, the British summarily imposed an interim constitution. No one liked the document. Both the royalists and the parties felt it insufficiently recognized their positions and gave too much power to their rivals. Sobhuza registered his disapproval of the new constitution by holding a country-wide referendum to gauge his subjects' opinion. This was a strategic move: Sobhuza knew he had little chance of reversing Britain's decision to impose the constitution, but he hoped the referendum's outcome would convince the British of mass support for the traditional regime. The referendum was, not surprisingly, a massive vote for Sobhuza, with 122,000 voting against the referendum and only 154 in its favor.[95]

Emboldened by his success, Sobhuza now decided to fight the political parties on their own terms. Shortly afterward, he formed a political party of his own to run in the elections of June 1964. Ever canny, Sobhuza, recognizing he was unable to change the constitution, which only allowed for representatives of political parties to stand, had decided to join one. Sobhuza and the traditionalists, given their former denigration of parties as un-Swati, dubbed their new organization the Imbokodvo National Movement. The stakes were high: the results of the 1964 election would determine the legislative council that would see Swaziland through to independence and beyond. The Imbokodvo National Movement ran on the independence of Swaziland from Britain and the retention of absolute power by Sobhuza. Imbokodvo energetically mobilized support for its cause, throwing the full weight of the monarchy and the funds of the Swazi national treasury behind its campaigning.[96]

Zionist churches, in particular, rallied around Sobhuza. By the early 1960s, the Zionists were as close to a national church as it came. Zionist prophets used key national events to argue that Sobhuza was divinely ordained, and they regularly lent their presence to key national rituals like the Incwala. During the Incwala of December 1963, Zionist prophets appeared in greater numbers than ever before, standing shoulder to shoulder in support of Sobhuza alongside traditional emaSwati warriors. Zionist ministers vocally urged members to attend Incwala as a show of support for their monarch. To fail to do was cast as a spiritual failing.[97] Zionist leaders also used a biblical grammar of divinely ordained kingship to argue for Sobhuza's legitimacy. In 1964, a prominent Zionist minister published rousing praises of Sobhuza in the national newspaper, *Izwi lama Swazi*: "Sobhuza is like Solomon of old in wisdom and his grandfather, Mbandzeni I, compares with Moses of old in Israel."[98] Jericho leader Vilakti similarly used his sermons throughout the early 1960s to remind believers the king was divinely ordained and that the democratic egalitarianism envisioned by the political parties ran counter to the Word of God: "It is good to respect your King, for even in heaven we shall not be equal, we shall still be made to stand around our kings of the earth."[99] When election day arrived, Zionist churches continued to play a key role in assuring monarchical rule, with "bus loads" of Zionists mobilized by their ministers to go to the polls for Imbokodvo candidates.[100]

Faced with the mobilization of church and king, this was a difficult campaign for the Progressives' political parties. Parties like the SPP and the NNLC lacked the financial resources to match the combined efforts of Sobhuza's Imbokodvo Movement and the Zionist churches. Much of the NNLC leadership was actually in jail (imprisoned by the British for their role in strike actions of the preceding year), and the organization was burdened with legal fees.[101] Money aside, all parties failed to reach the rural constituencies dominated by Zionists and traditionalists. Elite nationalists simply could not compete with the popular sway both Sobhuza and the Zionist churches held. Furthermore, the presence of several key women in the political parties—most of all, Regina Twala—seems to have harmed rather than helped their cause. During her campaigning for the 1964 election in rural communities, Twala would insist chairs be brought for the women rather than have them sit at the feet of their menfolk in the "traditional" style. Rural men deeply objected to this. Twala's neighbour and friend, Janet Aphane, remembered to me how "[Twala] used to argue with men; they would say she was enlightening the women too much." While her daughter Zanele recalled that "men didn't like her; they said she was teaching women to disrespect men." [102] Twala, moreover, had recently written a controversial article in *Izwi lama Swazi* about the necessity of including women in the political process, noting that the new "constitution will be incomplete if women are not included; we want women to be able to vote."[103] Angry responses from outraged male readers immediately poured in. One suggested that "women cannot restrain themselves, especially when talking, and they thus ruin everything. . . . It is foolish to talk about women and the law!"[104] The combined royalist-Zionist bloc, on the other hand, resonated with patriarchal sentiment in continuing to favor male political authority and the exclusion of women from decision-making mechanisms.

The election outcome was a clean sweep for Sobhuza's Imbokodvo, and an utter defeat for all the parties, although the NNLC put up the most respectable showing of them all. Even in the city of Manzini, a hotbed of political activism and a hub for the educated elite, the Imbokodvo's A. K. Hlope (himself a prominent Zionist minister and a one-time president of the League of Churches) defeated Regina Twala by margins of eleven to one.[105] Imbokodvo hailed the outcome as a great victory for Sobhuza and for Swati traditionalism, and a refutation of "unscrupulous parties and their leaders [who] fought us with vicious and false propaganda."[106] Yet rumours circulated of intimidation from traditionalist chiefs toward voters in rural areas. People whispered that chiefs threatened their subjects with dispossession of their lands if they voted against Imbokodvo.[107] In the aftermath of the election, Regina Twala wrote a single bitter article for *Izwi lama Swazi*, describing an imagined conversation between two baffled voters, one asking his friend, "Tell me, this 'of the people, by the people,' in whose land will this work, because Swaziland is a feudal land, the tikhulu [chiefs] exercise their powers in his name, who-that-never-tells-a-lie, umlomo ongaqalimanga?" His friend replied: "My friend, I feel scared. I have no land of my own, let us part. I have no voice of my own, yet the truth is there."[108]

In the aftermath of the election, Sobhuza worked to neutralize the Christian Progressives. Through his strategic deployment of "tradition," he now possessed near-hegemonic control over the political process, with Imbokodvo controlling the legislative council that would set the agenda for independence. The British threw up their hands in defeat, deciding they could do little to change the course that Swaziland was set upon.[109] Soon most parties other than the NNLC and the SPP had folded. Throughout the next year or two, several prominent politicians defected to Imbokodvo, seeing the writing on the wall, and the impossibility of maintaining resistance to Sobhuza.[110] Not all did. Regina Twala, for one, would not betray her principles in this way. But she felt she could not continue along the same path, either. By 1965, Twala had announced her resignation from politics, using *The Times of Swaziland* to inform the nation that "she had decided to spend her full time doing social welfare work, which had always been her calling."[111] Political leaders who insisted upon maintaining an active presence underwent severe harassment over the coming years; John Nquku, for example, had his home and car burned in mysterious acts of arson throughout the 1960s.[112]

Conclusion

After the British departed in 1968, the monarchy's power only increased. Initially, however, Sobhuza continued to be plagued by political opposition, as the British-derived constitution still made provision for the participation of political parties in a semi-democratic electoral process. Startled and worried by the success of the NNLC in the 1972 elections, Sobhuza abolished the constraining inconvenience of parliamentary procedure by declaring a state of emergency in early 1973, which is still in force today.[113] In 1973, Sobhuza named himself the holder of "supreme power," and outlawed all political parties on the grounds of being counter to "tradition": they were "highly undesirable political practices alien to and incompatible with the way of life in our society . . . designed to disrupt and destroy our own peaceful, constructive and essentially democratic methods of political activity."[114] Brief flare-ups of resistance occurred in the 1990s, but were quickly squashed by the then-regent, Sobhuza's son, Mswati III.[115] More recently, however, protest has arisen again in Eswatini (as Swaziland is now named), with 2021 bringing a number of turbulent uprisings on the part of emaSwati. Repression from the state has been swift and violent. To date, more than sixty emaSwati are reported to have been murdered by the country's army. The coming years will show whether the sway of theocratic monarchy can continue to convince the bulk of emaSwati citizens, or whether alternative forms of "worldmaking" will gain ascendance.

In sum, Swaziland's decolonizing process reveals a different story to the more optimistic one usually applied to the end of colonial rule in Africa. Rather than an emancipatory triumph, Swaziland's independence from Britain signalled the squashing of the democratic process. And rather than a victory for a particular liberal vision of the nation-state, decolonization marked the ascent of a monarchical-theocratic vision for statehood. The intertwined stories of the Progressives, royalty, and the Zionist churches highlight the competing forms of Christian nationalism alive throughout the 1960s. There was no such thing as a single Christian template for decolonization in Africa. Instead, multiple Christian players and organizations espoused rival political theologies. Throughout the 1960s and far beyond, lively arguments have persisted about the nature of an African continent free from colonial rule yet still bound to other masters, both new and old.

CHAPTER 10

"International Law as God's Law": The Promise and Limits of Christian-Suffused Nationalisms After Empire

Lydia Walker

Before the Second World War, Zapuvisie Lhousa learned English and music from American Baptist missionaries in Nagaland, a region of what was then British India, located at the junction of India, Burma, and China.[1] After the war, stimulated by the speeches and nationalist imagination of the Naga nationalist leader Angami Zapu Phizo, Zapuvisie spent a decade living and fighting in the jungle (1954–1964), rejoining his village and family after a ceasefire in September 1964.[2] In the decades since, he became a community and church leader for the village of Mezoma, outside the Naga capital of Kohima. Always historically minded, Zapuvisie kept records—correspondence from his insurgent days and copies of the letters and petitions his people sent to the United Nations, the United States, and other governments in their search for international sponsorship of their demand for independence from India.

Also a prolific scholar, Zapuvisie has used this archive for his collaboratively written books on the Naga struggle.[3] A recent book is titled *Bethlehem to Nagaland*, articulating the arc of a shared Christian heritage that underpins significant elements of the Naga nationalist claim.[4] For Zapuvisie, "God enables the world to live very close," even as "vast oceans, mountains and valleys separate our nations."[5] From this perspective, shared Christian heritage connected the Naga claim to wider circles of international power and governance. These spheres were explicitly and implicitly aligned with

Western, Christian, and, during the Cold War, anti-Communist ideological connections, even when most in those international circles had little knowledge of (or interest in) Naga nationalism or in Nagaland itself.

The Naga Hills, where Zapuvisie was born, became the Indian state of Nagaland in 1963.[6] It had been and continues to be a place of restricted travel under British and then Indian rule.[7] Nagas resided in both India and Burma, which shared an unfixed frontier until 1952. As with many colonial regions, international-legal borders did not take into consideration the movement and residence of the peoples who resided in these borderlands. It is important to note that the Indian state of Nagaland is nearly 90 percent Christian and 75 percent Baptist.[8] By this calculation, Nagaland is more Baptist than the American state of Mississippi.[9] The accuracy of these numbers is hampered by the methodological and political limits of census categories and undertakings, but they articulate the significant impact Baptist Christianity has had upon the region.

American Baptist missionaries first arrived in the Naga Hills in the 1870s. In the subsequent decades, and accelerating following the Second World War, they sparked substantial conversion and English-language education rates. However, most conversion was carried out by Naga (rather than American) missionaries and occurred after American missionaries were banned from the Naga Hills by the Indian government in 1953. The American-Naga missionary encounter demonstrated a set of global-historical connections that bypassed New Delhi in both colonial and independent India. They significantly influenced the language and religion of the region, and crafted affective connections between individuals rather than strong linkages between institutions, organizations, or governments.

The American missionary who was also the schoolmaster in Kohima possessed a printing press that Nagas used to print an English-language newssheet, the *Naga Nation*, starting in the mid-1940s.[10] Earlier, in the 1930s, they had printed a newssheet in Tenyidie, the Angami language of the Kohima District, on the same press.[11] The idea and terminology of a "Naga Nation" predated Indian independence and directly contrasted with the concept of Nagas as a pre-modern "tribal" people. This notion fit in with the long history of how imperial rulers defined many peoples as tribes rather than nations in order to legitimize colonial conquest over them and undermine the status of any treaties made with them.[12] Globally, transforming peoples into tribes subordinated them within the colonial expansionist and eventual postcolonial national consolidation projects. In the Indian context, a Naga nation also escaped the structures of caste in a Hindu-dominated society and rejected the Indian constitutional category of tribe with its connotations of colonial anthropological classification.[13] The concept of "nation" also linked Nagas to the idea of a biblically chosen people such as the Hebrew nation of Israel.[14] Whether and how Nagas are (or became) a nation, or a set of tribes, or both, is a subject of contentious debate among Nagas today.[15] Calling a community a nation utilized a language of power that was in dialogue with Western ideological and religious discourses but also a rejection of another Western-originated construction—that of tribe—that was of subordination.

Language and education are important tools of both Christian conversion and nation-making.[16] Missionary education policies made many Nagas speak, read, and write English, particularly in the Kohima region.[17] The English language and (Baptist) Christianity provided the avenues for Naga nationalists to attempt to access international politics in their pursuit of political recognition.[18] During the Cold War era, Christianity also aligned certain minority or indigenous nationalist claimants with the First World against the prospect of "godless" Communism.[19] These religious networks also created forms of connection and affinity that did not move through states, creating useful political pathways for claimants who lacked international recognition.

The content and character of these claims beg an array of questions: Who is a visible subject of international legal-order and how do shifting conceptions of "civilization" and "humanity" impact that visibility?[20] Did Christianity remain a sign of shared (Western) civilization and humanity when transposed to peoples from the formerly colonial world, particularly for peoples for whom formal decolonization did not necessarily lead to the political recognition they sought? Did this religious marker help make them visible as "civilized" international subjects or did it become one more characteristic that reinscribed colonial difference? Did it shape their portrayal as not quite modern enough to be legitimate political claimants, as institutions of international order became professionalized, bureaucratized, and even secularized over the course of the twentieth century?[21]

This chapter explores these interlinked questions, demonstrating how Nagas' use of Christian networks and discourse in their nationalist claims-making articulated a narrative of global decline, of weakness and erosion: a decline in Christianity as a signifier of "civilized" "worthiness" for international recognition and, eventually, a decline in the influence that the ecumenical Protestant, Western missionary project had on national liberation movements. As decolonization progressed during the second half of the twentieth century, the international language of Christianity was not necessarily a source of political influence for particular disenfranchised groups in the postcolonial world. In contrast to situations where colonial subjects appropriated the language of their oppressors to serve anti-colonial ends—such as in this volume's chapters by Darcie Fontaine and Phi-Vân Nguyen—Naga nationalist claims-making shows the potential for political constraint when Christian language and networks were utilized to counter the sovereignty of postcolonial states.

The Civilizing Mission Reordered by Decolonization

Nagas were not unique in their use of Christian language in their political claims-making. In one example of many, Hereros from the former League of Nations mandate of South West Africa/Namibia drew upon similar themes even as they had greater international access.[22] Ethnic groups in South West Africa have petitioned institutions of international order since the interwar era.[23] The German colony of South West Africa, which had carried out a genocide against the Herero and Nama peoples, became a League of Nations mandate administered by South Africa after the First World War. When South Africa's postwar attempt to annex South West Africa was halted by the United Nations, the territory remained in international limbo as a former League of Nations mandate, rather than legally integrated into South Africa or defined as a United Nations trust territory and set on a developmental path toward independence, as other former German African colonies were. Claimants and advocates for an eventually independent Namibia constantly and consistently called South West Africa a "sacred trust" held by the United Nations.[24] This repeated word choice combined strong paternalist and religious connotations.

On the walls of the United Nations library in New York City is the personal prayer of the Namibian Herero Chief Hosea Kutako, who petitioned the UN annually through representatives from 1949 until his death in 1970:

> O Lord help us who roam about.
> Help us who have been placed in Africa and have no dwelling place of our own.
> Give us back our dwelling place, O God.[25]

Kutako defines a state as a dwelling place—a home, not simply a country. Those who "roam about," such as nomads or tribal peoples, need their own home, one recognized and provided by God through the aegis of international law, which Kutako called God's Law.[26] It was no accident that the UN found this formula worthy of permanent display on the walls of its headquarters. Kutako's prayer combined the mixture of sacred and secular concepts that were embedded in the historical and ideological foundations of the United Nations itself as an institution of international order.

Before 1945, ideas of an international order—the system of norms that structure political units and their relationships with each other—grew from conceptions of a unified, implicitly Christian (as well as white and Western) civilization defined in opposition to "uncivilized," colonized, and non-Christian peoples.[27] This "structuring" of metropolitan political units into an international order was intertwined in time and theme with nineteenth- and twentieth-century imperial expansion.[28] Through missionary conversion, Christianity served as an uneven avenue of colonialism, as well as a defining characteristic of civilization. There is a well-told history of the Christian missionary networks that stretched across European and American empires, articulating the contestation and cooperation between conversion, "civilizing" development projects, and imperialism.[29] Over time, the intertwining of civilization, Christianity, colonialism, and the formulation of an international order grew so naturalized as to seem organic rather than historically constructed. At least until postwar decolonization, when the international order formalized in the United Nations came to be dominated—in number if not necessarily in terms of influence—by non-Western, recently postcolonial member states.

Simultaneously, Christianity, particularly ecumenical Protestantism, was undergoing a process that came to be termed the secularization thesis: it became so ingrained within Anglo-American ruling elites and organizations that it no longer needed to be demonstrated in actual worship practice and public discourse.[30] This naturalization of Christian universalist discourses was also occurring within the building and transforming of the United Nations.[31] The United Nations that ecumenical protestants such as John Foster Dulles had hoped to construct before 1945 would have been an institution underpinned by a sense of shared Atlantic world Protestant internationalism.[32] When Dulles felt that the institution unveiled in San Francisco in 1945 lacked that shared ideological foundation, and instead had the potential to infringe upon national state (i.e., in his priority, US) sovereignty, his earlier support—grounded in the implicit Christian civilizational bonds of previous structures of international order (such as the League of Nations, at whose founding conference he had been the United States' legal counsel)—dropped away. Dulles became a fierce critic of the UN.

In spite of Dulles's perception that the UN as constructed in 1945 was a rejection of a "gentleman's agreement" of Atlantic world Protestant internationalism, a sense of Christian mission privately remained within many in the UN's upper echelons, at least through Dag Hammarskjöld's tenure as secretary-general (1953–1961). Hammarskjöld's posthumously published diary is full of Christian imagery, and he repeatedly compared his work to that of biblical heroes in poetry and prose while he attempted to manage the Congo Crisis, a political challenge where he envisioned himself working to "heal the sores" of a "divided" land, operating from "slippery places"—alluding to particular Bible verses.[33] This historical background of Christianity, colonialism, and ecumenical Protestant international institution-making served as important context for the professions and utilizations of Christian language and themes by minority or indigenous claimants from within postcolonial states. They were drawing upon a well-trodden political and religious landscape even as the terrain of "legitimate" political discourse was shifting beneath them, and public Christian displays carried diminishing political returns as a language of international-legal legitimacy.

"Fourth World" Nationalists and Religious Claims-Making

While Christian language receded from Western-dominated governments and elite political institutions, the reverse occurred in parts of former colonies that had experienced influential missionary contact. In British colonial India, missionary conversion had generally been restricted to "tribal" groups in the Northeast or communities in the South. These regions had less political sway on the Delhi-based colonial government, or were ruled indirectly as princely states, or were perceived as less likely to be subject to Hindu-Muslim conflict that could be potentially exacerbated by missionary intervention.[34] Even after formal decolonization, for these "peripheral" Christians from the "Fourth World,"[35]—a term popularized by the Canadian indigenous leader George Manuel to refer to minority or indigenous groups excluded from international, state-centric, political organization—a sense of connection to a wider global community grew from notions of a shared Christian "civilization" that had been crafted by missionary networks and relationships. This belief in Christian global belonging contained elements of reaction and rejection to the perceived socialism (or secularism) of dominating governments or majoritarian nationalist movements. The prospect of an international audience allowed a minority nationalism to attempt to circumnavigate the coercion of its rulers in order to appeal to wider publics. In this scheme, requesting international attention and even intervention was an appeal to a higher power, toward a universal aspiration of self-determination and self-rule.

Angami Zapu Phizo, the Naga nationalist leader who had studied with American Baptist missionaries at Kohima School, believed that the Naga nationalist claim had divine backing, that "God forbids that we give away our homeland."[36] This call upon a higher authority was also inherent to a people's petition to an international forum above that of the state that ruled them. In some ways, international petitioning shared an analytical structure with that of prayer. Phizo wrote to the President of the UN General Assembly regularly, entreating the UN for "deliverance" form Indian oppression.[37] Separate from a direct appeal to the divine, international claims-making had moral valence: to appeal for help, a people had to present themselves as in need and deserving of aid. Phizo's personal prayer served as a statement of personal belief in his cause and its divine backing: "I believe I am divinely guided. I believe I will always take the right road. I believe God will always make a way where there is no way."[38]

During the Cold War, religious discourses provided a language of liberty that was recognizable and sympathetic to First World audiences, even as the United States and its allies were often ambivalently or even explicitly supportive of European empire as well as certain authoritarian postcolonial states. Assistance to those regimes was justified as necessary to fight global Communism. Fourth World claimants, seeking aid from the First World to circumnavigate the limits of their ruling (generally Third World) governments, sought to utilize the threat of Communism's global threat to gain support for their causes, since they could intimate the possibility of aligning with the communist Second World if their needs were not met.

The Naga Baptist Church leader, Kijungluba Ao, looking for support and funding from friends in the American Baptist Convention, wrote that he worried Nagas were not "very far from the dangerous disease" of Communism, if their political rights and humanitarian needs were not addressed by Western backers.[39] For the Nagas who made appeals for Western support during this period, Communism loomed much larger as a threat than the potential of encroachment from Hinduism or Islam. In part this was due to strategic reasons—their Western network was much more concerned with Communism and certain Naga claimants also received a degree of support from the Hindu Sarvodaya movement.[40] But also, before the mid-twentieth century, they had had very little contact from those religious communities.[41]

Christian networks and international organizations facilitated engagement and connection between groups that otherwise would have little financial or logistical means to interact. One of the very few occasions when Nagas rubbed shoulders with African anti-colonial nationalists occurred at the World Council of Churches' 1961 Assembly in New Delhi. The Naga Baptist Church sent a delegation under the leadership of Rev. Longri Ao, the most successful Naga missionary and eventual head of the Nagaland Baptist Church Council, to the 1961 Delhi Assembly.[42] There, Longri was quite impressed by the governor of Eastern Nigeria and former medical missionary Francis Akanu Ibiam, who gave a speech on the African Christian as an independent, global (rather than national) citizen.[43] Ibiam went on to mobilize international humanitarian aid for an independent Biafra during the Nigerian Civil War (1967–1970), drawing upon his network within the World Council of Churches for prestige and contacts to support his country and countrymen. Longri's feelings of affinity with Ibiam significantly predated the Biafran War. In addition, Naga clergy never had the international reach that Ibiam would be able to draw upon in the late 1960s. However, it is not surprising that one Christian leader from a minority within a postcolonial state might draw inspiration from another.

At the Delhi Assembly, the World Council of Churches' director of international affairs, O. Frederick Nolde, delivered a keynote address. Nolde was a prominent American Protestant ecumenical diplomat who wrote the religious freedom section of the Universal Declaration of Human Rights. In his speech, he asked nations to "relinquish those aspects of sovereignty, which are outworn and self-defeating." Instead, nations should accept their "submission to the jurisdiction of the International Court of Justice, to international regulations affecting trade and commerce, to international inspections to ensure compliance with treaties—these and similar commitments must replace the former claims of sovereignty."[44] In this formulation, "higher" level international-legal institutions of justice, economics, and politics could solve the problems and limits of "lower" level national government. While Nolde did not explicitly invoke the divine, or conflate international law with a "higher power," his elevation of institutions of international order to a level above that of national governments lent itself to that interpretation, especially to elements of his religiously oriented audience.[45]

In the 1980s, decades after Nolde's address, Rev. V. K. Nuh, a prominent Naga Baptist Church leader (who had been a chaplain for Naga nationalist armed forces in his youth), explicitly linked the UN's Universal Declaration of Human Rights to Christian textual understandings of human behavior. He analyzed the Universal Declaration article-by-article, through biblical verses as comparison and explanation.[46] In doing so, Nuh made international-legal doctrine resonate for a biblically literate, Naga public. He also excavated some of the Christian underpinnings of the Universal Declaration in a manner much more direct than Nolde's more circumspect allusions.

Back in his 1961 speech, Nolde had argued that "submission" to institutions of international order should have priority over demands for national sovereignty. Speaking during a moment of rapid decolonization—seventeen countries became independent in 1960, the year prior, including Ibiam's Nigeria—Nolde articulated a religious call for internationalism and the need for "new" limits on sovereignty because of the formation of these new postcolonial states. These expressions of constrained sovereignties drew upon older forms of international trusteeship and oversight from the League of Nations era. They held echoes of the paternalism that underpinned the notion that the UN owed a "sacred trust" to its international-legal predecessor's former mandates that it now held in "trust," such as Namibia (a former League of Nations mandate), as well as literal trust territories such as Tanganyika or New Guinea.

Regardless of paternalist connotations rooted in ideas and practices of international oversight, disenfranchised groups saw the prospect of such oversight and intervention as an improvement upon their circumstances. In 1964, a few years after the World Council of Churches' Delhi Assembly, Naga nationalists called for peace talks "under the witness of the United Nations" or for a World Council of Churches "fact finding mission" to be sent to the region.[47] For a nationalist movement whose claim of independence was considered a domestic matter by its ruling government (and which never reached the UN as a nationalist claim because of this reason), international investigation was a desirable outcome. However, for the World Council of Churches, it was far outside the realm of possibility to send fact finding missions into countries whose governments did not approve them. Nor could the United Nations intervene without being invited by the government(s) whose international-legal territory was involved—that is, India and Burma. Therefore, from the perspective of international institutions (such as the UN) or global civil society organizations (such as the World Council of Churches) these requests underscored the unrealizability of the Naga claim. That Naga nationalists saw these bodies as sources of potential political legitimacy articulated the arenas in which they sought to operate. That these entities did not reciprocate that belief demonstrated those organizations' own limits to be significant sources of support as well as validation.

When researching the public, internationally projected, religious expressions of Naga nationalist thinking, an explanatory note is needed about the methodological challenges involved. This is not simply a linguistic question, since the language of international petitioning was (and remains) English as a means of accessing global power and influence, though scholarship using Tenyidie and other Naga languages would illuminate important avenues of insight. Nagas were acutely aware of the impact and utility of English and how it demonstrated active connection to Western (Christian) networks of potential support. However, challenges arise because a nationalist movement that does not achieve independence lacks a state archive.

Certain Naga nationalists have kept and maintained personal archives, such as Zapuvisie Lhousa. Other "movement-intellectuals," such as Rev. Nuh, have self-published accounts that are filled with letters and petitions to the UN and other potentially interested outside entities. Yet those of some of the most prominent and most articulate leaders (such as T. Sakhrei, viewed as the intellectual progenitor of the Naga nationalism movement, or of Phizo himself) have been lost or obscured. They have been seized and most probably destroyed by the Indian military, misplaced when shifting houses and countries, or given into the hands of Western advocates for safekeeping and subsequently are logistically difficult or impossible to access. These questions of national, intellectual patrimony and its loss are complex issues that shape how histories are written, collected, and organized, as well as which narratives are promulgated and to which audiences. They also underscore the processes that have prioritized Western understandings of the Naga cause, and the double-edged role Christianity has played in both Westernizing and indigenizing—sometimes even simultaneously—Naga national claims-making.

Ambivalently Anti-colonial

The most prominent Western advocate for the Naga cause in the early 1960s, during the period of "high" decolonization on the African continent and the alleged universalizing of national self-determination as an international norm, was the British Anglican minister Michael Scott. Scott himself was an emblem of postwar Protestant ecumenical internationalism, if somewhat of a rogue figure.[48] He had served as Hosea Kutako's personal representative before the UN's Committee on South West Africa, helped bring Phizo past British immigration into London during the summer of 1960, and worked to monitor a peace agreement between Naga nationalists and the Indian government in 1964. In the spring of 1960, Scott was drafting an article on the ambivalent role of the Western advocate for anti-colonial nationalist causes for *The Observer* newspaper. Considering himself inspired and provoked by Psalm 17, Scott pondered how the "the human race needs to be saved from those who would save the human race from itself."[49]

He continued: "So long as man looks for a Savior, whether it be Christ or Buddha or Gandhi, and fails to look within himself, not relying upon Saviors, Saints, or Heroes to bring him Salvation, is there any hope that he can be saved?" Eventually, Scott decided not to publish the draft because, while he had tried "to keep it soft and inoffensive, an African would be hurt by it."[50] In private, Scott acknowledged the paternalism as well as the religious undercurrents embedded in many of the individuals involved in facilitating decolonization and national liberation—components that swirled below the surface of what was publicly presented as a great liberatory, egalitarian, (secular) nationalizing process.

Scott's anti-colonial advocacy endeavors were funded by a group of Western philanthropists who thought of him as their "guru in the religion of doubt."[51] These financial backers saw Scott's "theology" as safely non-communist and non-revolutionary. In the words of the journalist Richard Kershaw, Scott's endeavors were funded by "mandarins, ex-intelligence, millionaires," who "mistrusted the movement for colonial freedom."[52] "These Establishment figures wanted to remedy injustice but not advance communism. . . . They wanted freedom, but not at all costs." These "rich, tough, old-fashioned imperialists" backed Scott and his projects as an "action wedge" during decolonization.[53] Kershaw's interpretation articulated how the Cold War context shaped a certain subset of ambivalent Western backing for national liberation, as well as how that backing was hedged with limits. Though they received significantly less active support due to their small population and distant geopolitical placement, Nagas were one of many groups (such as Tibetans and certain African national liberation movements) that fit this general advocacy profile.

While they remained sympathetic, many Western advocates found explicit Christian appeals to international bodies on matters that fell outside seemingly realistic political possibility to be noble, naïve, and even silly, because they did not conform to their understandings of the appropriate way to address international-legal forums.[54] The utilization of Christian-infused international petitioning for Nagas and other groups cut in multiple directions: on the one hand, it provided a palpable, anti-Communist and civilizational affinity with their Western supporters. On the other, it was then perceived as too overt, too public, perhaps even too uneducated in the norms of international-legal discourse, serving as a further signal of the seeming unrealizability of these groups' national claims.

At the same time, the symbol of the minority nationalist (eventually termed an indigenous) claimant was deeply appealing to institutions of international order—so appealing that the United Nations wrote Kutako's prayer on their walls as a public demonstration of the institution's relevance to dispossessed communities. The importance these petitioners placed upon the United Nations outstripped the institution's actual influence. Yet it mirrored how the United Nations and its affiliated structures wanted to be viewed, and how they wanted to publicly portray themselves, even and especially as the perception of influenced outstripped the institution's effective clout.

The dissemination and recitation of Hosea Kutako's prayer—first allegedly performed before Scott in 1948 when he left Windhoek South West Africa on his way to carry Herero petitions to the United Nations, subsequently used as a rallying cry at global anti-apartheid rallies, eventually included in one of Scott's prayers before a Naga nationalist armed unit in Northeast India, and finally inscribed on the interior walls of the United Nations[55]—has a curious corollary. According to a South African intelligence operative, Kutako was illiterate.[56] The repetition of the written words of an illiterate man, and the need to annually refute them, infuriated the South African delegation at the UN.[57] While an unsurprising matter in a country with limited available education, Kutako served as the face and words for a host of international petitions written, sent, and presented on his behalf, while he most likely did not read or write them. This circumstance underscores the strategic ingenuity of nationalist claimants, the utility of prayer as a mode for expressing claims, the constrained conditions in which they operated, and how their causes and words were abstracted to suit a variety of audiences.

Besides independence from apartheid South Africa, Kutako's Hereros wished to distinguish themselves from (and resist amalgamation with) the central Namibian nationalist movement of SWAPO (the South West African People's Organization), which was dominated by the Ovambo ethnic group.

As the 1960s progressed into the 1970s, SWAPO came to embrace Marxist-Leninist public ideology and private aid from China and Cuba. As part of this shift, SWAPO members formed the "Yu Chi Chen club," a reading group for studying the writings of Mao and Che Guevara,[58] and participated in global tricontinentalist circles.[59] In contrast, Herero petitioners, and their repetition of the international community's "sacred trust" owed to South West Africa (alluding to South West Africa's status as a former League of Nations mandate), remained attractive claimants for First World, anti-Communist interests. This appeal was mutually constitutive with their structural weakness within international politics: the same religious and "civilizational" characteristics that made certain groups appealing candidates for Western advocacy underscored the underlying limitations of their claims-making. It might even have become a defining feature of their appeal since the unrealizability of their claims removed the realizable prospect of international intervention. Advocacy for these causes, either through networks of personal affinity or by inscribing the words of their leaders on to the walls of international institutions, could exclude the blood, treasure, or political blowback that actively supporting nationalist insurgent movements with a (seemingly) more viable path to self-government required.

Conclusion: Billy Graham in Nagaland

As the late 1950s and 1960s' window of rapid nationalist possibility closed at the United Nations, many claimants shifted their primary attention away from international-legal institutions. The 1970s were a period of heightened "radicalization" and violence in Northeast India and elsewhere, as well as increased ideological and logistical backing from communist countries among anti-colonial nationalists.[60] In response, certain communities who felt marginalized from dominant nationalist movements compromised with their ruling regimes or sought out forms of international recognition that did not rely on international institutions or state governments. For Nagas, international evangelical networks were one of the few sources available for such global connection.

In November 1972, celebrating a century of Baptist conversion in Nagaland, the American evangelical minister Billy Graham came to Kohima to lead one of his crusades, which locals termed the "Kohima miracle." The year 1972 was a violent period in the Naga Hills, and the Indian government had severely limited the presence of foreigners, particularly American Baptist missionaries, in the region since the 1950s. Against this landscape of insurgency, assassination, and violence between Naga nationalists and the Indian state, and India's virtual ban on international visitors, it was striking that the government of Indira Gandhi not only gave Graham and his party inner line permits to enter Nagaland (as well as visas to enter India), they also facilitated their travel in and out of Kohima with Russian-manufactured military helicopters—a point of interest for Graham, the American religious Cold Warrior.[61]

The elusive inner line permits were procured on Graham's behalf by three Northeastern Baptist leaders from the Indian Minister of Defense with relative ease, since the Indian government saw Graham's visit as a chance to placate rather than antagonize ordinary Nagas.[62] Graham's visit represented two significant changes from Naga nationalists' engagement with global Christian networks a decade prior. First, Graham's crusade demonstrated evangelical rather than ecumenical Protestant internationalism. And second, this religious internationalism took place under the auspices of the Indian state rather than working to subvert it.

For Naga participants in Graham's Kohima visit, "it was as if God was coming"; the entire city was packed with people from almost all Naga regions, and it was the biggest gathering one of the attendees, Makenla Ao, had ever seen.[63] The visit also made a significant impression on Graham, who would hire the local organizer of the crusade on to his permanent US-based staff. In Graham's public sermon, he alluded briefly to the violent insurgency ongoing around him, but an outside listener unfamiliar with events would not know why Nagaland was riven by warfare, what were its causes, or the identity of its participants.[64] Of course, his listeners knew well the circumstances in which they lived, and saw Graham's visit as an opportunity to escape that violence. Contemporaneous international reporting provided some of the brutal context: According to *Time* magazine, "just three miles away from the site [in Kohima] where Graham was speaking to 60,000 people [other observers put the figure at closer to one million],[65] Naga guerrillas ambushed an Indian army convoy, killed one soldier and wounded four others. The evangelist called off the last day of his revival and flew back to rest in New Delhi, where he had scheduled a meeting th[at] week with Prime Minister Indira Gandhi."[66] Graham's crusade meant that events such as these were reported globally, and this reporting may help explain why the Indian government did not facilitate a subsequent high-profile American Baptist visit.

The Christian globalism of Graham's crusade in Nagaland showed the separation between religion and nationalist claims-making and its international advocacy by the 1970s. During the early Cold War era, the Christian language and affiliation that made these claimants attractive and unthreatening to First World–dominated international institutions also underscored their movements' weaknesses and limitations, as those institutions shifted religion to private spheres and away from public political claims-making. Graham was himself an active Cold Warrior, but his crusade worked to reconcile Nagas to the Indian state (and facilitate greater Christian missions within India) rather than support their independence. His evangelical internationalism underscored both the weakness of Christianity as a mobilizing force for national liberation for Nagaland *and* that of ecumenical Protestant networks in reaching and addressing these groups. Because he did not address Naga nationalism, it was Billy Graham who was able to come to Nagaland in 1972, not the World Council of Churches or a UN mission. Christianity, once a language of power within international politics, had shifted to one of weakness, in these particular circumstances. This shift demonstrated that utilizing a tool of colonialism by disenfranchised peoples did not necessarily empower what had been. Rather, it had the potential to undermine the efficacy of the tool itself.

Nagas used the language and promise of self-rule embedded in "Western" Christian "civilization," hoping that these formerly imperial ideas and networks would help them achieve independence. Yet, as Western powers refused to intervene on behalf of Christian minorities, this pursuit undermined Naga claims-making in an era of secular national liberation and bureaucratized international-legal institutions. Simultaneously, these institutions, which had themselves been forged by international Protestant ecumenical networks (such the World Council of Churches and those that underpinned the founding of the United Nations), lost their effectiveness both for protecting the rights of minority groups and in mobilizing faith-based communities. Instead, explicit, public professions of Christianity shifted from those who built institutions of international order to those who were positioned on the outside, looking in. The relationship between Christianity and nationalism for Nagas, as well as other minority or indigenous peoples, showed that while decolonization opened new opportunities for national liberation, it could also foreclose political possibilities for minorities left behind by empire.

CHAPTER 11

Decolonizing Theology: EATWOT and the Rise of Third World Theologies

Sarah Shortall

In August 1976, President Julius Nyerere of Tanzania gave a speech at the inaugural conference of the Ecumenical Association of Third World Theologians (EATWOT), which he was hosting in Dar es Salaam. In his remarks, Nyerere gave voice to the frustration of many recently decolonized nations with how little had changed since they had gained their independence from European colonial powers. Despite the achievement of political or "flag" independence, Nyerere pointed out that most African nations remained in a state of economic dependency on foreign powers and multinational corporations that prevented them from achieving full sovereignty and self-determination. "True liberation has not started in Africa," he told the assembled theologians.[1] In order to overcome this situation of "neocolonialism," it was necessary to restructure the global economy in such a way as to level the playing field between rich and poor nations—a project that Nyerere and others hoped to realize through the establishment of a New International Economic Order (NIEO).[2] Only then could the process of decolonization be completed.

Postcolonial leaders such as Nyerere were thus keenly aware in the 1970s of everything that political decolonization had left undone. At the very same moment, Christian theologians and intellectuals from the Global South were coming to a similar realization about the extent to which political decolonization had not fundamentally altered the relations of power within their churches. "Why," asked the Cameroonian theologian Jean-Marc Ela, "twenty years after the local churches were handed over to an indigenous clergy, are these churches still treated as spiritual colonies of a foreign religion?"[3] Theologians like Ela were sensitive to the relationship between European colonial expansion and the spread of Christianity, which meant that the theology that missionaries had brought with them was by no means universal. Instead, Ela argued, it was the expression of a particular European culture and its imposition on non-European peoples tended to alienate them from themselves. As a result, he concluded, "we find ourselves in what may be called a 'religious concubinage,' which results from practicing our faith in a way that does not allow our living spirit to speak."[4] It was necessary, in other words, to decolonize Christian theology itself.

The organization to which Nyerere spoke in 1976 (and of which Ela was a member) represented just such a project. Born that very same year, the Ecumenical Association of Third World Theologians declared its independence from the European theological tradition brought by the missionaries who had accompanied European colonizers. Instead, it sought to develop a distinctive Third World theology by bringing theologians from Latin America, Asia, Africa, and minority groups in North America into dialogue. They committed themselves to articulating a theology anchored in their own political, cultural, and economic contexts and attentive to the practical needs of their communities. Because, like Nyerere, they were alive to the challenge of neocolonialism, they foregrounded the necessity for structural economic change and, taking their cue from the work of Latin American liberation theologians, sought to write theology from the perspective of the poor and oppressed. But, as we shall see, the commitment to a contextual theology soon revealed powerful differences of approach within this remarkably diverse group of theologians, as they began to realize that the priorities of Christians in Sri Lanka might not be the same as those in São Paulo, undermining the possibility of a single unifying Third World theology.

EATWOT thus suffered from many of the same pressures that beset other Third World movements in the 1970s—internal fractures among the diverse nations of the Global South and disinterest or hostility from their counterparts in Europe and North America. But the history of EATWOT also differs in important respects from the trajectory of secular Third Worldism. 1975 is often seen as the end of the "Bandung Era" of Third World activism, with the NIEO serving as both its high-water mark and swansong, before the unfavorable economic and political climate of the 1980s definitively brought an end to such projects.[5] And yet, EATWOT got its start in 1976 and it continued to maintain a prominent public profile in both the Global South and the

North well into the 1990s (indeed, it continues to exist today). Moreover, recent developments within the Catholic Church, in particular, have brought renewed attention to the concerns raised by EATWOT and suggest that its impact is far from spent. These contrasts indicate the limits of a history of Third Worldism written from the perspective of secular actors or forces. Integrating the history of theology into this story reveals not just the extent to which economic and political questions were bound up with religious and theological ones, but also provides a less fatalistic view of the legacy and lasting import of Third Worldism.

The Genesis of EATWOT

The effort to develop a distinctive Third World theology emerged in the mid-1970s out of developments within the Christian churches, as well as the rise of Third World consciousness more broadly. The notion of a self-conscious "Third World" identity that refused the choice between the capitalist West and the communist East made its entry onto the world stage at the Bandung Conference in 1955, along with regionalist identities such as Pan-Africanism.[6] As the wave of anti-colonial uprisings across Africa and Asia brought a raft of new states into being from the 1950s to the 1970s, there was a very real sense that the Third World could become a leading force in global affairs. Such sentiments reached their highest expression in the project to establish a New International Economic Order under the aegis of the United Nations in 1974.[7] As the export-oriented economies of the Global South faced a sharp drop in commodity prices and declining terms of trade, many economists abandoned the theory of development that had been in vogue since the war in favor of new theories of dependency. It was not that poorer states simply needed to "catch up" to the industrialized economies of the North Atlantic; instead, the development of the North was itself premised on the underdevelopment and dependency of the Global South.[8] The only way to redress this structural imbalance was to regulate the global economy in such a way as to level the playing field. To this end, the NIEO demanded preferential and nonreciprocal trade agreements that favored the South, stabilization of commodity prices, technology transfers from wealthier to poorer nations, and regulations designed to limit the power of multinational corporations. As politicians like Nyerere pointed out, only in this way could newly independent nations achieve the economic sovereignty they needed to complete the process of decolonization. Though the NIEO would rapidly unravel under pressure from internal differences among the G-77 nations, resistance from the wealthy nations, and the UN's lack of enforcement mechanisms, the project nevertheless marked the "highpoint of anticolonial worldmaking" and of Third Worldism more generally.[9]

In conjunction with these developments, Christian churches were undergoing their own transformation in the wake of decolonization. Though the challenges of decolonization and global inequality had been peripheral to the discussion at the Second Vatican Council (1962–1965), the council did foster a new sense of regional solidarity among the bishops of the Global South and inaugurated a number of theological changes that Third World theologians would take up and radicalize. Two of the most significant were the council's teaching on the liturgy, which allowed the Mass to be said in the vernacular and promoted the incorporation of local music and culture, as well as Vatican II's opening to the world beyond the church's borders, by which it acknowledged that the Catholic Church did not have an exclusive monopoly on salvation and recognized the value in non-Christian religions. In addition, the council insisted on the need to interpret Catholic teaching in light of the historical "signs of the times," rather than treating it as a timeless, unchanging set of doctrines.[10] In the wake of Vatican II, Catholics outside Europe and North America would build on these developments while prioritizing the socioeconomic questions that the council had sidestepped. Meanwhile, as several essays in this volume have shown, the World Council of Churches was moving in a similar direction, reckoning more fully with the political imperatives of the Gospel, the scourge of racism, and even allowing that armed revolution might be justified in some instances.[11]

It was in Latin America that these developments first bore fruit. Buoyed by the spirit of opening at Vatican II but anxious to go further, Catholic theologians such as Gustavo Gutiérrez, Leonardo Boff, and Juan Luis Segundo, and Protestants such as José Míguez Bonino and Julio de Santa Ana began to develop a distinctive theology of liberation written from the perspective of the poor. Many of these theologians had studied at European institutions but recognized that European theological models were inadequate to the demands of the Latin American context.[12] Above all, they insisted, theology had to tackle the problem of poverty and economic injustice that dominated the lives of the faithful in the region. In paradigmatic works such as Gustavo Gutiérrez's *A Theology of Liberation* (1971), these theologians argued that the church could not claim to remain neutral and above politics in the face of sinful social structures because silence was itself a political choice in favor of the status quo and the ruling class.[13] In this context, they argued, the church must self-consciously side with the poor and oppressed, adopting what they called a "preferential option for the poor." In making this claim, these theologians broke with the logic of economic development, drawing instead on the insights of Marxist economics and dependency theory and calling for radical structural change. Liberation theology also found expression in new ways of organizing church life known as "base ecclesial communities" (CEBs), lay-led grassroots groups that combined a shared engagement with scripture and commitment to social justice. In 1968, liberation theology was enshrined at the Conference of Latin American Bishops (CELAM) meeting in Medellín and would continue to dominate the Latin American church through the 1970s.

1975 was a decisive year for the development of Third World theology. That year, the Theology in the Americas conference in Detroit brought theologians from North, Central, and South America into dialogue. Latin American liberation theologians such as Gutiérrez, Sergio Torres, and Enrique Dussel were among the leading voices, and the meeting gave them an opportunity to connect with Black theologians in North America and forge a common Christian front against American imperialism in the region.[14] That same year, the idea for EATWOT was born at the Catholic University of Louvain. It was the brainchild of Oscar Bimwenyi-Kweshi, a Congolese theology student, with the support of Enrique Dussel (then in exile from Argentina) and François Houtart, a leftist priest and sociologist at Louvain. The infrastructure for the group was initially provided by the Brussels-based Servicio Europeo de Universitarios Latinoamericanos, a Catholic organization that served Latin American students in Belgium. In its initial phase, the project was very much a Catholic one, but when the Chilean theologian Sergio Torres joined the team, he helped to transform it into a self-consciously ecumenical project with a strong liberationist bent. The goal was to organize an intercontinental congress involving theologians from Asia, Africa, and Latin America, with an equal balance between Catholic and Protestant voices. A newly formed secretariat decided to use the 1975 World Council of Churches meeting in Nairobi to secure funding for the congress, while President Nyerere offered to host the event in Tanzania.[15]

Twenty-two participants from sixteen countries and three religious traditions gathered in Dar es Salaam in August 1976 for what the celebrated French theologian Marie-Dominique Chenu heralded as the "Bandung of Theology."[16] The meeting crystallized the main aims of EATWOT. As

Torres explained in his opening remarks, the primary objective was to create a space for Third World theologians to connect with each other outside of Christian institutions run by Europeans and North Americans. Doing so, he insisted, would allow them to make an "epistemological break" with theologies imported from Europe, which were necessarily bound up with the history of colonialism.[17] "For centuries," Torres explained, "the Third World had passively received the culture, Gospel, and theology of the conquerors."[18] This was the theology that European missionaries had brought with them and, despite their noble intentions, these missionaries could not escape their entanglement with colonialism. As the conference's final statement explained, "the churches were allies in the colonization process. They spread under the aegis of colonial powers; they benefited from the expansion of empire. In return they rendered a special service to western imperialism by legitimizing it and accustoming their new adherents to accept compensatory expectations of an eternal reward for terrestrial misfortunes, including colonial exploitation."[19] Moreover, "the sense of military and commercial superiority" of the colonial powers "was underpinned with the view that Christianity was superior to other religions."[20]

In addition to reinforcing secular colonial projects, the theologians at Dar es Salaam also charged the missionaries with a "theological imperialism" that imposed the categories of European Christianity on the peoples of the Third World.[21] While missionaries had presented their theology as universal, the theologians at Dar es Salaam insisted that this "'universal theology' of the Church was in fact a geographically localised and culturally conditioned interpretation. Theology was not universal but European."[22] Rather than mimicking European Christianity, EATWOT therefore promoted the development of contextual theologies that reflected the particular culture, history, and needs of Christians across the Global South. In doing so, it built upon a longer history of efforts to "inculturate" Christianity in non-European cultures. In the Catholic world, such efforts had yielded some fruits in the interwar period and especially from the 1950s, as the church made a push to ordain indigenous priests in Africa and Asia.[23] But the Congolese theologian Ngindu Mushete insisted that such efforts were purely cosmetic, for they remained bound to a logic of adaptation that did not fundamentally challenge the European categories in which theology was expressed. Not only was European culture not "the locus and highpoint of human universality," Mushete insisted, but the very "notion of a universal theology, like that of a universal philosophy, is a myth."[24] In keeping with this logic, EATWOT's various regional constituencies tended to adopt slightly different theological approaches that reflected their respective contexts. While the Latin Americans foregrounded the role of socioeconomic oppression, Black theologians from the United States and apartheid South Africa stressed the scourge of racial oppression, while Asian theologians focused instead on the encounter between Christianity and non-Christian religions.

What united these disparate constituencies was a common identification as "Third World theologians," reflecting the rise of Third World consciousness since Bandung. The theologians at EATWOT, however, tended not to conceive of the "Third World" as a geographical entity or as an ideological marker based on the logic of the Cold War. Instead, they treated it as a "supra-geographical" category, the defining feature of which was "a social condition characterized by poverty and oppression."[25] Such a definition included not just the peoples of Asia, Africa, and Latin America, but also the marginalized minorities of the "First World," though they were not admitted as members of EATWOT until 1979. As we shall see, the question of how precisely to define the Third World, as well as the relationship between poverty and other forms of oppression, was highly contested within EATWOT. But at least initially, the definition that prevailed tended to privilege socioeconomic markers as well as the legacies of European imperialism—and indeed, in the context of neocolonialism, the two were necessarily intertwined. The theologians of EATWOT therefore insisted that colonialism was by no means a thing of the past. Like Nyerere, they were keenly aware of the limits of "flag independence" and the extent to which political decolonization had not transformed the basic relations of economic (and theological) dependency between the First and Third Worlds.

As this conception of the Third World suggests, the unifying theological framework for EATWOT was provided by liberation theology, broadly construed. "The starting point for Third World theologies," proclaimed EATWOT's first general assembly, "is the struggle of the poor and the oppressed against all forms of injustice and domination."[26] This commitment was written into the organization's constitution, which limited membership to those whose "theological work is rooted in socio-political action and . . . interprets the Gospel of Jesus Christ as the power of God enabling people to participate in the struggle of the poor and oppressed for a just society."[27] EATWOT thus made a self-conscious break, not just with the content of European and North American theology, but also with its methodology. Abandoning its abstract, academic style, they instead conceived of theology as a "critical reflection on praxis."[28] As Gutiérrez explained at Dar es Salaam, this meant that "active commitment to liberation comes first and theology develops from it."[29] Rather than starting from eternal principles, such a theology began from an analysis of the concrete sociopolitical context, drawing on the insights of social-scientific theory. EATWOT's constitution therefore listed as one of the organization's primary objectives: "promoting the mutual interaction between theological formulation and social analysis." Such an approach was reflected in the structure of the final statement for each EATWOT conference, which began with an analysis of the social, political, and economic context before drawing theological conclusions. In addition, EATWOT's constitution insisted on the importance of "keeping close contacts as well as involvement with action-oriented movements for social change."[30] Members thus committed themselves to playing an active role in the secular movements for liberation in their regions, "reject[ing] as irrelevant an academic type of theology that is divorced from action."[31]

This praxis-oriented methodology had important theological implications for everything from ecclesiology to biblical hermeneutics to the nature of salvation. In the first place, it broke with the theological dualism that these theologians associated with European Christianity, which tended to stress the distinction between history and eternity, the temporal and the spiritual, church and world. Instead, Third World theologians viewed the temporal struggle for liberation as the key locus for the encounter with the divine. God could only be met within history, they insisted, and to participate in the earthly struggle for a more just society was therefore to participate in God's salvific plan. As Gutiérrez explained in *A Theology of Liberation*, "there are not two histories, one profane and one sacred, 'juxtaposed' or 'closely linked.' Rather there is only one human destiny, irreversibly assumed by Christ, the Lord of history. His redemptive work embraces all the dimensions of existence and brings them to their fullness."[32] Consequently, Gutiérrez concluded, "the struggle for a just society is in its own right very much a part of salvation history."[33] This approach informed how Third World theologians read the Bible, leading them to stress the political and liberating message of the Gospel, communicated most forcefully in the Exodus story. It also led them to emphasize the relationship between evangelization and "conscientization," in an effort to transform social structures as well as individual hearts.

The other signal feature of EATWOT's emerging program was its openness to non-Christian religions. Vatican II had opened the way to this engagement by acknowledging that "elements of truth and grace are to be found among the nations, as a sort of secret presence of God," and that it was possible for people of goodwill to be saved even if they remained outside the formal structures of the Catholic Church.[34] The theologians of EATWOT drew upon these pronouncements but took them considerably further, asking how the dialogue with non-Christian traditions might transform Christian theology itself. This position reflected the influence of the Asian representatives at EATWOT, many of whom worked in contexts where Christians were a small minority. For African theologians, too, opening Christianity up to other religions allowed for a greater engagement with traditional African religions and the practice of ancestor worship. Some, for instance, sought to pioneer a distinctively African Christology by figuring Christ himself as an ancestor who mediates between God and humans, initiating the faithful into grace by making them sons of God.[35] Others argued that engaging with African religions should inspire a more communal and expansive definition of salvation, one that could incorporate the ancestors of African Christians even if they had not been baptized.[36]

The Asian theologians at EATWOT likewise made the case for a more inclusive view of salvation, in an effort to break down the barriers between Christians and non-Christians. In doing so, they invoked the concept of the "cosmic Christ," which was rooted in the work of the Church Fathers but had been popularized much more recently by the idiosyncratic priest-paleontologist Pierre Teilhard de Chardin.[37] D. S. Amalorpavadass, a pioneer of liturgical renewal in India, explained this concept at the Dar es Salaam meeting. Christ had not come into the world at the time of the historical incarnation of Jesus Christ, he argued, but had always been present in creation. He was "universally operative and effective both in time and space, hence before the foundation of the institutional church by Christ and outside it too today." And this meant that "the revelation and realization of God's universal plan of salvation for humankind is older than the church; it is wider than the narrow, linear, and limited Judeo-Christian history of four thousand years. . . . Thus the religions of the world and the realities of the temporal order must be viewed as included in God's universal saving plan."[38] The Sri Lankan theologian Tissa Balasuriya took the argument even further. Though the concept of the cosmic Christ was firmly anchored in scripture, he argued, Christians had lost sight of it thanks to the dualism of the Western theological tradition, which was anxious to distinguish the Creator from the created world. Limiting Christ to the historical person of Jesus had led Christians to claim "a monopoly of Christ," treating the church as "the unique medium of salvation" and limiting revelation to the Judeo-Christian scriptures.[39] This exclusivist view of salvation, and the contempt for other religions it implied, was precisely the logic that had informed colonial Christianity, Balasuriya argued, but the encounter with Asian religions should inspire Christian theologians to question the assumptions baked into this model. Indeed, he credited the pantheistic elements of Asian religions with helping Asian theologians to recover the vision of the cosmic Christ, allowing for "a more universal understanding of Jesus and of Christianity."[40] And as with Amalorpavadass, the concept of the cosmic Christ underwrote Balasuriya's commitment to both religious pluralism and social justice, thus anchoring a "theology and spirituality for a New International Economic Order."[41]

Internal Fractures Emerge

Despite this shared set of priorities, tensions began to emerge among the various constituencies represented at EATWOT. From the first, many Asian and African theologians resented the dominance of Latin American liberation theology, a privilege they felt was reflected in the final statement of the Dar es Salaam meeting. They feared that the Latin American approach, which had a much higher international profile, would crowd out other models and claim to speak for all Third World theologies. In doing so, it threatened to replicate the imperialist tendencies of European theology and become "the next 'universal' theology to dominate the Third World."[42] These concerns came to a head at the general assembly of EATWOT in New Delhi in 1981. Held in the wake of the three continental conferences in Africa (Ghana, 1977), Asia (Sri Lanka, 1979), and Latin America (Brazil, 1980), the goal in New Delhi was to synthesize the discrete approaches of the continental groups into an overarching Third World theology. But it quickly became apparent that no such synthesis was possible, and African and Asian theologians complained that any effort to establish a unifying Third World theology would simply mean the "institutionalization of the Latin American theology of liberation."[43]

Such concerns reflected important differences between the Latin Americans, who tended to privilege economic and political questions, and Asian and African theologians who prioritized cultural questions and the dialogue with non-Christian religions. This divergence was often characterized as a split between "liberationist" and "inculturationist" approaches, or between "socio-economic" and "religio-cultural" concerns. Added to this, for many in the latter camp, was the sense that Latin American Christianity remained essentially "occidental," reflecting a European settler-colonial and predominantly

Christian context. The Sri Lankan theologian Aloysius Pieris therefore lamented that "the only Third World theology presently being given substance is circumscribed by the exclusively Latin and Christian context of its origin."[44]

At issue was a particular disagreement about how to define the "poor and oppressed" on behalf of whom Third World theology claimed to speak, and what analytic tools were best suited to understanding the challenges they faced. Latin American theologians tended to draw on social-scientific modes of analysis, such as Marxist or dependency theory, in order to understand the economic structures responsible for poverty and injustice. But Asian and especially African theologians argued that such models failed to grasp key dimensions of the life of the poor in these regions, whether it be the role of racism or of sexism, or the importance of drawing on local religious and cultural traditions that had been devalued by European colonialism. They pointed out that Marxism was very much bound by the limitations of its nineteenth-century European context of origin, including the secular and rationalist tendencies of European thought. As Pieris explained, this had led Marx to devalue religion as a mere ideological auxiliary of capitalism and to endorse European colonialism as a necessary conduit for the globalization of capitalism that would prepare the way for the eventual proletarian revolution.[45] Hamstrung by his Eurocentrism, Marx had been unable to imagine the possibility of a distinctively Asian path to socialism, or to appreciate the liberating potential of religion. It was therefore necessary to supplement and correct Marxist analysis with resources better suited to the Asian context, such as "the psychological tools of *introspection*" pioneered by the Asian religious traditions.[46]

The Cameroonian theologian Engelbert Mveng likewise denounced the methodological imperialism of Marxist analysis at EATWOT and sought to elaborate a more complex understanding of poverty. For Africans, he argued, poverty involved much more than material or economic deprivation; it was rooted in a deeper form of impoverishment born of colonialism—what he called "anthropological poverty." This kind of impoverishment consisted in "despoiling human beings not only of what they have, but of everything that constitutes their being and essence—their identity, history, ethnic roots, language, culture, faith, creativity, dignity, pride, ambitions, right to speak."[47] It was a product of the colonial imposition of a Western anthropology "based on domination," which had robbed Africans of their personhood and devalued or displaced their indigenous traditions. And it continued to find expression in "neocolonialism, racism, apartheid, and the universal derision that has always accompanied the 'civilized' world's discourse upon and encounter with Africa—and still accompanies it today."[48] For Mveng, anthropological poverty seemed much more fundamental than the material poverty analyzed by Marx. The priority for African theologians, he insisted, was to reverse the process of anthropological impoverishment by renewing and reviving African cultural and religious traditions, as the Negritude movement had been doing since the 1930s.[49] The fact that EATWOT did not seem to take such a priority seriously and instead privileged the Latin American approach was, for Mveng, evidence of the internal "struggles for hegemony" within the Third World. "Even in the Third World itself, in an association of theologians," he lamented, "Africa remains the everlastingly marginalized—not to say forgotten!—continent."[50]

But the battle between "inculturationists" and "liberationists" was not always so acrimonious, and it led many theologians to acknowledge the limits of their own approach and the need to incorporate alternative perspectives. This was clear from Pieris's critique of liberation theology at the New Delhi conference.[51] For the Sri Lankan Jesuit, liberation theology was simply the most recent manifestation of a tradition he labelled "Christ-*against*-religions" theology, which he associated with the European missionaries who had come to Asia to spread Western civilization and battle "false religion." In its most unsophisticated (i.e., Marxist) form, Pieris implied, liberation theology was thus "crypto-colonialist" and tended to underestimate the liberating power of religion generally and non-Christian religions in particular.[52] But Pieris was just as critical of the opposing tradition—what he called "Christ-*of*-religions" theology—of which the inculturationists were the latest representatives. He associated this tradition with early efforts to bring Christianity into dialogue with Asian religions, including the approach enshrined at Vatican II, which presented Christianity as the culmination of the highest impulses in other religions. Whereas the Christ-*against*-religions tradition underestimated the value of religion, the problem with this second tradition was that it neglected the role of material and economic forces. The current debate between liberationists and inculturationists was simply the latest iteration of this age-old conflict, Pieris argued, and both sides were missing a key piece of the puzzle. Neither could appreciate the extent to which all religions could be a force for liberation as well as oppression, and Pieris insisted that it was precisely the role of Third World theology to identify and foster those elements of religion that were liberating. Crucially, for Pieris, this project could not be confined to Christianity since Christians were a tiny minority (3 percent) of the poor in Asia.

Though the conflict between liberationists and inculturationists was never fully resolved, most theologians accepted the need to incorporate both modes of analysis. Latin Americans such as Torres and Gutiérrez were generally alive to the concerns of their Asian and African counterparts, and the New Delhi meeting's final statement insisted on the need to balance an attention to both socioeconomic forces and religion and culture. Indeed, EATWOT's constitution was altered at New Delhi to add "promoting the interaction of theology with the diversity of cultures and religions of the people of the Third World" to the existing emphasis on socioeconomic liberation.[53] It is likewise important to note that these regional differences were never hard and fast. There were many African and Asian theologians, for instance, who were deeply sympathetic to the Marxist/liberationist paradigm. But the effect of the debate between liberationists and inculturationists was to make theologians from all regions more aware of the limitations of their own analytic tools and the need to address multiple forms of oppression. This realization was driven home most powerfully by the contributions of Black and feminist theologians.

If Asian and African theologians pointed out the blind spots in Marxist analysis of religion and culture, Black theologians from the United States and South Africa were quick to criticize the way Latin American liberation theology privileged socioeconomic oppression over racial injustice. Doing so, Cornel West suggested, had the effect of blinding these theologians to the particular depredations suffered by the Indigenous and Black communities in their midst.[54] For their part, Latin American theologians pressed Black theologians to pay greater attention to class and adopt a sharper critique of US imperialism.[55] As the celebrated Black theologian James Cone acknowledged, "in this dialogue with Latin theologians, we have come to realize the importance of Marxism as a tool for social analysis" and of situating the struggle against racism in a wider international context. "I am firmly convinced," he concluded, "that black theology must not limit itself to the race struggle in the United States but must find ways to join in solidarity with the struggles of the poor in the Third World."[56] Such a commitment was in fact a key plank of the Black Theology Project, which emerged out of the Theology in the Americas conference in 1975 and participated in the activities of EATWOT.[57] And yet, while Black theologians took the Latin Americans to task for privileging class over race, they also tended to criticize African theologians for paying insufficient attention to economic exploitation. Because they prioritized culture and "Africanization" over economic analysis, argued the South

African theologian Frank Chikane, African theologians had failed to see how the ruling elites in their own society had taken the place of colonial authorities and represented the interests of international capital at the expense of their fellow Africans.[58] For Chikane and Cone, then, it was critical to incorporate both a commitment to socioeconomic liberation and an awareness of racial oppression because each alone was inadequate.

At the 1981 conference in New Delhi, women raised similar concerns about the blindness to women's oppression within EATWOT. Like Black theologians, they pointed out that attention to sexism tended to take a back seat to socioeconomic analysis and, indeed, the initial meeting in Dar es Salaam had included only one woman (the Argentinian theologian Beatriz Melano Couch). These concerns sparked vigorous debate in New Delhi, prompted by the intervention of the Ghanaian feminist theologian Mercy Amba Oduyoye. If the rise of EATWOT had signaled the "irruption of the third world" into theology, she argued, women's struggle for representation within EATWOT constituted an "irruption within the irruption."[59] Oduyoye challenged her male counterparts to consider whether, despite their commitment to liberation, they themselves might be "the oppressors who are so well concealed behind the mask of liberation concerns."[60] At issue was not just the representation of women at EATWOT meetings, in its publications, and on its decision-making bodies—a problem that reflected the paucity of women in church leadership and the discipline of theology more broadly—but also the lack of serious engagement with feminist theology. These issues took center stage at the 1986 general assembly in Oaxtepec, Mexico. As the final statement explained, the presence of women at EATWOT "should not only complement men's theology but change the whole style of doing theology."[61] Such sentiments led to the creation of a women's commission and a slew of conferences and publications devoted to feminist theology, thanks largely to the tireless efforts of Virginia Fabella, a Filipina Maryknoll sister who played a pivotal role in the development of EATWOT, though often behind the scenes.[62] The organization's constitution was also changed in 1986 to mandate gender balance in membership and leadership positions, adding to the existing requirements for regional and confessional balance.[63] Similar concerns about representation also prompted efforts to include more Native American and Latino voices within EATWOT.

Thanks to these developments, EATWOT came to represent a much wider range of voices and approaches by the 1980s. By then, its membership had expanded from the initial group of twenty-two to one hundred twenty-five and the organization had launched its own journal, *Voices from the Third World*.[64] Perhaps because of this growing internal diversity, the attempt to synthesize the various approaches that was broached in New Delhi was never renewed, and members had to content themselves with the more modest goal of "cross-fertilization." Precisely because of EATWOT's commitment to contextualist theology, members were forced to recognize that no single approach could claim to represent the Third World as a whole. And consequently, Third World theologies had to remain plural and plural*ist*, by definition. This is not to say, however, that members simply retreated into their local or regional silos to produce what Chikane called "ghetto theologies."[65] Instead, the confrontation between Latin American liberation theology, African and Asian inculturationists, Black, and feminist theologians forced each of these constituencies to confront their own blind spots and made them more attentive to the relationship between different forms of oppression—what we would now call "intersectionality." Moreover, these groups were united by a common theological methodology that involved a praxis-based theology, a rigorous analysis of the structures of oppression, and interpreting the Bible from the perspective of the poor and oppressed. This shared methodology allowed EATWOT to escape the fate of so many other Third World movements at a time when the international climate was becoming increasingly hostile to such projects.

The First World Responds

EATWOT did not confine itself to nurturing exchanges among Third World theologians, however. Echoing the logic of the NIEO, it also sought to establish a dialogue between First and Third World theologians, based on the premise that the Third World could not escape its situation of dependency without a fundamental restructuring of the global economy and, by extension, of the global churches. "It behooves Christians of the Third World and those of the North Atlantic countries," Sergio Torres explained at Dar es Salaam, "to work together for a new International Economic Order as well as for a new theological formulation."[66] The delegates at the 1981 general assembly in New Delhi therefore resolved that EATWOT's next intercontinental conference would be a conversation with First World theologians, to be followed eventually by a dialogue between Second and Third World theologians.[67] Though this second project never came to fruition, the first took place in Geneva in

1983. From its inception, EATWOT had established support committees in Europe and North America that included some of the most eminent progressive theologians of the day, such as Marie-Dominique Chenu, Johann Baptist Metz, and Jürgen Moltmann, and the organization relied heavily on funding from Europe and North America.[68] But when the committee tasked with preparing for the Geneva dialogue solicited European theologians who might be interested in participating, the initial response was disappointing.[69] As a result, the dialogue with Third World theologians was confined to the most radical and progressive wing of the Northern churches—an eclectic and internally divided group drawn from the ranks of the feminist movement, labor activism, Christians for Socialism, base ecclesial communities, and academic theology.[70]

In the leadup to the Geneva meeting, EATWOT encouraged its partners in Europe and North America to hold preparatory meetings in order to discuss the impact of Third World theology and how its methods might be taken up in the First World. In 1978, the Pan-American organization that had emerged from the 1975 Theology in the Americas (TIA) conference in Detroit organized a meeting to discuss the question: "Is Liberation Theology for North America? The Response of First World Churches to Third World Theologies."[71] The goal of the conference was to apply the methods of liberation theology to the North American context and promote solidarity with the Third World. A similar preparatory meeting was held for European theologians in the Netherlands in 1981, bringing together nearly one hundred participants from nine national support groups that EATWOT had inspired throughout Western Europe, as well as observers from the Second and Third Worlds.[72] As with the TIA meeting, the goal was to apply the methods of liberation theology to the European context and lay a foundation for the upcoming dialogue with EATWOT, on the grounds that Third World theology should inspire Europeans to "question our way of doing theology."[73] In keeping with this method, subgroups on immigration, feminism, labor, culture, and peace began with an analysis of the oppressive structures in place in Europe and the church's relationship to them before proposing a theological response. Participants stressed the commonalities between Third World countries and the "Third World in Europe"—marginalized or oppressed communities in their own midst.[74] And they probed the ways in which European theology had been complicit in shoring up capitalism and colonialism, becoming in some instances little more than an "ideo-theology." "A new way has opened at the core of our European existence through the irruption of the Third World," the participants proclaimed. It promised "a new theological existence" founded on "solidarity with the oppressed" and "a conversion to the poor."[75]

By the time ninety-five delegates from the First and Third Worlds gathered in Geneva in 1983, then, Third World theology had already made important inroads among a subset of Euro-American theologians. Recognizing that any effort to restructure the global economy would require the cooperation of wealthy nations, one of the goals of the conference was to establish a common front of progressive theologians against neocolonialism. This meant developing a liberation theology for both the First and Third Worlds and strengthening the solidarity between the Third World and oppressed groups within Europe and North America. To this end, delegates eschewed the methods of traditional theology in favor of a liberationist approach grounded in concrete praxis, social analysis, and the preferential option for the poor. Feminist theologians seem to have played a particularly important role at the conference and helped to mediate between the two constituencies. The American theologian Rosemary Radford Ruether, for instance, drew attention to the "double oppression" that Third World women faced "both as women and as members of oppressed classist and racial groups."[76] One major consequence of the meeting was to shift the conversation away from the problem of secularization, which had long preoccupied First World theologians. According to the final statement, the most pressing religious challenge confronting the wealthy nations was not secularization but *idolatry*—the worship of false gods such as consumerism, individualism, the free market, and national security. "The question about God in the world of the oppressed," the document explained, "is not knowing whether God exists or not, but knowing on which side God is."[77]

For the influential political theologian Johann Baptist Metz, the Geneva conference and the irruption of Third World theology signaled nothing less than "*the end of the European-centered era of Christianity*."[78] The history of European Christianity, he explained, had been dominated by the conflict with modernity, whether in the form of the Enlightenment, democratic revolutions, technology, capitalism, or secularization. As a result of its confrontation with, and eventual adaptation to, these forces, European Christianity had become a privatized, bourgeois religion. For Metz, the rise of Third World theologies represented nothing less than a "second Reformation," one which promised to rescue Christianity from its privatization and make it a force for liberation once again. In doing so, it would overcome the false choice that European theology had established between rejecting and embracing modernity; between the "the old theocratic monism" and "the modern bourgeois-liberal dualism" of religion and politics.[79] Just as Judeo-Christianity had given way to European Christianity, Metz concluded that Christianity was now undergoing another major transformation "from a Eurocentric church to a culturally polycentric world church."[80] Some Third World participants resented his notion of a linear development from Judeo-Christianity through Europe to the rest of the world, however, as well as Metz's focus on the Holocaust as the paradigmatic scandal of modern history.[81] Even as they embraced Third World theologies, in other words, many First World theologians had not fully divested themselves of their Eurocentric assumptions.

Metz's prediction about the death of the Eurocentric church is a testament to the extent to which Third World theologies had penetrated Euro-American theological discourse by the 1980s. But it was also somewhat premature. Even as the delegates gathered in Geneva, the global economic and political climate had shifted decisively against the sort of restructuring envisioned by Third Worldist projects such as the NIEO. The 1980s instead saw much of the Global South hamstrung by a spiraling cycle of debt and "structural adjustment" imposed by international lending agencies such as the IMF and the World Bank, which increasingly came to supplant the UN as the arbiters of international development.[82] With the elections of Ronald Reagan and Margaret Thatcher, neoliberal economics, free trade, and deregulation became the order of the day.[83] The final statement of the EATWOT conference in Oaxtepec in 1986 acknowledged the changed situation. "In contrast to the years 1976–1981, which were boom years for the Third World and provided much cause for hope, the years 1981–1986 were difficult ones for most countries in Asia, Africa, and Latin America," the document explained. "The First World nations have regained their control of the international situation. In the Third World the outlook has turned grim."[84]

Meanwhile, the document pointed out, the climate within the Christian churches had also changed considerably. The churches had become "suspicious of Third World movements and liberation theologies" and "a wave of neoconservatism and fundamentalism threaten[ed] to engulf the gains of recent struggles and insights."[85] With the election of John Paul II in 1978 and the rise of the religious right in the United States, Christians in Europe and North America increasingly shifted their focus to questions of marriage, sexuality, and reproduction rather than the socioeconomic concerns so central to liberation theology. Meanwhile, the renewal of the Cold War and John Paul II's own struggle against Communism in Poland made the Catholic hierarchy rather less sympathetic to theologies professing any kind of sympathy for Marxism. In 1984, the Congregation for the Doctrine of the Faith, under the leadership of Joseph Ratzinger (the future Pope Benedict XVI), issued a forceful condemnation of liberation theology, moderated only slightly by a second document in 1986. At issue was its use of Marxist categories, including the notion of the class struggle and "a disastrous confusion between the 'poor' of the Scripture and the 'proletariat' of Marx," as well as the way it politicized the Bible.[86] After this confrontation with liberation theology, Cardinal Ratzinger turned his attention to the danger of religious pluralism, which he associated with one of the greatest threats facing the church at the turn of the new millennium—the "dictatorship of relativism."[87]

One of the people to fall afoul of this campaign was the Sri Lankan theologian Tissa Balasuriya, a founding member of EATWOT and a key player within the organization. In 1997, the Vatican took the unprecedented step of excommunicating Balasuriya. The immediate trigger was the publication of *Mary and Human Liberation*, in which the Sri Lankan theologian criticized Catholic teaching on Mary for reinforcing the structures of patriarchal oppression, and even went so far as to question the doctrine of original sin. But perhaps the key point of contention was Balasuriya's commitment to the kind of religious pluralism that Asian theologians at EATWOT had been championing for years. From the perspective of the Roman authorities, its effect was to deny "the supernatural, unique and irrepeatable character of the revelation of Jesus Christ, by placing its presuppositions on the same level as those of other forms of religion."[88] EATWOT protested vigorously against the decision to excommunicate Balasuriya, denouncing it as a violation of the church's commitment to ecumenism and contextual theology, and calling on the pope "to respect the sentiments of the churches in the Third World."[89] The excommunication was eventually lifted, but the severity of the response indicates the distance that separated the Vatican from the priorities of EATWOT by the 1990s.

The organization struggled to withstand these pressures from within and beyond the church. After the 1992 general assembly in Nairobi, EATWOT ceased publishing its conference proceedings and the organization seems to have lost some steam, though it continues to exist and to publish its journal to this day. The leading progressive Catholic theological journal *Concilium* also continued to provide a platform for members of EATWOT, several of whom served on its editorial board, by publishing issues devoted to Third World theology.[90] But EATWOT's moment seemed to have passed, even if it lasted longer than most secular Third Worldist projects.

And yet, the last chapter of this story has not yet been written. The election of Pope Francis in 2013—the first modern pope from the Global South—has brought many of the concerns raised by Third World theologians in the 1970s and 1980s back to the fore. Not only has Francis signaled a greater openness to liberation theology, symbolized by the canonization of Óscar Romero in 2018, but he has also been a vigorous critic of global capitalism. Speaking in Bolivia in 2015, the pope offered an apology for the church's role in European colonialism and also warned against a "new colonialism" enforced by "corporations, loan agencies, certain 'free trade' treaties, and the imposition of measures of 'austerity,'" which prevent poorer nations from achieving true sovereignty. "Colonialism, both old and new, which reduces poor countries to mere providers of raw material and cheap labor," he explained, "engenders violence, poverty, forced migrations and all the evils which go hand in hand with these . . . by placing the periphery at the service of the center."[91] Such sentiments, so reminiscent of the critiques of EATWOT, suggest that the project to decolonize Christianity, launched by Third World theologians in the 1970s, is far from dead. Indeed, as the demographic balance of the church increasingly shifts to the Global South, such voices are only likely to grow louder.[92]

NOTES

Introduction

1. Albert Tévoédjrè, *L'Afrique révoltée* (Paris: Présence africaine, 1958).

2. Tévoédjrè and his MLN co-militants traveled to Africa to persuade people to reject Charles de Gaulle's proposed French Community, a restructuring of the empire that would give African members more internal autonomy but would retain the metropole's authority in the domains of foreign policy, defense, and currency, among others. In the end, Guinea under Sékou Touré was the only territory in French sub-Saharan Africa that voted no. Guinea acceded to independence in 1958, but the French retaliated by withdrawing all financial technical and medical assistance almost overnight. On the MLN, see Elizabeth A. Foster, *African Catholic: Decolonization and the Transformation of the Church* (Cambridge, MA: Harvard University Press, 2019), 149–51.

3. Gwendolen Margaret Carter, ed., *Five African States* (Ithaca, NY: Cornell University Press, 1963).

4. Albert Tévoédjrè, *Poverty: The Wealth of Mankind* (Oxford: Pergamon, 1978).

5. Tévoédjrè, *L'Afrique révoltée*, 111 (emphasis in original), 123.

6. The figure of 9 percent derives from the Catholic Church's own records for 1955, cited in Foster, *African Catholic*, 19. The recent statistics are based on the 2013 census, as analyzed in the US Department of State 2019 report on religion in Benin, available in the CIA's "World Factbook," https://www.cia.gov/the-world-factbook/countries/benin/.

7. Philip Jenkins, *The Next Christendom: The Coming of Global Christianity*, 3rd edition (New York: Oxford University Press, 2011), 3.

8. Frantz Fanon, *Wretched of the Earth*, trans. Richard Philcox (New York: Grove Atlantic, 2007), 45.

9. The scholarship on this topic is vast. For a few helpful examples, see Hilary M. Carey, *God's Empire: Religion and Colonialism in the British World* (Cambridge, UK: Cambridge University Press, 2011); Andrew N. Porter, *Religion versus Empire: British Protestant Missionaries and Overseas Expansion* (Manchester: Manchester University Press, 2004); J. P. Daughton, *An Empire Divided: Religion, Republicanism, and the Making of French Colonialism* (New York: Oxford University Press, 2006); Richard Hölzl, *Gläubige Imperialisten* (Frankfurt: Campus Verlag, 2021).

10. A good example is Hugh McLeod's excellent *The Religious Crisis of the 1960s* (Oxford: Oxford University Press, 2007), which provides a rare pan-European perspective but does not discuss encounters between Europeans and non-Europeans. On liberation theology, see Lilian Calles Barger, *The World Come of Age: An Intellectual History of Liberation Theology* (New York: Oxford University Press, 2018). Recent works that have begun to explore decolonization's

impact on religious life include Ari Waskar, *Earth Politics: Religion, Decolonization, and Bolivia's Indigenous Intellectuals* (Durham, NC: Duke University Press, 2014); Olufemi Vaughan, *Religion and the Making of Nigeria* (Durham, NC: Duke University Press, 2016); and Clemens Six, *Secularism, Decolonisation, and the Cold War in South and Southeast Asia* (London: Routledge, 2019).

11. On Christian anti-Communism from the interwar period to the Cold War era, see Giuliana Chamedes, *A Twentieth Century Crusade* (Cambridge, MA: Harvard University Press, 2019). The quote is from Pius XII, *Decree Against Communism* (1949), available online at http://www.montfort.org.br/eng/documentos/decretos/anticomunismo/.

12. See Frederick Cooper, *Citizenship between Empire and Nation: Remaking France and French Africa, 1945–1960* (Princeton: Princeton University Press, 2014); Alanna M. O'Malley, *The Diplomacy of Decolonisation: America, Britain and the United Nations during the Congo Crisis 1960–64* (Manchester: Manchester University Press, 2018); and Martin Thomas, *Fight or Flight: Britain, France, and the Roads from Empire* (Oxford: Oxford University Press, 2014). For the West's response, see Samuel Moyn, *Not Enough: Human Rights in an Unequal World* (Cambridge, MA: Harvard University Press, 2018), esp. 119–45, and Vanessa Ogle, "Funk Money: The End of Empires, the Expansion of Tax Havens, and Decolonization as an Economic and Financial Event," *Past & Present* 249, no. 1 (2020): 213–49. The quote is from Pankaj Mishra, *Bland Fanatics: Liberals, Race, and Empire* (New York: Farrar, Straus and Giroux, 2020), 195.

13. See Michael Goebel, *Anti-Imperial Metropolis: Interwar Paris and the Seeds of Third World Nationalism* (New York: Cambridge University Press, 2015); Tony Ballantyne and Antoinette Burton, *Empires and the Reach of the Global* (Cambridge, MA: Harvard University Press, 2012), 131–81.

14. Miguel A. De La Torre, *Decolonizing Christianity* (Grand Rapids, MI: Eerdmans, 2021).

Chapter 1

Epigraphs: Paul Abrecht, *The Churches and Rapid Social Change* (London: SCM Press, 1961), 28; and Hans Hoekendijk, "Christ and the World in the Modern Age," an address delivered at the World Student Christian Federation's World Teaching Conference in Strasbourg, France, July 1960, 1 (World Council of Churches Archives, 213.15.7).

1. The major statement of this argument is in David Hollinger, *After Cloven Tongues of Fire: Protestant Liberalism in Modern American History* (Princeton: Princeton University Press, 2013); see also his *Protestants Abroad: How Missionaries Tried to Change the World but Changed America* (Princeton: Princeton University Press, 2017). For accounts that follow in this vein, see Andrew Preston, "Peripheral Visions: American Mainline Protestants and the Global Cold War," *Cold War History* 13, no. 1 (2013); Gene Zubovich, *Before the Religious Right: Liberal Protestants, Human Rights, and the Polarization of the United States* (Philadelphia: University of Pennsylvania Press, 2022); Zubovich, "The Protestant Search for 'The Universal Christian Community' Between Decolonization and Communism," *Religions* 8, no. 2 (2017); and David Sehat, "Political Atheism: The Secularization and Liberalization of American Public Life," *Modern Intellectual History* 17, no. 1 (2020), which is also a contextualizing analysis of Hollinger's arguments. Though these works focus on American Protestants, they often make wider claims about ecumenical Protestantism in its international dimensions. Albert Wu's *From Christ to Confucius: German Missionaries, Chinese Christians, and the Globalization of Christianity, 1860–1950* (New Haven, CT: Yale University Press, 2016) develops a similar account from the point of view of German missionaries and Chinese Christians in China.

2. See, for example, Michael Thompson, *For God and Globe: Christian Internationalism in the United States from the Great War to the Cold War* (Ithaca, NY: Cornell University Press, 2015); Andrew Preston, *Sword of the Spirit, Shield of Faith: Religion in American War and Diplomacy* (New York: Penguin Press, 2012); James Kennedy, "Protestant Ecclesiastical Internationals," in *Religious Internationals in the Modern World: Globalization and Faith Communities since 1750,* ed. Abigail Green and Vincent Viaene (New York: Palgrave Macmillan, 2012), 292–318; and Elisabeth Engel, James Kennedy, and Justin Reynolds, "Editorial—The Theory and Practice of Ecumenism: Christian Global Governance and the Search for World Order, 1900–1980," *Journal of Global History* 13, no. 2 (2018).

3. *Report of Commission I: Carrying the Gospel to All the Non-Christian World* (London: Oliphant, Anderson & Ferrier, 1910), 24. Published for the World Missionary Conference 1910.

4. Quoted in Brian Stanley, *The World Missionary Conference: Edinburgh 1910* (Grand Rapids, MI: Eerdmans, 2009), 219.

5. Emil Brunner, "Secularism as a Problem for the Church," *International Review of Missions* 19, no. 76 (January 1930). See also Udi Greenberg, "Protestants, Decolonization, and European Integration," *Journal of Modern History* (June 2017): 319–27, for a similar account of interwar developments.

6. "Report on Church and Community," in *The Churches Survey Their Task: The Report of the Conference at Oxford, July 1937, on Church, Community, and State* (London: George Allen & Unwin, 1937), 67.

7. *Man's Disorder and God's Design: The Amsterdam Assembly Series* (New York: Harper, 1948).

8. Greenberg, "Protestants, Decolonization, and European Integration," 328.

9. Justin Reynolds, "From Christian anti-imperialism to Post-colonial Christianity: M. M. Thomas and the Ecumenical Theology of Communism in the 1940s and 1950s," *Journal of Global History* 13, no. 2 (2018): 246.

10. C. W. Li, "Theology and Revolution," *Student World* 41, no. 2 (1948): 162. For a discussion of pro-Communist Chinese Christians immediately before and during the Communist era, see Philip Wickeri, *Reconstructing Christianity in China: K. H. Ting and the Chinese Church* (Maryknoll: Orbis Books, 2007), esp. 77–78.

11. M. M. Thomas and Davis McCaughey, "The Christian in the World Struggle," Report of the Commission on "Where is the SCM in the World Struggle?" to the General Committee of the World Student Christian Federation Meeting at Whitby, Canada, August 1949 (World Council of Churches Archives, 213.13.2), pg. 1.

12. See for instance John Karefa-Smart and Rena Karefa-Smart, *The Halting Kingdom: Christianity and the African Revolution* (New York: Friendship Press, 1959); Richard Shaull, *Encounter with Revolution* (New York: Haddam House, 1955); and Mauricio Lopez, "The Political Dynamics of Latin American Society Today" in *The Church Amid Revolution*, ed. Harvey Cox (New York: Association Press, 1967).

13. Kenneth Scott Latourette and William Richey Hogg, *Tomorrow Is Here: The Mission and Work of the Church as Seen from the Meeting of the International Missionary Council at Whitby, Ontario, July 5–24, 1947* (New York: Friendship Press, 1948), 17.

14. Stephen Neill, *Cross Over Asia* (London: Canterbury Press, 1948), 16.

15. "Findings of the Eastern Asia Christian Conference, Bangkok, 3–11 December 1949: The Church in Social and Political Life," in *Statements of the World Council of Churches on Social Questions* (Geneva: World Council of Churches, 1955), 27.

16. “World Council of Churches Study Department Staff Meeting Minutes,” Ecumenical Institute, Bossey, Switzerland, November 25–30, 1954 (World Council of Churches Archives, 422.005), pg. 10.

17. A summary of these reports appears in *Christ: The Hope of Asia, Papers and Minutes of the Ecumenical Study Conference for East Asia, Lucknow, India, December 27–30, 1952* (Madras: Study Department of the World Council of Churches, 1953).

18. The program has received little attention in recent scholarship on the ecumenical movement by non-church historians, but see Paul Abrecht, “The Development of Ecumenical Social Thought and Action” in *A History of the Ecumenical Movement, Volume II: 1948–1968*, ed. Harold Fey (Geneva: World Council of Churches, 1968), 235–59. One of the few accounts of this program outside of in-house movement historiography is Darcie Fontaine, *Decolonizing Christianity: Religion and the End of Empire in France and Algeria* (Cambridge, UK: Cambridge University Press, 2016), which focuses on the program’s activities in France and Algeria.

19. Pierre van der Eng, “An Observer of 65 Years of Socio-Economic Change in Indonesia: Egbert de Vries,” *Bulletin of Indonesian Economic Studies* 27, no.1 (August 2006).

20. For instance, Egbert de Vries, “Problems of Agriculture in Indonesia,” *Pacific Affairs* 22, no. 2 (June 1949), and de Vries, “Population Growth and Christian Responsibility,” *Ecumenical Review* 13, no. 1 (October 1960).

21. On Munby’s background and work (also discussed below), see A. M. C. Waterman, “Denys Munby on Economics and Christianity,” *Theology* 93, no. 752 (1990).

22. On Lebret, see Giuliana Chamedes, “The Catholic Origins of Economic Development after World War II,” *French Politics, Culture, & Society* 33, no. 2 (Summer 2015).

23. For a sample of the debates around this issue within the RSC, see “Minutes and Reports of the Eleventh Meeting of the Central Committee,” Nyborg Strand, Denmark, August 21–29, 1958, https://archive.org/stream/eleventhmeetingo00unse/eleventhmeetingo00unse_djvu.txt.

24. For an account of the Geneva conference in relation to ecumenical economic ideas, see Udi Greenberg, “The Rise of the Global South and the Protestant Peace with Socialism,” *Contemporary European History* 29, no. 2 (2020): 1–18.

25. Paul Ramsey, *Who Speaks for the Church?* (Nashville, TN: Abington Press, 1967), 108.

26. *The Common Christian Responsibility Towards Areas of Rapid Social Change: Second Statement* (Switzerland: World Council of Churches, 1956), 70.

27. *The Common Christian Responsibility*, 69.

28. Reports on many of these study groups and consultations were published in the Christian Institute for the Study of Religion and Society journal *Religion and Society* and the Social Concerns series edited by Thomas and Devanandan (Calcutta: YMCA Publishing House).

29. For a description, see Thomas, *My Ecumenical Journey* (Bangalore: P. M. Oommen, 1990), 173–95.

30. M. M. Thomas, *Christian Participation in Nation-Building* (Bangalore: National Christian Council of India), 155–56.

31. Kevin Schultz, *Tri-Faith America: How Catholics and Jews Held Postwar America to Its Protestant Promise* (New York: Oxford University Press, 2011). For an illuminating account of competing conceptions of pluralism, Christianity, and democracy in the United States, see Healan Gaston, *Imagining Judeo-Christian America: Religion, Secularism, and the Redefinition of Democracy* (Chicago: University of Chicago Press, 2019).

32. Martin Marty, “Protestantism Enters Third Phase,” *Christian Century*, January 18, 1961, 72–75.

33. W. A. Visser 't Hooft, "Pluralism—Temptation or Opportunity," *Ecumenical Review* 18, no. 2 (1966): 145.

34. S. J. Samartha, "Dialogue as a Continuing Christian Concern," *Ecumenical Review* 23, no. 2 (1971): 129.

35. Complete transcripts of the addresses are available in the World Council of Churches Archives, 213.15.7.

36. Denys Munby, *The Idea of a Secular Society and Its Significance for Christians* (Oxford: Oxford University Press, 1963), 13–14.

37. Arend Th. van Leeuwen, *Christianity in World History: The Meeting of the Faiths of East and West*, trans. H. H. Hoskins (New York: Scribner's, 1964).

38. Harvey Cox, *The Secular City* (New York: Macmillan, 1965), 267.

39. Cox, *The Secular City*, 4.

40. Cox, *The Secular City*, 268.

41. Important recent studies of this era have mostly adopted a national frame. See especially Sam Brewitt-Taylor, *Christian Radicalism in the Church of England and the Invention of the British Sixties, 1957–1970* (New York: Oxford University Press, 2018); Alexander Christian Widmann, *Wandel mit Gewalt? Der deutsche Protestantismus und die politisch motivierte Gewaltanwendung in den 1960er und 1970er Jahren* (Göttingen: Vandenhoeck & Ruprecht, 2013); and Jill Gill, *Embattled Ecumenism: The National Council of Churches, the Vietnam War, and the Trials of the Protestant Left* (DeKalb: Northern Illinois University Press, 2011). For a discussion of relevant literature and an interpretation of the root causes of mainline Protestant church decline in the United States, see Hollinger, *After Cloven Tongues*, 18–55 (esp. 36–38).

42. Thomas J. J. Altizer and William Hamilton, eds., *Radical Theology and The Death of God* (Indianapolis: Bobbs-Merrill, 1966).

43. John A. T. Robinson, *Honest to God* (London: SCM Press, 1963). For Robinson's defense of *Lady Chatterley's Lover*, see Brewitt-Taylor, *Christian Radicalism*, 184–89.

44. For example, Ian Macqueen, "Students, Apartheid, and the Ecumenical Movement in South Africa, 1960–1975," *Journal of Southern African Studies* 39, no. 2 (June 2013).

45. Van Leeuwen, *Christianity in World History*, 20.

46. Munby, *Idea of a Secular Society*, 12.

47. Thomas, "Review of *Christianity in World History*," *Ecumenical Review* 16, no. 5 (October 1964): 550.

48. On the WCC's "Program to Combat Racism," see David C. Kirkpatrick's contribution to this volume.

49. Ernst Feil, "Aspekte der Bonhoeffererinterpretation," *Theologische Literaturzeitung* 117, nos. 1 & 2 (January and February 1992): 1–18, 81–100. For an overview in English of Bonhoeffer's reception, see John W. de Grouchy, "The Reception of Bonhoeffer's theology," in *The Cambridge Companion to Bonhoeffer*, ed. John W. de Grouchy (Cambridge, UK: Cambridge University Press, 1999).

50. Wayne Whitson Floyd, "Dietrich Bonhoeffer," in *Modern Theologians: An Introduction to Christian Theology since 1918*, eds. David Ford and Rachel Muers (Cambridge, UK: Cambridge University Press, 2005), 43–61.

51. Martin Marty, ed., *The Place of Bonhoeffer: Problems and Possibilities in His Thought* (New York: Association Press, 1952). The Robinson quote appears in "The Saint of the Secular," a sermon preached on April 4, 1965, reprinted in Dietrich Bonhoeffer, *Letters and Papers from Prison* (revised edition), ed. Eberhard Bethge (New York: Macmillan, 1967), 9.

52. Cox, *The Secular City*, 4.

53. Elisabeth Adler, "Secularisation," *Student World* 56, no. 1 (1963): 1.

54. W. A. Visser 't Hooft, "Dietrich Bonhoeffer, 1945–1965," *Ecumenical Review* 17, no. 3 (January 1965): 224.

55. Quoted in Floyd, "Dietrich Bonhoeffer," 55.

56. Friedrich Gogarten also filled this role for 1960s ecumenists, especially Cox in *The Secular City*.

Chapter 2

1. On the growth of anti-colonial thought among ecumenical Protestants prior to the Cold War, see William R. Hutchison, *Errand to the World: American Protestant Thought and Foreign Missions* (Chicago: University of Chicago Press, 1987); David A. Hollinger, *Protestants Abroad: How Missionaries Tried to Change the World but Changed America* (Princeton, NJ: Princeton University Press, 2017); and Michael G. Thompson, *For God and Globe: Christian Internationalism in the United States between the Great War and the Cold War* (Ithaca, NY: Cornell University Press, 2015). For other work that emphasizes American ecumenical Protestant international engagement, see Cara Lea Burnidge, *A Peaceful Conquest: Woodrow Wilson, Religion, and the New World Order* (Chicago: University of Chicago Press, 2016); Andrew Preston, "Peripheral Visions: American Mainline Protestants and the Global Cold War," *Cold War History Cold War History* 13, no. 1 (2013): 109–30; Nicholas T. Pruitt, *Open Hearts, Closed Doors: Immigration Reform and the Waning of Mainline Protestantism* (New York: New York University Press, 2021); and James D. Strasburg, *God's Marshall Plan: American Protestants and the Struggle for the Soul of Europe* (New York: Oxford University Press, 2021).

2. On the close relationship between international affairs and anti-racist activism, see Keisha N. Blain, *Set the World on Fire: Black Nationalist Women and the Global Struggle for Freedom* (Philadelphia: University of Pennsylvania Press, 2019); Thomas Borstelmann, *The Cold War and the Color Line: American Race Relations in the Global Arena* (Cambridge, MA: Harvard University Press, 2001); Mary L. Dudziak, *Cold War Civil Rights: Race and the Image of American Democracy* (Princeton, NJ: Princeton University Press, 2011); and Penny M. Von Eschen, *Race Against Empire: Black Americans and Anticolonialism, 1937–1957* (Ithaca, NY: Cornell University Press, 1997).

3. Nico Slate, *Colored Cosmopolitanism* (Cambridge, MA: Harvard University Press, 2012); Sarah Azaransky, *This Worldwide Struggle: Religion and the International Routes of the Civil Rights Movement, 1935–1959* (New York: Oxford University Press, 2017).

4. Carol Anderson, *Bourgeois Radicals: The NAACP and the Struggle for Colonial Liberation, 1941–1960* (New York: Cambridge University Press, 2015); Steven L. B. Jensen, *The Making of International Human Rights: The 1960s, Decolonization, and the Reconstruction of Global Values* (New York: Cambridge University Press, 2017); Sarah B. Snyder, *From Selma to Moscow: How Human Rights Activists Transformed U.S. Foreign Policy* (New York: Columbia University Press, 2018).

5. Udi Greenberg, "Protestants, Decolonization, and European Integration, 1885–1961," *Journal of Modern History* 89, no. 2 (June 1, 2017): 314–54.

6. Elizabeth A. Foster, "'Theologies of Colonization': The Catholic Church and the Future of the French Empire in the 1950s," *Journal of Modern History* 87, no. 2 (June 1, 2015): 281–315.

7. Melani McAlister, *The Kingdom of God Has No Borders: A Global History of American Evangelicals* (New York: Oxford University Press, 2018); Lauren Frances Turek, *To Bring the Good News to All Nations: Evangelical Influence on Human Rights and U.S. Foreign Relations* (Ithaca, NY: Cornell University Press, 2020); Molly Worthen, *Apostles of Reason: The Crisis of Authority in American Evangelicalism* (New York: Oxford University Press, 2016).

8. See Emily Conroy-Krutz, *Christian Imperialism: Converting the World in the Early American Republic* (Ithaca: Cornell University Press, 2015); Kathryn Gin Lum, *Heathen: Religion and Race in American History* (Cambridge, MA: Harvard University Press, 2022); Margaret D. Jacobs, *White Mother to a Dark Race: Settler Colonialism, Maternalism, and the Removal of Indigenous Children in the American West and Australia, 1880–1940* (Lincoln: University of Nebraska Press, 2011).

9. Paul A. Kramer, *The Blood of Government: Race, Empire, the United States, and the Philippines* (Chapel Hill: University of North Carolina Press, 2006); Christopher McKnight Nichols, *Promise and Peril: America at the Dawn of a Global Age* (Cambridge, MA: Harvard University Press, 2015).

10. "Last Day of Conference," *New York Times*, May 2, 1900, 6.

11. "Last Day of Conference," 6.

12. Brian Stanley, *The World Missionary Conference, Edinburgh 1910* (Grand Rapids, MI: William B. Eerdmans, 2009).

13. See H. Richard Niebuhr, *The Social Sources of Denominationalism* (New York: Holt, 1929).

14. For these reasons, several denominations stayed away from the ecumenical movement. The largest were the Southern Baptist Convention and Missouri Synod Lutherans.

15. Joseph Kip Kosek, *Acts of Conscience: Christian Nonviolence and Modern American Democracy* (New York: Columbia University Press, 2011).

16. Eddy quoted in Michael G. Thompson, "Sherwood Eddy, the Missionary Enterprise, and the Rise of Christian Internationalism in 1920s America," *Modern Intellectual History* 12, no. 1 (April 2015): 23.

17. William Ernest Hocking, *Re-Thinking Mission: A Laymen's Inquiry after One Hundred Years* (New York: Harper, 1937). Hutchison, *Errand to the World*, 158–77. On Hocking's confrontation with neoorthodoxy, see J. Wesley Robb, "Hendrik Kraemer Versus William Ernest Hocking," *Journal of the American Academy of Religion* 29, no. 2 (1961): 93–101.

18. Donald B. Meyer, *The Protestant Search for Political Realism, 1919–1941*, 2nd ed. (Middletown, CT: Wesleyan University Press, 1988).

19. "American Malvern," *Time*, March 16, 1942, 44, 46–48, quote at 48.

20. Gene Zubovich, "For Human Rights Abroad, against Jim Crow at Home: The Political Mobilization of American Ecumenical Protestants in the World War II Era," *Journal of American History* 105, no. 2 (September 1, 2018): 267–90. Dulles quoted at 277.

21. Anne M. Blankenship, *Christianity, Social Justice, and the Japanese American Incarceration during World War II* (Chapel Hill: University of North Carolina Press, 2016); Sarah Marie Griffith, *The Fight for Asian American Civil Rights: Liberal Protestant Activism, 1900–1950* (Urbana: University of Illinois Press, 2018); David A. Hollinger, *Protestants Abroad: How Missionaries Tried to Change the World but Changed America* (Princeton, NJ: Princeton University Press, 2018); Robert Shaffer, "Cracks in the Consensus: Defending the Rights of Japanese Americans During World War II," *Radical History Review* 1998, no. 72 (1998): 84–120.

22. Kosek, *Acts of Conscience*, 176–77. See also Blankenship, *Christianity, Social Justice, and the Japanese American Incarceration during World War II*; and Pruitt, *Open Hearts, Closed Doors.*

23. Zubovich, "For Human Rights Abroad, against Jim Crow at Home."

24. *The Church and Race Relations*, pamphlet (New York: Federal Council of Churches, 1946), 5.

25. Anderson, *Bourgeois Radicals*; Mark Thomas Edwards, *The Right of the Protestant Left: God's Totalitarianism* (New York: Palgrave Macmillan, 2012); Andrew Preston, "The Limits of Brotherhood: Race, Religion, and World Order in American Ecumenical Protestantism," *American Historical Review* 127, no. 3 (September 1, 2022): 1222–51; Heather A. Warren, *Theologians of a New World Order: Reinhold Niebuhr and the Christian Realists, 1920–1948* (New York: Oxford University Press, 1997).

26. Preston, "The Limits of Brotherhood"; Michael G. Thompson, *For God and Globe*.

27. Anne M. Blankenship, *Christianity, Social Justice, and the Japanese American Incarceration during World War II*; Griffith, *The Fight for Asian American Civil Rights*; Pruitt, *Open Hearts, Closed Doors*; Gene Zubovich, *Before the Religious Right: Liberal Protestants, Human Rights, and the Polarization of the United States* (Philadelphia: University of Pennsylvania Press, 2022).

28. "The Churches and Human Rights: An Official Statement adopted by the Federal Council of Churches of Christ in America," December 1948, pp. 4–6, Folder 16, Box 57, Federal Council of Churches Papers, Presbyterian Historical Society, Philadelphia, PA.

29. On the links between human rights, the UN, and decolonization, see Jensen, *The Making of International Human Rights*.

30. Jill K. Gill, *Embattled Ecumenism: The National Council of Churches, the Vietnam War, and the Trials of the Protestant Left* (DeKalb: Northern Illinois University Press, 2011); Mark Hulsether, *Building a Protestant Left: Christianity and Crisis Magazine, 1941–1993* (Knoxville: University of Tennessee Press, 1999).

31. Jonathan P. Herzog, *The Spiritual-Industrial Complex: America's Religious Battle Against Communism in the Early Cold War* (New York: Oxford University Press, 2011); Stephen J. Whitfield, *The Culture of the Cold War: The American Moment* (Baltimore: Johns Hopkins University Press, 1991).

32. K. Healan Gaston, *Imagining Judeo-Christian America: Religion, Secularism, and the Redefinition of Democracy* (New York: Oxford University Press, 2019); Kevin Michael Schultz, *Tri-Faith America: How Catholics and Jews Held Postwar America to Its Protestant Promise* (New York: Oxford University Press, 2011).

33. J. B. Matthews, "Reds and Our Churches," *American Mercury*, July 1953, 3.

34. Reinhold Niebuhr, *The Children of Light and the Children of Darkness, a Vindication of Democracy and a Critique of Its Traditional Defence* (New York: C. Scribner's Sons, 1944). On Niebuhr, see Richard Wightman Fox, *Reinhold Niebuhr: A Biography* (New York: Pantheon Books, 1985). On the Protestant divisions over foreign policy during the early Cold War, see William Inboden, *Religion and American Foreign Policy: 1945–1960: The Soul of Containment* (New York: Cambridge University Press, 2010).

35. Justin Reynolds, "Against the World: International Protestantism and the Ecumenical Movement between Secularization and Politics, 1900–1952" (Ph.D. diss., Columbia University, 2016), 316–324.

36. Barbara D. Savage, "Benjamin Mays, Global Ecumenism, and Local Religious Segregation," *American Quarterly* 59, no. 3 (2007): 785–806.

37. Benjamin Mays, "The Church Will Be Challenged at Evanston," *Christianity and Crisis*, August 9, 1954, 106–8.

38. George Daniels, "WCC Approves Mays' Plan for Brotherhood," *Chicago Defender*, September 11, 1954, 1.

39. *The Evanston Report: Second Assembly of the World Council of Churches, 1954*, ed. W. A. Visser 't Hooft (New York: Harper & Brothers, 1955), 156–57.

40. Quoted in Chesly Manly, "Segregation Is a Scandal, World Council Told," *Chicago Tribune*, August 22, 1954, 8. See also George Dugan, "Bias in Churches Held False Trend," *New York Times*, August 22, 1954, 66.

41. Quoted in Jurjen A. Zeilstra, *Visser 't Hooft, 1900–1985: Living for the Unity of the Church* (Amsterdam: Amsterdam University Press, 2018), 320.

42. Philip Edgcumbe Hughes, "Review of Current Religious Thought," *Christianity Today*, May 13, 1957, 39.

43. "South African Race Tensions," *Christianity Today*, September 1, 1958, 30.

44. Ben J. Marais, "Missions in South Africa," *Christianity Today*, December 22, 1958; Marais, "The Church's Role in Africa (Part I), *Christianity Today*, May 23, 1960; Marais, "The Storm over South Africa (Part II)," *Christianity Today*, June 6, 1960.

45. Letter from Daisuke Kitagawa, April 1960, YDL-WCC 0038, Programme to Combat Racism Papers, World Council of Churches.

46. Loretta Kreider Andrews and Herbert D. Andrews, "The Church and the Birth of a Nation: The Mindolo Ecumenical Foundation and Zambia," *Journal of Church and State* 17, no. 2 (Spring 1975): 202.

47. Daisuke Kitagawa, *Race Relations and Christian Mission* (New York: Friendship Press, 1964).

48. Kitagawa, *Race Relations*, 26–29.

49. Kitagawa, *Race Relations*, 26–27.

50. Kitagawa, *Race Relations*, 18.

51. Kitagawa, *Race Relations*, 164–66, 170.

52. Inboden, *Religion and American Foreign Policy*, 190–225; Zubovich, *Before the Religious Right*, 190–208.

53. "Meeting at the II General Assembly of the National Student Christian Federation," Folder 584, Box 45, RG 247, National Student Christian Federation Papers, Yale Divinity School Special Collections, New Haven, CT; Gene Zubovich, "U.S. Protestants, Globalization, and the International Origins of the Sixties," *Diplomatic History* 45, no. 1 (2021): 28–49.

54. Lilian Calles Barger, *The World Come of Age: An Intellectual History of Liberation Theology* (New York: Oxford University Press, 2018), 13–30.

55. James Baldwin, "White Racism or World Community?" in *Unity of Mankind: Speeches from the Fourth Assembly of the World Council of Churches, Uppsala, 1968*, ed. Albert H. van den Heuvel (Geneva: World Council of Churches, 1969), 50.

56. "World Council Admits First African Church," *Bay State Banner*, October 23, 1969, 10. Between 1968 and 1972, the World Council also admitted denominations from Kenya, Southern Africa, Brazil, Jamaica, Burma, Tanzania, Indonesia, and the Philippines.

57. Ernest W. Lefever, *Amsterdam to Nairobi: The World Council of Churches and the Third World* (Washington, DC: Ethics and Public Policy Center, 1979), 27.

58. On Shaull, see Zubovich, *Before the Religious Right*. On Thomas, see Justin Reynolds, "From Christian Anti-Imperialism to Postcolonial Christianity: M. M. Thomas and the Ecumenical Theology of Communism in the 1940s and 1950s," *Journal of Global History* 13, no. 2 (2018): 230–51.

59. M. M. Thomas, "Issues Concerning the Life and Work of the Church in a Revolutionary World," in *Unity of Mankind: Speeches from the Fourth Assembly of the World Council of Churches, Uppsala 1968*, ed. Albert H. van den Heuvel (Geneva: World Council of Churches, 1969), 92.

60. Thomas, "Issues Concerning the Life and Work of the Church," 93.

61. See Claude E. Welch, "Mobilizing Morality: The World Council of Churches and Its Program to Combat Racism, 1969–1994," *Human Rights Quarterly* 23, no. 4 (2001): 863–910. See also Elisabeth Adler, *A Small Beginning: An Assessment of the First Five Years of the Programme to Combat Racism* (Geneva: World Council of Churches, 1996).

Chapter 3

1. "L'Église au Sud Vietnam," *Informations Catholiques Internationales* 188 (March 1963): 17–18.

2. On Washington's influence, see Ronald H. Spector, "Phat Diem: Nationalism, Religion, and Identity in the Franco-Viet Minh War," *Journal of Cold War Studies* 15, no. 3 (2013): 40; Seth Jacobs, *America's Miracle Man in Vietnam: Ngo Dinh Diem, Religion, Race and U.S. Intervention in Southeast Asia, 1950–1957* (Durham, NC: Duke University Press, 2005); and Avro Manhattan, *Vietnam, Why Did We Go? The Shocking Story of the Catholic "Church's" Role in Starting the Vietnam War* (Ontario, CA: Chick Publications, 1984). On Rome's influence, see Trần Thị Liên, "Les catholiques vietnamiens pendant la guerre d'indépendance (1945–1954) entre la reconquête coloniale et la résistance communiste" (diss., Institut d'études politiques, 1996); and Charles Keith, *Catholic Vietnam: A Church from Empire to Nation* (Berkeley: University of California Press, 2012).

3. Christopher E. Goscha, *Historical Dictionary of the Indochina War (1945–1954): An International and Interdisciplinary Approach* (Copenhagen: NIAS Press, 2011), 90–91. Protestants came to Indochina, but there were only 30,000 in 1959, according to Pierre Médard, "Catholiques et Protestants au Vietnam," *Église vivante* 11 (1959), 446.

4. Keith, *Catholic Vietnam.*

5. Frédéric Mantienne, *Pierre Pigneaux, évêque et mandarin de Cochinchine, 1744–1799* (Paris: Les Indes savantes, 2012); David E. Mungello, "The Chinese Rites Controversy, Its History and Meaning," in *International conference on the significance of the Rites Controversy in Sino-Western history* (London: Routledge, 1994).

6. Michéal Thompson, "Choosing Among the Long Spoons: The MEP, The Catholic Church and Manchuria: 1900–1400," *Comparative Culture* 14 (2008): 85.

7. Thomas David Dubois, *Religion and the Making of Modern East Asia* (Cambridge, UK: Cambridge University Press, 2011), 192–197.

8. Régis Ladous, *Le Vatican et le Japon dans la guerre de la Grande Asie orientale: la mission Marella* (Paris: Desclée de Brouwer, 2010).

9. Jean Decoux, *À la barre de l'Indochine, Histoire de mon gouvernement général (1940–1945)* (Paris: Plon, 1949), 237, 239.

10. "Étude n.1300/Z-C.I," June 8, 1951, 10R95, Service de documentation extérieure et de contre-espionnage (SDECE), Service historique de l'Armée de Terre (SHAT). The report refers to the "Institute of Cultural Relations," but its name was the "Japanese Cultural Center." See also Kiyoko Kurusu Nitz, "Independence without Nationalists? The Japanese and Vietnamese National during the Japanese Period, 1940–45," *Journal of Southeast Asian Studies* 15, no. 1 (1984): 117–118, 121.

11. Ellen J. Hammer, *The Struggle for Indochina, 1940–1955* (Palo Alto, CA: Stanford University Press, 1955), 31.

12. Anne Raffin, *Youth Mobilization in Vichy Indochina and Its Legacies, 1940–1970* (Lanham, MD: Lexington Books, 2005).

13. Eric Jennings, *Vichy in the Tropics: Pétain's National Revolution in Madagascar, Guadeloupe, and Indochina, 1940–1944* (Palo Alto, CA: Stanford University Press, 2001).

14. Đoàn Thanh Liễm, "Chuyện về bức tranh cuối cùng của họa sĩ Nguyễn Gia Trí," *Diễn Đàn Giáo Dân* (2015), 158–159.

15. Alexis Cras, "L'Église missionnaire et la culture occidentale," *La Vie Intellectuelle* 15, no. 1 (1947). See also Alexis Cras, "La charité chrétienne et le principe confucéen de la réciprocité," *La Vie intellectuelle* 15, no. 3 (1947); Đỗ Minh Vọng, "Nhân vị trong "Hồn bước mơ tiên"," *Đại Học* (1958), 4–5; and Alexis Cras, *Le Cercle "Renaissance" . . . et les Dominicains de Hanoi* (Hanoi: Imp. Taupin, 1941). On French intelligence claims that Cras's lectures were propaganda for existentialism, see "Extrait du BR n. 16/C11, documents datant de 1950," January 5, 1953, 10R95, SDECE, SHAT, 18.

16. R. P. Edouard Blais, *Souvenirs d'un missionnaire* (Québec: 1965), 214.

17. "Étude n.1300/Z-C.I," June 8, 1951, 10R95, SDECE, SHAT, 3. The French divided the Đại Việt empire into three zones: Cochinchina, Annam, and Tonkin. Unless otherwise indicated, all translations are my own.

18. Msgr. Hồ Ngọc Cẩn, the bishop of Bùi Chu, chaired the Tonkin Advisory Council in the government. On support to the Japanese, see Forces terrestres du Nord Vietnam, " Notice concernant les évêchés de Phat Diem & Bui Chu," n.d., 10R95, SDECE, SHAT, 5. On the Catholic Youth saying the Te Deum, see "Étude n.1300/Z-C.I," June 8, 1951, 10R95, SDECE, SHAT 4.

19. David Marr, *Vietnam, 1945: The Quest for Power* (Berkeley: University of California Press, 1997), 109; Greg Huff, "The Great Second World War Vietnam and Java Famines," *Modern Asian Studies* 54, no. 2 (2020).

20. Đoàn Đọc Thu and Xuân Huy, *Giám mục Lê Hữu Từ & Phát Diệm* (Saigon: 1973), 38.

21. "Étude n.1300/Z-C.I," June 8, 1951, 10R95, SDECE, SHAT, 4–5.

22. T. B. C. [Trương Bá Cẩn], "Người Việt Nam công giáo với cách mạnh tháng tám," *Công giáo và dân tộc* (1975), 5.

23. "Dossier de la quinzaine: Un million de catholiques devant le régime Vietminh, Lettre du vicaire apostolique de Phat-Diem au Souverain Pontife, 23 septembre 1945," *L'Actualité religieuse dans le monde* 9 (1954), 15–16.

24. Trần Thị Liên, "Les catholiques vietnamiens," 45.

25. Forces terrestres du Nord Vietnam, "Notice concernant les évêchés de Phat Diem & Bui Chu," n.d., 10R95, SDECE, SHAT, 1.

26. David Marr, *Vietnam, State, War, Revolution 1945–1946* (Berkeley: University of California Press, 2013), 432.

27. Đoàn Đọc Thu and Xuân Huy, *Giám mục Lê Hữu Từ*, 36–37; Trần Thị Liên, "Les catholiques vietnamiens," 46.

28. Pastoral letter, May 17, 1946 as quoted in "Les catholiques du Vietnam après 1946," n.d., 10R95, SDECE, SHAT, 3–4.

29. "Le point de vue communiste sur l'Église en Chine," *Église vivante* 3 (1951), 54–56.

30. Tch'ang Djen Tsuain, "Fidélité de l'Église de Chine," *Église vivante* 3 (1951), 299.

31. Pius XII, "L'Église et la Chine, Lettre apostolique Cupimus Imprimis du 18 janvier 1952," *Église vivante* 4 (1952).

32. General Nguyễn Sơn was an officer in both armies, see Goscha, *Historical Dictionary of the Indochina War (1945–1954): An International and Interdisciplinary Approach* (Honolulu: University of Hawaii Press, 2012). On Hồ Chí Minh, see Sophie Quinn-Judge, *Ho Chi Minh, The Missing Years* (Berkeley: University of California Press, 2003).

33. Christopher E. Goscha, *Vietnam: Un état né de la guerre, 1945–1954* (Paris: Armand Colin, 2011), ch. 9.

34. Viễn, "Việt Minh với công giáo," in *Dân mới, Cơ quan tuyên truyền và huấn luyện của Việt Minh Thanh Nghệ Tĩnh*, 31/5/1946.

35. Phạm Bá Trực, "Ta hãy vì chúa vì chính nghĩa mà kháng chiến oanh liệt," in *Kính chúa yêu nước, Đoàn kết giáo lương, 25/12/1948*, ed. Phạm Bá Trực (Hà Nội: Ủy ban Liên Việt toàn quốc, 1954).

36. Phạm Bá Trực, "Lời kêu gọi ngụy binh công giáo, 1/6/1951," in *Kính chúa yêu nước, Đoàn kết giáo lương*, ed. Phạm Bá Trực (Hà Nội: Ủy ban Liên Việt toàn quốc, 1954).

37. Phạm Bá Trực, "Lời kêu gọi đồng bào và ngụy binh công giáo, 1/6/1951."

38. Phạm Bá Trực, "Lời kêu gọi đồng bào và ngụy binh công giáo, 1/6/1951."

39. Phạm Bá Trực, "Đồng bào tôn giáo chúng ta vô cùng phấn khởi và hết sức biết ơn Hồ chủ tịch, chính phủ đã ban hành chính sách tôn trọng tự do tín ngưỡng, chính sách cải cách ruộng đất, 25/12/1953," in *Kính chúa yêu nước, Đoàn kết giáo lương*, ed. Phạm Bá Trực (Hà Nội: Ủy ban Liên Việt toàn quốc, 1954).

40. David E. Mungello, *The Catholic Invasion of China: Remaking Chinese Christianity* (Lanham, MD: Rowman & Littlefield, 2015), 58; Paul Mariani, *Church Militant: Bishop Kung and Catholic Resistance in Communist Shanghai* (Cambridge, MA: Harvard University Press, 2011), 47–52.

41. "Muốn lập đạo binh Đức bà phải làm gì?" *Đạo Binh Đức Mẹ*, March 1, 1952, 16.

42. "Tình hình công giáo Trung Hoa," *Đạo Binh Đức Mẹ*, March 1, 1952; Trịnh Trấn Nguyên, "Giáo hội với quốc gia," *Đạo Bình Đức Mẹ*, July 31, 1952, 5; "Thế nào chúng tà cùng phải đấu tranh với cộng sản," *Đạo Bình Đức Mẹ*, July 1, 1954, 17. On Korea, see "Tình hình giáo hội Cao Ly," *Đạo Bình Đức Mẹ*, May 31, 1952; and "Hội Thanh niên Công giáo Triều Tiên," *Đạo Bình Đức Mẹ*, August 15, 1952. On church-state relations, see Trịnh Trấn Nguyên, "Giáo hội với quốc gia," 5.

43. Các Đức giám mục Việt Nam, "Thư chung các giám mục Đông Dương, 1951," in *Hàng giáo phẩm công giáo Việt Nam (1960–1995)*, ed. Trần Anh Dũng (Paris: Mission catholique vietnamienne, 1996). Vietnamese Party historians argue General de Lattre de Tassigny's visit to the Pope in Rome prompted the bishops to take this position. See T. B. C. [Trương Bà Cấn], "Các Đức giám mục Việt Nam hôm nay với thư chung của các Đức giám mục Đông Dương năm 1951," *Công giáo và dân tộc* (1976): 40–41. To make this claim, they rely on a hagiographic French history of the officer, underscoring the General's influence over the prelate. See Pierre Darcourt, *De Lattre au Viet-Nam, Une année de victoires* (Paris: La Table ronde, 1965), 265.

44. The French called it "le régime des moines mandarins." See Forces terrestres du Nord Vietnam, "Notice concernant les évêchés de Phat Diem & Bui Chu," n.d., 10R95, SDECE, SHAT, 2–3; 5.

45. Các Đức giám mục Việt Nam, "Thư chung, 1952," in *Hàng giáo phẩm công giáo Việt Nam (1960–1995)*, ed. Trần Anh Dũng (Paris: Mission catholique vietnamienne, 1996), 101; Các Đức giám mục Việt Nam, "Thư, 1953," in *Hàng giáo phẩm công giáo Việt Nam (1960–1995)*, ed. Trần Anh Dũng (Paris: Mission catholique vietnamienne, 1996), 117.

46. Wladimir d'Ormesson, "Lettre à Georges Bidault, Ministre des Affaires étrangères, Direction d'Asie-Océanie, " December 23 1953, 10R95, SDECE, SHAT, 2–3; Jean Naussannes, "Opinions: Le catholicisme est-il l'ennemi numéro un du Viet Minh?," July 23, 1953, 10R95, SDECE, SHAT.

47. Trần Thị Liên, "Les catholiques vietnamiens," 24–25; Keith, *Catholic Vietnam*, 241.

48. C. Pierre Bodin, "Choses vues à Hong Kong: Fête religieuse, événement politique: le sacre du 10ème évêque vietnamien," *Journal d'Extrême-Orient*, March 23, 1953.

49. C. Pierre Bodin, "Le Discours de M. Nguyen Huy Lai au sacre de Mgr. Dai," *Journal d'Extrême-Orient*, March 23, 1953.

50. "Dossier de la quinzaine: Un million de catholiques devant le régime Vietminh, Lettre du vicaire apostolique de Phat-Diem au Souverain Pontife, 23 septembre 1945," 18–19; "Extrait de n.3564 IISFS, Au Vietnam, Attitude des autorités ecclésiastiques du Nord à l'égard de l'évacuation des populations civiles," August 25, 1954, 10R95, SDECE, SHAT.

51. Peter Hansen, "The Virgin Heads South: Northern Catholic Refugees in South Vietnam, 1954–1964" (diss., Melbourne College of Divinity, 2008), 119.

52. Général de Brigade Brebisson, "Lettre n.3483/CMC, Enquête de la Commission internationale à Luu My," March 16, 1955, 10H5783, Fonds Indochine, SHAT; George Naïdenoff, "Vainqueurs aux mains nues, les réfugiés viêt-namiens demandent justice à l'opinion," *Missi* 5 (1955).

53. Bernard Broussole and Lucien Provençal, "L'évacuation des catholiques du Tonkin en 1954–1955," *Bulletin de l'Association amicale santé navale et d'Outremer* 125 (2013).

54. On these figures, see Phi-Vân Nguyen, "Réfugiés, religion et politique: La signification du regroupement de 1954," in *Travail, migrations et culture au Viêt-Nam, du début du 19e s. à nos jours*, ed. Éric Guérassimoff, Thi Phuong Ngoc Nguyen, and Emmanuel Poisson (Paris: Maisonneuve Larose, 2020).

55. For an example of the party's instructions, see "Thông tư của Ban bí thư số 19-TT/TW về việc tổ chức lễ Phúc sinh cho đồng bào công giáo và đề phòng địch lợi dụng dịp này để dụ dỗ cưỡng ép đồng bào di cư, 24-3-1955," in *Văn Kiên Đảng, Tập 16*, ed. Đảng Cộng Sản Việt Nam (Hà Nội: Nhà Xuất Bản Chính Trị Quốc Gia, 2002).

56. Ủy Ban Liên Lạc Công giáo toàn quốc, *Báo cáo kỷ niệm 5 năm ngày thành lập Ủy Ban liên lạc công giáo yêu tổ quốc, yêu hòa bình toàn quốc* (Hà Nội: Đồng Tiến, 1960).

57. Hoang Nguyen, "La Catholicité vietnamienne en 1983," *Le Courrier du Vietnam*, January 1984. See also Stephen Denney, "The Catholic Church in Vietnam," in *Catholicism and Politics in Communist Societies*, ed. Pedro Ramet (Durham, NC: Duke University Press, 1990), 274.

58. Lucas Ly, "Respects aux révérends pères, Salut aux frères coreligionnaires," April 31, 1951, 10R95, SDECE, SHAT, 3.

59. ". . . des quatre vents: Schisme en Chine?," *Église vivante* 10 (1958).

60. "Le point de vue communiste sur l'Église en Chine," *Église vivante* 3 (1951).

61. Ngo Dinh Diem, "Letter to Cardinal Spellman," 1954, Funds/S/C-49/To Card, Spellman/Folder 4, Archdiocese of New York.

62. Raymond de Jaegher, *The Enemy Within: An Eyewitness Account of the Communist Conquest of China* (New York: Doubleday, 1952).

63. Ngô Đình Diệm, "Lời tuyên bố ông Ngô Đình Diệm." *Tinh Thần*, June 16, 1949. For an analysis, see Edward Miller, *Misalliance, Ngo Dinh Diem, The United States, and the Fate of South Vietnam* (Cambridge: Harvard University Press, 2013), 35–36; and Duy Lap Nguyen, *The Unimagined Community: Imperialism and Culture in South Vietnam* (Manchester: Manchester University Press, 2020).

64. Jessica Chapman, *Cauldron of Resistance: Ngo Dinh Diem, the United States, and 1950s Southern Vietnam* (Ithaca, NY: Cornell University Press, 2013); Pierre Grosser, "La France et l'Indochine (1953–1956): Une 'carte de visite' en 'peau de chagrin'" (diss., Institut d'études politiques, 2002); David Anderson, *Trapped by Success: The Eisenhower Administration and Vietnam, 1953–1961* (New York: Columbia University Press, 1991).

65. Phi-Vân Nguyen, "A Secular State for a Religious Nation: The Republic of Vietnam and Religious Nationalism, 1946–1963," *Journal of Asian Studies* 77, no. 3 (2018).

66. Trần Thái Định, "La notion de personne dans la philosophie bouddhiste primitive," diss., Institut Catholique de Paris, 1958), 10.

67. Alexis Cras, "Les Chances de l'apostolat au Viet-Nam," *L'Actualité religieuse dans le monde* 28 (1954). See also Alain Riou, *Mémoires dominicaines 24: Alexis Cras, un frère dans la tourmente* (Paris: Éditions du Cerf, 2009), 153.

68. Fernand Parrel, "Jeunesse vietnamienne d'aujourd'hui," *Bulletin des Missions étrangères de Paris* (1957): 1036.

69. Fernand Parrel, "Nhìn vào một thế giới bất công," *Sacerdos Linh mục* 22, no. 1 (1962); Fernand Parrel, "Huấn luyện đức công bình xã hội," *Sacerdos Linh mục* 22, no. 4 (1962).

70. Fernand Parrel, "De l'emploi des armes spirituelles ou 43 ans de vie missionnaire au Viet-Nam," unpublished manuscript (1974), 115.

71. Banque nationale du Viêt-Nam, *Mission "Économie et humanisme" Étude sur les conditions de vie et les besoins de la population du Viêt-Nam, 1957–1959* (Saigon: EHBN, 1959).

72. Darcourt, *De Lattre au Viet-Nam, Une année de victoires*, 257; "Extrait du n.68/IISFS," January 6, 1954, 10R95, SDECE, SHAT; Amaury De Saint Martin, "La contribution de la SAM (Société Auxiliaire des Missions) auprès du monde catholique vietnamien entre 1945 et 1975," in *Vincent Lebbe et son héritage*, ed. Arnaud Join-Lambert et al. (Louvain-la-Neuve: Presses Universitaires de Louvain, 2017), 160; Claire Trần Thị Liên, "The Role of Education Mobilities and Transnational Networks in the Building of a Modern Vietnamese Catholic Elite (1920s–1950s)," *SOJOURN* 35, no. 2 (2020): 259.

73. Ngo Dinh Diem, "Letter to Cardinal Spellman," November 30, 1957, Funds/S/B-10/To Card, Spellman Korea/Folder 8, Archdiocese of New York; "Vie des missions: Dalat," *Bulletin des Missions étrangères de Paris* (1961).

74. Lý Chánh Trung, "Sứ mệnh giáo dục của giáo hội," *Đức Mẹ Lavang* 2, no. 10 (1963).

75. "L'Église au Sud Vietnam," *Informations Catholiques Internationales* 188, no. mars (1963), 17–18.

76. Ngô Đình Diệm resented the decision not to choose his brother. See "Rapport sur les cadeaux de la présidence à MM. SS. Nguyen Van Hien et Nguyen Van Binh," January 9, 1956, 10R95, SDECE, SHAT.

77. "Bức thư Đức khâm sứ Giuseppe Caprio gửi bề trên các địa phận về vấn đề giáo sĩ di cư," *Đường Sống*, June 25, 1956; "Giáo quyền với di cư, Bức thư Đức khâm sứ Giúeppe Caprio gửi bề trên địa phận về vấn đề giáo sĩ di cư, 20 tháng 8 1956," *Sao Việt* 10 (1956).

78. Các đức giám mục miền Nam, "Thư chung về vấn đề Cộng sản vô thần của các Đức giám mục miền Nam, mùa chay 1960," *Sacerdos Linh mục* 24, no. 30 (1964).

79. "Du 17 au 22 août 1961, Une semaine glorieuse à La-Vang pour les Catholiques du Viet-nam et pour la Chrétienté toute entière, La Consécration de la Basilique, le congrès Marial, le Pèlerinage National et la Consécration du Vietnam à la Vierge Marie," *Extrême Asie* 104 (1961).

80. Ngô Đình Thục, "Mấy lời phi lộ," *Đức Mẹ Lavang* 1, no. 1 (1961).

81. Ngô Đình Thục, "Lời hiệu triệu của Đức cha Ngô Đình Thục tổng giám mục Huế về Đại Hội Lavang," *Đức Mẹ Lavang* 1, no. 1 (1961): 43.

82. "Gíao hội công giáo và Cộng sản," *Đức Mẹ Lavang* 1, no. 10 (1962). A French version, signed by Father Raymond de Jaegher, appeared the following year. See Raymond de Jaegher, "Comment détuire l'Église," *Église vivante* 15 (1963).

83. J. M. T., "Lavang và đức mẹ Lavang," *Đức Mẹ Lavang* 1, no. 1 (1961): 5.

84. "L'Église au Sud Vietnam," 26.

85. Bùi Châu Thi, "Trong khuôn khổ 'Liên hiệp giáo sỹ truyền giáo': Mấy ý kiến về vấn đề tổ chức hành thày giảng Giáo dân tại Việt Nam," *Sacerdos Linh mục* 22, no. 9 (1962): 532.

86. Nguyễn Tiến Huynh, "Người Việt Nam truyền giáo tại Phi-Châu?" *Sacerdos Linh mục* 22, no. 11 (1962): 642–43.

87. Trần Thị Liên, "The Challenge for Peace within South Vietnam's Catholic Community: A History of Peace Activism," *Peace and Change* 38, no. 4 (2013).

Chapter 4

1. Jin Luxian, *The Memoirs of Jin Luxian, Volume One: Learning and Relearning, 1916–1982*, trans. William Hanbury-Tenison (Hong Kong: Hong Kong University Press, 2012), 82.

2. Bith helped the French Resistance hide Jews from the Gestapo in Poitiers. See Vincent Lapomarda, "The Jesuits and the Holocaust," *Journal of Church and State* 23, no. 2 (1981): 241–58.

3. See Elizabeth A. Foster, *African Catholic: Decolonization and the Transformation of the Church* (Cambridge, MA: Harvard University Press, 2019).

4. For an overview of this historiography, see D. E. Mungello, "Reinterpreting the History of Christianity in China," *Historical Journal* 55, no. 2 (June 2012): 533–52.

5. For more on Jin's "controversial" career, see Adam Minter, "Keeping Faith," *Atlantic Monthly*, July/August 2007. For a response, see Joseph Kung, "A Rebuttal to Keeping Faith," Cardinal Kung Foundation, accessed December 20, 2021, http://www.cardinalkungfoundation.org/ar/pdf/ARebuttaltoAdamMinter.pdf.

6. See A. G. Hopkins, "Globalization and Decolonization," *Journal of Imperial and Commonwealth History* 45, no. 5 (2017): 736–37.

7. Scholars have long debated how "informal empire" in China fit within the European imperial system of the nineteenth and twentieth centuries. For a classic formulation, see Jürgen Osterhammel, "Semicolonialism and Informal Empire in Twentieth-Century China: Towards a Framework of Analysis," in *Imperialism and After: Continuities and Discontinuities*, ed. Wolfgang J. Mommsen and Jürgen Osterhammel (London: Allen and Unwin, 1986), 290–314.

8. See Ernest P. Young, *Ecclesiastical Colony: China's Catholic Church and the French Religious Protectorate* (Oxford: Oxford University Press, 2013).

9. See Steven Pieragastini, "Imperium inter Imperia: The Catholic Church in Shanghai, 1842–1957" (PhD diss., Brandeis University, 2017), 3–4.

10. Jin, *Memoirs*, 7.

11. Jin, *Memoirs*, 8.

12. Jin, *Memoirs*, 9.

13. Jin, *Memoirs*, 37.

14. For a detailed history of *Maximum illud* and the centrality of China to its formation, see Young, *Ecclesiastical Colony*, 185–232.

15. For more on the ordination of the six Chinese bishops, see Paul P. Mariani, "The First Six Chinese Bishops of Modern Times: A Study in Church Indigenization," *Catholic Historical Review* 100, no. 3 (2014): 486–513.

16. Young, *Ecclesiastical Colony*, 216.

17. For instance, the influential public education reformer, Ma Xiangbo, began his career as a Jesuit. See Ruth Hayhoe and Lu Yongling, eds., *Ma Xiangbo and the Mind of Modern China* (Armonk: M. E. Sharpe, 1996).

18. For a collection of Xu's writing, see Xu Zongze, *Suisi suibi* [*Pencillus Liber*, A Free Pencil] (Shanghai: Shengjiao zazhi she, 1940).

19. Chloë Starr, *Chinese Theology: Text and Context* (New Haven: Yale University Press, 2016), 208.

20. For a more comprehensive overview of Wang's career, see Lu Jin, "From Pagan Virtues to the Salvation of Non-Christians: Father Wang Changzhi's Contribution to Chinese Christianity," *Ching Feng* 17, nos. 1–2 (2018): 5–26.

21. Jin, *Memoirs*, 58.

22. Jin, *Memoirs*, 44–45.

23. Jin, *Memoirs*, 57–58.

24. Jin, *Memoirs*, 45.

25. Jin, *Memoirs*, 72.

26. Jin, *Memoirs*, 72.

27. Jin, *Memoirs*, 82.

28. Jin, *Memoirs*, 83. Most scholarly accounts of the Jesuit mission agree with Jin's argument that the Jesuits implemented *Maximum illud* much later than other more progressive orders, like the Lazarists. Other than Ernest Young's *Ecclesiastical Colony*, see David Strong, *A Call to Mission: A History of the Jesuits in China, 1842–1954, Volume 1: The French Romance* (Adelaide: ATF, 2018).

29. Jin, *Memoirs*, 83.

30. Jin, *Memoirs*, 71.

31. Jin, *Memoirs*, 71.

32. Jin, *Memoirs*, 142.

33. Jin, *Memoirs*, 93.

34. Cited in Gabriel Flynn, "The Church in a Pluralistic World: The Public Vision of *Ressourcement*," *Religions* 10, no. 11 (2019): 3.

35. For more on the development of the movement later coined as *nouvelle théologie*, see Sarah Shortall, *Soldiers of God in a Secular World: Catholic Theology and Twentieth-Century French Politics* (Cambridge, MA: Harvard University Press, 2021). There has been a recent explosion of literature on Catholicism's engagement with "modernity" more broadly. A non-comprehensive list includes John Connelly, *From Enemy to Brother: The Revolution in Catholic Teaching on the Jews, 1933–1965* (Cambridge, MA: Harvard University Press, 2012); Samuel Moyn, *Christian Human Rights* (Philadelphia: University of Pennsylvania Press, 2015); James Chappel, *Catholic Modern: The Challenge of Totalitarianism and the Remaking of the Church* (Cambridge, MA: Harvard University Press, 2018); Giuliana Chamedes, *A Twentieth-Century Crusade: The Vatican's Battle to Remake Christian Europe* (Cambridge, MA: Harvard University Press, 2019).

36. Jin, *Memoirs*, 96–97.

37. Jin, *Memoirs*, 121.

38. Jin, *Memoirs*, 138.

39. Shortall, *Soldiers of God*, 161.

40. Piotr Kosicki, *Catholics on the Barricades: Poland, France, and "Revolution," 1891–1956* (New Haven: Yale University Press, 2018), 206.

41. Jin, *Memoirs*, 101–2.

42. Jin, *Memoirs*, 101–3.

43. Darcie Fontaine, "Decolonizing Christianity: Grassroots Ecumenism in France and Algeria, 1940–1965" (PhD diss., Rutgers University, 2011), 167.

44. Shortall, *Soldiers of God*, 158.
45. Shortall, *Soldiers of God*, 229.
46. Jin, *Memoirs*, 100.
47. Jin, *Memoirs*, 136.
48. Jin, *Memoirs*, 63.
49. Jin, *Memoirs*, 110.
50. Jin, *Memoirs*, 165–66.
51. Jin, *Memoirs*, 195.
52. Jin, *Memoirs*, 190.
53. Jin, *Memoirs*, 151. Of course, Jin wrote this statement in 2012, so he may have been providing justification after the fact. But László Ladány, in *The Catholic Church in China* (New York: Freedom House, 1987), 74–81, suggests that Jin was drawn to Communism even before the Communist victory.
54. Jin, *Memoirs*, 174.
55. See Paul Mariani, *Church Militant: Bishop Kung and Catholic Resistance in Communist Shanghai* (Cambridge, MA: Harvard University Press, 2011), 56.
56. Jin, *Memoirs*, 200.
57. Mariani, *Church Militant*, 57.
58. Mariani, *Church Militant*, 37.
59. Jin, *Memoirs*, 166.
60. Albert R. O'Hara, "China Mission in Exile," *Woodstock Letters* 80, no. 4 (1951): 327.
61. The most comprehensive account of the Chinese Jesuit diaspora is found in Fernando Mateos, "China Jesuits in East–Asia: Starting from Zero" (unpublished manuscript, 1995), typescript.
62. See Jean Lefeuvre, *Les Enfants dans la ville: Chronique de la vie chrétienne à Shanghaï, 1949–1955* (Paris: Témoignage Chrétien, 1956), 156.
63. Anthony E. Clark, *China's Catholics in an Era of Transformation: Observations of an "Outsider"* (Singapore: Springer Nature), 150.
64. Simon Leys, "The Art of Interpreting Nonexistent Inscriptions Written in Invisible Ink on a Blank Page," *New York Review of Books,* October 11, 1990.
65. László Ladány, *The Catholic Church in China* (New York: Freedom House, 1987), 65.
66. Jan C. Jansen and Jürgen Osterhammel, *Decolonization: A Short History*, trans. Jeremiah Riemer (Princeton, NJ: Princeton University Press, 2017), 1–6.
67. Jin, *Memoirs*, 77.
68. For a comprehensive biography and bibliography of Hofinger's work, see Mark Markuly, "Johannes Hofinger," Database: Christian Educators of the 20th Century, Biola University, accessed December 20, 2021, https://www.biola.edu/talbot/ce20/database/johannes-hofinger.
69. Johannes Hofinger, "Institute for Mission Apologetics," *Philippine Studies* 3, no. 2 (1955): 212. I am grateful to Udi Greenberg and Elizabeth Foster for pointing me to Hofinger's work.
70. See Markuly, "Johannes Hofinger."
71. Jin, *Memoirs*, 155.

Chapter 5

1. Billy Graham, "Salvation for Brazil," *Hour of Decision* radio program, September 30, 1962, Billy Graham Center Archives, Wheaton College, Illinois, T664c, g.
2. Graham, "Salvation for Brazil."

3. See David C. Kirkpatrick, "The Latin American Bullring: U.S. Evangelical Internationalism and Anti-Protestant Violence in Cold War Colombia," unpublished manuscript.

4. Andrew Preston, "Evangelical Internationalism: A Conservative Worldview for the Age of Globalization," in *The Right Side of the Sixties: Reexamining Conservatism's Decade of Transformation*, ed. Laura Jane Gifford and Daniel K. Williams (New York: Palgrave Macmillan, 2012), 232.

5. *The Uppsala Report 1968: Official Report of the Fourth Assembly of the World Council of Churches* (Switzerland: World Council of Churches, 1968), p. XV. General assemblies of the WCC meet in seven-year intervals.

6. Carl F. H. Henry was editor and passed the baton to Harold Lindsell that year; both were staunchly anti-Communist.

7. Udi Greenberg, "The Rise of the Global South and the Protestant Peace with Socialism," *Contemporary European History* 29 (2020): 203.

8. Claude E. Welch, "Mobilizing Morality: The World Council of Churches and its Program to Combat Racism, 1969–1994," *Human Rights Quarterly* 23 (2001): 866.

9. See also Giuseppe Alberigo and Joseph A. Komonchak, eds., *History of Vatican II. Vol. II: The Formation of the Council's Identity. First Period and Intersession. October 1962–September 1963* (Maryknoll, NY: Orbis; and Leuven: Peeters, 1997), 171–72.

10. Paul Davies, *Faith Seeking Effectiveness: The Missionary Theology of José Míguez Bonino* (Zoetermeer: Boekencentrum, 2006), 18. For more on the SCM and ISAL, see Robin Boyd, *The Witness of the Student Christian Movement: Church Ahead of the Church* (London: SPCK, 2007).

11. Christian Smith, *The Emergence of Liberation Theology: Radical Religion and Social Movement* Theory (Chicago: University of Chicago Press, 1991), 117.

12. Richard Shaull, *The New Revolutionary Mood in Latin America* (New York: Committee on Cooperation in Latin America, 1962), 19–20.

13. Smith, *The Emergence of Liberation Theology*, 116; Neely, "Protestant Antecedents of the Latin American Theology of Liberation" (PhD diss., American University, 1977), 189. See also Alan P. Neely, "Liberation Theology in Latin America: Antecedents and Autochthony," *Missiology: An International Review* 6, no. 3 (1978): 363.

14. Iglesia y Sociedad en América Latina (ISAL), *Social Justice and the Latin Churches* (Richmond, VA: John Knox Press, 1969), cited in Neely, "Liberation Theology in Latin America: Antecedents and Autochthony," 363.

15. "Desafió revolucionario a la Iglesia y la Teología," *Cristianismo y revolución* 2, no. 3 (October–November 1966): 28.

16. "Desafió revolucionario," 28.

17. Lilian Calles Barger, *The World Come of Age: An Intellectual History of Liberation Theology* (New York: Oxford University Press, 2018), 143.

18. Neely, "Protestant Antecedents," 253.

19. Harold E. Fey, "Letter from Geneva," *Christian Century*, August 9, 1967, 1015.

20. See especially Risto Lehtonen, *Story of a Storm: The Ecumenical Student Movement in the Turmoil of Revolution, 1968 to 1973*, Publications of the Finnish Society of Church History (Grand Rapids, MI: Eerdmans, 1998), 66–67.

21. "Roman Catholics: Burden of Responsibility," *Time*, June 6, 1969, 88.

22. Lehtonen, *Story of a Storm*, 68.

23. Lehtonen, *Story of a Storm*, 68.

24. Greenberg, "Rise of the Global South," 204.

25. Brian Stanley, *Christianity in the Twentieth Century: A World History* (Princeton, NJ: Princeton University Press, 2018), 211.

26. Greenberg, "Rise of the Global South," 204.

27. Stanley, *Christianity in the Twentieth Century*, 209.

28. "Back to Violence as Usual," *Christianity Today*, July 5, 1968, 45.

29. David C. Kirkpatrick, *A Gospel for the Poor: Global Social Christianity and the Latin American Evangelical Left* (Philadelphia: University of Pennsylvania Press, 2019); David C. Kirkpatrick, "Reforming Fundamentalism in Latin America: Power, Politics and Paternalism in Univeridad Bíblica Latinoamericana," *Journal of the American Academy of Religion* 87, no. 1 (March 2019): 122–55; David C. Kirkpatrick, "C. René Padilla and the Origins of Integral Mission in Post-War Latin America," *Journal of Ecclesiastical History* 67, no. 2 (April 2016): 351–71.

30. Kirkpatrick, "C. René Padilla."

31. C. René Padilla, "Student Witness in Latin America Today," *IFES Journal* 19, no. 2 (1966): 20; C. René Padilla, "El testimonio Cristiano en la universidad Latinoamericana," *Pensamiento Cristiano* Año 14, no. 55 (1967). Padilla began writing for the IFES in 1962, but his first reference to the political situation of Latin America was not until 1966.

32. Padilla, "Student Witness," 19; Padilla, "El testimonio Cristiano en la universidad Latinoamericana."

33. Padilla, "Student Witness," 15–16.

34. Padilla, "Student Witness," 16.

35. C. René Padilla, "Teología Latinoamericana: ¿Izquierdista o Evangélica?" *Pensamiento Cristiano* 17, no. 66 (1970): 133.

36. C. René Padilla, "Teología Latinoamericana," 133.

37. Orlando Costas, "Latin American Revolutions and the Church," *Foundations* 14, no. 2 (1971): 122.

38. Costas, "Latin American Revolutions and the Church," 127.

39. C. René Padilla, "Theology of Liberation," *Christianity Today*, November 9, 1973. Padilla's article followed an earlier issue in which Harold Brown reviewed Gustavo Gutiérrez's *Theology of Liberation*. See Harold O. J. Brown, "A Theology of Liberation: History, Politics, and Salvation," *Christianity Today*, June 22, 1973.

40. Padilla, "Theology of Liberation," 70.

41. Padilla, "Theology of Liberation," 70.

42. Congreso Latinoamericano de Evangelización (CLADE), *Acción en Cristo para un continente en crisis* (San Jose, Costa Rica: Editorial Caribe, 1970). Personal correspondence, planning, and general papers from CLADE I can be found in collection 324 at the Billy Graham Center Archives (BGCA).

43. CLADE, *Acción en Cristo.*

44. Samuel Escobar, "Divided Protestantism Struggles with Latin American Problems," *World Vision Magazine*, November 1969.

45. Clyde Taylor, letter to Richard Sturz, March 28, 1969, BGCA 324, box 2, folder 3. The pastor in question was the influential Pentecostal Manuel de Mello, head of the "Brazil Para Cristo" denomination.

46. Peter Wagner, *Latin American Theology: Radical or Evangelical? The Struggle for the Faith in a Young Church* (Grand Rapids, MI: Eerdmans, 1970).

47. Samuel Escobar, interview, translated by the author, Valencia, Spain, October 21–22, 2013.

48. Orlando Costas, "Teólogo en la encrucijada," in *Hacia una teología Evangélica Latinoamericana: Ensayos en honor de Pedro Savage*, ed. C. René Padilla (Miami; San José, Costa Rica: Editorial Caribe, 1984), 26.

49. Escobar, interview.

50. Carlos Lastra, "Plan para América Latina," in *Acción en Cristo para un continente en crisis* (San José, Costa Rica: Editorial Caribe, 1970), 72–73.

51. Lastra, "Plan para América Latina."

52. Padilla quoted in Daniel Salinas, *Latin American Evangelical Theology in the 1970's: The Golden Decade* (Leiden; Boston: Brill, 2009), 76.

53. Billy Graham Center Archives, Wheaton College, collection number 685, VIP Notebooks, "Richard Nixon file."

54. Padilla, "Teología Latinoamericana," 133.

55. Peter Wagner, "The Latin American Congress on Evangelism," BGCA, collection 506, box 7, folder 1.

56. Samuel Escobar, "Responsabilidad social de la iglesia," in *Acción en Cristo para un continente en crisis* (San Jose, Costa Rica: Editorial Caribe, 1970), 35.

57. Escobar, "Responsabilidad social de la iglesia," 35.

58. Escobar, "Responsabilidad social de la iglesia," 34.

59. Escobar, "Responsabilidad social de la iglesia," 38.

60. Escobar, interview.

61. René Padilla Papers, Buenos Aires, "FTL Consulta 1," undated; C. René Padilla, "My Theological Pilgrimage," 133. Padilla, "My Theological Pilgrimage," in *Shaping a Global Theological Mind*, ed. Darren C. Marks (Burlington, VT: Ashgate, 2008), 133.

62. Carl F. H. Henry, "Latin American Visit, July–August, 1973," Carl F. H. Henry Archives at Trinity Evangelical Divinity School, box 5, folder 26. Leon Morris and Michael Green also made similar trips.

63. Henry, "Latin American Visit."

64. Peter Goodwin Heltzel, *Jesus and Justice: Evangelicals, Race and American Politics* (New Haven, CT: Yale University Press, 2009), xix.

65. C. René Padilla, "Personal Letter from René Padilla, August 10, 1972," Carl F. H. Henry Archives at Trinity Evangelical Divinity School, box 5, folder 26.

66. Carl F. H. Henry, "Personal Letter to Professor Pedro Savage, Co-Ordinator of the Fraternity, January 3, 1974," Carl F. H. Henry Archives at Trinity Evangelical Divinity School, box 5 folder 26.

67. Padilla, "Personal Letter from René Padilla."

68. Carl F. H. Henry, *The Uneasy Conscience of Modern Fundamentalism* (Grand Rapids, MI: Eerdmans, 1947).

69. Padilla, "Personal Letter from René Padilla."

70. Padilla, "Personal Letter from René Padilla."

71. "A Challenge from Evangelicals," *Time*, Monday, August 5, 1974.

72. Axel Schäfer, *Piety and Public Funding: Evangelicals and the State in Modern America* (Philadelphia: University of Pennsylvania Press, 2012), 1–11.

Chapter 6

1. Oissila Saaïdia, "Le cas de l'Église catholique en Algérie avant la Première Guerre mondiale," in *Religions et colonization XVIe-XXe siècle*, ed. D. Borne and B. Falaize (Paris: Éditions

de l'Atelier/Éditions ouvrières, 2009), 174. There was also a small group of Protestants (approximately 6,000) and a Jewish population of approximately 140,000 who lived among the nearly 9 million Muslim Algerians, however, this chapter will focus specifically on history of the Catholic Church, individual Catholics, and Catholic institutions in the colonial and postcolonial Maghreb.

2. The French established a protectorate in Tunisia in 1881; the French occupation of Morocco began in 1907 and was made permanent with the protectorate in 1912. Statistics on Catholics in Tunisia are in Maria Chiara Cugusi, *Una testimonianza silenziosa: Storia della Chiesa cattolica in Tunisia dal Trattato del Bardo alla "rivoluzione dei gelsomini"* (Arricia: Aracne, 2016), 167. Jamaâ Baida and Vincent Feroldi, *Présence chrétienne au Maroc (XIXème-XXème siècles)* (Rabat: Éditions & Impressions Bouregreg, 2005), 108, lists statistics from 1947 of Catholics in Morocco.

3. The dioceses of Oran and Constantine & Hippo were established in 1857, and Laghouat, covering the entire Saharan region, was established as the apostolic prefecture of Ghardaïa in 1901 and as the diocese of Laghouat in 1955.

4. See Sarah Curtis, *Civilizing Habits: Women Missionaries and the Revival of the French Empire* (New York: Oxford University Press, 2010); Kyle Francis, "Catholic Missionaries in Colonial Algeria: Faith, Foreigners, and France's Other Civilizing Mission, 1848–1883," *French Historical Studies* 39, no. 4 (October 2016): 685–715.

5. Lavigerie is notorious in Algeria for his creation of two new missionary orders called the Missionaries of Africa (better known as the "White Fathers" and "White Sisters") in the 1870s. Lavigerie was an adherent of the "Kayble myth," which posited that Kabyle Berbers were direct descendants of Roman Christians, including Saint Augustine. He created the Missionaries of Africa specifically to focus on converting Kabyle Berbers "back" to Christianity in the wake of the Catholic failure to convert the Muslim Arab population of Algeria. See Patricia Lorcin, *Imperial Identities: Stereotyping, Prejudice and Race in Colonial Algeria* (London: I. B. Tauris, 1995), 62–63, 179; and Karima Dirèche-Slimani, *Chrétiens de Kabylie, 1873–1954* (Paris: Éditions Bouchène, 2004).

6. See Julia Clancy-Smith, *Mediterraneans: North Africa and Europe in an Age of Migration, c. 1800–1900* (Berkeley: University of California Press, 2010), 5, ch. 1; Daniel E. Coslett, "(Re)Creating a Christian Image Abroad: The Catholic Cathedrals of Protectorate-Era Tunis," in *Sacred Precincts: The Religious Architecture of Non-Muslim Communities Across the Islamic World*, ed. Mohammed Gharipour (Leiden: Brill, 2015), 353–75.

7. Moussa Marguich, "L'Église catholique au Maroc sous le protectorat français: Rabat-Paris-Rome ou le heurt des logiques (1912–1956)," *Histoire, Monde et Cultures Religieuses* 4, no. 44 (2017): 33–54.

8. Jacques Alexandropoulos, "Entre archaéologie, universalité et nationalismes: le trentième congrès eucharistique international de Carthage (1930)," *Anabases* 9 (2009): 53–70.

9. Kenneth Perkins, *A History of Modern Tunisia*, 2nd ed. (New York: Cambridge University Press, 2014), 95.

10. "Un Congrès Eucharistique va se tenir dans Alger, ville de l'Islam, pendant que le décret du 8 mars baillonne la langue arabe: N'est-ce pas là une provocation?" *El-Ouma* no. 71, April 1939, Archives nationales d'outre mer (ANOM), Aix-en-Provence, France, Fonds ministériels (FM)/Ministre des Affaires Algériennes/81f/828.

11. See, for example, André Mandouze, "Impossibilités algériennes ou le mythe des trois départements," *Esprit*, July 1947.

12. Yvon Tranvouez, *Catholiques et communists: La crise du progressisme chrétien, 1950–1955* (Paris: Cerf, 2000).

13. Tangi Cavalin and Nathalie Viet-Depaule, *Une histoire de la Mission de France: La riposte missionnaire, 1941–2002* (Paris: Karthala, 2007).

14. On Scotto's role in Algeria, see Darcie Fontaine, *Decolonizing Christianity: Religion and the End of Empire in France and Algeria* (New York: Cambridge University Press, 2016).

15. Pierre Chaulet and Claudine Chaulet, *Le choix de l'Algérie* (Algiers: Éditions Barzakh, 2012), 88–94.

16. For more on the AJAAS, see Fontaine, *Decolonizing Christianity*, chapter 1.

17. Evelyne Lavalette Safir, interview, Médéa, Algeria, January 31, 2009; see also Evelyne Safir Lavalette, *Juste Algérienne: Comme une tissure* (Algiers: Éditions Barzakh, 2013).

18. "Lettre collective de l'épiscopat algérien," September 15, 1955, Archives of Cardinal Duval, Archdiocese of Algiers, casier 262, file 31.

19. See Elizabeth Foster, "'Theologies of Colonization': The Catholic Church and the Future of the French Empire in the 1950s," *Journal of Modern History* 87 (2015): 281–315.

20. On French Catholicism and decolonization in other locations of the French empire, see Elizabeth Foster, *African Catholic: Decolonization and the Transformation of the Church* (Cambridge, MA: Harvard University Press, 2019); Charles Keith, *Catholic Vietnam: A Church from Empire to Nation* (Berkeley: University of California Press, 2012); and several essays in this volume.

21. C. Alix, "Le Vatican et la décolonisation," in *Les églises chrétiennes et la décolonisation*, ed. M. Merle (Paris: Armand Colin, 1967), 36.

22. "Lettre collective de l'épiscopat algérien."

23. Msgr. Duval's January 1955 statement that quoted large sections of Pope Pius XI's discourses on "natural rights" as a means to critique the French military's use of torture and violence against civilians did not go over well at all with the French military and led General Jacques Massu to order the French military chaplain of the Tenth Parachute Division in Algiers, R. P. Delarue, to write his own theological treatise in support of the use of torture in March 1957. See R.P. Delarue, "Réflexions d'un Prêtre sur le terrorisme urbain," Centre des archives du monde du travail (CAMT), Fonds de la Mission de France (MDF), 1999014 0154/Janvier–Juin 1957, Roubaix, France.

24. Raphaëlle Branche, *La torture et l'armée pendant la guerre d'Algérie* (Paris: Gallimard, 2001).

25. See Fontaine, *Decolonizing Christianity*, chapters 2 and 3.

26. "Rapport très confidential sur les incidences religieuses des événements d'Algérie du 1 août 1955 au 25 mars 1956," Archives of Cardinal Duval, Archdiocese of Algiers, casier 284.

27. Jean Scotto, *Curé pied-noir évêque algérien* (Paris: Desclée de Brouwer, 1991), 149.

28. Léon-Étienne Duval and Marie-Christine Ray, *Le Cardinal Duval:* Évêque en Algérie (Paris: Le Centurion, 1984), 70.

29. Anne-Marie Duranton-Crabol, *Le temps de l'OAS* (Brussels: Editions Complèxe, 1995), 217.

30. Susan Gilson Miller, *A History of Modern Morocco* (Cambridge, UK: Cambridge University Press, 2013), ch. 5.

31. Cited in Baida and Feroldi, *Présence chrétienne au Maroc*, 110–11.

32. Baida and Feroldi, *Présence chrétienne au maroc*, 114–15. On the role of Morocco in the development of the Catholic anti-colonial left in France, see David Stenner, *Globalizing*

Morocco: Transnational Activism and the Postcolonial State (Stanford, CA: Stanford University Press, 2019), ch. 3; and Daniel Rivet, ed., "Le Comité France-Maghreb: réseaux intellectuels et d'influence face à la crise marocaine (1952–1955)," *Cahiers de l'Institut d'histoire du temps présent* 38 (1997): 1–176.

33. See Ben M'Barek Sabah, *La réinstallation des agriculteurs Français rapatriés de Tunisie (1956–1965)* (master's thesis, Université d'Evry Val d'Essonne, 2008), 13.

34. See, for example, Jean-Marc Largeaud, "Violences urbaines, Maroc 1956," *Annales de Bretagne et des Pays de l'Ouest* 123, no. 2 (2016): 107–29; and Pierre Vermeren, *Histoire du Maroc depuis l'indépendance* (Paris: La Découverte, 2016), 20.

35. Miller, *A History of Modern Morocco*, 154.

36. See Marguich, "L'Église catholique au Maroc sous le protectorat français," 53; and Baida and Feroldi, *Présence chrétienne au Maroc*, 133–36.

37. The influence of Charles de Foucauld, and consequently Louis Massignon, who helped found the seminaries that trained the congregations of the Little Brothers and Sisters of Jesus, can be found throughout leftist Catholic ideas and movements in France and North Africa from the 1930s to the present.

38. Baida and Feroldi, *Présence chrétienne au Maroc*, 143–44.

39. Cardinal Paul Marella, handwritten letter to Msgr. Lefevre, summer 1964, located in the Archives of the Archdiocese of Rabat, cited in Baida and Feroldi, *Présence chrétienne au Maroc*, 144.

40. Baida and Feroldi, *Présence chrétienne au Maroc*, 151–52.

41. Cited in Diocèse de Rabat, "Dossier de Presse – Venue du Pape," http://www.dioceserabat.org/venue_du_pape/dossier-presse/dossier-en.pdf, accessed November 27, 2022.

42. Perkins, *A History of Modern Tunisia*, 136–37.

43. Perkins, *A History of Modern Tunisia*, 140.

44. Pierre Soumille, "L'Église catholique et l'État tunisien après l'indépendance," in *Les relations Églises-État en situation postcoloniale*, ed. Philippe Delisle and Marc Spindler (Paris: Karthala, 2003), 161.

45. Soumille, "L'Église catholique et l'État tunisien après l'indépendance," 162–63.

46. Cugusi, *Una testimonianza silenziosa*, 167.

47. Michel Prignot, "L'Église catholique en Tunisie," 1960, CAMT/MDF/1997015 0187/1960.

48. Cited in Cugusi, *Una testimonianza silenziosa*, 168.

49. Cugusi, *Una testimonianza silenziosa,* 163; Mission de France team in Tunis, letter to Msgr. Jean Vinatier, March 29, 1960, CAMT/MDF/1997015 0187/1960.

50. P. Judet, "Après les événements de Kairouan: Quelques notes pour faire le point," Nov.–Dec. 1959, CAMT/MDF/1997015 0187/1959 and M. Prignot, "L'Église catholique en Tunisie."

51. "Devant les problèmes de la Tunisie actuelle: Réflexions et questions d'un groupe de chrétiens," CAMT/MDF/1997015 0187/1960.

52. "Devant les problèmes de la Tunisie actuelle."

53. Soumille, "L'Église catholique et l'État tunisien après l'indépendance," 171.

54. See the diplomatic convention between the Tunisian government and the Vatican known as the *Modus Vivendi*, 1964, https://www.iuscangreg.it/conc/tunisia-1964.pdf, accessed November 7, 2021.

55. *Modus Vivendi,* https://www.iuscangreg.it/conc/tunisia-1964.pdf, accessed November 7, 2021.

56. Soumille, "L'Église catholique et l'État tunisien après l'indépendance," 187–88.

57. Soumille, "L'Église catholique et l'État tunisien après l'indépendance," 178–79; Cugusi, *Una testimonianza silenziosa*, 167.

58. Alexis Artaud de la Ferrière, "The Catholic Church in Tunisia: A Transliminal Space," *The Journal of North African Studies* 25, no. 3 (2020): 420–21.

59. Artaud de la Ferrière, "The Catholic Church in Tunisia," 425.

60. See, for example, Claire Eldridge, *From empire to exile: History and memory within the* pied-noir *and* harki *communities, 1962–2012* (Manchester: Manchester University Press, 2016); and Yann Scioldo-Zürcher, *Devenir métropolitain: politique d'intégration et parcours de rapatriés d'Algérie en métropole* (Paris: Les Éditions de l'EHESS, 2011).

61. André Nozière, *Algérie: Les chrétiens dans la guerre* (Paris: Éditions Cana, 1979), 241.

62. Duval and Ray, *Le Cardinal Duval*, 157–60; Chaulet and Chaulet, *Le choix de l'Algérie*, 219–20.

63. "Memorandum du G.P.R.A. à N.N.S.S. les Évêques d'Algérie," Archives of Cardinal Duval, Archdiocese of Algiers, casier 280.

64. Duval and Ray, *Le Cardinal Duval*, 162.

65. Msgr. Giroud, letter to M. Hervé Bourges, Directeur du Cabinet du Président du Conseil, October 23, 1962, Archives of Cardinal Duval, Archdiocese of Algiers, casier 472.

66. Document of transfer of the Cathédrale d'Alger, signed in Rome by Msgr. Duval, October 25, 1962, Archives of Cardinal Duval, Archdiocese of Algiers, casier 472. See also Ralph Ghoche, "Erasing the Ketchaoua Mosque: Catholicism, Assimilation, and National Identity," in *Neocolonialism and Built Heritage*, ed. Daniel E. Coslett (London: Routledge, 2019), 87–105.

67. Minutes of the Association d'études, 1962–64, from the private archives of Paul and Josette Fournier. See, for example, "L'Avenir de l'Église dans une Algérie nouvelle," June 24, 1962.

68. Minutes of the Association d'études, 1962-64.

69. On postcolonial *coopérants* in Algeria, see Jean-Robert Henry and Jaen-Claude Vatin, eds., *Le temps de la coopération: Sciences sociales et décolonisation au Maghreb* (Paris: Karthala, 2012).

70. Duval and Ray, *Le Cardinal Duval*, 70.

71. Soumille, "L'Église catholique et l'État tunisien après l'indépendance," 189.

72. Msgr Duval, "Remarques sur le Schema 13, présentées par le Cardinal Duval, Archevêque d'Alger," Archives of Cardinal Duval, Archdiocese of Algiers, casier 293.

73. Martine de Sauto, *Henri Teissier, un évêque en Algérie* (Paris: Bayard, 2006), 107. There is much disagreement among experts on the role played by the French Catholic scholar of Islam Louis Massignon in the formulation of *Nostra aetate*. However, his influence was clear in Algeria, particularly among Foucauldian groups like the Little Brothers and Sisters of Jesus.

Chapter 7

1. "Lettre du député Barthélémy Boganda à Mgr. Cucherousset, 1 décembre 1949 après sa suspension," Archives Générales Spiritaines, Chevilly-Larue (hereafter ACCSp.), 2D71.2a5/103217; letters of Père le Comte, 1950–1951, ACSSp. 3J3.31a4/108151. See also Klaas van Walraven, "Barthélémy Boganda between Charisma and Cosmology," in *The Individual in African History*, ed. Klaas van Walraven (Leiden: Brill, 2020), 246–74.

2. Côme Kinata, "Barthélémy Boganda et l'Église Catholique en Oubangui-Chari," *Cahiers d'Études Africaines* 191, no. 3 (September 27, 2008): 560.

3. Kinata, "Barthélémy Boganda et l'Église Catholique en Oubangui-Chari"; Antoine-Denis N'Dimina-Mougala, "Une Personnalité de l'Afrique Centrale: Barthélémy Boganda (1910–1959)," *Guerres mondiales et conflits contemporains*, no. 181 (1996): 27–51.

4. The Lobaye region was part of Moyen Congo until 1933, when it became incorporated into Oubangui-Chari. See Jacqueline M. C. Thomas, *Les Ngbaka de la Lobaye: le dépeuplement rural chez une population forestière de la République centrafricaine*, Deuxième série (Monde d'outre-mer, passé et présent, 1963), 23–34.

5. Pierre Kalck, *Barthélemy Boganda, 1910–1959: Élu de Dieu et des Centrafricains* (Saint-Maur-des-Fossés: Editions Sépia, 1995), 40–56. For discussion of the ravages of concessionary company extractions and ethnic competition for labor and slaves in Moyen Congo and Oubangui-Chari, see Catherine Coquery-Vidrovitch, *Le Congo Au Temps Des Grandes Compagnies Concessionnaires* (Paris-La Haye: Mouton, 1972); and Charles Tisserant, *Ce que j'ai connu de l'esclavage en Oubangui-Chari* (Paris: Société antiesclavagiste de France, 1955). For further discussion of Catholic mission education and clerical training in Central Africa, see Jean Paul Messina and Jaap Van Slageren, *Histoire Du Christianisme Au Cameroun: Des Origines à Nos Jours: Approche Oecuménique* (Paris: Éditions Karthala, 2005).

6. Barthélemy Boganda, "lettre du 30 décembre 1933 à Mgr. Grandin," ACCSp. SF-241.14/113537; Barthélemy Boganda, "lettre du 8 janvier 1937 au Père Auguste Fayet," ACCSp. SF-241.14/113537; Barthélemy Boganda, "lettre du 22 octobre 1937 au Père Auguste Fayet," ACCSp. SF-241.14/113537.

7. Cahiers de Barthélemy Boganda (in particular March 1939), ACCSp. SF-241.14/113537. See also Kinata, "Barthélémy Boganda et l'Église Catholique En Oubangui-Chari."

8. Kalck, *Barthélemy Boganda*.

9. The starvation, forced labor, and torture in Oubangui Chari is documented in detail in documents in the Archives Nationales d'Outre-Mer (ANOM): "Politique économique en AEF," 1AFFPOL 657; "La Vie Agricole dans un District Cotonnier d'Oubangui-Chari," 3ECOL 116; and "Indigénat et internement," 1AFFPOL 663, among others.

10. Congrès National MRP, 14 mars 1947, "Problèmes sociaux et culturels dans les Territoires d'Outre-Mer" Discours prononcé par M. l'abbé Boganda, Député d'Oubangui-Chari, AEF, printed in Jean-Dominique Pénel, *Barthélémy Boganda: Ecrits et discours 1946–1951: La lutte décisive* (Paris: Editions L'Harmattan, 1995), , 122–33.

11. Not coincidentally, the paper of his political party, MESAN (Mouvement de l'Évolution Sociale en Afrique Noire), was *Terre Africaine*. See *Pour Sauver un Peuple: Bulletin Mensuelle d'action politique, économique et sociale en A.E.F*, ANOM AFFPOL 2253-54. See also, Barthélemy Boganda "1949 lettres," ACSSp. 5J1.5b1/108549. For more on equatorial cosmology, see Jan Vansina, *Paths in the Rainforests: Toward a History of Political Tradition in Equatorial Africa* (Madison: University of Wisconsin Press, 1990); Florence Bernault, "Body, Power and Sacrifice in Equatorial Africa," *Journal of African History* 47, no. 2 (2006): 207–39.

12. Antoine-Denis N'Dimina-Mougala, "Une Personnalité de l'Afrique Centrale: Barthélémy Boganda (1910–1959)," *Guerres mondiales et conflits contemporains*, no. 181 (Janvier 1996), 49–51; "L'Oubangui autonome" février 1960, ACSSp. SF-241.15/113538.

13. For example, Boganda's letters to the administration were printed in *Le Libertaire*, an international anarchist newspaper. See "L'Enfer colonial: M'Baiki- le bagne Auschwitz Africain," *Le Libertaire*, no. 264, 13 April 1951.

14. Elizabeth Foster and Darcie Fontaine have both extensively documented the morally and politically fraught debates within the Catholic Church during decolonization. See Elizabeth A.

Foster, "Theologies of Colonization: The Catholic Church and the Future of the French Empire in the 1950s," *Journal of Modern History* 87, no. 2 (June 2015): 281–315; Darcie Fontaine, *Decolonizing Christianity: Religion and the End of Empire in France and Algeria, 1940–1965* (London: Cambridge University Press, 2016).

15. Barthélemy Boganda, "Lettre du député Barthélémy Boganda à Mgr. Cucherousset, 1 déc. 1949," ACCSp. 2D71.2a5 /103217.

16. Barthélemy Boganda, "Discours récemment prononcé à l'Assemblée territorial de l'Oubangui par M. Boganda, mai 1956," ANOM AFFPOL 1/2254. Arbitrary mutilation, extreme beatings, torture, and murder of colonial subjects in Oubangui-Chari are documented in "Indigénat et internement," ANOM 1AFFPOL 663; Jacques Augendre, "La legislation du travail indigene en Afrique Equatoriale Française," 6 January 1946, 3ECOL 58; and "Tournées de police," 2AFFPOL 19, among many others.

17. The history of Central Africa at the end of the French empire provides some of the starkest evidence for this. See Thomas Deltombe, Marcel Domergue, and Jacob Tatsitsa, *Kamerun! Une Guerre Caché aux Origines de la Françafrique, 1948–1971* (Paris: La Découverte, 2011); François-Xavier Verschave, *Françafrique: Le Plus Long Scandale de la République* (Paris: Stock, 1998); Kaye Whiteman, "The Man Who Ran Françafrique," *National Interest*, no. 49 (1997): 92–99.

18. Foster, "Theologies of Colonization"; Elizabeth A. Foster, *African Catholic: Decolonization and the Transformation of the Church* (Cambridge, MA: Harvard University Press, 2019); Fontaine, *Decolonizing Christianity*; Giuliana Chamedes and Elizabeth A. Foster, "Introduction: Decolonization and Religion in the French Empire," *French Politics, Culture & Society* 33, no. 2 (2015): 1–10.

19. ACSSp. 5J1.2b9, Réflexions du Père Joseph Bouchaud, 31 janvier 1947.

20. Barthélémy Boganda, parole à l'Assemblée nationale, 5 mars 1947, Commission des Territoires d'Outre Mer, printed in Jean-Dominique Pénel, *Barthélémy Boganda: Ecrits et discours 1946–1951: La lutte décisive* (Paris: Editions L'Harmattan, 1995), , 121–22.

21. Rapport du Gouverneur de la France d'Outre-Mer, Chef du Territoire de l'Oubangui-Chari, sur les agissements du député B. Boganda et éléments de réponse au Mémorandum présenté par ce parlementaire à l'Assemblé nationale le 23 janvier 1951, Bangui, cited in Jean-Dominique Pénel, *Barthélémy Boganda: Ecrits et discours 1946–1951: La lutte décisive* (Paris: Editions L'Harmattan, 1995, 377–88; Barthélemy Boganda, "lettres à Mgr. le Hunsec," ACSSp. 5J1.2b9.

22. Jacques Augendre, "La legislation du travail indigene en Afrique Equatoriale Française," 6 janvier 1946, ANOM 3ECOL 58. See also J. P. Daughton, *In the Forest of No Joy: The Congo-Océan Railroad and the Tragedy of French Colonialism* (New York: W. W. Norton, 2021); Gilles Sautter, "Notes sur la Construction du Chemin de Fer Congo-Océan," *Cahiers d'Etudes Africaines* 7 (1967): 269–99; Julien Gautier, "La Culture du Cotonnier en Afrique Équatoriale Française," *Journal d'Agriculture Traditionnelle et de Botanique Appliquée* 26, no. 279 (1946): 3–10.

23. Misner carefully traces the emergence of advanced social consciousness among Catholics in northern Europe in the nineteenth as well as twentieth centuries and depicts the radical challenge it presented to the "residual and recrudescent paternalism of the church." See Paul Misner, *Social Catholicism in Europe: From the Onset of Industrialization to the First World War* (New York: Crossroad, 1991), 318. Moyn discusses the 1940s Catholic Church's perceptions of social and economic rights as particularly "treacherous" for their potential to lead to materialistic or totalitarian ends, as well as Catholic skepticism toward human rights conceived as

anything other than religious freedom. See Samuel Moyn, *Christian Human Rights* (Philadelphia: University of Pennsylvania Press, 2015), 113–15.

24. Coquery-Vidrovitch, *Le Congo Au Temps Des Grandes Compagnies Concessionnaires*; J. P. Daughton, "The 'Pacha Affair' Reconsidered: Violence and Colonial Rule in Interwar French Equatorial Africa," *Journal of Modern History* 91, no. 3 (August 21, 2019): 493–524.

25. Daughton, *In the Forest of No Joy*.

26. Jacques Augendre, "La legislation du travail indigene en Afrique Equatoriale Française," 6 January 1946, ANOM 3ECOL 58.

27. "Subdivision de Kouango: Journal du poste de Kouango (extraits de 1913 à 1926)" ACSSp. SF-240.6/113516; Père Taise "lettere du Père Taise, Kouango, 7 décembre 1920," ACSSp. SF-240.6/113516.

28. Victor Bissengue and Prosper Indo, *Barthélémy Boganda: Héritage et vision* (Paris: Editions L'Harmattan, 2018), 93–94.

29. *Arrêté du 1 juillet 1924* ANOM Travaux Publiques (hereafter TP) Série 1 420/11; *Arrêté du 9 mars 1927*, ANOM TP Série 1 420/11.

30. Catherine Coquery-Vidrovich, "The Colonial Economy of the Former French, Belgian, and Portuguese Zones, 1914–35," in *General History of Africa VII: Africa Under Colonial Domination 1880–1935*, ed. A. Adu Boahen (Berkeley: University of California Press and Heinemann, 1985), 360.

31. "Lettre n° 458 du lieutenant-gouverneur par intérim de l'Oubangui-Chari au gouverneur général au sujet du problème de la main d'œuvre, 21 décembre 1927," ANOM, Gouvernement Général de l'AEF, 1 h 10. See also P. Mollion, "Le portage en Oubangui-Chari (1890–1930)," *Revue d'histoire moderne et contemporaine* 33, no. 4 (October–December 1986): 546. The *laissez-passer* is also mentioned by Father Charles Tisserant in his observations of ongoing slavery practices in Oubangui-Chari, as slave/laborer requisitions were not recorded in laissez-passer documentation. See Tisserant, *Ce que j'ai connu de l'esclavage en Oubangui-Chari*, 30–33.

32. Bissengue and Indo, *Barthélémy Boganda*, 104.

33. Thomas O'Toole, "The 1928–1931 Gbaya Insurrection in Ubangui-Shari: Messianic Movement or Village Self-Defense?" *Canadian Journal of African Studies / Revue Canadienne Des Études Africaines* 18, no. 2 (1984): 329–44; Philip Burnham and Thomas Christensen, "Karnu's Message and the 'War of the Hoe Handle': Interpreting a Central African Resistance Movement," *Africa: Journal of the International African Institute* 53, no. 4 (1983): 3–22; Elikia M'Bokolo, "French Colonial Policy in Equatorial Africa in the 1940s and 1950s," in *The Transfer of Power in Africa: Decolonization 1940–1960*, ed. Prosser Gifford and William Roger Louis (New Haven: Yale University Press, 1982), 173–210; Pierre Mollion, "Le Portage en Oubangui-Chari, 1890–1930," *Revue d'histoire moderne et contemporaine (1954-)* 33, no. 4 (1986): 542–68.

34. See, among others, Burnham and Christensen, "Karnu's Message"; O'Toole, "The 1928–1931 Gbaya Insurrection in Ubangui-Shari"; Pierre Kalck, *Histoire de la République centrafricaine: des origines préhistoriques à nos jours* (Paris: Berger-Levrault, 1974), 240–47; and Barthélémy Boganda, Lettre ouverte à M. le Haut Commissaire en AEF, Paris, 1 October 1950, cited in Antoine-Denis N'Dimina-Mougala, "Une Personnalité de l'Afrique Centrale: Barthélémy Boganda (1910–1959)," *Guerres Mondiales et Conflits Contemporains* 181 (1996): 27–51.

35. Brian Weinstein, "Felix Eboue and the Chiefs: Perceptions of Power in Early Oubangui-Chari," *Journal of African History* 11, no. 1 (1970): 107–26.

36. Mario Azevedo, "The Human Price of Development: The Brazzaville Railroad and the Sara of Chad," *African Studies Review* 24, no. 1 (1981): 1–19; René Lemarchand, "The Politics of Sara Ethnicity: A Note on the Origins of the Civil War in Chad," *Cahiers d'Études Africaines* 20, no. 80 (1980): 56–74; Kinata, "Barthélémy Boganda et l'Église Catholique En Oubangui-Chari."

37. Barthélémy Boganda, "Terreur et travaux forcés en Oubangui-Chari," *L'Observateur*, 12 November 1953, ACSSp. 5J1.5b1/108549.

38. Jean Aubame, "La Conférence de Brazzaville," in *Afrique Equatoriale Française*, ed. E. Guernier (Paris: Office français d'édition, 1950); Claude Levy, "Les Origines de La Conférence de Brazzaville, Le Contexte et La Décision," in *Ville Janvier-Fevrier 1944: Aux Sources de la Décolonisation*, ed. Institut Charles de Gaulle and Institut d'Histoire du Temps Présent (Paris: Plon, 1988).

39. The scant literature includes key primary research by Weinstein, "Felix Eboue and the Chiefs"; and Azevedo, "The Human Price of Development."

40. Barthélemy Boganda, "lettres du 8 janvier 1937 et 22 octobre 1937 au Père Auguste Fayet," ACCSp SF-241.14/113537.

41. "Programme du candidat Boganda 1947," ACSSp. 5J1.5b1/108549; Barthélémy Boganda, "Terreur et travaux forcés en Oubangui-Chari"; Barthélémy Boganda, député-Maire de Bangui, "Enfin on décolonise," 5 October 1957, ACSSp. 5J1.5b1/108549.

42. Charlotte Walker-Said, "Fabrique du Genre et Sens National dans les Organisations de la Jeunesse Chrétienne au Cameroun (Années 1940–1950)," *Le Mouvement Sociale*, no. 255 (2016): 119–35; Giuliana Chamedes, "The Catholic Origins of Economic Development After World War II," *French Politics, Culture & Society* 33, no. 2 (2015): 57–59.

43. Msgr. Grandin, "Candidat Boganda," ACSSp. 5J1.5b1 108549. See also Foster, *African Catholic*, 129–32; Roger Pasquier, *La jeunesse ouvrière chrétienne en Afrique noire (1930–1950)* (Paris: Karthala, 2013).

44. Caroline Sappia and Olivier Servais, *Mission et engagement politique après 1945: Afrique, Amérique latine, Europe* (Paris: Karthala, 2010); Chamedes, "The Catholic Origins of Economic Development After World War II," 57.

45. Barthélémy Boganda, "Pour Sauver un Peuple," no. 5 et 6, August 1949, printed in Jean-Dominique Pénel, *Barthélémy Boganda: Ecrits et discours 1946–1951: La lutte décisive* (Paris: Editions L'Harmattan, 1995), 211–16. See also Kinata, "Barthélémy Boganda et l'Église Catholique en Oubangui-Chari."

46. Boganda's early conceptions of "civilization" and "development" emphasized these terms. See Lettre de Boganda à Abel Goumba, Paris, 26 January 1947, printed in Jean-Dominique Pénel, *Barthélémy Boganda: Ecrits et discours 1946–1951: La lutte décisive* (Paris: Editions L'Harmattan, 1995),, 116–17.

47. Msgr. Grandin, "lettres de 1947, Msgr. Grandin sur Boganda," ACSSp. 5J1.3a8 108522; Msgr. Le Hunsec, "lettres de Msgr. Le Hunsec, 18 avril 1947," ACSSp. 5J1.3a8 108522; Msgr. Cucherousset, "Lettres du avril, août 1947," ACSSp. 5J1.3a8 108522.

48. Frederick Cooper et al., "The History and Politics of Development Knowledge," in *The Anthropology of Development and Globalization: From Classical Political Economy to Contemporary Neoliberalism* (London: Blackwell, 2005), 126–39; Chamedes, "The Catholic Origins of Economic Development After World War II."

49. Chamedes, "The Catholic Origins of Economic Development After World War II," 66.

50. Chamedes, "The Catholic Origins of Economic Development After World War II."

51. Giuliana Chamedes, "Pius XII, Rights Talk and the Dawn of the Religious Cold War," in *Religion and Human Rights*, ed. David Pendas (New York: Routledge, forthcoming).

52. Jessica Pearson-Patel, "Promoting Health, Protecting Empire: Inter-Colonial Medical Cooperation in Postwar Africa," *Monde(s)* 7, no. 1 (September 18, 2015): 213–30; Jessica Lynne Pearson, *The Colonial Politics of Global Health: France and the United Nations in Postwar Africa* (Cambridge, MA: Harvard University Press, 2018), 67–95. See also Mark Mazower, *No Enchanted Palace: The End of Empire and the Ideological Origins of the United Nations* (Princeton, NJ: Princeton University Press, 2009).

53. Pearson, *The Colonial Politics of Global Health*, 67–95.

54. Foster, *African Catholic*, 7.

55. Raymond Susset, *La Vérite sur le Cameroun et l'Afrique Équatoriale Française* (Paris: Nouvelle revue critique, 1934); Jules Alcandre, "Le Désastre Financier de l'Afrique Équatoriale Française," *Europe-Colonies*, August 1934. See also Weinstein, "Felix Eboue and the Chiefs."

56. These included the French orders of the Society of Jesus, the Congregation of the Holy Ghost, and Priests of the Sacred Heart of Saint Quentin, along with the French Protestant Mission (which included the French Evangelical Lutheran Church, the Fraternal Lutheran Church, the Union of Baptist Churches, and the Paris Society of Evangelical Missions, and, perhaps most notably, the Presbyterian Mission of the USA). See ANOM Affaires Politiques (hereafter AFF-POL) 3349/2; ACSSp. 2J1.7a4, construction des églises et monastères; SMEP/DEFAP Section Eglise Evangélique du Cameroun (hereafter EEC), Inventaire du Fonds Brutsch (hereafter FB) 2/2, EEC Divers, vie des eglises I; PHS West Africa Mission, Mission Meeting Minutes 1952, Elat, July–August 1952.

57. André Gide, *Voyage Au Congo* (Paris: Gallimard, 1927); René Maran, "L'AEF ou La Colonie Rouge," *Journal du Peuple*, April 24, 1926.

58. Barthélemy Boganda, "Lettre du député Barthélémy Boganda à Mgr. Cucherousset, 1 décembre 1949, après sa suspension," ACSSp. 2D71.2a5 /103217.

59. Lettre de B. Boganda à Mgr. Grandin, Grimari, 15 mars 1946, printed in Jean-Dominique Pénel, *Barthélémy Boganda: Ecrits et discours 1946–1951: La lutte décisive* (Paris: Editions L'Harmattan, 1995, 99–100.

60. Barthélemy Boganda, "Lettre de l'abbé Boganda en réponse à Msgr Biéchy, 10 janvier 1948," ACSSp. 5J1.2b9/108513; Memorandum sur l'arrestation, la détention préventive et la traduction en police correctionnelle de M. Boganda ACSSp. 2D*94/111523; "Derniers moments de Mgr Grandin, 4 septembre 1947," ACSSp. 2D*94/111523.

61. Vansina, *Paths in the Rainforests.*

62. Vansina, *Paths in the Rainforests*, 247.

63. Vansina, *Paths in the Rainforests*, 247; Chinua Achebe, *Things Fall Apart* (London: Doubleday, 1994). For critical analysis of Achebe's work, see Òlakunle George, "The 'Native' Missionary, the African Novel, and In-Between," *NOVEL: A Forum on Fiction* 36, no. 1 (2002): 5–25.

64. Charlotte Walker-Said, *Faith, Power & Family: Christianity and Social Change in French Cameroon* (Oxford: James Currey, 2018).

65. For greater context of this level of under-investment in education, see David E. Gardinier, "The Impact of French Education on Africa, 1817–1960," *Proceedings of the Meeting of the French Colonial Historical Society* 5 (1980): 70–82.

66. Père Morandeau, "Lettres de 1947, P. Morandeau, 23 février 1947," ACSSp. SF-240.11/113521.

67. Barthélemy Boganda, "Lettres de 1947," "Lettre de P. Boganda à Msgr. Grandin, 17 mai 1947," ACSSp. SF-240.11/113521; Père Cucherousset, "Lettre de Cucherousset, 4 avril 1947," ACSSp. SF-240.11/113521; Msgr. Grandin, "Lettre de Msgr. Grandin 6 mai 1947," ACSSp. SF-240.11/113521.

68. Lettre de Boganda à son évêque, Bambari, 21 December 1943, cited in Benoît Basile Siango, *Barthélémy Boganda: Premier Prêtre Oubanguien, Fondateur de La République Centrafricaine* (Pierrefitte-sur-Seine: Bajag-Meri, 2004), 122.

69. See, among other writings, Barthélémy Boganda, "Labor improbus omnia vincit," *Terre Africaine* 121, April 1966, 5; Barthélémy Boganda, *Enfin on décolonise*, Brazzaville, Imprimerie officielle, 1958, 5. See also, Barthélémy Boganda, "Une grande figure missionaire," ACSSp. SD-E10.3/111567.

70. Elizabeth Schmidt, *Mobilizing the Masses: Gender, Ethnicity, and Class in the Nationalist Movement in Guinea, 1939–1958* (Portsmouth, NH: Heinemann, 2005); Jean Marie Allman, *The Quills of the Porcupine: Asante Nationalism in an Emergent Ghana* (Madison: University of Wisconsin Press, 1993).

71. Frederick Cooper, *Citizenship between Empire and Nation: Remaking France and French Africa, 1945–1960* (Princeton, NJ: Princeton University Press, 2014), 1.

72. Henry Grimal, *La décolonisation de 1919 à nos jours* (Paris: Armand Colin, 1965), 335.

73. Philippe Guillemin, "Les Élus d'Afrique Noire à l'Assemblée Nationale Sous la Quatrième République," *Revue Française de Science Politique* 8, no. 4 (1958): 861–77.

74. L. J. Lebret, "Le gigantesque effort à entreprendre," ACSSp. SD-F8.2/111720; "Lebret lettres 1958," ACSSp. SD-H2 111900.

75. Ruth Marshall, "The Sovereignty of Miracles: Pentecostal Political Theology in Nigeria," *Constellations* 17, no. 2 (2010): 204.

76. Robert Mbe Akoko, *"Ask and You Shall Be Given": Pentecostalism and the Economic Crisis in Cameroon*, African Studies Collection Series (Leiden: African Studies Centre, 2007); Babatunde A. Adedibu and Benson O. Igboin, "Eschato-Praxis and Accountability: A Study of Neo-African Pentecostal Movement in the Light of Prosperity Gospel," *Verbum et Ecclesia* 40, no. 1 (2019): 1–8; Ruy Llera Blanes, "Politics of Sovereignty: Evangelical and Pentecostal Christianity and Politics in Angola," in *The Anthropology of Global Pentecostalism and Evangelicalism*, ed. Simon Coleman and Rosalind I. J. Hackett (New York: NYU Press, 2015), 197–213.

77. See Barthélemy Boganda, "Griefs contre les missionaires; Barthélemy Boganda: 'Terreur et travail forcé,' lettres 1949," ACSSp. 5J1.5B1.

78. Ruth Marshall, *Political Spiritualities: The Pentecostal Revolution in Nigeria* (Chicago: University of Chicago Press, 2009).

79. Michael Kpughe Lang, "The Patterns of Corruption in Christian Churches of Cameroon: The Case of the Presbyterian Church in Cameroon," *Transformation* 31, no. 2 (2014): 132.

80. Naomi Haynes, "Pentecostalism and the Morality of Money: Prosperity, Inequality, and Religious Sociality on the Zambian Copperbelt," *Journal of the Royal Anthropological Institute* 18, no. 1 (2012): 123–39.

81. Comaroff and Comaroff's work strongly emphasizes neoliberalism as a primary motivator of the emergence of wealth-centered Christian and religious movements in Africa. See Jean Comaroff and John L. Comaroff, *Millennial Capitalism and the Culture of Neoliberalism* (Durham, NC: Duke University Press, 2001); Jean Comaroff, "Pentecostalism, Populism, and the Politics of Affect: In Africa and Elsewhere," in *Pentecostalism and Development: Churches, NGOs and Social Change in Africa*, ed. Dana Freeman (Basingstoke: Palgrave Macmillan, 2012), 41–66.

Chapter 8

1. Among others, see Amélia Neves de Souto, *Caetano e o ocaso do "império": Administração e guerra colonial em Moçambique durante o Marcelismo, 1968–1974* (Oporto: Edições Afrontamento, 2007), ch. 9; and Teresa Cruz e Silva, *Protestant Churches and the Formation of Political Consciousness in Southern Mozambique (1930–1974)* (Basel, Switzerland: P. Schlettwein, 2001).

2. Eric Morier-Genoud, "The Vatican vs. Lisbon: The Relaunching of the Catholic Church in Mozambique, ca. 1875–1940," *Basler Afrika Bibliographien Working Papers* no. 4, 2002; James Duffy, *Portuguese Africa* (Cambridge, MA: Harvard University Press, 1959), ch. 5; and Pinto Rema, "A actividade missionária de Portugal nos séculos XIX e XX: I. A missionação portuguesa em geral," *Itinerarium* (Braga, Portugal), no. 43 (1997): 251–332.

3. Eric Morier-Genoud, *Catholicism and the Making of Politics in Central Mozambique, 1940–1986* (Rochester, NY: University of Rochester Press, 2019), 66.

4. Numbers calculated on the basis of Francisco Maria Pinheiro, *Na entrega do testemunho 1975: Acção missionária portuguesa em Moçambique* (Torres Novas, Portugal: Paróquia de S. João de Deus, 1992).

5. Luís Benjamin Serapião, "The Roman Catholic Church and the Principle of Self-Determination: A Case Study in Mozambique," *Journal of Church and State* 23, no. 2 (1981): 323–35; and Morier-Genoud, *Catholicism and the Making of Politics*, ch.4.

6. Morier-Genoud, *Catholicism and the Making of Politics*, 96–108.

7. Claudia Castelo, *"O modo português de estar no mundo": O luso-tropicalismo e a ideologia colonial portuguesa (1933–1961)* (Oporto: Afrontamento, 1998); and Warwick Anderson, Ricardo Roque, and Ricardo Ventura Santos, eds., *Luso-Tropicalism and Its Discontents: The Making and Unmaking of Racial Exceptionalism* (New York: Berghahn, 2019).

8. Morier-Genoud, *Catholicism and the Making of Politics*, 29–30.

9. White Fathers, *Mozambique: Une église, signe de salut . . . pour qui?* (Rome: Société des Missionnaires d'Afrique, 1973), 187. Author's translation—all quotes in this chapter from non-English sources have been translated by the author.

10. Morier-Genoud, *Catholicism and the Making of Politics*, ch. 5.

11. Among others, see "White Fathers encouraged Africans to rebel," *The Times* (London), 29 May 1971; and "Padres Brancos e Padres Vermelhos," *Diário de Notícias* (Lisbon), 15 July 1971.

12. "Reunion Del Grupo IEME em Mozambique," 1971, 4 p., Box 32(9)/9, Jesuit Archives, Lisbon, Portugal,

13. Morier-Genoud, *Catholicism and the Making of Politics*, 42–43. More broadly, see Félix Lopes, *Missões franciscanas em Moçambique, 1898–1970* (Braga: Editorial Franciscana, 1972).

14. Zélia Pereira, *Jésuitas em Moçambique (1941–1974): a construção do modelo imperial do Estado Novo* (master's thesis, Instituto Universitário de Lisboa, 1998), 174 (published without page numbers as *Africanos e Jesuítas: Experiência missionária dos jesuítas em Moçambique* [Lisbon: Theya, 2017]). On lusotropicalism, see Claudia Castelo, *"O modo português de estar no mundo."* About the plans for a Portuguese federal empire, see Norrie Macqueen, "António de Spínola and the decolonization of Portuguese Africa," *Diplomacy and Statecraft* 7, no. 2 (1996): 436–65.

15. White Fathers, *Mozambique: Une église, signe de salut*, 313–14.

16. Direcção Geral de Segurança, Delegação em Moçambique, Pº 23.26.01/SR-1, *Informação* no. 2598/73/DI/2/SC, 15-6-73, *secret*, Assunto: "Perfil político da religiosa Maria de Carli," Pide archives, Instituto dos Arquivos Nacionais / Torre de Tombo (IAN/TT), Lisbon, Portugal.

17. Father de Sousa struggled at first, he explains in his autobiography, but he developed into a bridge-builder and became a very influential member of the diocese, as well as a most successful and lasting vicar-general. See José Augusto Alves de Sousa, *Memórias de um 'jesuíta missionário em Moçambique: 1960–2004 quarenta e quatro anos de compromisso na igreja e na sociedade moçambicana; uma nova face da missão* (Braga, Portugal: Editorial Apostolado da Oração, 2015), 255.

18. Sister Paulina de Pozo Ureña, cited in Soares Tomás, *Irmãs franciscanas missionárias da Mãe do Divino Pastor em Moçambique* (Braga: Livraria Apostolado da Imprensa, 1998), 109. About these meetings, see José Augusto Alves de Sousa, *Memórias de um jesuíta missionário em Moçambique: 1960–2004*, 257.

19. "Curso de Pastoral—Renovação das estruturas pastorais, Matola 20–15.11.1972," 10 p., No. 131, Box Prov. 6.26, "Correspontie III," Archives of the Picpus Congregation, Breda, The Netherlands (hereafter cited as APICC).

20. Florent Bourgeault, *Un geste prophétique: Le retrait des Pères Blancs du Mozambique* (PhD dissertation, Université de Montréal, 1974), 84–85.

21. Bourgeault, *Un geste prophétique*, 84–85.

22. For the details of the meetings in Rome, see Morier-Genoud, *Catholicism and the Making of Politics*, 143–46.

23. Morier-Genoud, *Catholicism and the Making of Politics*, 143–46.

24. Frank Nolan, *The Departure of the Missionaries of Africa (The White Fathers) from Mozambique in 1971* (Rome: Missionaries of Africa Society, 2017), ch. 5.

25. "Projet de communiqué des instituts missionnaires [rédigé] par le R. P. Walbert Bülhmann, ofm. cap. (transmis par téléphone au P. W. Neven)," s/d., No. 11b, Doc. 6.26, Dossier "Moz 1971-I," APICC.

26. For the White Fathers' superior general's recollections of the process, see Theo van Asten, *A Maverick in a missionary church: Memories of Theo van Asten*, author's edition (Saint Gély-du Fesc, France: 2020), 77–78.

27. Cesare Bertulli, *A Cruz e a Espada em Moçambique* (Lisbon: Portugalia editora, 1974), 227–30.

28. For an extreme case, see Bertulli, *A cruz e a espada*, 65.

29. Carlos Alberto Alves, "*Esperar pela hora de Deus: O exílio forçado de sacerdotes angolanos em Portugal entre 1960 a 1974* (Luanda: Mayamba Editora, 2015).

30. Morier-Genoud, *Catholicism and the Making of Politics*, 150–51.

31. For statistics of the clergy, see Conferência Episcopal de Moçambique, *Cartas Pastorais: Documentos CEM* (Oporto: Humbertipo, 1984), 46.

32. Cited in Benedito Marime, *Lições de História da Igreja Católica em Moçambique* (Maputo, Mozambique: author's edition, 2011), 118.

33. Service oecuménique de presse et d'information (SOEPI),"La décision des Pères Blancs proposée en exemple aux protestants: 2-11-71," 1 November 1971, reproduced in White Fathers, *Mozambique: Une église, signe de salut*, 356–57.

34. Caroline Jeannerat, Eric Morier-Genoud, and Didier Péclard, *Embroiled: Swiss Churches, South Africa and Apartheid* (Berlin: LIT-Verlag, 2011), ch. 5.

35. Caroline Jeannerat et al., *Swiss Churches*, 220–21; and Georges Andrié, *Au creuset de l'épreuve, 1972–1974* (Lausanne: DM. Echange et Mission, 2010), 7–10. For the minutes of the meetings, see handwritten notes of a meeting in Lausanne, 19 May 1971, 6 p., and handwritten

notes of a meeting in Geneva, 17 June 1971, 5p., Box 275, Program to Combat Racism, Archives of the World Council of Churches (WCC), Geneva, Switzerland.

36. Report on a meeting between the Provincial Superior and the Picpus local council of Lisbon, VCMI no. 6, 1956, 3 p., Folder "Divers," Box Prov. 6.21, APICC. For a history of the congregation, see I. M. Rademaker, *Called to Serve: History of the Congregation of the Sacred Hearts of Jesus and Mary (1800–1988)* (Dublin: Fathers and Brothers of the Sacred Hearts, 1988).

37. Edmund Blommaert, *Mozambique: A Hopeful Return? A Suffering Nation . . . People with a Mission* (Breda: Missiecentrum Pater Damiaan: 1993), 9.

38. Dossier "Portugal na vitwijzing" and "Pro Memoria à secrétairerie d'Etat," 16 March 1970, and "Pro Memoria," 20 February 1970, No. 8 and No. 26, Prov. 6.22, APICC.

39. Letter by Father Antonio to Father Verdaarsdonk, 25 May 1971, No. 15a, Dossier "Moz 1971-I," Doc 6.26, APICC.

40. Letter by A. Verdaasdonk [to Father Antonio?], 25 May 1971, No. 15b, Dossier "Moz 1971-I," Doc 6.26, APICC.

41. Letter Secretariado da CNIR, Lisbon to Provincial, 18 January 1973, Folder Corr. G. Spokel / M. Verney, No. 3, Prov 6.23, APICC.

42. Letter [Brito?] to Vice-Provincial, 5 Abril de 1973, Corr. Sprokel / Verney, No. 18, Prov. 6.23, APICC. For the Frelimo guerrilla, the "fourth front" was the southern part of Mozambique.

43. Assembleia Regional, Nazaré, 20–24 August 1973, 14 p., No.139, Prov. 6.26 "Correspondentie II,"APICC.

44. Assembleia Regional, Nazaré, 20–24 August 1973, 14 p., , Correspondentie II., No. 139, Prov. 6.26, APICC.

45. *Recentes Massacres em Moçambique. Abril de 1974. Relatório dos Missionários de Inhaminga* (Lisbon: Edição do movimento Justiça e Paz). More generally, see Jorge Ribeiro, *Inhaminga: O último massacre* (Oporto: Edições Afrontamento, 2015).

46. Letter 28 March 1974, Prov. 1.01 (divers), APICC.

47. Letter of the Superior General to all missionaries in Mozambique, 28 March 1974, No. 155, Folder "Correspondie III," Prov. 6.26, APICC.

48. Norrie Macqueen, "António de Spínola and the decolonization of Portuguese Africa," *Diplomacy and Statecraft* 7, no. 2 (1996), 436–65.

49. Letter 4 May 1974 with annexes, , No. 71, Folder "Documentum unit . . . II," Doc. 6.24, APICC.

50. Letter to the Départment missionnaires des Eglises protestantes de la Suisse Romande, 2 July 1974, No. 8, Folder "Oecumenische Kontaketen. M.b.t. Mozambique," Prov. 6.27, APICC.

51. Folder "Kontakt mith missionarissen . . . ," No.1, Prov. 6.27, APICC. See also Cesare Bertulli, *A Cruz e a Espada,* 402–4.

52. Teresa Cruz e Silva, "Zedequias Manganhela: Notas para Uma Releitura das Relações Estado-Igrejas Protestantes na Década de 70," *Estudos Moçambicanos*, no. 13 (1993): 29–49.

53. Letter 22 May 1974, 2p., No. 3, Folder "Oecumenische Kontaketen. M.b.t. Mozambique," APICC.

54. Letter 14 June 1974, 3 p., no. 5, Folder "Oecumenische Kontaketen. M.b.t. Mozambique," Prov. 6.27, APICC.

55. Letter 2 July 1974, 2 p., No. 8, Folder "Oecumenische Kontaketen. M.b.t. Mozambique," Prov. 6.27, APICC.

56. Letter 17 July 1974, 1 p., no. 9, Folder "Oecumenische Kontaketen. M.b.t. Mozambique," Folder 6.27, APICC.

57. "Breve relatório do encontro em Lausanne, no dia 24 de Setembro de 1974," 7 p., no. 22, Folder "Folder Oecumenische Kontaketen. M.b.t. Mozambique," Prov. 6.27, APICC.

Chapter 9

1. E. A. Ayandele, *The Missionary Impact on Modern Nigeria, 1842–1942* (London: Longmans, 1966); David Maxwell, "Decolonization," in *Missions and Empire*, ed. Norman Etherington (Oxford: Oxford University Press, 2005), 297.

2. Adom Getachew, *Worldmaking after Empire: The Rise and Fall of Self-Determination* (Princeton, NJ: Princeton University Press, 2019); Manu Goswami, "Imperial Futures and Colonial Internationalisms," *American Historical Review* 117, no. 5 (2012): 1461–85

3. Robert Vinson, *The Americans Are Coming* (Athens: Ohio University Press, 2011); James Campbell, *Songs of Zion: The African Methodist Episcopal Church in the United States and South Africa* (New York: Oxford University Press, 1995).

4. EmaSwati refers to the people of Eswatini (formerly Swaziland). The singular is liSwati.

5. Norman Etherington, "Mission Station Melting Pots as a Factor in the Rise of South African Black Nationalism," *International Journal of African Historical Studies* 9, no. 4 (1976): 600–1.

6. Hilda Kuper, *The Uniform of Color: A Study of White-Black Relationships in Swaziland* (Johannesburg: Wits University Press, 1947), 107, 113–14.

7. Kuper, *Uniform of Color*, 118.

8. Kuper, *Uniform of Color*, 120.

9. Norman Etherington, *Peasants, Peasants and Politics in Southeast Africa, 1835–1880: African Christian Communities in Natal, Pondoland and Zululand* (London: Royal Historical Society, 1978), 122.

10. *Times of Swaziland*, November 5, 1936.

11. Kuper, *Uniform of Color*, 121.

12. *Times of Swaziland*, March 1, 1945.

13. *Times of Swaziland*, October 22, 1936.

14. Hilda Kuper, *Sobhuza II: Ngwenyama and King of Swaziland* (New York: Duckworth, 1978), 103.

15. *Times of Swaziland*, May 14, 1936.

16. *Times of Swaziland*, May 14, 1940.

17. *Times of Swaziland*, May 14, 1936.

18. *Times of Swaziland*, April 30, 1936.

19. *Times of Swaziland*, October 27, 1949.

20. J. S. M. Matsebula, *A History of Swaziland* (Cape Town: Longmans, 1972), 206.

21. Kuper, *Sobhuza II*, 103.

22. *Times of Swaziland*, May 14, 1936.

23. *Times of Swaziland*, September 4, 1941.

24. *Times of Swaziland*, February 13, 1941.

25. *Times of Swaziland*, December 20, 1945.

26. *Times of Swaziland*, November 13, 1941.

27. Christian P. Potholm, *Swaziland: The Dynamics of Political Modernization* (Berkeley: University of California Press, 1972), 33.

28. Potholm, *Swaziland*, 33–35.

29. *Times of Swaziland*, September 8, 1956.

30. *Times of Swaziland*, May 2, 1953.

31. Thula Simpson, "The Bay and the Ocean: A History of the ANC in Swaziland, 1960–1979," *African Historical Review* 41, no. 1 (2009): 90–117.

32. Interview with Anne Twala, Kwaluseni, Eswatini, July 29, 2019. For Douglas Lukhele, see also Kuper, *Sobhuza II*, 224.

33. *Times of Swaziland*, November 27, 1947.

34. *Times of Swaziland*, August 25, 1949.

35. *Times of Swaziland*, October 27, 1949.

36. *The Swazilander* 1, no. 1 (April 1955), Swaziland National Archives, Lobamba (hereafter SNA), Swaziland Progressive Association, File No. 3311.

37. *Times of Swaziland*, November 14, 1946; *Times of Swaziland*, October 14, 1949; *Times of Swaziland*, April 7, 1956.

38. *Times of Swaziland*, November 14, 1959.

39. J. J. Nquku, letter to the Government Secretary, Mbabane, May 18, 1959, SNA, Swaziland Secretariat, File No. 3444; Bengt Sundkler, *Zulu Zion and Some Swazi Zionists* (Oxford: Oxford University Press, 1976), 224–26.

40. Sundkler, *Zulu Zion*, 227.

41. J. Hlathikhulu, Letters to the Editor, *Times of Swaziland*, January 16, 1935.

42. A.N.G. from Matapa, Letters to the Editor, *Times of Swaziland*, March 5, 1936.

43. Kuper, *Sobhuza II*, 104.

44. *Times of Swaziland*, February 15, 1945.

45. *Times of Swaziland*, November 25, 1948.

46. *Times of Swaziland*, October 28, 1942.

47. *Izwi lama Swazi*, February 21, 1959.

48. *Izwi lama Swazi*, July 2, 1960.

49. A. G. Marwick, Letters to the Editor, *Times of Swaziland*, July 14, 1961.

50. J. J. Nquku, letter to the Government Secretary, Mbabane, November 2, 1953, SNA, Swaziland Secretariat, File No. 3444.

51. Potholm, *Swaziland*, 52.

52. Potholm, *Swaziland*, 45.

53. For an account of the Zionists' relationship with the church in the United States, see J. Cabrita, *The People's Zion: Southern Africa, the USA and a Transatlantic Faith-Healing Movement* (Cambridge, MA: Harvard University Press, 2018).

54. Kuper, *Uniform of Color*, 122.

55. Assistant District Commissioner Mankanyane, letter to Government Secretary, Mbabane, November 5, 1936, SNA, RCS 791/36.

56. Swaziland Police, letter to Chief of Police, January 6, 1937, SNA, RCS 791/36.

57. Fiona Armitage, "The Zionist Movement in Swaziland: Origins and Bid for League Recognition, 1936–1958," Botswana History Workshop (unpublished paper, August 1973), 15; Sundkler, *Zulu Zion*, 228.

58. J. J. Nquku, UCCA, letter to Government Secretary, Mbabane, May 21, 1948, Bengt Sundkler Papers, Uppsala University (hereafter BSP), Box 91.

59. Armitage, "Zionist Movement in Swaziland," 11, 15.

60. Interview with Soul Sibandze, Lobamba Lomdzala, Swaziland, June 29, 2016.

61. District Commissioner, letter to Mbabane to Government Secretary, February 11, 1937, SNA, RCS 791/36.

62. Assistant District Commissioner Mankaiyana, letter to Government Secretary, Mbabane, November 5, 1936, SNA, RCS 791/36.

63. District Commissioner Central District, letter to Government Secretary Mbabane, October 21, 1941, SNA, RCS 282/1941.

64. Hugh MacMillan, "A Nation Divided: The Swazi in Swaziland and the Transvaal, 1865–1986," in *The Creation of Tribalism in Southern Africa*, ed. Leroy Vail (Berkeley: University of California Press, 1986).

65. MacMillan, "A Nation Divided," 301.

66. Interview with Simon/Dabete Mavimbela, Mbabane, Swaziland, July 11, 2016.

67. Anders Fogelqvist, "Red-Dressed Zionists: Symbols of Power in a Swazi Independent Church" (Uppsala: Uppsala University Press, 1986), 349.

68. Interview with Meshack Dlamini, Matsapha, Swaziland, August 19, 2016.

69. *Fulfilling the Vision: Swaziland Evangelism Task Report* (no publisher, 1995), 67.

70. "The Swazi National Council Challenges Statutory Marriage," June 18, 1959, BSP, Box 92.

71. Interview with Khanyakwezwe Vilakati, Makanyane, Swaziland, July 30, 2016; *Times of Swaziland*, April 11, 1998.

72. Fogelqvist, *Red-Dressed Zionists*, 114.

73. Fiona Armitage, "Abakamoya: People of the Spirit" (PhD thesis, University of Aberdeen, 1986), 350.

74. Interview with Vusimuzi Mkhatshwa, Mbabane, Swaziland, August 17, 2016; G. C. Oosthuizen, *The Healer-Prophet in Afro-Christian Churches* (Leiden: E. J. Brill, 1992), 32.

75. Interview with Meshack Dlamini, Matsapha, Swaziland, August 19, 2016; J. P. Kiernan, "Prophet and Preacher: An Essential Partnership in the Work of Zion," *MAN* 11, no. 3 (1976): 356–66.

76. Fogelqvist, *Red-Dressed Zionists*, 63.

77. Interview with Bishop Maziya, Manzini, Swaziland (interview conducted by Dr. Sonene Nyawo), August 4, 2016.

78. Hebron Ndlovu, Sonene Nyawo, David Nhlabatsi, and Patrick Mkhonta, "The League of African Christian Churches in Swaziland: Challenges and Prospects" (unpublished paper, Kwaluseni: University of Swaziland, 2011), 34.

79. Notes on a service at Lozithehlezi Royal Kraal, July 27, 1958, Leo Kuipers, BSP, Box 92.

80. J. F. Holleman, *Experiment in Swaziland: Report of the Random Sample Survey, 1960* (Swaziland: University of Natal, Institute for Social Research, 1964), 232, 236.

81. Armitage, "Zionist Movement in Swaziland," 16.

82. Armitage, "Zionist Movement in Swaziland," 20.

83. Report of Good Friday Council, March 28–31, 1959, BSP, Box 110.

84. Nquku, General Secretary of the UCCA, letter to Government Secretary, Mbabane, August 8, 1949, BSP, Box 110.

85. District Commissioner, Manzini, letter to Government Secretary, Mbabane, July 7, 1950, SNA, Swaziland Secretariat, File No. 3444.

86. Holleman, "Experiment in Swaziland," 232, 236.

87. "Ahlukaniswa yini amabandla na?" Kadebona, *Izwi lama Swazi*, August 3, 1963.

88. "Andiswa yini amabandla enkolo na?" Kadebona, *Izwi lama Swazi*, June 8, 1963.

89. Potholm, *Swaziland*, 48–49.

90. Kuper, *Sobhuza II*, 223.

91. J. S. M. Matsebula, *A Tribute to the Late His Majesty King Sobhuza II* (Mbabane: Webster, 1983), 28.

92. "Ingwenyama Warns Swazi Nation," *Times of Swaziland*, October 14, 1960.

93. A. Z. Khumalo, "Open Letter to All the Political Leaders by Mr. A. Z. Khumalo," *Times of Swaziland*, January 4, 1963.

94. *Times of Swaziland*, July 1, 1960.

95. Kuper, *Sobhuza II*, 248.

96. "Swaziland Fighting News: Issued by NNLC, 21 September 1964," SOAS Archives, PP.SQ Ngwane National Liberatory Congress.

97. Fogelqvist, *Red-Dressed Zionists*, 80.

98. *Izwi lama Swazi*, December 8, 1964, cited in Sundkler, *Zulu Zion*, 233.

99. Fogelqvist, *Red-Dressed Zionists*, 80.

100. Paul Cummergen, "Zionism and Politics in Swaziland," *Journal of Religion in Africa* 30, no. 3 (2000): 376.

101. "Swaziland Fighting News: Issued by NNLC, September 21, 1964," SOAS Archives, PP.SQ Ngwane National Liberatory Congress.

102. Interview with Janet Aphane, Kwaluseni, Eswatini, August 12, 2018; interview with Zanele Twala, Mbabane, Eswatini, August 8, 2019.

103. "Zenzele Women at Matsapha by R. D. Twala," *Izwi lama Swazi*, April 20, 1963,

104. Letters to the Editor, Unsigned, *Izwi lama Swazi*, May 4, 1963.

105. Potholm, *Swaziland*, 112; "Clean Sweep for Sobhuza," *Times of Swaziland*, July 4, 1964; Christian Potholm, "Changing Political Configurations in Swaziland," *Journal of Modern African Studies* 4, no. 3 (1966): 316.

106. "Victory Message from Imbhokodvo," *Times of Swaziland*, July 3, 1964.

107. Richard Levin, *When the Sleeping Grass Awakens* (Johannesburg: Wits University Press, 1997), 77.

108. "Our Elections by Intombazana," *Times of Swaziland*, July 10, 1964.

109. Potholm, *Swaziland*, 115.

110. Potholm, *Swaziland*, 115.

111. "Mrs. Twala Resigns," *Times of Swaziland*, May 14, 1965.

112. Interview with Zanele Twala, Mbabane, Eswatini, August 8, 2019.

113. Levin, *Sleeping Grass*, 95–103.

114. Kuper, *Sobhuza II*, 336.

115. Levin, *Sleeping Grass*.

Chapter 10

1. Burma (independent since 1948) changed its name to Myanmar in 1989. Unless referring directly to the current government of Myanmar, this chapter refers to Burma because most action takes place before 1989 and because most Nagas use the term Burma historically as well as in the present day.

2. For a detailed study of the early Naga nationalist movement, see Jelle Wouters, "Difficult Decolonization: Debates, Divisions, and Deaths Within the Naga Uprising, 1944–1963," *Journal of North East India Studies* 9, no. 1 (2019): 1–28. For the history of the Naga nationalist claim in an international context, see Lydia Walker, "Chapter 1: Sovereignty in the Hills," in

States-in-Waiting: Global Decolonization and its Discontents (Cambridge: Cambridge University Press, forthcoming).

3. Zapuvise Lhousa, *Strange Country: My Experience in Naga Nationalism* (Kohima, India: self-pub., 2015); the Naga nationalist source book, Zapuvise Lhousa, *Phizo and Medina* (Kohima, India: self-pub., 2011)

4. Correspondence with Sede Lhousa, 6 July 2021.

5. Correspondence with Zapuvisie Lhousa, 14 September 2017.

6. In 1957, India combined the British district of Nagaland and the Tuensang Frontier Division into an administrative unit governed by the state of Assam called the Naga Hills-Tuensang Area, which became the Indian state of Nagaland in 1963.

7. On state-making in Northeast India, with a focus on the creation of NEFA/Arunachal Pradesh (in which some Nagas reside), see Bérénice Guyot-Réchard, *Shadow States: India, China and the Himalayas, 1910–1962* (Cambridge: Cambridge University Press, 2017), particularly 102–10.

8. Indian Census, 2011. The next Indian census is scheduled to be carried out in 2023. Available at https://www.census2011.co.in/.

9. As of 2007, Mississippi was 34 percent Baptist, according to Paul Harvey, *Freedom's Coming: Religious Culture and the Shaping of the South from the Civil War through the Civil Rights Era* (Chapel Hill: University of North Carolina Press, 2007), 255.

10. The missionary was George Supplee. This history is discussed in Keviyiekielie Linyïe, "Christianity and Society in Nagaland: Media, Newspapers, News, and Christianity," *Nagaland Today*, 19 January 2019. Rev. Linyïe has a personal collection of these newsheets.

11. Copies of *The Naga Nation* and *Kewhira Kielie* from the collections of Rev. Keviyiekielie Linyïe, Kohima, Nagaland.

12. The British colonial chronicler, Mountstuart Elphinstone, draws comparisons between Pashtuns and American Indians in *An Account of the Kingdom of Caubul* (London: Bentley, 1842). For the Elphinstone and the "tribalization" of Afghan society, see Benjamin Hopkins, *Making of Modern Afghanistan* (London: Palgrave Macmillan, 2008), 23–33. For the North American comparison, see Elizabeth Colson, "Political Organization in Tribal Societies: A Cross-Cultural Comparison," *American Indian* Quarterly 10, no. 1 (1986): 5–19. I am grateful to Elisabeth Leake for articulating this point.

13. On caste, see John Thomas, *Evangelising the Nation: Religion and the Formation of Naga Political Identity* (New Delhi: Routledge, 2015), 194–95. Accepting the 6th Schedule of the Indian constitution, which applies to Nagas, was one of the requirements of the creation of an Indian state of Nagaland in 1963. The categorization remains controversial today, though Nagas appreciate that it means that non-Nagas cannot buy property in Naga areas. On the discourses of "tribe" versus "adivasi," see Willem van Schendel, "The Dangers of Belonging: Tribes, Indigenous Peoples and Homelands in South Asia," in *The Politics of Belonging in India: Becoming Adivasi*, ed. Daniel J. Rycroft and Sangeeta Dasgupta (Oxford: Routledge, 2011), 19–43. Across much of the world (though not necessarily in India), "tribe" often has a pejorative connotation; see Archie Mafeji, "The Ideology of Tribalism," *Journal of Modern African Studies* 9, no. 2 (1971): 253–61.

14. Some Nagas feel an affinity with Israel through evangelical Christian theology and a sense of shared national struggle—declaring independence within a year of each other and both being small, religiously-oriented states/states-in-waiting with antagonistic neighbors of a different religion. In addition, certain Mizos from neighboring Mizoram and Manipur have called themselves a lost tribe of Israel, were recognized as such by the Israeli chief rabbi, and

some have since emigrated to Israel on that basis. See Eetta Prince-Gibson, '"Lost' Indian Jews Come Home," *Tablet Magazine*, 12 December 2017, https://www.tabletmag.com/jewish-news-and-politics/120195/lost-indian-jews-come-home.

15. For a recent exposition, see Akum Longchari, "Did Tribes Exist Before Colonialism?" *Morung Express*, 10 August 2022, https://www.morungexpress.com/did-tribes-exist-before-colonialism. Longchari invokes both Mahmood Mamdani and Nicholas Dirks in his argument. The op-ed became a subject of debate among Naga intellectuals in private correspondence.

16. Eugen Weber, *Peasants into Frenchman: The Modernization of Rural France, 1870–1914* (Stanford, CA: Stanford University Press, 1976); F. K. Ekechi, "Colonialism and Christianity in West Africa: The Igbo Case, 1900–1915," *Journal of African History* 12, no. 1 (1971): 103–15. There is a long tradition of missionaries translating the Bible into vernacular languages, and Supplee tried to do so in Tenyidie. However, his language skills were not sufficient (interview with Niketu Iralu, 23 December 2018). Most Naga church services today are in Naga languages, as most conversion was carried out by Nagas. However, the number of Naga languages and initial identification of Christianity with English, and the English language with elements of nationalism, made English a dominant language of Naga nationalist claims-making.

17. George Supplee correspondence, 1940–1953, American Baptist Foreign Mission Society Archives, Reel 348.

18. Arkotong Longkumer, "'Along Kingdom's Highway': The Proliferation of Christianity, Education, and Print Amongst the Nagas in Northeast India," *Contemporary South Asia* 27, no. 2 (2019): 160–78.

19. Anna Su, *Exporting Freedom: Religious Liberty and American Power* (Cambridge, MA: Harvard University Press, 2016): 114–15, describes how the United States weaponized religion, particularity Christianity, during the Cold War. For a general overview, see Andrew Preston, *Sword of the Spirit, Shield of Faith: Religion in American War and Diplomacy* (New York: Random House, 2012), 418–40; and Philip E. Muehlenbeck, ed., *Religion and the Cold War* (Nashville, TN: Vanderbilt University Press, 2012).

20. On petitioning and international-legal visibility, see Natasha Wheatley, "New Subjects in International Law and Order," in *Internationalisms: A Twentieth-Century History*, ed. Patricia Clavin and Glenda Sluga (Cambridge: Cambridge University Press, 2017), 265–86; and Susan Pedersen, *The Guardians: The League of Nations and the Crisis of Empire* (Oxford: Oxford University Press, 2015). On evolving civilizational discourses, see Ntina Tzouvala, *Capitalism as Civilisation: A History of International Law* (Cambridge: Cambridge University Press, 2020).

21. For the ever-mutating notion of "readiness" under empire, see Partha Chatterjee, *The Black Hole of Empire* (Princetone, NJ: Princeton University Press, 2012): 273–76. On "legitimacy" and international claims-making, see Lydia Walker, "Minority Nationalisms during Postwar Decolonization," in "Reflections: Nationalism's Tangled Histories," ed. Michael Goebel, special issue, *American Historical Review* 127, no. 1 (2022): 351–54.

22. Regarding South West Africa/Namibia: The UN General Assembly adopted the name "Namibia" in 1966. Mburumba Kerina allegedly coined the name "Namibia" in conversation with Sukharno sometime between 1960 and 1961; by 1962 many Namibian nationalists used it, but it was not agreed upon by all.

23. Tilman Dedering, "Petitioning Geneva: Transnational Aspects of Protest and Resistance in South West Africa/Namibia after the First World War," *Journal of Southern African Studies* 35, no. 4 (2009): 785–801.

24. Michael Scott, *A Time to Speak* (London: Faber and Faber, 1958), 35.

25. Kutako allegedly prayed in public before the Rev. Michael Scott when he left Windhoek, South West Africa, to carry the Herero petitions to New York in 1948.

26. "Meeting with Hosea Kutako and SWAPO," Windhoek, 15 May 1962, UN General Assembly Report of the Special Committee for South West Africa, 20 September 1962, National Archives of Namibia, BB/1000.

27. Martti Koskenniemi, Mónica García-Salmones Rovira, and Paolo Amorosa, eds., *International Law and Religion: Historical and Contemporary Perspectives* (Oxford: Oxford University Press, 2017); Samuel Moyn, *Christian Human Rights* (Philadelphia: University of Pennsylvania Press, 2015).

28. Claire Vergerio, "The Berlin and Hague Conferences," in *The Oxford Handbook of History and International Relations*, ed. Mlada Bukovanski, Edward Keene, Christian Reus-Smit, and Maja Spanu (Oxford: Oxford University Press, forthcoming 2022).

29. Some examples include Ian Tyrell, *Reforming the World: The Creation of America's Moral Empire* (Princeton, NJ: Princeton University Press, 2010); John Thomas, *Evangelising the Nation: Religion and the Formation of Naga Political Identity* (Routledge India, 2017); Harald Fischer-Tiné, "The YMCA and Low-Modernist Rural Development in South Asia, c.1922–1957," *Past & Present* 240, no. 1 (2018): 193–234; Hilary M. Carey, *God's Empire: Religion and Colonialism in the British World, c.1801–1908* (Cambridge: Cambridge University Press, 2011); Andrew N. Porter, *Religion versus Empire? British Protestant Missionaries and Overseas Expansion, 1700–1914* (Manchester: Manchester University Press, 2004); and Elizabeth Foster, *African Catholic: Decolonization and the Transformation of the Church* (Cambridge, MA: Harvard University Press, 2019).

30. David A. Hollinger, *After Cloven Tongues of Fire: Protestant Liberalism in Modern American History* (Princeton, NJ: Princeton University Press, 2013).

31. John Nurser, *For All People and All Nations: The Ecumenical Church and Human Rights* (Washington, DC: Georgetown University Press, 2005).

32. On the unraveling of this ecumenical internationalism, its relationship to US global power projection through institutions of international order, and John Foster Dulles' role, see Andrew Preston, "The Limits of Brotherhood: Race, Religion, and World Order in American Ecumenical Protestantism," *American Historical Review* 127, no. 3 (2022): 1222–51.

33. Dag Hammarskjöld, *Markings* (London: Faber and Faber, 1964), 217, references to Psalm 60:2 and Psalm 73:17–18.

34. For a recent articulation of the restricted scope of missionary activity, see Manikarnika Dutta, "The Sailors' Home and Moral Regulation of White European Seamen in Nineteenth-Century India," *Cultural and Social History* 18, no. 2 (2021): 201–20.

35. George Manuel and Michael Posluns, *The Fourth World: An Indian Reality* (New York: Free Press, 1974).

36. Angami Zapu Phizo, 1946 speech, included in a manuscript collection held by the Nagaland Baptist Church Council Library, Kohima, *The Naga National Rights and Movement* (Publicity and Information Department, Naga National Council, 1993), 12.

37. Pieter Steyn, *Zaphuphizo* (Routledge, 2002), 119.

38. Steyn, *Zaphuphizo*, 119.

39. Kijungluba Ao, letter to AF Merrill, 2 August 1966, American Baptist Foreign Mission Society Archives, Reel 426K.

40. Lydia Walker, "Jayaprakash Narayan and the Politics of Reconciliation for the Postcolonial State and its Imperial Fragments," *Indian Economic and Social History Review* 56, no. 2 (2019): 147–69.

41. Interview with Niketu Iralu, 4 February 2016: "The Hindu swamis didn't climb the hills. The American missionaries did and the Nagas were impressed." That dynamic has changed in recent years; see Arkotong Longkumer, *The Greater India Experiment: Hindutva and the Northeast* (Stanford, CA: Stanford University Press, 2020).

42. Frederick S. Downs, "Ao, Longri (Longritangchetba)," in *Biographical Dictionary of Christian Missions*, ed. Gerald H. Anderson (Grand Rapids, MI: William B. Eerdmans, 1999), 25. Downs was born to American Baptist missionary parents in Assam in 1930 and was one of the last Americans to live in the Northeast, as a professor at Eastern Theological College in Jorhat, Assam, and the vice president of the Council of Baptist Churches in North East India. Longri was a close friend and colleague of Fred Downs.

43. *Assam Baptist Leader*, September 1961, Council of Baptist Churches North East India Archives, Guwahati Assam, India.

44. Dr. O. F. Nolde, "The Future Is Now," speech, New Delhi, 23 November 1961, Dingle Macintosh Foot Papers, Churchill College, Cambridge UK, DGTS II 4/8.1.

45. *Assam Baptist Leader*, September 1961.

46. Rev. V. K. Nuh, *Nagaland Church and Politics* (Kohima, Nagaland: self-pub., 1986), 31–39. For a wider discussion of Nuh's intellectual and personal work, see Arkotong Longkumer, "The Alter-Politics of Rev. Nuh," in *Life and Works of V. K. Nuh* (Dimapur, India: Heritage Publishers, 2017).

47. Scato Swu, Kedahge, Federal Government of Nagaland, letter to Michael Scott, 4 April 1964, Guthrie Michael Scott Papers Box 17. "Kedahge" was the title for the president of the federal government, the in-country leadership of Phizo's Naga National Council political party. Emphasis added.

48. For the full story, see Lydia Walker, "Decolonization in the 1960s: On Legitimate and Illegitimate National Claims-Making," *Past & Present* 242, no. 1 (2019): 227–64. For Scott's extended biography, see Anne Yates and Lewis Chester, *The Troublemaker* (London: Aurum Press, 2004).

49. "Savior, Save thyself from the saved," was Scott's gloss of Psalm 17:7 King James Version, "Shew thy marvellous loving kindness, O thou that savest by thy right hand them which put their trust *in thee* from those that rise up *against them*."

50. Michael Scott, letter to David Astor, 3 April 1960, Guthrie Michael Scott (GMS) Papers, Box 25, The Weston Library, Oxford University (capitalization in original). Prominent among this group were David Astor (of *The Observer* newspaper), Ronald Praine (of the Rhodesian Selection Trust mining company), and Jock Campbell (of Booker Brothers, McConnell & Co., the British Guiana sugar company).

51. Cyril Dunne interview with David Astor, 1975, GMS Papers, Box 25.

52. Anne Yates interview with Richard Kershaw, undated, GMS Papers, Box 103.

53. Anne Yates interview with Richard Kershaw.

54. Examples include Jane Symonds, letter to Michael Scott, 23 Nov 1962, GMS Papers, Box 40; Ursula Graham Bower Betts, letter to George Patterson, 2 Jan 1963, GMS Papers, Box 63.

55. Michael Scott, account to Cyril Dunne, 1964, GMS Papers, Box 77.

56. Kurt Dahlmann, "One Man Many Parties: The Parties of the Non-Whites in SWA," undated manuscript notebook used in South Africa's South West Africa International Court of Justice testimony, p. 76, Kurt Dahlmann Papers, PA 85, Basler Afrika Bibliographien, Basel, Switzerland.

57. Dahlmann, "One Man Many Parties," 76.

58. Andreas Shipanga, director of SWAPO Information Service and member of the national executive, interview, 1973, Tony Emmett Papers, PA 48, Basler Afrika Bibliographien, Basel, Switzerland.

59. R. J. Parrott and M. A. Lawrence, eds., *The Tricontinental Revolution: Third World Radicalism and the Cold War* (Cambridge: Cambridge University Press, 2022).

60. Jeremy Friedman, *Shadow Cold War: The Sino-Soviet Competition for the Third World* (Chapel Hill: University of North Carolina Press, 2015).

61. Billy Graham, *Just as I Am: The Autobiography of Billy Graham* (New York: HarperCollins, 1999). On getting the permit, see 276. On Mrs. Gandhi providing helicopters to facilitate Graham's travel, see 279.

62. Rev. L. Suohie Mhasi, "Dr. Billy Graham's Kohima Crusade 1972," *Eastern Mirror* (Nagaland), 10 March 2018, https://easternmirrornagaland.com/dr-billy-grahams-kohima-crusade-1972/.

63. *Morung Express* (Nagaland), 23 February 2018.

64. Billy Graham, "Why We Came to Nagaland," speech, probably given 17 November 1972. Video available via Worldwide Index of Sermons https://www.youtube.com/watch?v=FpEi8vwa54E (accessed 8 December 2022).

65. Thomas, *Evangelising the Nation*, 157–58.

66. *Time*, 4 December 1972.

Chapter 11

1. Quoted in M. P. Joseph, *Theologies of the Non-Person: The Formative Years of EATWOT* (New York: Palgrave Macmillan, 2015), 59.

2. The term "neocolonialism" came into use following Kwame Nkrumah's *Neo-Colonialism: The Last Stage of Imperialism* (New York: International Publishers, 1966). On the NIEO, see note 7 below.

3. Jean-Marc Ela, *African Cry*, trans. Robert J. Barr (Eugene, OR: Wipf and Stock, 1986), 102.

4. Jean-Marc Ela, *My Faith as an African*, trans. John Pairman Brown and Susan Perry (Eugene, OR: Wipf and Stock, 1988), 139.

5. On the "Bandung Era" and the NIEO, see Bret Benjamin, "Bookend to Bandung: The New International Economic Order and the Antinomies of the Bandung Era," *Humanity* 6, no. 1 (Spring 2015): 33–46. Vijay Prashad presents the NIEO as "the highest point of the Third World Project," in *The Poorer Nations: A Possible History of the Global South* (London: Verso, 2014), 3.

6. On the Bandung Conference, see Luis Eslava, Michael Fakhri, and Vasuki Nesiah, eds., *Bandung, Global History, and International Law: Critical Pasts and Pending Futures* (Cambridge: Cambridge University Press, 2017); George MacTurnan Kahin, *The Asian-African Conference, Bandung, Indonesia* (Ithaca, NY: Cornell University Press, 1956). The coining of the term "Third World" is usually attributed to the French economist Alfred Sauvy. See Sauvy, "Trois mondes, une planète," *L'Observateur*, August 14, 1952.

7. On the NIEO, see the essays in *Humanity* 6, no. 1 (2015); Adom Getachew, *Worldmaking after Empire: The Rise and Fall of Self-Determination* (Princeton, NJ: Princeton University Press, 2019), ch. 5; Jagdish Bhagwati, *The New International Economic Order: The North-South Debate* (Cambridge, MA: MIT Press, 1977).

8. On this shift, see Getachew, *Worldmaking after Empire*, 146–60. The key text of dependency theory was Andre Gunder Frank, *Capitalism and Underdevelopment in Latin America: Historical Studies of Chile and Brazil* (New York: Monthly Review Press, 1967).

9. Getachew, *Worldmaking After Empire*, 167; Prashad, *The Poorer Nations*, 3.

10. For an excellent introduction to Vatican II, see John O'Malley, *What Happened at Vatican II* (Cambridge, MA: Belknap/Harvard University Press, 2008); Stephen Schloesser, "Against Forgetting: Memory, History, Vatican II," *Theological Studies* 67, no. 2 (2006): 275–319.

11. See the chapters by Justin Reynolds, Gene Zubovich, and David Kirkpatrick in this volume.

12. Ivan Petrella, "The Intellectual Roots of Liberation Theology," in *The Cambridge History of Religions in Latin America*, ed. Virginia Garrard, Paul Freston, and Stephen C. Dove (Cambridge: Cambridge University Press, 2016), 362.

13. For an introduction to Latin American liberation theology, see Lilian Calles Barger, *The World Come of Age: An Intellectual History of Liberation Theology* (Oxford: Oxford University Press, 2018); Christopher Rowland, ed., *Cambridge Companion to Liberation Theology* (Cambridge: Cambridge University Press, 2008).

14. Joseph, *Theologies of the Non-Person*, 26–28.

15. See the account of the origins of EATWOT in Joseph, *Theologies of the Non-Person*, 31–35; Sergio Torres, "Dar-es-Salaam, 1976," in "Theologies of the Third World: Convergences and Divergences," ed. Leonardo Boff and Virgil Elizondo, *Concilium* 199, no. 5 (Edinburgh: T&T Clark, 1988), 109.

16. Quoted in Sergio Torres, "Memo to Participants, Delhi Conference: Background Materials," WAB: EATWOT, series 1B, box 11, folder 6, Burke Library at Union Theological Seminary, Columbia University in the City of New York.

17. Sergio Torres, "Opening Address," in *The Emergent Gospel: Theology from the Underside of History; Papers from the Ecumenical Dialogue of Third World Theologians, Dar es Salaam, August 5–12, 1976*, ed. Sergio Torres and Virginia Fabella (Maryknoll, NY: Orbis, 1978), 4.

18. Torres, "Dar-es-Salaam, 1976," 108.

19. "Final Statement," in *The Emergent Gospel: Theology from the Underside of History; Papers from the Ecumenical Dialogue of Third World Theologians, Dar es Salaam, August 5–12, 1976*, ed. Sergio Torres and Virginia Fabella (Maryknoll, NY: Orbis, 1978), 266.

20. "Final Statement," *The Emergent Gospel*, 266.

21. Torres, "Opening Address," 5.

22. Torres, "Dar-es-Salaam, 1976," 111.

23. On the interwar moment, see Charles Keith, *Catholic Vietnam: A Church from Empire to Nation* (Berkeley: University of California Press, 2012), ch. 3–4; Albert Wu, "On Chinese Rites and Rights," in *Christianity and Human Rights Reconsidered*, ed. Sarah Shortall and Daniel Steinmetz-Jenkins (Cambridge: Cambridge University Press, 2020), 207–22. On the postwar moment, see Elizabeth A. Foster, *African Catholic: Decolonization and the Transformation of the Church* (Cambridge, MA: Harvard University Press, 2019).

24. Ngindu Mushete, "The History of Theology in Africa: From Polemics to Critical Irenics," in *African Theology en Route: Papers from the Pan-African Conference of Third World Theologians, December 17–23, 1977, Accra, Ghana* ed. Kofi Appiah-Kubi and Sergio Torres (Maryknoll, NY: Orbis, 1979), 29–30.

25. Virginia Fabella, quoted in Joseph, *Theologies of the Non-Person*, 44.

26. "Final Statement," in *Irruption of the Third World: Challenge to Theology; Papers from the Fifth International Conference of the Ecumenical Association of Third World Theologians, August 17–29, 1981, New Delhi, India*, ed. Virginia Fabella and Sergio Torres (Maryknoll, NY: Orbis, 1983), 199.

27. "Constitution (As approved by the General Assembly, Oaxtepec, Mexico, 12 December, 1986)," WAB: EATWOT, series 2A, box 14, folder 1, Burke Library at Union Theological Seminary, Columbia University in the City of New York.

28. Gustavo Gutiérrez, *A Theology of Liberation: History, Politics, and Salvation*, trans. Sister Caridad Inda and John Eagleson (Maryknoll, NY: Orbis, 1973), 5.

29. Gustavo Gutiérrez, "Two Theological Perspectives: Liberation Theology and Progressivist Theology," in *The Emergent Gospel: Theology from the Underside of History; Papers from the Ecumenical Dialogue of Third World Theologians, Dar es Salaam, August 5–12, 1976*, ed. Sergio Torres and Virginia Fabella (Maryknoll, NY: Orbis, 1978), 247.

30. "Working Constitution," December 1977, WAB: EATWOT, series 1A, box 1, folder 1, Burke Library at Union Theological Seminary, Columbia University in the City of New York.

31. "Final Statement," *The Emergent Gospel*, 269.

32. Gutiérrez, *A Theology of Liberation*, 86.

33. Gutiérrez, *A Theology of Liberation*, 97.

34. *Ad Gentes* (1965), section 9, https://www.vatican.va/archive/hist_councils/ii_vatican_council/documents/vat-ii_decree_19651207_ad-gentes_en.html.

35. See Bruno Chenu, *Théologies chrétiennes des tiers mondes* (Paris: Le Centurion, 1987), 154–55; Engelbert Mveng, "African Liberation Theology," in "Theologies of the Third World: Convergences and Divergences," ed. Leonardo Boff and Virgil Elizondo, *Concilium* 199, no. 5 (Edinburgh: T&T Clark, 1988): 28–30.

36. See Ela, *My Faith as an African*, ch. 2.

37. See James A. Lyons, *The Cosmic Christ in Origen and Teilhard de Chardin: A Comparative Study* (Oxford: Oxford University Press, 1982).

38. D. S. Amalorpavadass, "The Indian Universe of a New Theology," in *The Emergent Gospel: Theology from the Underside of History; Papers from the Ecumenical Dialogue of Third World Theologians, Dar es Salaam, August 5–12, 1976*, ed. Sergio Torres and Virginia Fabella (Maryknoll, NY: Orbis, 1978), 138.

39. Tissa Balasuriya, *Planetary Theology* (London: SCM Press, 1984), 188–89.

40. Tissa Balasuriya, "Divergences: An Asian Perspective," in *Third World Theologies: Commonalities and Divergences; Papers and Reflections from the Second General Assembly of the Ecumenical Association of Third World Theologians, December 1986, Oaxtepec, Mexico*, ed. K. C. Abraham (Maryknoll, NY: Orbis, 1990), 119.

41. Balasuriya, *Planetary Theology*, 191.

42. Virginia Fabella, "Preface," in *Irruption of the Third World: Challenge to Theology; Papers from the Fifth International Conference of the Ecumenical Association of Third World Theologians, August 17–29, 1981, New Delhi, India*, ed. Virginia Fabella and Sergio Torres (Maryknoll, NY: Orbis, 1983), xv. See also Engelbert Mveng, "Third World Theology—What Theology? What Third World? Evaluation by an African Delegate," in the same volume, 217–21; Frank Chikane, "EATWOT and Third World Theologies: An Evaluation of the Past and Present," in *Third World Theologies: Commonalities and Divergences; Papers and Reflections from the Second General Assembly of the Ecumenical Association of Third World Theologians, December 1986, Oaxtepec, Mexico*, ed. K. C. Abraham (Maryknoll, NY: Orbis, 1990), 165–67.

43. Mveng, "Third World Theology," 217.

44. Aloysius Pieris, "The Place of Non-Christian Religions and Theologies in the Evolution of Third World Theologies," in *Irruption of the Third World: Challenge to Theology; Papers*

from the Fifth International Conference of the Ecumenical Association of Third World Theologians, August 17–29, 1981, New Delhi, India, ed. Virginia Fabella and Sergio Torres (Maryknoll, NY: Orbis, 1983), 114.

45. Pieris, "The Place of Non-Christian Religions," 118.

46. Aloysius Pieris, "Towards an Asian Theology of Liberation: Some Religio-Cultural Guidelines," in *Asia's Struggle for Full Humanity: Towards a Relevant Theology; Papers From the Asian Theological Conference, January 7–20, 1979, Wennapuwa, Sri Lanka*, ed. Virginia Fabella (Maryknoll, NY: Orbis, 1980), 88, emphasis in original.

47. Mveng, "Third World Theology," 220.

48. Mveng, "Third World Theology," 220.

49. On the role of Negritude in Catholic thought, see Foster, *African Catholic*, esp. ch. 2. On Negritude and decolonization, see Gary Wilder, *Freedom Time: Negritude, Decolonization, and the Future of the World* (Durham, NC: Duke University Press, 2015).

50. Mveng, "Third World Theology," 218.

51. Pieris, "The Place of Non-Christian Religions," 113–39.

52. Pieris, "The Place of Non-Christian Religions," 114.

53. See the version of the constitution proposed at the New Delhi General Assembly, August 29, 1981, WAB: EATWOT, series 1A, box, 1, folder 1, Burke Library at Union Theological Seminary, Columbia University in the City of New York.

54. Cornel West, "The North American Blacks," in *The Challenge of the Basic Christian Communities: Papers from the International Ecumenical Congress of Theology, February 20–March 2, 1980, São Paulo, Brazil* (Maryknoll, NY: Orbis Books, 1981), 255–57. See also Chikane, "EATWOT and Third World Theologies," 156.

55. See, for instance, "History of the Contribution of EATWOT to Third World Theology," WAB: EATWOT, series 1B, box 11, folder 6, Burke Library at Union Theological Seminary, Columbia University in the City of New York.

56. James H. Cone, "Reflections from the Perspective of U.S. Blacks," in *Irruption of the Third World: Challenge to Theology; Papers from the Fifth International Conference of the Ecumenical Association of Third World Theologians, August 17–29, 1981, New Delhi, India*, ed. Virginia Fabella and Sergio Torres (Maryknoll, NY: Orbis, 1983), 243, 244.

57. See the draft of the organization's mission statement in box 1, folder 1, Black Theology Project records, Sc MG 286, Schomburg Center for Research in Black Culture, Manuscripts, Archives and Rare Books Division, The New York Public Library.

58. Chikane, "EATWOT and Third World Theologies," 161.

59. Mercy Amba Oduyoye, "Reflections from a Third World Woman's Perspective: Women's Experience and Liberation Theologies," in *Irruption of the Third World: Challenge to Theology; Papers from the Fifth International Conference of the Ecumenical Association of Third World Theologians, August 17–29, 1981, New Delhi, India*, ed. Virginia Fabella and Sergio Torres (Maryknoll, NY: Orbis, 1983), 247.

60. Quoted in Joseph, *Theologies of the Non-Person*, 190.

61. "Commonalities, Divergences, and Cross-fertilization among Third World Theologies," in *Third World Theologies: Commonalities and Divergences; Papers and Reflections from the Second General Assembly of the Ecumenical Association of Third World Theologians, December 1986, Oaxtepec, Mexico*, ed. K. C. Abraham (Maryknoll, NY: Orbis, 1990), 209.

62. See, for instance, Virginia Fabella and Mercy Amba Oduyoye, eds., *With Passion and Compassion: Third World Women Doing Theology* (Maryknoll, NY: Orbis, 1988).

63. "Constitution (As approved by the General Assembly, Oaxtepec, Mexico, 12 December, 1986)."

64. For the membership numbers, see WAB: EATWOT, series 2A, box 16, folder 12, Burke Library at Union Theological Seminary, Columbia University in the City of New York.

65. Chikane, "EATWOT and Third World Theologies," 150.

66. Torres, "Opening Address," 5.

67. A task force for dialogue with the Second World was set up after the 1986 general assembly in Oaxtepec and plans were made in conjunction with Bishop Károly Tóth to host a conference in Hungary in June 1989. The archives do not explain why the event did not take place, but the fall of Communism across Eastern Europe likely had something to do with it. See WAB: EATWOT, series 3B, box 35, folder 1, Burke Library at Union Theological Seminary, Columbia University in the City of New York.

68. EATWOT's dependence on European and North American funding was a source of some consternation among members. For instance, the 1990 financial report indicates that all of its funding came from organizations in Europe and North America, apart from about 1 percent of its revenue, which came from membership dues and royalties. See WAB: EATWOT, series 3A, box 31, folder 13, Burke Library at Union Theological Seminary, Columbia University in the City of New York. For the list of theologians on the European Support Committee, see WAB: EATWOT, series 1A, box 3, folder 5a.

69. See the memo from the organizing committee to observers and guests of the symposium "The Future of Europe: A Challenge to Theology," December 1980, WAB: EATWOT, series 2B, box 21, folder 12, Burke Library at Union Theological Seminary, Columbia University in the City of New York.

70. See Joseph, *Theologies of the Non-Person*, 46, 145, 162. On the internal divisions among progressive European Christians, see the minutes from the second meeting of the European Coordinating Committee for the Preparation of the Dialogue with EATWOT, April 30–May 1, 1982, WAB: EATWOT, series 2B, box 21, folder 12, Burke Library at Union Theological Seminary, Columbia University in the City of New York.

71. Theology in the Americas, *Is Liberation Theology for North America? The Response of First World Churches to Third World Theologies* (New York: Theology in the Americas, 1978).

72. Jacques van Nieuwenhove and Georges Casalis, eds., *Towards a Dialogue with Third World Theologians/Pour un dialogue avec des théologiens du tiers monde* (Zeist, Netherlands: s.n., 1981).

73. Memo from the organizing committee to observers and guests of the symposium "The Future of Europe: A Challenge to Theology."

74. "A Report of the Symposium/ Un compte-rendu du symposium," in *Towards a Dialogue with Third World Theologians/Pour un dialogue avec des théologiens du tiers monde*, ed. Jacques van Nieuwenhove and Georges Casalis (Zeist, Netherlands: s.n., 1981), 177.

75. "A Report of the Symposium/ Un compte-rendu du symposium," 196.

76. Rosemary Radford Ruether, "A Feminist Perspective," in *Doing Theology in a Divided World: Papers of the Sixth International Conference of the Ecumenical Association of Third World Theologians, January 5–13, 1983, Geneva, Switzerland*, ed. Virginia Fabella and Sergio Torres (Maryknoll, NY: Orbis, 1985), 69.

77. "Doing Theology in a Divided World: Final Statement of the Sixth EATWOT Conference," in *Doing Theology in a Divided World: Papers of the Sixth International Conference of the Ecumenical Association of Third World Theologians, January 5–13, 1983, Geneva, Switzerland*, ed. Virginia Fabella and Sergio Torres (Maryknoll, NY: Orbis, 1985), 190.

78. Johann Baptist Metz, "Standing at the End of the Eurocentric Era of Christianity," in *Doing Theology in a Divided World: Papers of the Sixth International Conference of the Ecumenical Association of Third World Theologians, January 5–13, 1983, Geneva, Switzerland*, ed. Virginia Fabella and Sergio Torres (Maryknoll, NY: Orbis, 1985), 85, emphasis in original.

79. Metz, "Standing at the End of the Eurocentric Era of Christianity," 86, 88.

80. Metz, "Standing at the End of the Eurocentric Era of Christianity," 89.

81. Joseph, *Theologies of the Non-Person*, 141–42.

82. See Getachew, *Worldmaking After Empire*, 171–75; Robert E. Wood, *From Marshall Plan to Debt Crisis: Foreign Aid and Development Choices in the World Economy* (Berkeley: University of California Press, 1986).

83. On the origins of neoliberalism, see Quinn Slobodian, *Globalists: The End of Empire and the Birth of Neoliberalism* (Cambridge, MA: Harvard University Press, 2018).

84. "Commonalities, Divergences, and Cross-fertilization," 196.

85. "Commonalities, Divergences, and Cross-fertilization," 196.

86. Sacred Congregation for the Doctrine of the Faith, "Instruction on Certain Aspects of the 'Theology of Liberation,'" https://www.vatican.va/roman_curia/congregations/cfaith/documents/rc_con_cfaith_doc_19840806_theology-liberation_en.html.

87. Joseph Ratzinger, "Homily of His Eminence Cardinal Ratzinger, Dean of the College of Cardinals," https://www.vatican.va/gpII/documents/homily-pro-eligendo-pontifice_20050418_en.html. On Ratzinger's opposition to religious pluralism, see Ian Linden, *Global Catholicism: Diversity and Change Since Vatican II* (London: Hurst, 2009), 240–41, 252; Ambrose Mong, *Dialogue Derailed: Joseph Ratzinger's War Against Pluralist Theology* (Cambridge: James Clarke, 2017).

88. Sacred Congregation for the Doctrine of the Faith, "Notification Concerning the Text *Mary and Human Liberation*," in Tissa Balasuriya, *Mary and Human Liberation: The Story and the Text*, ed. Helen Stanton (Harrisburg, PA: Trinity, 1997), 236.

89. "A Resolution Unanimously Adopted by the EATWOT IV Assembly in Manila, December 16, 1996," WAB: EATWOT, series 4A, box 38, folder 18, Burke Library at Union Theological Seminary, Columbia University in the City of New York.

90. See, for instance, "Theologies of the Third World: Convergences and Divergences," ed. Leonardo Boff and Virgil Elizondo, *Concilium* 199, no. 5 (Edinburgh: T&T Clark, 1988); "Tensions between the Churches of the First World and the Third World," ed. Virgil Elizondo and Norbert Greinacher, *Concilium* 144, no. 4 (Edinburgh: T&T Clark, 1981).

91. Pope Francis, "Address of the Holy Father at the Second World Meeting of Popular Movements," July 9, 2015, https://www.vatican.va/content/francesco/en/speeches/2015/july/documents/papa-francesco_20150709_bolivia-movimenti-popolari.html.

92. See Philip Jenkins, *The Next Christendom: The Coming of Global Christianity* (Oxford: Oxford University Press, 2011).

CONTRIBUTORS

Joel Cabrita is Associate Professor of African History and the Susan Ford Dorsey Director of the Center for African Studies at Stanford University. She is also Senior Research Associate in the Department of Historical Studies at the University of Johannesburg. Her work focuses on religion, gender, and the politics of knowledge production in Africa and globally. She is the author of *Text and Authority in in the South African Nazaretha Church* (Cambridge University Press, 2014) and *The People's Zion: Southern Africa, the United States, and a Transatlantic Faith-Healing Movement* (Harvard University Press, 2018). Her forthcoming book, *Written Out: The Silencing of Regina Gelana Twala* (Ohio University Press, 2023), is a biography of Regina Twala, an unjustly neglected Black literary figure in apartheid-era South Africa and colonial Eswatini.

Darcie Fontaine is Associate Professor of History at the University of South Florida. She is a historian of the modern French empire, focusing on North Africa, and is the author of *Decolonizing Christianity: Religion and the End of Empire in France and Algeria* (Cambridge University Press, 2016).

Elizabeth A. Foster is Professor of History at Tufts University. She is the author of *Faith in Empire: Religion, Politics, and Colonial Rule in French Senegal, 1880–1940* (Stanford University Press, 2013) and *African Catholic: Decolonization and the Transformation of the Church* (Harvard University Press, 2019), as well as articles and essays on religion, colonialism, and decolonization in Africa. She is currently writing a history of four intersecting lives in colonial French Sudan (today's Mali) and Guinea, ca. 1885–1955.

Udi Greenberg is Associate Professor of History at Dartmouth College. He is the author of *The Weimar Century: German Émigrés and the Ideological Foundations of the Cold War* (Princeton University Press, 2015), and of articles and essays on the history of European religion, politics, and thought. He is currently writing a book about the transformation of Catholic-Protestant relations in Europe from animosity to peace.

David C. Kirkpatrick is Associate Professor of Religion at James Madison University and the executive director of the Madison Center for Civic Engagement. He is the author of *A Gospel for the Poor: Global Social Christianity and the Latin American Evangelical Left* (University of Pennsylvania Press, 2019) and co-editor with Jason Bruner of *Global Visions of Violence: Agency and Persecution in World Christianity* (Rutgers University Press, 2022).

Eric Morier-Genoud is Professor of African History at Queen's University Belfast. He works on religion, politics, and the history of Southern Africa and is the author of *Catholicism and the Making of Politics in Central Mozambique, 1940–1986* (University of Rochester Press, 2019). His latest book, *Convertir l'Empereur?* (Antipodes, 2020), is the critical edition of the diary of a Swiss Protestant missionary and medical doctor, Georges Liengme, who lived and worked in the capital of the African Gaza empire until its conquest by the Portuguese in 1895.

Phi-Vân Nguyen is Associate Professor of History at the University of Saint-Boniface in Winnipeg, Canada. She is the author of multiple articles and essays on the history of the war, mobility, and religions in modern Vietnam.

Justin Reynolds is a historian of religion and global politics from the mid-nineteenth century to the present, with a focus on Protestant ecumenism and missionary movements. He has taught at Harvard University, Columbia University, and Deep Springs College. He is co-founder and co-director of the Gull Island Institute, an immersive liberal arts program based in Woods Hole, Massachusetts.

Sarah Shortall is Assistant Professor of History at the University of Notre Dame. She is the author of *Soldiers of God in a Secular World: Catholic Theology and Twentieth-Century French Politics* (Harvard University Press, 2021), and co-editor of *Christianity and Human Rights Reconsidered* (Cambridge University Press, 2020).

Lydia Walker is Assistant Professor and Myers Chair in Global Military History at The Ohio State University. A historian of postwar decolonization, she is the author of *States-in-Waiting: Global Decolonization and its Discontents* (Cambridge University Press, forthcoming), as well as articles in *The American Historical Review* and *Past & Present.*

Charlotte Walker-Said is Associate Professor of Africana Studies at John Jay College of Criminal Justice, CUNY, where she is also the Director of Graduate Studies for the Human Rights MA Program. Her scholarship focuses primarily on the intersections of law and religion in West and Central Francophone Africa, and she has also published essays and articles on human rights and LGBT rights in Africa. She is the author of *Faith, Power and Family: Christianity and Social Change in French Cameroon* (James Currey, 2018), and the editor of *Corporate Social Responsibility? Human Rights in the New Global Economy* (Chicago University Press, 2015). Her forthcoming book investigates crimes of policing and criminal justice in colonial French Central Africa.

Albert Wu is Associate Research Fellow at the Institute of History and Philology at Academia Sinica in Taipei, Taiwan. He is the author of *From Christ to Confucius: German Missionaries, Chinese Christians, and the Globalization of Christianity, 1860–1950* (Yale University Press, 2016), as well as articles and essays on global Christianity. He is currently writing a book on the global history of medicine and mistrust.

Gene Zubovich is Assistant Professor of History at the University at Buffalo, SUNY. He is the author of *Before the Religious Right: Liberal Protestants, Human Rights, and the Polarization of the United States* (University of Pennsylvania Press, 2022). He is currently writing a global history of the US culture wars.

INDEX

ACKNOWLEDGMENTS

This book has been supported by several institutions and individuals, and it is our great pleasure to be able to thank them. At Dartmouth College, we are grateful to Rebecca Elizabeth Biron and Mary Fletcher at the Leslie Center for the Humanities, and to Cecilia Gaposchkin and Bruch Lehmann at the Department of History. At Tufts University, we appreciate the support of Dean Bárbara M. Brizuela and the School of Arts and Sciences. We also thank the two anonymous readers, who offered generous and incisive criticism of the book. We owe a special debt to our editor, Elisabeth Maselli of the University of Pennsylvania Press, who provided invaluable guidance and support. This book would not have been published without her. And, finally, we extend our warm gratitude to all of the contributors. Despite the many difficulties posed by Covid-19, they remained committed to this collective endeavor. After two scheduled in-person conferences fell victim to the pandemic, they participated avidly in a series of three virtual workshops in the fall of 2021, which helped to refine arguments and highlight common themes. We are most grateful for their generosity, patience, and persistence in challenging times.

CPSIA information can be obtained
at www.ICGtesting.com
Printed in the USA
JSHW020718310523
42007JS00002B/2

9 781512 824964